THE OXFORD BOOK OF
CREATURES

The
Oxford Book of
CREATURES

Edited by

Fleur Adcock

and

Jacqueline Simms

Oxford   New York

OXFORD UNIVERSITY PRESS

1995

Oxford University Press, Walton Street, Oxford OX2 6DP

Oxford New York
Athens Auckland Bangkok Bombay
Calcutta Cape Town Dar es Salaam Delhi
Florence Hong Kong Istanbul Karachi
Kuala Lumpur Madras Madrid Melbourne
Mexico City Nairobi Paris Singapore
Taipei Tokyo Toronto
and associated companies in
Berlin Ibadan

Oxford is a trade mark of Oxford University Press

Introduction and compilation © Fleur Adcock and Jacqueline Simms
For additional copyright information see pp. 373–9

First published 1995

British Library Cataloguing in Publication Data

Data available

Library of Congress Cataloging in Publication Data

The Oxford book of creatures / edited by Fleur Adcock and Jacqueline Simms.
p.   cm.   Includes index.
1. Animals—Literary collections.   I. Adcock, Fleur.   II. Simms, Jacqueline, 1940– .
PN6071.A7094   1995   808.8′036—dc20   94—45355
ISBN 0–19–214226–7

1 3 5 7 9 10 8 6 4 2

Typeset by Pure Tech Corporation, Pondicherry, India
Printed in Great Britain on acid-free paper by
Bookcraft (Bath) Ltd
Midsomer Norton, Avon

CONTENTS

Editors' Note   vi

Introduction   vii

Prologue: Reflections   1

Design   17

Procreation   45

Habitat   71

Companionship   121

Talkers   175

Workers   205

Habits   235

Red in Tooth and Claw   255

Monsters   307

Death and Extinction   335

Epilogue: Celebration   361

Acknowledgements   373

Index of Creatures   381

Index of Authors   385

EDITORS' NOTE

We should like to record our gratitude to all the people who gave us helpful advice and suggestions. They are too many to name in full, but Jacqueline Simms thanks in particular Dr Donald Parry, Stella Booth, Brad Leithauser, Mark Wormald, Peter Scupham and Margaret Steward (who plied her with books and ideas in the library that is Old Hall), and especially D. J. Enright, exemplary anthologist, for his encouragement. Our editor at the Oxford University Press, Judith Luna, gave us an exceptionally useful first reading. Fleur Adcock would like above all to mention the late Angela Carter, who loved the idea of this anthology but did not live to see it realized.

INTRODUCTION

This is only one of several possible Books of Creatures we might have compiled. It would be easy to fill a whole shelf (or a whole wall, even a whole room) with collections of prose and verse on the ridiculously enormous subject we have chosen; but the point of an anthology is to select. The very richness of the field meant that we were free to impart our own particular flavour to the resulting confection, while the fact that there were two of us helped to prevent it from being too idiosyncratic. We came to the task by different routes and from different backgrounds of reading but with open minds, prepared to be surprised by our discoveries and to show flexibility in our choices. Animals inspire strong emotions (one of us was in mourning for a cherished family of spiders when she felt the first impulse to embark on this book), and they also tend to attract writers with a taste for precise observation, whether scientifically or aesthetically motivated. We are creatures ourselves; it is natural for human beings to be fascinated by the behaviour of the other species with which we share this planet. The prospect of exploring how this fascination had found literary expression was irresistible.

What we have aimed for, on the whole, is range: a wide range of styles, periods, genres, and tones, but above all a wide variety of creatures—although it must be admitted that about 250 cannot be more than a sample, when the total number of animal species in the world (many of them varieties of beetles) has been estimated at upwards of 30 million. What is a creature? A living being, real or imaginary, belonging to the animal kingdom. For the purposes of this book human creatures are excluded from our definition, but we have spread our boundaries wide enough to embrace anything else, from the microbe to the whale. Cell DNA, as a constituent of all life, got in—we couldn't resist Les Murray's poem—and also plankton; the exact status of plankton had never been quite clear to us (was it animal or vegetable?) but it seemed a pity to reject Norman Nicholson's description of it, and sure enough a zoological dictionary reassured us that 'zoo plankton' (from the Greek *plagtos*, wandering) was the animal form.

Our first rule, even before we began our serious reading, was 'Not too many cats, dogs, or horses'. Cat-lovers in particular can find any number of anthologies to satisfy their craving. Spider-lovers are less well catered for, and slug-lovers are apparently ignored. We soon became aware that certain creatures crop up regularly in literature, and forced ourselves to be sparing with them. Bees have been of interest to writers from the Old Testament onwards; birds, particularly song-birds (most notably the nightingale), have always been popular; foxes have had quite a following (in more senses than one); the lion, useful as a symbol, and widely featured in folklore as well as hunting tales, is well documented. Creatures such as poultry and cattle, which have been domesticated or farmed, naturally get written about; and we had to be rather ruthless with silkworms.

Towards the end of our researches (or rather, since the task could have occupied us for the rest of our lives, towards the date of our deadline), we found ourselves falling gleefully upon the literary mention of any species not yet represented: a gecko, a sea mouse, a hairy armadillo. On the other hand, we refrained from combing zoological textbooks for esoteric creatures just for the sake of comprehensiveness; even if our chosen extracts may not be consistently by the most elegant stylists (although many are), we were careful not to include anything badly written or lacking in interest and bite. Some of the naturalists, travel writers, and innocent onlookers in these pages may have lacked literary training, but they are readable, lively, sometimes funny, always observant.

The attitude of the writer was also important. We tried to avoid pieces where a creature was mentioned merely as an adjunct or accessory to some other theme. Whatever the emotions involved—love, loathing, curiosity, wonder, or scientific detachment—our creatures had to be in full focus, as themselves, not as mere symbols or excuses for philosophizing. When it came to rats, for example, Richmal Crompton's William showed a proper enthusiasm; and Mayhew's grisly account of rat-catching as a sport, concentrating on the dogs as much as on their victims, is equally graphic. This is not to say that we excluded broader speculations about the place of creatures in the scheme of things, or their relationships with human beings and with each other; our Prologue, 'Reflections', opens with some of these, but the creatures mentioned (Darwin's lion-ant, Judith Wright's pelican) are nevertheless vividly present. Fables also found their way into this section; too many would have overloaded it with abstractions, but they have their place in literature, as well as in the oral tradition, and needed to be represented. On the whole we have avoided anthropomorphism, though we have let in some particularly compelling examples, especially coming from children's literature.

It was interesting to find how much the presence or absence of creatures through centuries of poetry has been influenced by literary fashion. John Skelton, in the sixteenth century, cast his quirky gaze on several; Michael Drayton, a little later, wallowed in them; Milton surveyed them in his account of the Creation. After this they rather thinned out. Certain birds and animals have never quite been out of the poetic view, but in the hard-headed eighteenth century only a few eccentrics such as Blake, Cowper, and Smart took any serious interest in the lesser orders. You had to be mildly or seriously mad to enjoy creatures in that rational age. With the dawn of Romanticism, however, they came back, and have never since lost their attraction. Twentieth-century poets have naturally been affected by a growing concern for ecology and the risk to numerous species; indeed, a whole book might have been produced from contemporary poems on creatures.

Poetry was perhaps relatively simple to deal with: poems come in small units, on the whole, and have titles which are sometimes helpful. Prose in all its forms (fiction, letters, journals, travel books, natural history, scientific studies) is more unwieldy and it was hard to know where to begin. Although at first we divided our territory (the poet scouring the poems, the proser the prose), in the end we naturally shared a certain amount of the research, and contributed to one another's work. The final decisions as to contents, pruning of the prose, thematic arrangement, and divisions into sections were joint operations, and mutually agreed.

We wanted to mix up styles and periods, allowing for a succession of contrasts and surprises, while preserving some element of overall logic, or at least flow. A thematic order seemed best in what is primarily a literary anthology, a book to be read, and the themes presented themselves quite readily from the material we had found. After 'Reflections' we begin by examining creatures as visual objects—what they look like, how they are constructed and move. From the 'wonderful machinery' of A. R. Ammons's crab, through a more intricate and dense passage by D'Arcy Thompson on the effect of gravity on size, and Leonardo's jotting about a goose's foot, to Eeyore's *lack* of a tail (one of our few whimsical moments), 'Design' opens our eyes to the fantastic variations between creatures.

In 'Procreation', the anthology then turns to aspects of behaviour, first in mating, giving birth, and parenthood. The poets in particular have observed some curious copulations; young creatures are—more or less—cared for (a salutary 'cage of instruction' here). Miriam Rothschild observes the parasitical connection between the reproduction of fleas and rabbits; which brings us to John Donne who, in a tone of scientific accuracy combined with witty intent, bids his beloved to 'mark but this flea'. Where creatures live, their 'Habitat', necessarily follows, and this section includes the elements in which creatures move: air, earth, water, even fire. From insects and beetles to two-toed sloth and waterhog, all need shelter. Maeterlinck's bees swarm in search of a new hive; birds build their varied nests—except, that is, for swifts, which (in Anne Stevenson's poem) reject 'Soft nests in the wet fields, slimehold of worms' to live on the wing.

The relationships creatures have with other creatures and with human beings (a chance here for the domestic animals to make themselves felt) fill 'Companionship', a section that includes more passing acquaintances, best described as 'visitors', welcome or unwelcome. Konrad Lorenz's tame raven grooms 'with wonderful precision' Lorenz's facial hair; Cowper's tame hare has lost, after ten years, 'Much of her vigilant instinctive dread' of him; dogs fall prey to jealousy and need human wiles to reassure them; spiders creep in at a window to listen to a piano playing. David Lack firmly states of the robin that 'trusting it often becomes, but friendly never', to be contradicted in the more sentimental circumstances of *The Secret Garden*.

That animals communicate with one another using sounds, if not language, is demonstrated in a brief section called 'Talkers'. Birds—including those that imitate the human voice—are predominant, but Jane Goodall looks at the sign language of chimpanzees, and Lopez discusses the various sounds made by wolves. E. T. A. Hoffman's cat speaks for itself, and Dr Doolittle gets vital instruction on animal languages from his parrot.

Creatures work both on their own behalf, as in the case of bees, spiders, or Fabre's dung-beetles, and under compulsion for their human owners: carrying burdens, performing to entertain us (Angela Carter's chimps; Montaigne's dancing elephants), hunting, or providing milk and eggs (two Hardy passages from *Tess of the D'Urbervilles* are outstanding here). The last pit pony in Britain was retired in 1994; and Jefferies describes an old horse put out to grass after a long hard-working career. In the group called 'Habits' we have assembled pieces that take a closer look at some ordinary, and some specific, often odd, examples of animal behaviour. These range from the reactions of weak or young wolves under attack from their superiors (they literally 'turn the other cheek') to Hudson's peremptory gander; Darwin's paper of 1881 demonstrates the sensitivity of worms to vibrations, and Louis Roule shows how a calcareous 'tomb' forms round the pearl in the oyster.

Perhaps the most contentious section is 'Red in Tooth and Claw', which covers a great variety of hostile or predatory activities, both from the creatures' point of view (bedbugs, mosquitoes, vultures) and that of their more deliberate exploiters—us, usually, as exemplified in a couple of recipes for eating our victims. Samuel Johnson is a lone voice speaking against the vivisection of animals. Shooting lions as sport makes a wretched appearance; D. H. Lawrence comes to mourn one slaughtered in Mexico; and reversing the charges, as it were, Jim Corbett says in a note to his *Man-Eaters of Kumaon* that 'a man-eating tiger is one that has been compelled . . . to adopt a diet alien to it'. We may not have pleased the Buddhist or the vegetarian, but hope to have shown things as they are.

'Monsters' is a slightly anomalous section. Mythical or imaginary and invented creatures occur occasionally elsewhere, but here is a gallery of them, ranging from Belloc's multicoloured microbe to the Loch Ness Monster and the ngarara of Maori legend; from siren to unicorn. It also includes several 'transformations', in what can be no more than a mere glimpse of this fabulous land. Then comes 'Death and Extinction', which again could have been extended indefinitely if we had included all the laments and mournful elegies we came across; and lastly the Epilogue, 'Celebration', whose title encapsulates the feelings of wonder, delight, and praise we most wanted to convey.

FLEUR ADCOCK
JACQUELINE SIMMS

Unto men we owe Justice, and to all other creatures that are capable of it, grace and benignity.

Montaigne

All the animals are very good at being animals.
As usual, we are not up to being us.

Penelope Shuttle

With an ass I can commune for ever.

Laurence Sterne

Even a worm an inch long has a soul half-an-inch long.

Japanese Buddhist proverb

Altogether elsewhere, vast
Herds of reindeer move across
Miles and miles of golden moss,
Silently and very fast.

W. H. Auden

PROLOGUE

REFLECTIONS

[Australia, Jan. 1836]

A little time before . . . I had been lying on a sunny bank, and was reflecting on the strange character of the animals of this country as compared with the rest of the world. An unbeliever in every thing beyond his own reason might exclaim, 'Two distinct Creators must have been at work; their object, however, has been the same, and certainly the end in each case is complete.' While thus thinking, I observed the hollow conical pitfall of the lion-ant: first a fly fell down the treacherous slope and immediately disappeared; then came a large but unwary ant; its struggles to escape being very violent, those curious little jets of sand, described by Kirby as being flirted by the insect's tail, were promptly directed against the expected victim. But the ant enjoyed a better fate than the fly, and escaped the fatal jaws which lay concealed at the base of the conical hollow. There can be no doubt but that this predacious larva belongs to the same genus with the European kind, though to a different species. Now what would the sceptic say to this? Would any two workmen ever have hit upon so beautiful, so simple, and yet so artificial a contrivance? It cannot be thought so: one Hand has surely worked throughout the universe.

CHARLES DARWIN, *Journal of Researches* (*Voyage of the Beagle*), 1839

Cell DNA

I am the singular
in free fall.
I and my doubles
carry it all;

life's slim volume
spirally bound.
It's what I'm about,
it's what I'm around.

Presence and hungers
imbue a sap mote
with the world as they spin it.
I teach it by rote

but its every command
was once a miscue
that something rose to,
Presence and freedom

re-wording, re-beading
strains on a strand
making I and I more different
than we could stand.

LES MURRAY (b. 1938)

Wonderful, perplexing divisibility of Life. It is related by D. Unzer, an authority wholly to be relied on, that an Ohrwurm (Earwig?) cut in half ate its own hinder half. The Head of the rattlesnake severed from the body bit at, and squirted out its poison. Related by Bevereley in his Hist. of Virginia. Lyonnet in his Insect-theology tore a wasp in half, and 3 days after the fore-half bit whatever was presented to it of its former food, and the hind-half darted out its sting on being touched. Boyle mentions a female butterfly that when beheaded not only admitted the male but laid eggs in consequence of the impregnation. But a Turtle has lived six months with his Head off and wandered about, yea, six hours after its heart and bowels (all but the Lungs) were taken out. How shall we think of this compatible with the *monad* Soul? If I say what has Spirit to do with space, what odd dreams it would suggest? Or is every animal a republic *in se*? Or is there one Breeze of Life, at once the soul of each and God of all? Is it not strictly analogous to generation, and no more contradictory to unity than *it?* But *it?* Aye! there's the Twist in the Logic. Is not the reproduction of the Lizard a complete generation! O it is easy to dream, and surely better of these things than of a 20,000 £ Prize in the Lottery, or of a Place at Court! 13 Dec. 1804. Malta.

SAMUEL TAYLOR COLERIDGE, *Notebooks*, 1804

Pelicans

Funnel-web spider, snake and octopus,
pitcher-plant and vampire-bat and shark—
these are cold water on an easy faith.
Look at them, but don't linger.
If we stare too long, something looks back at us;
something gazes through from underneath;
something crooks a very dreadful finger
down there in an unforgotten dark.

Turn away then, and look up at the sky.
There sails that old clever Noah's Ark,
the well-turned, well-carved pelican
with his wise comic eye;
he turns and wheels down, kind as an ambulance-driver,
to join his fleet. Pelicans rock together,
solemn as clowns in white on a circus-river,
meaning: this world holds every sort of weather.

JUDITH WRIGHT (b. 1915)

Do animals have less fear because they live without words?

It pains me that the animals will never rebel against us, the patient animals, the cows, the sheep, all the creatures in our control and unable to escape our control.

    I can imagine a rebellion in a slaughterhouse, spreading from there throughout a whole city; men, women, children, old people ruthlessly trampled to death; the animals pouring over streets and vehicles, smashing down gates and doors, dashing furiously up to the highest floor of the buildings, subway cars crushed by thousands of oxen running wild, and sheep tearing us apart with suddenly sharp teeth.

I would be relieved if just one bull would send those heroes, the toreadors, into a lamentable flight—a whole bloodthirsty arena too. But I would prefer an uprising by the lesser, gentle victims, the sheep and cows. I won't admit that it can never happen; that we will never tremble before them, before them of all creatures.

ELIAS CANETTI, *The Human Province*, 1973 (tr. Joachim Neugroschel, 1978)

Satire 2

My mother's maids, when they did sew and spin,
They sang sometime a song of the fieldmouse,
That for because her lyvelood was but thin
Would needs go seek her townish sister's house.
She thought herself endured too much pain:
The stormy blasts her cave so sore did souse
That when the furrows swimmed with the rain
She must lie cold and wet in sorry plight;
And worse than that, bare meat there did remain
To comfort her when she her house had dight—
Sometime a barley corn, sometime a bean,
For which she laboured hard both day and night
In harvest time whilst she might go and glean.
And when her store was 'stroyed with the flood,
Then wellaway, for she undone was clean.
Then was she fain to take instead of food
Sleep if she might, her hunger to beguile.
'My sister,' quod she, 'hath a living good,
And hence from me she dwelleth not a mile.
In cold and storm she lieth warm and dry
In bed of down. The dirt doth not defile
Her tender foot, she laboureth not as I:
Richly she feedeth, and at the rich man's cost,
And for her meat she needs not crave nor cry.
By sea, by land, of delicates the most
Her cater seeks, and spareth for no peril.
She feedeth on boiled bacon meat and roast,
And hath thereof neither charge nor travail,
And when she list, the liquor of the grape
Doth glad her heart, till that her belly swell.'
And at this journey she maketh but a jape,

---

lyvelood: i.e. livelihood   *meat*: food   *dight*: put in order   *cater*: i.e. caterer   *and . . . peril*: 'and no danger restrains him'   *charge*: burden; or: cost   *liquor*: i.e. juice

So forth she goeth, trusting of all this wealth
With her sister her part so for to shape
That if she might keep herself in health
To live a lady while her life doth last.
And to the door now is she come by stealth,
And with her foot anon she scrapeth full fast.
The other for fear durst not well scarce appear,
Of every noise so was the wretch aghast.
At last she asked softly who was there,
And in her language as well as she could,
'Peep,' quod the other, 'sister, I am here.'
'Peace,' quod the towny mouse, 'why speakest thou so loud?'
And by the hand she took her fair and well.
'Welcome,' quod she, 'my sister, by the rood!'
She feasted her that joy it was to tell
The fare they had—they drank the wine so clear,
And as to purpose now and then it fell
She cheered her with 'How, sister, what cheer?'
Amids this joy befell a sorry chance,
That wellaway the stranger bought full dear
The fare she had. For as she looked askance
Under a stool she spied two steaming eyes
In a round head with sharp ears: in France
Was never mouse so feared, for though the unwise
Had not yseen such a beast before,
Yet had nature taught her after her guise
To know her foe and dread him evermore.
The towny mouse fled: she knew whither to go.
The other had no shift, but wonders sore
Feared of her life; at home she wished her tho.
And to the door alas as she did skip,
The heaven it would, lo, and eke her chance was so,
At the threshold her seely foot did trip,
And ere she might recover it again
The traitor Cat had caught her by the hip,
And made her there against her will remain
That had forgotten her poor surety and rest
For seeming wealth wherein she thought to reign.

SIR THOMAS WYATT (1503–42)

---

steaming: flaming   *guise*: fashion   *shift*: solution, expedient   *wonders*:
prob. a verb; otherwise: wondrously   *tho*: then   *seely*: innocent, pitiful

After her little visitors were departed, Miss Harriet went into the drawing-room, and having paid her compliments, sat herself down, that she might improve her mind by the conversation of the company.

'I have', said a lady who was present, 'been for a long time accustomed to consider animals as mere machines, actuated by the unerring hand of Providence to do those things which are necessary for the preservation of themselves and their offspring; but the sight of the learned Pig, which has lately been shown in London, has deranged these ideas, and I know not what to think.'

As soon as they were gone, 'pray mamma', said Harriet, 'what does the learned Pig do? I had a great desire to ask Mrs Franks, but was fearful she would think me impertinent.' 'I commend your modesty, my dear,' replied Mrs Benson, 'but would not have it lead you into such a degree of restraint as to prevent your gratifying that laudable curiosity, without which young persons must remain ignorant of many things very proper for them to be acquainted with. . . . In respect to the learned Pig, I have heard things which are quite astonishing in a species of animals generally regarded as very stupid. The creature was shown for a sight in a room provided for the purpose, where a number of people assembled to view his performances. Two alphabets of large letters on card paper were placed on the floor; one of the company was then desired to propose a word which he wished the pig to spell. This his keeper repeated to him, and the Pig picked out every letter successively with his snout and collected them together till the word was completed. He was then desired to tell the hour of the day, and one of the company held a watch to him, which he seemed with his little cunning eyes to examine very attentively, and, having done so, picked out figures for the hour and minutes of the day. He showed a number of tricks of the same nature, to the great diversion of the spectators. For my own part, though I was in London at the time he was exhibited, and heard continually of this wonderful Pig from persons of my acquaintance, I never went to see him; for I am fully persuaded that great cruelty must have been exercised in teaching him things so foreign to his nature, and therefore would not give any encouragement to such a scheme.'

'And do you think, mamma,' said Harriet, 'that the Pig knows the letters and can really spell words?' 'I think it possible, my dear, for the Pig to be taught to know the letters one from the other, and that his keeper has some private sign by which he directs him to each that are wanted;— but that he has an idea of *spelling* I can never believe, nor are animals capable of attaining human sciences, because, for these, human faculties are requisite; and no art of man can *change* the nature of any thing, though he may be able to improve that nature to a certain degree, or at least to call forth to view, powers which would be hidden from us, because they would only be exerted in the intercourse of animals with each other. As far as this can be done by familiarizing them, and showing them such a degree of kindness as is consistent with our higher obligations, it may be an agreeable amusement, but will never answer any important purpose to mankind; and I would advise you, Harriet, never to give countenance to those people who show what they call *learned* animals; as you may assure yourself they exercise great barbarities upon them, of which starving them almost to death is most likely among the number. But, my dear, it is now time for you to retire to rest, I will therefore bid you good night.'

> Sarah Trimmer (1741–1810), *Fabulous Histories, &c.,* later known as *The History of the Robins*

Presumption is our naturall and originall infirmitie.

How knoweth [man] by the vertue of his understanding the inward and secret motions of beasts? By what comparison from them to us doth he conclude the brutishnesse, he ascribeth unto them? When I am playing with my Cat, who knowes whether she have more sport in dallying with me, than I have in gaming with her? We entertaine one another with mutuall apish trickes, If I have my houre to begin or to refuse, so hath she hers. *Plato* in setting forth the golden age under *Saturne,* amongst the chiefe advantages that man had then, reporteth the communication he had with beasts, of whom enquiring and taking instruction, he knew the true qualities, and differences of every one of them: by, and from whom he got an absolute understanding and perfect wisedome, whereby he led a happier life than we can doe. Can we have a better proofe to judge of mans impudency, touching beasts?

But to come to my purpose, I say therefore, there is no likelyhood, we should imagine, the beasts doe the very same things by a naturall inclination and forced genuitie, which we doe of our owne freewil and industrie. Of the very same effects we must conclude alike faculties; and by the richest effects infer the noblest faculties, and consequently acknowledge, that the same discourse and way, we hold in working, the very same, or perhaps some other better, doe beasts hold. Wherefore shall we imagine that naturall compulsion in them, that prove no such effect our selves?

> Michel Eyquem de Montaigne (1533–92), *An Apologie of Raymond Sebond,* 1580 (tr. John Florio, 1603)

A Bird and Her Chicks

Once upon a time a mother bird who had three chicks wanted to cross a river. She put the first one under her wing and started flying across. As she flew she said, 'Tell me, child, when I'm old, will you carry me under your wing the way I'm carrying you now?'

'Of course,' replied the chick. 'What a question!'

'Ah,' said the mother bird, 'you're lying.' With that she let the chick slip, and it fell into the river and drowned.

The mother went back for the second chick, which she took under her wing. Once more as she was flying across the river, she said, 'Tell me, child, when I'm old, will you carry me under your wing the way I'm carrying you now?'

'Of course,' replied the chick. 'What a question!'

'Ah,' said the mother bird, 'you're lying.' With that she let the second chick slip, and it also drowned.

Then the mother went back for the third chick, which she took under her wing. Once more she asked in mid-flight, 'Tell me, child, when I am old, will you carry me under your wing the way I'm carrying you now?'

'No, mother,' replied the third chick. 'How could I? By then I'll have chicks of my own to carry.'

'Ah, my dearest child,' said the mother bird, 'you're the one who tells the truth.' With that she carried the third chick to the other bank of the river.

Yiddish fable, ed. Angela Carter

for my part I love to look on nature with a poetic feeling which magnifys the pleasure I love to see the nightingale in its hazel retreat & the cuckoo hiding in its solitudes of oaken foliage & not to examine their carcasses in glass cases yet naturalists & botanists seem to have no taste for this practical feeling they merely make collections of dryd specimens classing them after Linnaeus into tribes & familys & there they delight to show them as a sort of ambitious fame with them 'a bird in the hand is worth two in the bush' well everyone to his hobby

I have none of this curiosity about me tho I feel as happy as they can about finding a new species of field flower or butterflye which I have not seen before yet I have no desire further to dry the plant or torture the butterflye by sticking it on a cork board with a pin—I have no wish to do this if my feelings woud let me I only crop the blossom of the flower or take the root from its solitudes if it woud grace my garden & wish the fluttering butterflye to settle till I can come up with it to examine the powderd colours on its wings & then it may dance off again from fancyd dangers &

welcome I think your feelings are on the side of Poetry for I have no specimens to send you so be as it may you must be content with my descriptions & observations

JOHN CLARE, Natural History Letters, 1825–37

The Lyon and the Gnat

To the still Covert of a Wood,
  About the prime of Day,
A *Lyon*, satiated with Food,
With stately Pace, and sullen Mood,
  Now took his lazy way.

To Rest he there himself compos'd,
  And in his Mind revolv'd,
How Great a Person it enclos'd,
How free from Danger he repos'd,
  Though now in Ease dissolv'd!

Who Guard, nor Centinel did need,
  Despising as a Jest
All whom the Forest else did feed,
As Creatures of an abject Breed,
  Who durst not him molest.

But in the Air a Sound he heard,
  That gave him some dislike;
At which he shook his grisly Beard,
Enough to make the Woods affeard,
  And stretch'd his Paw to strike.

When on his lifted Nose there fell
  A Creature, slight of Wing,
Who neither fear'd his Grin, nor Yell,
Nor Strength, that in his Jaws did dwell,
  But gores him with her Sting.

Transported with th'Affront and Pain,
  He terribly exclaims,
Protesting, if it comes again,
Its guilty Blood the Grass shall stain,
  And to surprize it aims.

The scoffing *Gnat* now laugh'd aloud,
    And bids him upwards view
The *Jupiter* within the Cloud,
That humbl'd him, who was so proud,
    And this sharp Thunder threw.

That Taunt no *Lyon*'s Heart cou'd bear;
    And now much more he raves,
Whilst this new *Perseus* in the Air
Do's War and Strife again declare,
    And all his Terrour braves.

Upon his haughty Neck she rides,
    Then on his lashing Tail;
(Which need not now provoke his Sides)
Where she her slender Weapon guides,
    And makes all Patience fail.

A Truce at length he must propose,
    The Terms to be her Own;
Who likewise Rest and Quiet chose,
Contented now her Life to close,
    When she'd such Triumph known.

You mighty Men, who meaner ones despise,
Learn from this Fable to become more Wise;
You see the Lyon *may be vext with* Flies.

ANNE FINCH, Countess of Winchilsea (1661–1720)

Many naturalists are of opinion that the animals which we commonly consider as mute have the power of imparting their thoughts to one another. That they can express general sensations is very certain; every being that can utter sounds has a different voice for pleasure and for pain. The hound informs his fellows when he scents his game; the hen calls her chickens to their food by her cluck, and drives them from danger by her scream.

Birds have the greatest variety of notes; they have indeed a variety which seems almost sufficient to make a speech adequate to the purposes of a life which is regulated by instinct, and can admit little change or improvement. To the cries of birds, curiosity or superstition has been always attentive; many have studied the language of the feathered tribes, and some have boasted that they understood it.

The most skilful or most confident interpreters of the silvan dialogues have been commonly found among the philosophers of the East, in a country where the calmness of the air, and the mildness of the seasons, allow the student to pass a great part of the year in groves and bowers. But what may be done in one place by peculiar opportunities may be performed in another by peculiar diligence. A shepherd of Bohemia has, by long abode in the forests, enabled himself to understand the voice of birds; at least he relates with great confidence a story of which the credibility may be considered by the learned.

'As I was sitting,' said he, 'within a hollow rock, and watching my sheep that fed in the valley, I heard two vultures interchangeably crying on the summit of the cliff. Both voices were earnest and deliberate. My curiosity prevailed over my care of the flock; I climbed slowly and silently from crag to crag, concealed among the shrubs, till I found a cavity where I might sit and listen without suffering, or giving disturbance.

'I soon perceived that my labour would be well repaid; for an old vulture was sitting on a naked prominence, with her young about her, whom she was instructing in the arts of a vulture's life, and preparing, by the last lecture, for their final dismission to the mountains and the skies.

' "My children," said the old vulture, "you will the less want my instructions because you have had my practice before your eyes; you have seen me snatch from the farm the household fowl, you have seen me seize the leveret in the bush, and the kid in the pasture, you know how to fix your talons, and how to balance your flight when you are laden with your prey. But you remember the taste of more delicious food; I have often regaled you with the flesh of man."

"Tell us," said the young vultures, "where man may be found, and how he may be known; his flesh is surely the natural food of a vulture. Why have you never brought a man in your talons to the nest?"

"He is too bulky," said the mother; "when we find a man, we can only tear away his flesh, and leave his bones upon the ground."

"Since man is so big," said the young ones, "how do you kill him? You are afraid of the wolf and of the bear; by what power are vultures superior to man; is man more defenceless than a sheep?"

"We have not the strength of man," returned the mother, "and I am sometimes in doubt whether we have the subtlety; and the vultures would seldom feast upon his flesh, had not Nature, that devoted him to our uses, infused into him a strange ferocity, which I have never observed in any other being that feeds upon the earth. Two herds of men will often meet and shake his earth with noise, and fill the air with fire. When you hear noise and see fire which flashes along the ground, hasten to the place with your swiftest wing, for men are surely destroying one another; you will then find the ground smoking with blood and covered with carcasses, of which many are dismembered and mangled for the convenience of the vulture."

"But when men have killed their prey," said the pupil, "why do they not eat it? When the wolf has killed a sheep, he suffers not the vulture to touch it till he has satisfied himself. Is not man another kind of wolf?"

"Man," said the mother, "is the only beast who kills that which he does not devour, and this quality makes him so much a benefactor to our species."

"If men kill our prey and lay it in our way," said the young one, "what need shall we have of labouring for ourselves?"

"Because man will, sometimes," replied the mother, "remain for a long time quiet in his den. The old vultures will tell you when you are to watch his motions. When you see men in great numbers moving close together, like a flight of storks, you may conclude that they are hunting, and that you will soon revel in human blood."

"But still," said the young one, "I would gladly know the reason of this mutual slaughter. I could never kill what I could not eat."

"My child," said the mother, "this is a question which I cannot answer, though I am reckoned the most subtle bird of the mountain." '

SAMUEL JOHNSON, *The Idler*, no. 22, 9 September 1758

You will remember, when we were in Naples, staying at the Locanda al Largo di Castello, you asked for a glass of water to drink, and when it was brought I could see there were lots of insects in it. I wanted to stop you from drinking it and asked for purer water, but was assured by the girl that it was the best they had and everybody drank it readily. You took the glass and drank calmly from it, saying, 'After all, we eat crabs and eels and they don't harm us, so neither will these delicate little creatures; perhaps they'll nourish us.' Then we asked them to show us the place, and we scooped up a glass of water from the bottom of the tank, in which there were countless creatures, monstrous in appearance.

Now I send you a drawing of a Neapolitan crab which I have often eaten, though only lately observed that it gives the impression of a human face. I send it not only because of its strangeness but so that you may see how I began my investigation of mankind with the most insignificant creatures, which none the less possess mechanical skills, and have worked my way up step by step, through all the species of animals, till I came to man; and I see there is a transition from the more perfect animals to the human species, and the faculties possessed by individual animals are found in their totality in the human species. Only they do not appertain to the individual man as they do to the individual animal, but to the whole of the human race, and therein lies the origin of perpetual concurrence and counteraction.

> JOHANN HEINRICH WILHELM TISCHBEIN, letter to Goethe, undated (tr. D. J. Enright, 1994). Goethe and Tischbein were in Naples together during February and March 1787

The Keys

> The Catterpiller on the Leaf
> Reminds thee of thy Mother's Grief.
>
> WILLIAM BLAKE (1757–1827), *The Gates of Paradise*

What a pitiful thing, what poor stuff it is to say that animals are machines deprived of knowledge and feeling, which always perform their operations in the same way, which learn nothing, which improve nothing, etc.!

What! this bird which makes its nest semi-circular when it is attached to a wall, which builds it in a quarter-circle when it is in a corner, and makes it circular in a tree, this bird does everything in the same way? This gun dog you have trained for three months: does he not know more at the end of that time than he knew before your lessons? Does the canary immediately repeat the tune you are teaching him? Have you not seen that it makes mistakes and corrects itself?

Judge this dog who has lost his master, who has searched for him with mournful cries in every path, who comes home agitated, restless, who runs up and down the stairs, who goes from room to room, who at last finds his beloved master in his study, and shows him his joy by the tenderness of cries, by his leaps, by his caresses.

Barbarians seize this dog who so prodigiously surpasses man in friendship. They nail him to a table and dissect him alive to show you the mesenteric veins. You discover in him all the same organs of feeling that you possess. Answer me, mechanist, has nature arranged all the springs of feeling in this animal in order that he should not feel? Does he have nerves to be impassive? Do not assume that nature presents this impertinent contradiction.

> VOLTAIRE (1694–1778), *Dictionnaire philosophique (Bêtes)*, 1764 (tr. Theodore Besterman, 1971)

Experience certainly educates the dog as it does the man. After long acquaintance and practice in the field we learn the habits and ways of game—

to know where it will or not be found. A young dog in the same way dashes swiftly up a hedge, and misses the rabbit that, hearing him coming, doubles back behind a tree or stole; an old dog leaves nothing behind him, searching every corner. This is acquired knowledge. Neither does all depend upon hereditary predisposition as exhibited in the various breeds—the setter, the pointer, the spaniel, or greyhound—and their especial drift of brain; their capacity is not wholly confined to one sphere. They possess an initiating power—what in man is called originality, invention, discovery: they make experiments.

I had a pointer that exhibited this faculty in a curious manner. She was weakly when young, and for that reason, together with other circumstances, was never properly trained: a fact that may perhaps have prevented her 'mind' from congealing into the stolidity of routine. She became an outdoor pet, and followed at heel everywhere. One day some ponds were netted, and of the fish taken a few chanced to be placed in a great stone trough from which cattle drank in the yard—a common thing in the country. Some time afterwards, the trough being foul, the fish—they were roach, tench, perch, and one small jack—were removed to a shallow tub while it was being cleansed. In this tub, being scarcely a foot deep though broad, the fish were of course distinctly visible, and at once became an object of the most intense interest to the pointer. She would not leave it; but stood watching every motion of the fish, with her head now on one side now on the other. There she must have remained some hours, and was found at last in the act of removing them one by one, and laying them softly, quite unhurt, on the grass.

I put them back into the water, and waited to see the result. She took a good look, and then plunged her nose right under the surface and half-way up the neck, completely submerging the head, and in that position groped about on the bottom till a fish came in contact with her mouth and was instantly snatched out. Her head must have been under water each time nearly a minute, feeling for the fish. One by one she drew them out and placed them on the ground, till only the jack remained. He puzzled her, darting away swift as an arrow and seeming to anticipate the enemy. But after a time he, too, was captured.

They were not injured—not the mark of a tooth was to be seen—and swam as freely as ever when restored to the water. So soon as they were put in again the pointer recommenced her fishing, and could hardly be got away by force. The fish were purposely left in the tub. The next day she returned to the amusement, and soon became so dexterous as to pull a fish out almost the instant her nose went under water. The jack was always the most difficult to catch, but she managed to conquer him sooner or later. When returned to the trough, however, she was done—the water was too deep. Scarcely anything could be imagined apparently more opposite to the

hereditary intelligence of a pointer than this; and certainly no one at-
tempted to teach her, neither did she do it for food. It was an original
motion of her own: to what can it be compared but mind proceeding by
experiment?

RICHARD JEFFERIES, The Gamekeeper at Home, 1890

The Jack Daw

There is a bird who by his coat,
And by the hoarseness of his note,
   Might be suppos'd a crow;
A great frequenter of the church,
Where bishop-like he finds a perch,
   And dormitory too.

Above the steeple shines a plate,
That turns and turns, to indicate
   From what point blows the weather;
Look up—your brains begin to swim,
'Tis in the clouds—that pleases him,
   He chooses it the rather.

Fond of the speculative height,
Thither he wings his airy flight,
   And thence securely sees
The bustle and the raree-show
That occupy mankind below,
   Secure and at his ease.

You think no doubt he sits and muses
On future broken bones and bruises,
   If he should chance to fall;
No not a single thought like that
Employs his philosophic pate,
   Or troubles it at all.

He sees that this great roundabout
The world, with all its motley rout,
   Church, army, physic, law,
Its customs and its businesses
Are no concern at all of his,
   And says, what says he? Caw.

Thrice happy bird! I too have seen
Much of the vanities of men,
    And sick of having seen 'em,
Would chearfully these limbs resign
For such a pair of wings as thine,
    And such a head between 'em.

WILLIAM COWPER (1731–1800), tr. from the Latin of Vincent Bourne

DESIGN

Help

From the inlet
surf a father
pulls in a crab—
a wonderful machinery
but
not a fish: kicks
it off the line &
up the beach
where three daughters
and two sons take
turns bringing cups
of water
to keep alive, to
watch work, the sanded
& disjeweled.

A. R. AMMONS (b. 1926)

Catch

There once was a fisherman of Scrabster
Caught in his pot a gey queer lapster.

Thought he, this lapster's a sure sellar,
A tail it has, and a wee propellor,

In fact, it's no ordinary lapster felly,
It looks far more like a peedie heli—

You know yon kind of hoverlapster,
A what do you call it, helicapster.

Aye, aye, it's a peedie helicapster:
There's lots are caught in the sea off Scrabster.

IAN HAMILTON FINLAY (b. 1925)

Starfish

'. . . and the waters shall no more become
a flood to destroy all flesh.
    And the bow shall be in the cloud;
and I will look upon it . . .'

Neither star nor fish, this
points the darker reaches of your thought.
Where the heart might be, a mouth hovers
under 5 pebbly rays
balefully tinted as gasoline on water,
enough raw power
to pry a clam apart. And
elusive . . . So fragile, starred a skeleton
no fossil survives intact. Who knows
how far back it goes?

                One summer, you
poised, spread-legged, dungareed
shin bruised by the rail of a lobster boat,
hefting a long handled hook.
Ahead, winking in and out the broken field
rose buoy after buoy

all banded day-glo colors:
picked off, the pots dragged
up into the cockpit,
backbreaking with the weight of bricks.
Your haul . . . an occasional blue green lobster
but starfish mostly
clinging to the wet laths, the twine netting,
barbarian hordes
sacking another citadel—gorged on
the salted, pinched alewives.

Mortal, spiny asteroids!
                              Imagine shining
arms hacked off, and the mouth saved.
Even a single ray. It grows back
a whole new animal.
Piecemeal was never enough.
That's what it's all about, you'd say
and litter the deck with starfish.
Allowed to die, then, out in the air—
delicate yellows, reds, pinks
blanched in crazy attitudes,
so many gracefully crippled pinwheels
incipient swastikas, brittle charms—
not one will last
even a million years. How strange, how hard
facing disintegration! Even now
under your own feet, you may see
neither star nor fish
the awful rainbow curling up, paler than cloud or stone.

JAMES SCULLY (b. 1937)

Gravity and other Size-limiting Factors

The forms as well as the actions of our bodies are entirely conditioned (save for certain exceptions in the case of aquatic animals) by the strength of gravity upon this globe; or, as Sir Charles Bell had put it some sixty years before, the very animals which move upon the surface of the earth are proportioned to its magnitude. Were the force of gravity to be doubled our bipedal form would be a failure, and the majority of terrestrial animals would resemble short-legged saurians, or else serpents. Birds and insects would suffer likewise, though with some compensation in the increased density of the air. On the other hand, if gravity were halved, we should get a lighter, slenderer, more active type, needing less energy, less heat, less heart, less lungs, less blood. Gravity not only controls the actions but also influences the forms of all save the least of organisms. The tree under its burden of leaves or fruit has changed its every curve and outline since its boughs were bare, and a mantle of snow will alter its configuration again. Sagging wrinkles, hanging breasts and many another sign of age are part of gravitation's slow relentless handiwork.

There are other physical factors besides gravity which help to limit the size to which an animal may grow and to define the conditions under which it may live. The small insects skating on a pool have their movements controlled and their freedom limited by the surface-tension between water and air, and the measure of that tension determines the magnitude which they may attain. A man coming wet from his bath carries a few ounces of water, and is perhaps 1 per cent heavier than before; but a wet fly weighs twice as much as a dry one, and becomes a helpless thing. A small insect finds itself imprisoned in a drop of water, and a fly with two feet in one drop finds it hard to extricate them.

The mechanical construction of insect or crustacean is highly efficient up to a certain size, but even crab and lobster never exceed certain moderate dimensions, perfect within these narrow bounds as their construction seems to be. Their body lies within a hollow shell, the stresses within which increase much faster than the mere scale of size; every hollow structure, every dome or cylinder, grows weaker as it grows larger, and a tin canister is easy to make but a great boiler is a complicated affair. The boiler has to be strengthened by 'stiffening rings' or ridges, and so has the lobster's shell; but there is a limit even to this method of counteracting the weakening effect of size. An ordinary girder-bridge may be made efficient up to a span of 200 ft or so; but it is physically incapable of spanning the Firth of Forth. The great Japanese spider-crab, *Macrocheira*, has a span of some 12 ft across; but Nature meets the difficulty and solves the problem by keeping the body small, and building up the long and slender legs out of short lengths of narrow tubes. A hollow shell is admirable for small animals, but Nature does not and cannot make use of it for the large.

D'ARCY WENTWORTH THOMPSON, *On Growth and Form*, 1917

Mollusc

By its nobship sailing upside down,
by its inner sexes, by the crystalline
pimplings of its skirts, by the sucked-on
lifelong kiss of its toppling motion,

by the viscose optics now extruded
now wizened instantaneously, by the
ridges grating up a food-path, by
the pop shell in its nick of dry,
by excretion, the earthworm coils, the glibbing,
by the gilt slipway, and by pointing
perhaps as far back into time as
ahead, a shore being folded interior,
by boiling on salt, by coming uncut over
a razor's edge, by hiding the Oligocene
underleaf may this and every snail sense
itself ornament the weave of presence.

LES MURRAY (b. 1938)

A Jellyfish

Visible, invisible,
   a fluctuating charm
an amber-tinctured amethyst
   inhabits it, your arm
approaches and it opens
   and it closes; you had meant
to catch it and it quivers;
   you abandon your intent.

MARIANNE MOORE (1887–1972)

But among outstanding marvels is the creature called the nautilus, and by others the pilot-fish. Lying on its back it comes to the surface of the sea, gradually raising itself up in such a way that by sending out all the water through a tube it so to speak unloads itself of bilge and sails easily. Afterwards it twists back its two foremost arms and spreads out between them a marvellously thin membrane, and with this serving as a sail in the breeze while it uses its other arms underneath it as oars, it steers itself with its tail between them as a rudder. So it proceeds across the deep mimicking the likeness of a fast cutter, if any alarm interrupts its voyage submerging itself by sucking in water.

PLINY THE ELDER (AD 23–79), *Natural History* (tr. H. Rackham, 1937)

Of true organic spirals we have no lack. We think at once of horns of ruminants, and of still more exquisitely beautiful molluscan shells—in which (as Pliny says) *magna ludentis Naturae varietas*. Closely related spirals may be traced in the florets of a sunflower; a true spiral, though not, by the way, so easy of investigation, is seen in the outline of a cordiform leaf; and yet again, we can recognise typical though transitory spirals in a lock of hair, in a staple of wool, in the coil of an elephant's trunk, in the 'circling spires' of a snake, in the coils of a cuttle-fish's arm, or of a monkey's or a chameleon's tail.

Among such forms as these, and the many others which we might easily add to them, it is obvious that we have to do with things which, though mathematically similar, are biologically speaking fundamentally different.

There is a difference between such a spiral conformation as is built up by the separate and successive florets in the sunflower, and that which, in the snail or *Nautilus* shell, is apparently a single and indivisible unit. And a similar if not identical difference is apparent between the *Nautilus* shell and the minute shells of the Foraminifera which so closely simulate it: inasmuch as the spiral shells of these latter are composite structures, combined out of successive and separate chambers, while the molluscan shell, though it may (as in *Nautilus*) become secondarily subdivided, has grown as one continuous tube. It follows from all this that there cannot be a physical or dynamical, though there may well be a mathematical *law of growth*, which is common to, and which defines, the spiral form in *Nautilus*, in *Globigerina*, in the ram's horn, and in the inflorescence of the sunflower.

Before we enter upon the mathematics of the equiangular spiral, let us carefully observe that the whole of the organic forms in which it is clearly and permanently exhibited, however different they may be from one another in outward appearance, in nature and in origin, nevertheless all belong, in a certain sense, to one particular class of conformations. In the great majority of cases, when we consider an organism in part or whole, when we look (for instance) at our own hand or foot, or contemplate an insect or a worm, we have no reason (or very little) to consider one part of the existing structure as *older* than another; through and through, the newer particles have been merged and commingled among the old; the outline, such as it is, is due to forces which for the most part are still at work to shape it, and which in shaping it have shaped it as a whole. But the horn, or the snail-shell, is curiously different; for in these the presently existing structure is, so to speak, partly old and partly new. It has been conformed by successive and continuous increments; and each successive stage of growth, starting from the origin, remains as an integral and unchanging portion of the growing structure.

We may go further, and see that horn and shell, though they belong to the living, are in no sense alive. They are by-products of the animal; they consist of 'formed material', as it is sometimes called; their growth is not of their own doing, but comes of living cells beneath them or around. The many structures which display the logarithmic spiral increase, or accumulate, rather than grow. The shell of nautilus or snail, the chambered shell of a foraminifer, the elephant's tusk, the beaver's tooth, the cat's claws or the canary-bird's—all these show the same simple and very beautiful spiral curve. And all alike consist of stuff secreted or deposited by living cells; all grow, as an edifice grows, by accretion of accumulated material; and in all alike the parts once formed remain in being, and are thenceforward incapable of change.

D'ARCY THOMPSON, *On Growth and Form*, 1917

The Snayl

Wise emblem of our politick world,
Sage Snayl, within thine own self curl'd,
Instruct me softly to make hast,
Whilst these my feet go slowly fast.

Compendious Snayl! thou seem'st to me
Large Euclid's strict epitome;
And in each diagram dost fling
Thee from the point unto the ring.
A figure now triangulare,
An oval now, and now a square,
And then a serpentine, dost crawl,
Now a straight line, now crook'd, now all.

Preventing rival of the day,
Th' art up and openest thy ray;
And ere the morn cradles the moon,
Th' art broke into a beauteous noon.
Then, when the Sun sups in the deep,
Thy silver horns e're Cinthia's peep;
And thou, from thine own liquid bed,
New Phœbus, heav'st thy pleasant head.

Who shall a name for thee create,
Deep riddle of mysterious state?

Preventing: anticipating, forerunning

Bold Nature, that gives common birth
To all products of seas and earth,
Of thee, as earth-quakes, is afraid,
Nor will thy dire deliv'ry aid.

Thou, thine own daughter, then, and sire,
That son and mother art intire,
That big still with thy self dost go,
And liv'st an aged embrio;
That like the cubbs of India,
Thou from thy self a while dost play;
But frighted with a dog or gun,
In thine own belly thou dost run,
And as thy house was thine own womb,
So thine own womb concludes thy tomb.

RICHARD LOVELACE (1618–57/8)

A narrow Fellow in the Grass
Occasionally rides—
You may have met Him—did you not
His notice sudden is—

The Grass divides as with a Comb—
A spotted shaft is seen—
And then it closes at your feet
And opens further on—

He likes a Boggy Acre
A Floor too cool for Corn—
Yet when a Boy, and Barefoot—
I more than once at Noon
Have passed, I thought, a Whip lash
Unbraiding in the Sun
When stooping to secure it
It wrinkled, and was gone—

Several of Nature's People
I know, and they know me—
I feel for them a transport
Of cordiality—

But never met this Fellow
Attended, or alone
Without a tighter breathing
And Zero at the Bone—

EMILY DICKINSON (1830–86)

So spake the Enemy of mankind, enclosed
In serpent, inmate bad, and toward Eve
Addressed his way, not with indented wave,
Prone on the ground, as since, but on his rear,
Circular base of rising folds, that tow'red
Fold above fold a surging maze; his head
Crested aloft, and carbuncle his eyes;
With burnished neck of verdant gold, erect
Amidst his circling spires, that on the grass
Floated redundant. Pleasing was his shape,
And lovely, never since of serpent kind
Lovelier; not those that in Illyria changed
Hermione and Cadmus, or the god
In Epidaurus; nor to which transformed
Ammonian Jove, or Capitoline was seen,
He with Olympias, this with her who bore
Scipio, the highth of Rome. With tract oblique
At first, as one who sought access, but feared
To interrupt, sidelong he works his way.
As when a ship by skilful steersman wrought
Nigh river's mouth or foreland, where the wind
Veers oft, as oft so steers, and shifts her sail,
So varied he, and of his tortuous train
Curled many a wanton wreath in sight of Eve,
To lure her eye; she busied heard the sound
Of rustling leaves, but minded not, as used
To such disport before her through the field
From every beast, more duteous at her call
Than at Circean call the herd disguised.
He bolder now, uncalled before her stood,
But as in gaze admiring. Oft he bowed
His turret crest, and sleek enameled neck,
Fawning, and licked the ground whereon she trod.
His gentle dumb expression turned at length
The eye of Eve to mark his play; he glad

Of her attention gained, with serpent tongue
Organic, or impulse of vocal air,
His fraudulent temptation thus began: . . .

JOHN MILTON (1608–74), *Paradise Lost*, Book IX, 1667

[*Bahia Blanca, Aug. 1833*]

Amongst the Batrachian reptiles, I found only one little toad, which was most singular from its colour. If we imagine, first, that it had been steeped in the blackest ink, and then when dry, allowed to crawl over a board, freshly painted with the brightest vermilion, so as to colour the soles of its feet and parts of its stomach, a good idea of its appearance will be gained. If it is an unnamed species, surely it ought to be called *diabolicus*, for it is a fit toad to preach in the ear of Eve. Instead of being nocturnal in its habits, as other toads are, and living in damp obscure recesses, it crawls during the heat of the day about the dry sand-hillocks and arid plains, where not a single drop of water can be found. It must necessarily depend on the dew for its moisture; and this probably is absorbed by the skin, for it is known, that these reptiles possess great powers of cutaneous absorption. At Maldonado, I found one in a situation nearly as dry as at Bahia Blanca, and thinking to give it a great treat, carried it to a pool of water; not only was the little animal unable to swim, but, I think, without help would soon have been drowned.

CHARLES DARWIN, *Journal of Researches* (*Voyage of the Beagle*), 1839

Toad

Stop looking like a purse. How could a purse
squeeze under the rickety door and sit,
full of satisfaction, in a man's house?

You clamber towards me on your four corners—
right hand, left foot, left hand, right foot.

I love you for being a toad,
for crawling like a Japanese wrestler,
and for not being frightened.

I put you in my purse hand, not shutting it,
and set you down outside directly under
every star.

A jewel in your head? Toad,
you've put one in mine,
a tiny radiance in a dark place.

NORMAN MacCAIG (b. 1910)

Selborne, Feb. 22, 1770.

Dear Sir,

Hedge-hogs abound in my gardens and fields. The manner in which they eat their roots of the plantain in my grass-walks is very curious: with their upper mandible, which is much longer than their lower, they bore under the plant, and so eat the root off upwards, leaving the tuft of leaves untouched. In this respect they are serviceable, as they destroy a very troublesome weed; but they deface the walks in some measure by digging little round holes. It appears, by the dung that they drop upon the turf, that beetles are no inconsiderable part of their food. In June last I procured a litter of four or five young hedge-hogs, which appeared to be about five or six days old; they, I find, like puppies, are born blind, and could not see when they came to my hands. No doubt their spines are soft and flexible at the time of their birth, or else the poor dam would have but a bad time of it in the critical moment of parturition: but it is plain that they soon harden; for these little pigs had such stiff prickles on their backs and sides as would easily have fetched blood, had they not been handled with caution. Their spines are quite white at this age; and they have little hanging ears, which I do not remember to be discernible in the old ones. They can, in part, at this age draw their skin down over their faces; but are not able to contract themselves into a ball as they do, for the sake of defence, when full grown. The reason, I suppose, is, because the curious muscle that enables the creature to roll itself up into a ball was not then arrived at its full tone and firmness. Hedge-hogs make a deep and warm *hybernaculum* with leaves and moss, in which they conceal themselves for the winter: but I never could find that they stored in any winter provision, as some quadrupeds certainly do.

GILBERT WHITE (1720–93), *The Natural History of Selborne*

'Mine is a long and a sad tale!' said the Mouse, turning to Alice and sighing.

'It *is* a long tail, certainly,' said Alice, looking down with wonder at the Mouse's tail; 'but why do you call it sad?' And she kept on puzzling about it while the Mouse was speaking, so that her idea of the tale was something like this:—

'Fury said to a
mouse, That he
met in the
house,
"Let us
both go to
law: *I* will
prosecute
you. Come,
I'll take no
denial; We
must have a
trial: For
really this
morning I've
nothing
to do."
Said the
mouse to the
cur, "Such
a trial,
dear Sir,
With
no jury
or judge,
would be
wasting
our
breath."
"I'll be
judge, I'll
be Jury."
Said
cunning
old Fury:
"I'll
try the
whole
cause,
and
condemn
you
to
death."

'You are not attending!' said the Mouse to Alice severely. 'What are you thinking of?'

'I beg your pardon,' said Alice very humbly: 'you had got to the fifth bend, I think?'

'I had *not!*' cried the Mouse, angrily.

'A knot!' said Alice, always ready to make herself useful, and looking anxiously about her. 'Oh, do let me help to undo it!'

'I shall do nothing of the sort,' said the Mouse, getting up and walking away. 'You insult me by talking such nonsense!'

LEWIS CARROLL, *Alice's Adventures in Wonderland*, 1865

In Which Eeyore Loses a Tail

The Old Grey Donkey, Eeyore, stood by himself in a thistly corner of the forest, his front feet well apart, his head on one side, and thought about things. Sometimes he thought sadly to himself, 'Why?' and sometimes he thought, 'Wherefore?' and sometimes he thought, 'Inasmuch as which?'—and sometimes he didn't quite know what he *was* thinking about. So when Winnie-the-Pooh came stumping along, Eeyore was very glad to be able to stop thinking for a little, in order to say 'How do you do?' in a gloomy manner to him.

'And how are you?' said Winnie-the-Pooh.

Eeyore shook his head from side to side.

'Not very how,' he said. 'I don't seem to have felt at all how for a long time.'

'Dear, dear,' said Pooh, 'I'm sorry about that. Let's have a look at you.'

So Eeyore stood there, gazing sadly at the ground, and Winnie-the-Pooh walked all round him once.

'Why, what's happened to your tail?' he said in surprise.

'What *has* happened to it?' said Eeyore.

'It isn't there!'

'Are you sure?'

'Well, either a tail *is* there or it isn't there. You can't make a mistake about it. And yours *isn't* there!'

'Then what is?'

'Nothing.'

'Let's have a look,' said Eeyore, and he turned slowly round to the place where his tail had been a little while ago, and then, finding that he couldn't catch it up, he turned round the other way, until he came back to where he was at first, and then he put his head down and looked between his front legs, and at last he said, with a long, sad sigh, 'I believe you're right.'

'Of course I'm right,' said Pooh.

'That Accounts for a Good Deal,' said Eeyore gloomily. 'It Explains Everything. No Wonder.'

'You must have left it somewhere,' said Winnie-the-Pooh.

'Somebody must have taken it,' said Eeyore. 'How Like Them,' he added, after a long silence.

Pooh felt that he ought to say something helpful about it, but didn't quite know what. So he decided to do something helpful instead.

'Eeyore,' he said solemnly, 'I, Winnie-the-Pooh, will find your tail for you.'

'Thank you, Pooh,' answered Eeyore. 'You're a real friend,' said he. 'Not like Some,' he said.

So Winnie-the-Pooh went off to find Eeyore's tail.

A. A. MILNE, *Winnie-the-Pooh*, 1926

The Bat

By day the bat is cousin to the mouse.
He likes the attic of an aging house.

His fingers make a hat about his head.
His pulse beat is so slow we think him dead.

He loops in crazy figures half the night
Among the trees that face the corner light.

But when he brushes up against a screen,
We are afraid of what our eyes have seen:

For something is amiss or out of place
When mice with wings can wear a human face.

THEODORE ROETHKE (1908–63)

Many and sundry sorts there be of Insects, as well among land creatures as those that fly in the aire.

In bodies of any bignes, or at least-wise in those of the greater sort, Nature had no hard piece of work to procreate, forme, and bring all parts to perfection; by reason that the matter wherof they be wrought, is pliable and will follow as she would have it. But in these so little bodies (nay pricks and specks rather than bodies indeed) how can one comprehend the reason, the power, and the inexplicable perfection that Nature hath therin shewed? How hath she bestowed all the five senses in a Gnat? and yet some there be, lesse creatures than they. But (I say) where hath she made the seat of her eies to see before it? where hath she set and disposed the tast? where hath she placed and inserted the instrument and organ of smelling? and above all, where hath she disposed that dreadful and terrible noise that it maketh, that wonderfull great sound (I say) in proportion of so little a body? can there be devised a thing more finely and cunningly wrought than the wings set to her body? Marke what long-shanked legs above ordinary she hath given unto them. See how she hath set that hungry hollow concavitie in stead of a belly: and hath made the same so thirstie and greedy after bloud, and mans especially.

Come to the weapon that it hath to pricke, pierce, and enter through the skinne, how artificially hath she pointed and sharpened it? and being so little as it is (as hardly the finenesse thereof cannot be seen) yet as if it were of bignesse and capacity answerable, framed it she hath most cunningly for a twofold use: to wit, most sharpe pointed, to pricke and enter; and withall, hollow like a pipe for to sucke in and convey the bloud through it. Come to the Wood-worme, what manner of teeth hath Nature given it, to bore holes and eat into the very heart of hard Oke? who heareth not the sound that she makes whiles she is at her work? For in wood and timber is in manner all her feeding.

We make a wonder at the monstrous and mighty shoulders of Elephants, able to carry turrets upon them. We marvell at the strong and stiffe necks of buls, and to see how terribly they will take up things and tosse them aloft into the aire with their hornes. We keepe a wondering at the ravening of Tygres, and in the shag manes of Lions: and yet in comparison of these Insects there is nothing wherein Nature and her whole power is more seene, neither sheweth she her might more than in the least creatures of all.

PLINY THE ELDER (AD 23–79), *Natural History* (tr. Philemon Holland, 1601)

Daddy-Long-Legs

It was an act of daring then to fling one at the girls,
a kind of modest proposal like requesting the pleasure
of a dance, and their cries, we understood, were pleasure.

Purring and rattling in the palms then out upon the world—
flop-flop across benches and the grass, these maddened ghosts
had their legs broken or pulled off, silent in their pain.

Little brown handkerchiefs animated by bluff currents,
blowing against windows where a veil of condensation
held back the damp larders of grass, bark, potato-leaf.

Those days were shorter. Our legs froze although properly speaking
it was hardly autumn. The television lay muzzled in
the front room. Tap and splay. They hung there, vegetal.

God save these daddies and all their young babies—
repulsive fry greasing the cellar, leathery nuisance.
Put salt on them like slugs, their curling slime.

They lilt against the lightbulb, out of control: in hell
they will be gorged with our blood, now they are brittle
girls proffering leaves and hands, ragged, memorial.

GEORGE SZIRTES (b. 1948)

The warm evening sunshine struck full and level against the bridge over the river not far from Pixton Park, and the May-flies sported in the rays. It is even warmer in the early part of a summer's evening than in the days; heat seems to accumulate and the air is dried by the long hours of sun that have passed. Heat came in the level rays of the sun and light was reflected up from the water and with it a sense if not the reality of more heat. But in the shade of an ash I watched the May-flies, or as they should be called the June-flies, without inconvenience. There was a draught of air flowing with the current of the river under the spans of the bridge, and against this the May-flies struggled facing the sunset. Though it was so slight they could but just make headway against it, and were continually carried back by a zephyr that would scarcely have disturbed the downward fall of a leaf. Their large broad wings seemed to possess no power and hardly supported them in the atmosphere, they were fanned in every direction by the least movement of the zephyr as the Japanese sent their fluttering paper butterflies. The pheasant of flies in estimation of the angler and all who frequent the stream, pheasant-like too in the proportion of length to breadth, is the opposite of the feathered pheasant in force of wing. The feathered pheasant flies like a clod of earth snatched from under a plough and hurled with some giant's strength crash into the nearest hedge; the pheasant of flies like helpless thistledown.

This singular feebleness is the reason apparently that the May-fly continually rises in the air, and as continually sinks. Instead of proceeding in an horizontal line the fly goes up vertically, and then goes down and so drifts rather than directs itself somewhere, it does not know where. Meeting the least current it is lifted up; the current ceases and it sinks; and again, as its little force momentarily increases and then decreases so it rises, and falls. Yet the length of the insect, its wide vanes, its tail, would at first sight indicate a straightforward and strong flight, while in fact it is the most hopelessly purposeless of flying creatures. Not only up and down, but sideways—now to the right, now to the left; presently sinking aslant, and shooting up straight, blown back, and blown forward; out into the sun's rays, aside into the shadow any way except the way it seems to want to go.

The wings gleam transparent in the sun, then in the shade by the bushes lose their illuminations, suddenly the creature floats past extended on the surface of the water helpless, and effortless as bloom from a flowering tree. Why do they sink to the water? Nothing throws them down, the current of air would assist them to rise rather than to fall; sometimes they go very near the surface and yet fly up; they are not obliged to fly over water for many wander away across the meadows; nor is the river broad so that a very little trouble would carry them to the banks. But sink to the surface they do, and instantly become entirely helpless—a complete and utter collapse, a paralysis seizes upon them, they do not even shake or lift the edge of a wing. The wings indeed look as if stuck to the surface, as if they immediately absorbed the water as linen would and so could not be lifted because too heavy.

RICHARD JEFFERIES, *Field and Farm*, 1884

The Caterpillar

I find among the poems of Schiller
No mention of the caterpillar,
Nor can I find one anywhere
In Petrarch or in Baudelaire,
So here I sit in extra session
To give my personal impression.
The caterpillar, as it's called,
Is often hairy, seldom bald;
It looks as if it never shaves;
When as it walks, it walks in waves;
And from the cradle to the chrysalis
It's utterly speechless, songless, whistleless.

OGDEN NASH (1902–71)

Upon a Wasp Child with Cold

The Bare that breaths the Northern blast
Did numb, Torpedo like, a Wasp
Whose stiffend limbs encrampt, lay bathing
In Sol's warm breath and shine as saving,
Which with her hands she chafes and stands
Rubbing her Legs, Shanks, Thighs, and hands.

Child: chilled

Her petty toes, and fingers ends
Nipt with this breath, she out extends
Unto the Sun, in greate desire
To warm her digits at that fire.
Doth hold her Temples in this state
Where pulse doth beate, and head doth ake.
Doth turn, and stretch her body small,
Doth Comb her velvet Capitall.
As if her little brain pan were
A Volume of Choice precepts cleare.
As if her sattin jacket hot
Contained Apothecaries Shop
Of Natures recepts, that prevails
To remedy all her sad ailes,
As if her velvet helmet high
Did turret rationality.
She fans her wing up to the Winde
As if her Pettycoate were lin'de,
With reasons fleece, and hoises sails
And hu'ming flies in thankfull gails
Unto her dun Curld palace Hall
Her warm thanks offering for all.

EDWARD TAYLOR (*c*.1644–1729)

The Wapiti

There goes the Wapiti,
Hippety-hoppity!

OGDEN NASH (1902–71)

The Kangaroo

mixtumque genus, prolesque biformis.
—Virgil, *Aeneid VI*

Kangaroo, Kangaroo!
Thou Spirit of Australia,
That redeems from utter failure,
From perfect desolation,
And warrants the creation
Of this fifth part of the Earth,
Which should seem an after-birth,

Not conceiv'd in the Beginning
(For GOD bless'd His work at first,
And saw that it was good),
But emerg'd at the first sinning,
When the ground was therefore curst;—
And hence this barren wood!

Kangaroo, Kangaroo!
Tho' at first sight we should say,
In thy nature that there may
Contradiction be involv'd,
Yet, like discord well resolv'd,
It is quickly harmoniz'd.
Sphynx or mermaid realiz'd,
Or centaur unfabulous,
Would scarce be more prodigious,
Or Labyrinthine Minotaur,
With which great Theseus did war,
Or Pegasus poetical.
Or hippogriff—chimeras all!
But, what Nature would compile,
Nature knows to reconcile;
And Wisdom, ever at her side,
Of all her children's justified.

She had made the squirrel fragile;
She had made the bounding hart;
But a third so strong and agile
Was beyond ev'n Nature's art.
So she join'd the former two
    In thee, Kangaroo!

To describe thee, it is hard:
Converse of the camélopard,
Which beginneth camel-wise,
But endeth of the panther size,
Thy fore half, it would appear,
Had belong'd to some 'small deer',
Such as liveth in a tree;
By thy hinder, thou should'st be
A large animal of chace,
Bounding o'er the forest's space;—
Join'd by some divine mistake,

None but Nature's hand can make—
Nature, in her wisdom's play,
On Creation's holiday.
For howsoe'er anomalous,
Thou yet art not incongruous,
Repugnant or preposterous.
Better-proportion'd animal,
More graceful or ethereal,
Was never follow'd by the hound,
With fifty steps to thy one bound.
Thou can'st not be amended: no;
Be as thou art; thou best art so.

When sooty swans are once more rare,
And duck-moles the Museum's care,
Be still the glory of this land,
Happiest Work of finest Hand!

BARRON FIELD (1786–1846)

The Amazonian tapir may be compared in size to a small ox; and weighs, I should think (for I have never actually seen one in the scales), about 400 pounds. It is a thick-set, heavily built animal, with a remarkably piggish external appearance, especially when lying down.

The skin is very smooth and tightly drawn on the animal, and is of a blackish brown hue, and sparsely covered with coarse hair. As a rule it is encased in mud, and its true colour is only seen when the animal is dead and cleaned; or when it emerges from a prolonged bath, or in very wet weather.

It is eminently a fluvial animal. I have never seen any of them except in the immediate neighbourhood of large rivers. They do not even visit lakes and pools, except some of those forest-surrounded lakes which form the head-waters of many of the affluents of the Purus and Madeira.

It is a habit of the tapir to lie in mud surrounded by reeds. Sometimes it reclines on its side, and sometimes on its knees, like an ox. When it thinks itself quite secure, and free from observation, it rolls over on its back in apparent enjoyment; and kicks its legs as we may see a horse do when given its liberty in a field. It seems to be an animal of a joyous disposition.

PAUL FOUNTAIN, *The River Amazon from its Sources to the Sea*, 1914

Selborne, March, 1770.

On Michaelmas-day 1768 I managed to get a sight of the female moose belonging to the Duke of Richmond, at Goodwood; but was greatly disappointed, when I arrived at the spot, to find that it died, after having appeared in a languishing way for some time, on the morning before. However, understanding that it was not stripped, I proceeded to examine this rare quadruped: I found it in an old green-house, slung under the belly and chin by ropes, and in a standing posture; but, though it had been dead for so short a time, it was in so putrid a state that the stench was hardly supportable. The grand distinction between this deer, and any other species that I have ever met with, consisted in the strange length of its legs; on which it was tilted up much in the manner of birds of the *grallæ* order. I measured it, as they do an horse, and found that, from the ground to the wither, it was just five feet four inches; which height answers exactly to sixteen hands, a growth that few horses arrive at: but then, with this length of legs, its neck was remarkably short, no more than twelve inches; so that, by straddling with one foot forward and the other backward, it grazed on the plain ground, with the greatest difficulty, between its legs: the ears were vast and lopping, and as long as the neck; the head was about twenty inches long, and ass-like; and had such a redundancy of upper lip as I never saw before, with huge nostrils. This lip, travellers say, is esteemed a dainty dish in North America.

This poor creature had at first a female companion of the same species, which died the spring before. In the same garden was a young stag, or red deer, between whom and this moose it was hoped that there might have been a breed; but their inequality of height must have always been a bar to any commerce of the amorous kind. I should have been glad to have examined the teeth, tongue, lips, hoofs, etc., minutely; but the putrefaction precluded all further curiosity.

GILBERT WHITE (1720–93), *The Natural History of Selborne*

A Black November Turkey

to A.M. and A.M.

Nine white chickens come
With haunchy walk and heads
Jabbing among the chips, the chaff, the stones
And the cornhusk-shreds,

And bit by bit infringe
A pond of dusty light,
Spectral in shadow until they bobbingly one
By one ignite.

Neither pale nor bright,
The turkey-cock parades
Through radiant squalors, darkly auspicious as
The ace of spades,

Himself his own cortège
And puffed with the pomp of death,
Rehearsing over and over with strangled râle
His latest breath.

The vast black body floats
Above the crossing knees
As a cloud over thrashed branches, a calm ship
Over choppy seas,

Shuddering its fan and feathers
In fine soft clashes
With the cold sound that the wind makes, fondling
Paper-ashes.

The pale-blue bony head
Set on its shepherd's-crook
Like a saint's death-mask, turns a vague, superb
And timeless look

Upon these clocking hens
And the cocks that one by one,
Dawn after mortal dawn, with vulgar joy
Acclaim the sun.

RICHARD WILBUR (b. 1921)

[*April, 1939*]

Good Friday. A magpie flies like a frying-pan.

T. H. WHITE (1906–64)

The Swan's Feet

Who is this whose feet
Close on the water,
Like muscled leaves darker than ivy

Blown back and curved by unwearying wind?
They, that thrust back the water,
Softly crumple now and close, stream in his wake.

These dank weeds are also
Part and plumage of the magnolia-flowering swan.
He puts forth these too—
Leaves of ridged and bitter ivy
Sooted in towns, coal-bright with rain.

He is not moved by winds in air
Like the vain boats on the lake.
Lest you think him too a flower of parchment,
Scentless magnolia,
See his living feet under the water fanning.
In the leaves' self blows the efficient wind
That opens and bends closed those leaves.

E. J. SCOVELL (b. 1907)

Observe the goose's foot: if it were always open or always closed the creature would not be able to make any kind of movement. While with the curve of the foot outwards it has more perception of the water in going forward than the foot would have as it is drawn back; this shows that the same weight the wider it is the slower is its movement. Observe the goose moving through the water, how as it moves its foot forward it closes it occupying but little water and consequently acquiring speed; and as it pushes it back it spreads it out and so makes itself slower, and then the part of the body that has contact with the air becomes swifter.

LEONARDO DA VINCI (1452–1519), *Notebooks*, 1505 (tr. Jean Paul Richter, 1939)

In medieval and Renaissance painting, Gabriel bears the wings of a bird, often elaborately spread and adorned. While visiting Florence last year, I became fascinated by the 'comparative anatomy' of Gabriel's wings as depicted by the great painters of Italy. The faces of Mary and Gabriel are so beautiful, their gestures often so expressive. Yet the wings, as painted by Fra Angelico or by Martini, seem stiff and lifeless, despite the beauty of their intricate feathering.

But then I saw Leonardo's version. Gabriel's wings are so supple and graceful that I scarcely cared to study his face or note the impact he had upon Mary. And then I recognized the source of the difference. Leonardo, who studied birds and understood the aerodynamics of wings, had painted a working machine on Gabriel's back. His wings are both beautiful and efficient. They have not only the right orientation and camber, but the correct arrangement of feathers as well. Had he been just a bit lighter, Gabriel might have flown without divine guidance. In contrast, the other Gabriels bear flimsy and awkward ornaments that could never work. I was reminded that aesthetic and functional beauty often go hand in hand (or rather arm in arm in this case).

In the standard examples of nature's beauty—the cheetah running, the gazelle escaping, the eagle soaring, the tuna coursing, and even the snake slithering or the inchworm inching—what we perceive as graceful form also represents an excellent solution to a problem in physics. When we wish to illustrate the concept of adaptation in evolutionary biology, we often try to show that organisms unconsciously 'know' physics—that they have evolved remarkably efficient machines for eating and moving.

STEPHEN JAY GOULD, *The Panda's Thumb*, 1980

A boy went in to a graveyard and shot a white owl. Then, seized with alarm, he rushed home in the greatest excitement screaming 'I've shot a cherubim'.

BEATRIX POTTER (1866–1943), *The Journal of Beatrix Potter from 1881 to 1897, transcribed . . . by Leslie Linder*, 1966

Robert's tea-cloth caught the golden egg and whisked it off the mantel-piece, and it fell into the fender and rolled under the grate.

'Oh, crikey!' said more than one voice.

And every one instantly fell down flat on its front to look under the grate, and there lay the egg, glowing in a nest of hot ashes.

'It's not smashed, anyhow,' said Robert, and he put his hand under the grate and picked up the egg. But the egg was much hotter than any one would have believed it could possibly get in such a short time, and Robert had to drop it with a cry of 'Bother!' It fell on the top bar of the grate, and bounced right into the glowing red-hot heart of the fire.

'The tongs!' cried Anthea. But, alas, no one could remember where they were.

'Never mind,' said Robert, 'we'll get it out with the poker and the shovel.'

'Oh, stop,' cried Anthea. 'Look at it! Look! look! look! I do believe something *is* going to happen!'

For the egg was now red-hot, and inside it something was moving. Next moment there was a soft cracking sound; the egg burst in two, and out of it came a flame-coloured bird. It rested a moment among the flames, and as it rested there the four children could see it growing bigger and bigger under their eyes.

Every mouth was a-gape, every eye a-goggle.

The bird rose in its nest of fire, stretched its wings, and flew out into the room. It flew round and round, and round again, and where it passed the air was warm. Then it perched on the fender. The children looked at each other. Then Cyril put out a hand towards the bird. It put its head on one side and looked up at him, as you may have seen a parrot do when it is just going to speak, so that the children were hardly astonished at all when it said, 'Be careful; I am not nearly cool yet.'

They were not astonished, but they were very, very much interested.

They looked at the bird, and it was certainly worth looking at. Its feathers were like gold. It was about as large as a bantam, only its beak was not at all bantam-shaped. 'I believe I know what it is,' said Robert. 'I've seen a picture—'

But when he came back into the room holding out a paper, and crying, 'I say, look here,' the others all said 'Hush!' and he hushed obediently and instantly, for the bird was speaking.

'Which of you,' it was saying, 'put the egg into the fire?'

'He did,' said three voices, and three fingers pointed at Robert.

The bird bowed; at least it was more like that than anything else.

'I am your grateful debtor,' it said with a high-bred air.

The children were all choking with wonder and curiosity—all except Robert. He held the paper in his hand, and he *knew*. He said so. He said—

'I know who you are.'

And he opened and displayed a printed paper, at the head of which was a little picture of a bird sitting in a nest of flames.

'You are the Phoenix,' said Robert; and the bird was quite pleased.

'My fame has lived then for two thousand years,' it said. 'Allow me to look at my portrait.'

It looked at the page which Robert, kneeling down, spread out in the fender, and said—

'It's not a flattering likeness. . . . And what are these characters?' it asked, pointing to the printed part.

'Oh, that's all dullish; it's not much about *you*, you know,' said Cyril, with unconscious politeness; 'but you're in lots of books—'

'With portraits?' asked the Phoenix.

'Well, no,' said Cyril; 'in fact, I don't think I ever saw any portrait of you but that one, but I can read you something about yourself, if you like.'

The Phoenix nodded, and Cyril went off and fetched Volume X of the old *Encyclopedia*, and on page 246 he found the following:—

'Phoenix—in ornithology, a fabulous bird of antiquity.'

'Antiquity is quite correct,' said the Phoenix, 'but fabulous—well, do I look it?'

Every one shook its head. Cyril went on—

'The ancients speak of this bird as single, or the only one of its kind.'

'That's right enough,' said the Phoenix.

'They describe it as about the size of an eagle.'

'Eagles are of different sizes,' said the Phoenix; 'it's not at all a good description.'

All the children were kneeling on the hearth-rug, to be as near the Phoenix as possible.

'You'll boil your brains,' it said. 'Look out, I'm nearly cool now;' and with a whirr of golden wings it fluttered from the fender to the table. It was so nearly cool that there was only a very faint smell of burning when it had settled itself on the table-cloth.

'It's only a very little scorched,' said the Phoenix, apologetically; 'it will come out in the wash. Please go on reading.'

The children gathered round the table.

'The size of an eagle,' Cyril went on, 'its head finely crested with a beautiful plumage, its neck covered with feathers of a gold colour, and the rest of its body purple; only the tail white, and the eyes sparkling like stars. They say that it lives about five hundred years in the wilderness, and when advanced in age it builds itself a pile of sweet wood and aromatic gums, fires it with the wafting of its wings, and thus burns itself; and that from its ashes arises a worm, which in time grows up to be a Phoenix. Hence the Phoenicians gave—'

'Never mind what they gave,' said the Phoenix, ruffling its golden feathers. 'They never gave much, anyway; they always were people who gave nothing for nothing. That book ought to be destroyed. It's most inaccurate. The rest of my body was *never* purple, and as for my tail—well, I simply ask you, *is* it white?'

It turned round and gravely presented its golden tail to the children.

'No, it's not,' said everybody.

'No, and it never was,' said the Phoenix. 'And that about the worm is just a vulgar insult. The Phoenix has an egg, like all respectable birds. It makes a pile—that part's all right—and it lays its egg, and it burns itself; and it goes to sleep and wakes up in its egg, and comes out and goes on living again, and so on for ever and ever. I can't tell you how weary I got of it—such a restless existence; no repose.'

'But how did your egg get *here?*' asked Anthea.

'Ah, that's my life-secret,' said the Phoenix. 'I couldn't tell it to any one who wasn't really sympathetic. I've always been a misunderstood bird. You can tell that by what they say about the worm. I might tell *you*,' it went on, looking at Robert with eyes that were indeed starry. '*You* put me on the fire—'

Robert looked uncomfortable.

'The rest of us made the fire of sweet-scented woods and gums, though,' said Cyril.

'And—and it was an accident my putting you on the fire,' said Robert, telling the truth with some difficulty, for he did not know how the Phoenix might take it. It took it in the most unexpected manner.

'Your candid avowal,' it said, 'removes my last scruple. I will tell you my story.'

E. NESBIT, The Phoenix and the Carpet, 1904

The Malay Dragon

We have ours; and they
    have theirs. Ours has a skin feather crest;
theirs has wings out from the waist which is snuff-brown or sallow.
    Ours falls from trees on water; theirs is the smallest
dragon that knows how to dive head first from a tree top to something dry.

Floating on spread ribs,
    the boatlike body settles on the
clamshell-tinted spray sprung from the nutmeg tree—minute legs
    trailing half akimbo—the true divinity
of Malay. Among unfragrant orchids, on the unnutritious nut-

tree, *myristica*
    fragrans, the harmless god spreads ribs that
do not raise a hood. This is the serpent dove peculiar
    to the East; that lives as the butterfly or bat
can, in a brood, conferring wings on what it grasps, as the air plant does.

MARIANNE MOORE (1887–1972), 'The Plumet Basilisk'

PROCREATION

For what seemed an incredible length of time [Tulip] showed no sign at all of the coming event. Then, quite suddenly, I observed the swell and sag of her belly and, in the first days of May, she began to flag and to take rests during our walks. This touched me. Hitherto, it had always been I who had sometimes felt fatigued, while she with her impatient high spirits had forced and teased me on; now it was she who could not stay the course. Soon Putney Common was as far as she could go, and even on these short strolls she would quietly halt and sink down upon the cool grass. Stretching myself beside her, I would smoke and read until she felt able to continue. A fortnight or so before she was due I asked Miss Canvey to be on hand in case we needed her, for bitches occasionally get into difficulties at their lying-in and require veterinary assistance.

But Tulip took us unawares. She whelped five days before her scheduled time and was alone in my flat when her labour began. The great unstaling pleasure of returning home was the welcome that she never failed to give me; there was no welcome that afternoon when I turned my key in the lock. The place was deathly, like a tomb. I hurried along to my bedroom. For some days I had been keeping the curtains there drawn; she would prefer, I knew, a dark, cool seclusion when her pains started. Standing now in the open doorway, I looked into the penumbrous room.

Tulip was in her box. She had understood its purpose after all. She was lying there in the shadows facing me, the front of her body upright, the rest reclined upon its side. Her ears crumpled back with pleasure at the sight of me; her amber eyes glowed with a gentle, loving look. She was panting. A tiny sound, like the distant mewing of gulls, came from the box; I could just discern, lying against her stomach, three small rat-like shapes. I think it is Major Hancock who says that a bitch is liable to hold up her labour if she is distracted or watched, and may even devour her children to protect them. I accepted this in a general way; I knew, at the same time, that Tulip was glad that I was there. Nevertheless, I did not approach her box. Moving to a chair at some distance from her, I hid my face in my hands and observed her without seeming to do so. Suddenly she stopped panting, her face took on a look of strain, she uttered a muted, shuddering sound like a sigh, a movement passed over her recumbent body, and she raised her great tail so that it stood out straight and rigid from her rump. Immediately a dark package was extruded beneath it, and to this, with a minimum of general effort, she brought her long nose round. Now I could not clearly see what she was doing, for her head interposed and obscured the operation; but I knew what was happening and I heard her tongue and teeth at work with liquid, guzzling noises. She was licking and nosing this package out of herself, severing the umbilical cord, releasing the tiny creature from its tissues and eating up the after-birth. In a few seconds she had accomplished all these tasks and was guiding her fourth child to her teats, cleansing it on the way.

It was a marvellous sight, to me very affecting; but I think that to anyone who did not know and love her as I did, it must have been a solemn and moving thing to see this beautiful animal, in the midst of the first labour of her life, performing upon herself, with no help but unerringly, as though directed by some divine wisdom, the delicate and complicated business of creation. I guessed now that she was thirsty. Quietly leaving the room I warmed some milk for her. When I returned with the bowl she stretched her head eagerly forward. Kneeling in front of her I held it to her while she lapped. She licked my hand and laid her head heavily back on the blanket.

Half an hour elapsed before her next delivery; then another sigh, another spasm, and her tail lifted to eject the fifth. She produced eight puppies at half-hourly intervals and was not done until evening fell. I sat with her in the darkened room throughout. It was a beautiful thing to have seen. When it was plain that she had finished I went and kissed her. She was quite wet. She allowed me to touch her babies. They were still blind. I took one up; she was frightened and gently nuzzled my hand as though to say 'Take care!' But she had too much confidence in me to suppose that I would hurt them.

J. R. ACKERLEY, *My Dog Tulip*, 1956

Seal

When the milk-arrow stabs she comes
water-fluent down the long green miles.
Her milk leaks into the sea, blue
blossoming in an opal.

The pup lies patient in his cot of stone.
They meet with cries, caress as people do.
She lies down for his suckling, lifts him
with a flipper from the sea's reach
when the tide fills his throat with salt.

This is the fourteenth day. In two days
no bitch-head will break the brilliance
listening for baby-cries.
Down in the thunder of that other country
the bulls are calling and her uterus is empty.

Alone and hungering in his fallen shawl
he'll nuzzle the Atlantic and be gone.
If that day's still his moult will lie
a gleaming ring on sand
like the noose she slips on the sea.

GILLIAN CLARKE (b. 1937)

About the Eel

Of which the specimen placed by Freddie Parr in Mary's knickers in July, 1940, was a healthy representative of the only, if abundant, freshwater species of Europe—namely *Anguilla anguilla*, the European Eel.

Now there is much that the eel can tell us about curiosity—rather more indeed than curiosity can inform us of the eel. Does it surprise you to know that only as recently as the nineteen-twenties was it discovered how baby eels are born and that throughout history controversy has raged about the still obscure life cycle of this snake-like, fish-like, highly edible, not to say phallically suggestive creature?

The Egyptians knew it, the Greeks knew it, the Romans knew it and prized its flesh; but none of these ingenious peoples could discover where the eel kept its reproductive organs, if indeed it had any, and no one could find (and no one ever will) in all the waters where the European Eel dwells, from the North Cape to the Nile, an eel bearing ripe milt.

Curiosity could not neglect this enigma. Aristotle maintained that the eel was indeed a sexless creature and that its offspring were brought forth by spontaneous generation out of mud. Pliny affirmed that when constrained by the urge to procreate, the eel rubbed itself against rocks and the young were formed from the shreds of skin thus detached. And amongst other explanations of the birth of this apparently ill-equipped species were that it sprang from putrefying matter; that it emerged from the gills of other fishes; that it was hatched from horses' hairs dropped in water; that it issued from the cool, sweet dews of May mornings; not to mention that peculiar tradition of our own Fenland, that eels are none other than the multiplied mutations of one-time sinful monks and priests, whom St Dunstan, in a holy and miraculous rage, consigned to eternal, slithery penance, thus giving to the cathedral city of the Fens its name: Ely—the eely place.

In the eighteenth century the great Linnaeus, who was no amateur, declared that the eel was viviparous, that is to say, its eggs were fertilised internally and its young were brought forth alive—a theory exploded (though never abandoned by Linnaeus) when Francesco Redi of Pisa clearly showed that what had been taken for young eelings in the adult's womb were no more than parasitic worms.

Womb? What womb? It was not until 1777 that one Carlo Mondini claimed to have located the miniscule organs that were, indeed, the eel's ovaries. A discovery which raised doubts in the mind of his countryman Spallanzani (a supporter of Redi contra Linnaeus) who asked the simple yet awkward question: if these were the ovaries then where were the eggs? And thus—after much refutation and counter-refutation and much hurling to and fro of scientific papers—it was not until 1850 that Mondini's discovery was confirmed (long after the poor man's death) by a Pole, Martin Rathke, who published in that year a definitive account of the female genitalia of *Anguilla anguilla*.

Graham Swift, *Waterland*, 1983

More on the Dinosaur

No wonder they almost died out,
with one full minute between stubbed tail and ouch,
their logic couldn't connect cause and effect.

Sex was an enigma—buoyed up in the mire,
cryptogams fringing their jaws
and their little eyes glassy with time-lag,
they'd quite forget, between effort and ecstasy,
just what they were at
(the other already wallowing off).
Imagine the bliss of brontosaurs—
embracing a mountain, incurring an earthquake—
love as a natural disaster.
But the urge to survive went deep,
they're with us still, in hindbrain, basal ganglion,
sometimes a stranger's eyes, and always
man's hidden part, blunt id,
barbed as the collared head of Triceratops,
a tip on tomorrow's winner.

JAN OWEN (b. 1940)

That vertebrates mate together for a considerable period is sufficiently explained by physiological causes—in the case of birds, for example, by the female's need of help during the brooding period . . . And if strict monogamy is the height of all virtue, then the palm must go to the tapeworm, which has a complete set of male and female sexual organs in each of its 50–200 proglottides, or sections, and spends its whole life copulating in all its sections with itself. Confining ourselves to mammals, however, we find all forms of sexual life—promiscuity, indications of group marriage, polygyny, monogamy. Polyandry alone is lacking—it took human beings to achieve that.

FREDERICK ENGELS, *The Origin of the Family*, 1934 (tr. Alick West and Dona Tow, 1940)

The Cephalopods, such as the octopus, the cuttlefishes, and the *teuthides*, all copulate in the same way: they intertwine by the mouth, fitting their tentacles into each other's. Thus one octopus will rest its so-called head upon the ground and spread out its tentacles, and then the other one will fit itself on to these spreading tentacles, and they bring their suckers into mutual contact. Some people allege that the male octopus has a sort of penis on one of his tentacles, *i.e.*, the one on which the two largest suckers are: they say that this organ is more or less sinewy, and that the whole of it is attached up as far as the middle of the tentacle, which it thus admits into the nostril of the female.

ARISTOTLE (384–322 BC), *History of Animals* (tr. A. L. Peck, 1965–70)

—So from his shell on Delta's showerless isle
Bursts into life the monster of the Nile;
First in translucent lymph with cobweb-threads
The brain's fine floating tissue swells, and spreads;
Nerve after nerve the glistening spine descends,
The red heart dances, the aorta bends;
Through each new gland the purple current glides,
New veins meandering drink the refluent tides;
Edge over edge expands the hardening scale,
And sheaths his slimy skin in silver mail.
—Erewhile, emerging from the brooding sand,
With tyger-paw he prints the brineless strand,
High on the flood with speckled bosom swims,
Helm'd with broad tail, and oar'd with giant limbs;
Rolls his fierce eye-balls, clasps his iron claws,
And champs with gnashing teeth his massy jaws;
Old Nilus sighs along his cane-crown'd shores,
And swarthy Memphis trembles and adores.

ERASMUS DARWIN (1731–1802)

An Emblem

Someone has nailed a lucky horse-shoe
beside my door while I was out—
or is it a loop of rubber? No:
it's in two sections. They glide about,
silently undulating: two
slugs in a circle, tail to snout.

The ends link up: it's a shiny quoit
of rippling slug-flesh, thick as a snake,
liquorice-black against the white
paint; a pair of wetly-nak-
ed tubes. It doesn't seem quite right
to watch what kind of love they'll make.

But who could resist? I'll compromise
and give them a little time alone
to nuzzle each other, slide and ooze
into conjunction on their own;
surely they're experts, with such bodies,
each a complete erogenous zone—

self-lubricating, swelling smooth
and boneless under grainy skin.
Ten minutes, then, for them to writhe
in privacy, to slither in-
to position, to arrange each lithe
tapered hose-pipe around its twin.

All right, now, slugs, I'm back; time's up.
And what a pretty coupling I find!
They're swinging from the wall by a rope
of glue, spun out of their combined
mucus and anchored at the top.
It lets them dangle, intertwined,

formally perfect, like some emblem:
heraldic serpents coiled in a twist.
But just in case their pose may seem
immodest or exhibitionist
they've dressed themselves in a cloud of foam,
a frothy veil for love-in-a-mist.

FLEUR ADCOCK (b. 1934)

Foam frogs use group sex in a bubblebath. These frogs live in trees often around swamps and marshes. They have dispensed with sex in the water, and package their eggs in nests of foam which they construct in foliage above pools and puddles. When the tadpoles hatch they wriggle free of their bubble nurseries and drop into the water, where they will continue their childhood. The foam frogs mate in the cool of the night. When a female finds herself a suitable spot above water, she is quickly sought after by the local males; they are smaller than she is, and she can, and often does, take on several. The first clasps her under the armpits, the next rides on top of the first mate and so on . . . She starts the ball rolling by producing a pale translucent fluid from her rear, and immediately she and her multiple lovers set to work whipping up the fluid into a stiff white foam with their hind legs. It looks like an erotic cooking session, semen and eggs being folded into the mixture to make a kind of 'meringue' for the benefit of the children! After a short while the mating frogs are nearly covered in froth. When the female is spent the group disperses, leaving between 100 and 200 eggs behind in the foam. The outside sets fairly hard, sealing in the soft moist centre into which the tadpoles hatch.

JOHN SPARKS, *The Sexual Connection: Mating the Wild Way*, 1977

The Turtle

The turtle lives twixt plated decks
Which practically conceal its sex.
I think it clever of the turtle
In such a fix to be so fertile.

OGDEN NASH (1902–71)

Thus every Creature, and of every Kind,
The secret Joys of sweet Coition find:
Not only Man's Imperial Race; but they
That wing the liquid Air; or swim the Sea,
Or haunt the Desart, rush into the flame:
For Love is Lord of all; and is in all the same.
    'Tis with this rage, the Mother Lion stung,
Scours o're the Plain; regardless of her young:
Demanding Rites of Love; she sternly stalks;
And hunts her Lover in his lonely Walks.
Tis then the shapeless Bear his Den forsakes;
In Woods and Fields a wild destruction makes.
Boars whet their Tusks; to battel Tygers move;
Enrag'd with hunger, more enrag'd with love.
Then wo to him, that in the desart Land
Of *Lybia* travels, o're the burning Sand.
The Stallion snuffs the well-known Scent afar;
And snorts and trembles for the distant Mare:
Nor Bitts nor Bridles, can his rage restrain;
And rugged Rocks are interpos'd in vain:
He makes his way o're Mountains, and contemns
Unruly Torrents, and unfoorded Streams.
The bristled Boar, who feels the pleasing wound,
New grinds his arming Tusks, and digs the ground.
The sleepy Leacher shuts his little Eyes;
About his churning Chaps the frothy bubbles rise:
He rubs his sides against a Tree; prepares
And hardens both his Shoulders for the Wars.

I pass the Wars that spotted *Linx's* make
With their fierce Rivals, for the Females sake:
The howling Wolves, the Mastiffs amorous rage;
When ev'n the fearful Stag dares for his Hind engage.
But far above the rest, the furious Mare,

Barr'd from the male, is frantick with despair.
For when her pouting Vent declares her pain,
She tears the Harness, and she rends the Rein;
For this; (when *Venus* gave them rage and pow'r)
Their Masters mangl'd Members they devour;
Of Love defrauded in their longing Hour.
For Love they force through Thickets of the Wood,
They climb the steepy Hills, and stem the Flood.
    When at the Spring's approach their Marrow burns,
(For with the Spring their Genial Warmth returns)
The Mares to Cliffs of rugged Rocks repair,
And with wide Nostrils snuff the Western Air:
When (wondrous to relate) the Parent Wind,
Without the Stallion, propagates the Kind.

        VIRGIL (70–19 BC), *Georgics*, book III, tr. JOHN DRYDEN (1631–1700)

Camels have a peculiarity which distinguishes them from all other quadrupeds: this is what is known as the 'hump' on their backs. The Bactrian camel differs from the Arabian in having two humps as against the latter's one, though this has a sort of hump below like the one above, on which it takes the weight of the whole body when it kneels down. The camel has four teats, like the cow, and a tail similar to the ass's; its privy member is directed backwards.

Camels copulate with the female seated: the male covers the female astride, not in the rearward position, but like the other quadrupeds; and they spend the whole day over it. When copulating they withdraw to some unfrequented place, and it is unsafe for anyone but their keeper to go near them. The camel's penis is so sinewy that bowstrings are actually made out of it.

        ARISTOTLE (384–322 BC), *History of Animals* (tr. A. L. Peck, 1965–70)

The ram

    is his testicles. Will serve
    a hundred ewes, easy. Fat

    wethers blether wifeless on
    the long moors, delectable,

    soft as shawls; but he, apart,
    accepts his special food. Tough

in his sour wool he grows old
and uneatable. Will butt,

from machismo, anyone
with tender hands. In autumn

he sets about his labour;
looks over his Roman nose,

selects where to begin. Thumps
in ramstam till it's done, black

scrotum tight with tottery lambs.

TED WALKER (b. 1934)

Lions Copulating

We caught lions copulating on the plains
Of Africa. Our landrover closed in,
I pressed so hard on my 8 mm. color film
I almost lost this gigantic naturalism,

Trying to preserve it for my friends and astoundees.
But saw the King of Beasts with his head high,
His mane imperial, no expression on his face,
Prodding in and out of the great female

As if he were a schizophrenic dualist
And had to put up with his baser nature,
For his great face had no expression at all
While his lower being worked mechanical,

Then he fell away, and stood off, and lay
His full length on the ancient earth
While the lioness with a sumptuous gesture
Rolled over as I have seen other females do

In the perfect surfeit of her animal nature,
And took ease as if nobody were looking on,
And after an interval of valuable rest
These great beasts of the African wilds

Stood in their historic posture of superiority
And ambled across the limitless plains in silence
Without a thought of the lucubration of man,
Trying to signify their big natures in empathy.

RICHARD EBERHART (b. 1904)

When I first came [to Camusfeàrna] the estate on whose land the house stood had long waged war upon the wildcats, and a tree by the deer-larder of the lodge, four miles away, was decorated with their banded tails hanging like monstrous willow catkins from its boughs. Now, since the estate has turned from general agriculture to forestry, the wildcats are protected, for they are the worst enemy of the voles, who are in turn the greatest destroyers of the newly planted trees. Under this benign régime the number of wildcats has marvellously increased. The males sometimes mate with domestic females, but the offspring rarely survives, either because the sire returns to kill the kittens as soon as they are born, and so expunge the evidence of his peasant wenching, or because of the distrust in which so many humans hold the taint of the untameable. It is the wild strain that is dominant, in the lynx-like appearance, the extra claw, and the feral instinct; and the few half-breeds that escape destruction usually take to the hills and the den life of their male ancestors. An old river-watcher at Lochailort, who for some reason that now eludes me was known as Tipperary, told me that one night, awoken by the caterwauling outside, he had gone to the door with a torch and in its beam had seen his own black-and-white she-cat in the fierce embrace of a huge wild tom. Thereafter he had waited eagerly for the birth of the kittens. When the time came she made her nest in the byre, and all that day he waited for the first birth, but at nightfall she had not yet brought forth. In the small hours of the morning he became conscious of piteous mewing at his door, and opened it to find his cat carrying in her mouth one wounded and dying kitten. In the dark background he heard a savage sound of worrying and snarling, and flashing his torch towards the byre he saw the wild tom in the act of killing a kitten. There was a green ember-glow of eyes, the flash of a big bottle-brush tail, and then the torch lit up nothing more but a pathetic trail of mangled new-born kittens. The single survivor, whom the mother had tried to carry to the house for sanctuary, died a few minutes later.

GAVIN MAXWELL, *Ring of Bright Water*, 1960

'Something is coming up hill,' said Mother Wolf, twitching one ear. 'Get ready.'

The bushes rustled a little in the thicket, and Father Wolf dropped with his haunches under him, ready for his leap. Then, if you had been watching, you would have seen the most wonderful thing in the world—the wolf checked in mid-spring. He made his bound before he saw what it was he was jumping at, and then he tried to stop himself. The result was that he shot up straight into the air for four or five feet, landing almost where he left ground.

'Man!' he snapped. 'A man's cub. Look!'

Directly in front of him, holding on by a low branch, stood a naked brown baby who could just walk—as soft and as dimpled a little atom as ever came to a wolf's cave at night. He looked up into Father Wolf's face, and laughed.

'Is that a man's cub?' said Mother Wolf. 'I have never seen one. Bring it here.'

A wolf accustomed to moving his own cubs can, if necessary, mouth an egg without breaking it, and though Father Wolf's jaws closed right on the child's back not a tooth even scratched the skin, as he laid it down among the cubs.

'How little! How naked, and—how bold!' said Mother Wolf, softly. The baby was pushing his way between the cubs to get close to the warm hide. 'Ahai! He is taking his meal with the others. And so this is a man's cub. Now, was there ever a wolf that could boast of a man's cub among her children?'

'I have heard now and again of such a thing, but never in our Pack or in my time,' said Father Wolf. 'He is altogether without hair, and I could kill him with a touch of my foot. But see, he looks up and is not afraid.'

RUDYARD KIPLING, 'Mowgli's Brothers', *The Jungle Book*, 1922

Mr Tebrick, his wife transformed into a fox (see p. 312 below), looks after her tenderly, until she runs off to live in the wild with a fox mate. Cubs are born . . .

Seeing the dog-fox thus surrounded by vixen and cubs was too much for Mr Tebrick; in spite of all his philosophy a pang of jealousy shot through him. He could see that Silvia had been hunting with her cubs, and also that she had forgotten that he would come that morning, for she started when she saw him, and though she carelessly licked his hand, he could see that her thoughts were not with him.

Very soon she led her cubs into the earth, the dog-fox had vanished and Mr Tebrick was again alone. He did not wait longer but went home.

Now was his peace of mind all gone, the happiness which he had flat-tered himself the night before he knew so well how to enjoy, seemed now but a fool's paradise in which he had been living. A hundred times this poor gentleman bit his lip, drew down his torvous brows, and stamped his foot, and cursed himself bitterly, or called his lady bitch. He could not forgive himself neither, that he had not thought of the damned dog-fox before, but all the while had let the cubs frisk round him, each one a proof that a dog-fox had been at work with his vixen. Yes, jealousy was now in the wind, and every circumstance which had been a reason for his felicity the night before was now turned into a monstrous feature of his nightmare. With all this Mr Tebrick so worked upon himself that for the time being he had lost his reason. Black was white and white black, and he was resolved that on the morrow he would dig the vile brood of foxes out and shoot them, and so free himself at last from this hellish plague.

All that night he was in this mood, and in agony, as if he had broken in the crown of a tooth and bitten on the nerve. But as all things will have an ending so at last Mr Tebrick, worn out and wearied by this loathed passion of jealousy, fell into an uneasy and tormented sleep.

After an hour or two the procession of confused and jumbled images which first assailed him passed away and subsided into one clear and powerful dream. His wife was with him in her own proper shape, walking as they had been on that fatal day before her transformation. Yet she was changed too, for in her face there were visible tokens of unhappiness, her face swollen with crying, pale and downcast, her hair hanging in disorder, her damp hands wringing a small handkerchief into a ball, her whole body shaken with sobs, and an air of long neglect about her person. Between her sobs she was confessing to him some crime which she had committed, but he did not catch the broken words, nor did he wish to hear them, for he was dulled by his sorrow. So they continued walking together in sadness as it were for ever, he with his arm about her waist, she turning her head to him and often casting her eyes down in distress.

At last they sat down, and he spoke, saying: 'I know they are not my children, but I shall not use them barbarously because of that. You are still my wife. I swear to you they shall never be neglected. I will pay for their education.'

Then he began turning over the names of schools in his mind. Eton would not do, nor Harrow, nor Winchester, nor Rugby. . . . But he could not tell why these schools would not do for these children of hers, he only knew that every school he thought of was impossible, but surely one could be found. So turning over the names of schools he sat for a long while holding his dear wife's hand, till at length, still weeping, she got up and went away and then slowly he awoke.

But even when he had opened his eyes and looked about him he was thinking of schools, saying to himself that he must send them to a private academy, or even at the worst engage a tutor. 'Why, yes,' he said to himself, putting one foot out of bed, 'that is what it must be, a tutor, though even then there will be a difficulty at first.'

At those words he wondered what difficulty there would be and recollected that they were not ordinary children. No, they were foxes— mere foxes. When poor Mr Tebrick had remembered this he was, as it were, dazed or stunned by the fact, and for a long time he could understand nothing, but at last burst into a flood of tears compassionating them and himself too. The awfulness of the fact itself, that his dear wife should have foxes instead of children, filled him with an agony of pity, and, at length, when he recollected the cause of their being foxes, that is that his wife was a fox also, his tears broke out anew, and he could bear it no longer but began calling out in his anguish, and beat his head once or twice against the wall, and then cast himself down on his bed again and wept and wept, sometimes tearing the sheets asunder with his teeth.

The whole of that day, for he was not to go to the earth till evening, he went about sorrowfully, torn by true pity for his poor vixen and her children.

At last when the time came he went again up to the earth, which he found deserted, but hearing his voice, out came Esther. But though he called the others by their names there was no answer, and something in the way the cub greeted him made him fancy she was indeed alone. She was truly rejoiced to see him, and scrambled up into his arms, and thence to his shoulder, kissing him, which was unusual in her (though natural enough in her sister Angelica). He sat down a little way from the earth fondling her, and fed her with some fish he had brought for her mother, which she ate so ravenously that he concluded she must have been short of food that day and probably alone for some time.

At last while he was sitting there Esther pricked up her ears, started up, and presently Mr Tebrick saw his vixen come towards them. She greeted him very affectionately but it was plain had not much time to spare, for she soon started back whence she had come with Esther at her side. When they had gone about a rod the cub hung back and kept stopping and looking back to the earth, and at last turned and ran back home. But her mother was not to be fobbed off so, for she quickly overtook her child and gripping her by the scruff began to drag her along with her.

Mr Tebrick, seeing then how matters stood, spoke to her, telling her he would carry Esther if she would lead, so after a little while Silvia gave her over, and then they set out on their strange journey.

Silvia went running on a little before while Mr Tebrick followed after with Esther in his arms whimpering and struggling now to be free, and indeed, once she gave him a nip with her teeth. This was not so strange a thing to him now, and he knew the remedy for it, which is much the same as with others whose tempers run too high, that is a taste of it themselves. Mr Tebrick shook her and gave her a smart little cuff, after which, though she sulked, she stopped her biting.

They went thus above a mile, circling his house and crossing the highway until they gained a small covert that lay with some waste fields adjacent to it. And by this time it was so dark that it was all Mr Tebrick could do to pick his way, for it was not always easy for him to follow where his vixen found a big enough road for herself.

But at length they came to another earth, and by the starlight Mr Tebrick could just make out the other cubs skylarking in the shadows.

Now he was tired, but he was happy and laughed softly for joy, and presently his vixen, coming to him, put her feet upon his shoulders as he sat on the ground, and licked him, and he kissed her back on the muzzle and gathered her in his arms and rolled her in his jacket and then laughed and wept by turns in the excess of his joy.

All his jealousies of the night before were forgotten now. All his desperate sorrow of the morning and the horror of his dream were gone. What if they were foxes? Mr Tebrick found that he could be happy with them. As the weather was hot he lay out there all the night, first playing hide and seek with them in the dark till, missing his vixen and the cubs proving obstreperous, he lay down and was soon asleep.

He was woken up soon after dawn by one of the cubs tugging at his shoelaces in play. When he sat up he saw two of the cubs standing near him on their hind legs, wrestling with each other, the other two were playing hide and seek round a tree trunk, and now Angelica let go his laces and came romping into his arms to kiss him and say 'Good morning' to him, then worrying the points of his waistcoat a little shyly after the warmth of his embrace.

That moment of awakening was very sweet to him. The freshness of the morning, the scent of everything at the day's rebirth, the first beams of the sun upon a tree-top near, and a pigeon rising into the air suddenly, all delighted him. Even the rough scent of the body of the cub in his arms seemed to him delicious.

At that moment all human customs and institutions seemed to him nothing but folly; for said he, 'I would exchange all my life as a man for my happiness now, and even now I retain almost all of the ridiculous conceptions of a man. The beasts are happier and I will deserve that happiness as best I can.'

DAVID GARNETT, *Lady into Fox*, 1923

Killiow Pigs

(From Killiow Country Park, near Truro)

Five adolescent suckling pigs
fanned out alongside their sleeping mamma;
each daughter big as an alsatian dog,
her five petticoat-pink starch-skinned girls.
They sleep with resolution and vitality.
Our admiration does not wake them.
Fed on apples, their flesh is ready-seasoned.
This afternoon heap of pig breathes a clean dusk
into the air; spring and dung,
rhododendrons, sour vapour of swill and straw.
With their sexy squiggle tails,
their ears soft as cats but big and lopped-over
like ambitious rabbits, with their long carefree
strokeable backs, their feet comic and smooth,
snouts succulent,
these sisters lie outspread, five cordial orchids
against mother's blushing pungent bulk,
dreaming of orchards
where an exiled male roots and roams,
his boar thighs tough and angelic,
his head lowered to the cool brisk echoes of morning,
his ringed nose a gleam of gravity,
his sudden stillness all swinish magnetism.
Dossing mother and daughters quiver in sleep,
the juice of desire lolloping over their lips;
snouts swell with love; tails uncurl, grow fine
and tender as silk;
each meets her orchard lover,
dreamy pigs in their matrilineal slumber.

As we watch these females, hope and desire
rise in us, a cloud of matrimonial heat,
blossoming and getting the better of us,
oh these shameless porcine arrangers of marriages!

PENELOPE SHUTTLE (b. 1947)

Kangaroos are really extraordinary creatures. When at full speed they jump
in prodigious bounds of their hind legs, with their tails stuck straight out
behind: leaps of well over thirty feet have been recorded, and speeds up to

30 miles an hour. In walking, however, their tail acts as a fifth limb, on which and on their tiny fore-limbs they support themselves while swinging their hind-legs forward for the next step. And when in fighting mood, they use the tail like a shooting stick, occasionally resting all their weight on it while bringing up their hind-legs with their formidable claws to rip at the enemy.

The baby kangaroo is born when no bigger than a human thumb-joint, and still extremely under-developed, a mere embryo thrust into the harsh outer world. But, like all newborn marsupials, it is endowed with a powerful instinct to climb up whatever surface it finds itself on. In nature, this is the skin of a female kangaroo's belly, which its mother has made smooth for it by licking. Eventually its efforts bring it to the lip of the wide-open pouch: it tumbles in, finds a teat, and becomes glued to it for several weeks. Later it becomes unstuck and only takes nourishment at intervals; and eventually it leaves the pouch to explore the outer world and learn the taste of grass, but returns to its mother when tired or at the threat of danger. It is amusing to see a well-grown young kangaroo or wallaby scramble head-first into a pouch only just big enough to hold him, and then turn round so that he can stick his head out and survey the world.

JULIAN HUXLEY, Kingdom of the Beasts, 1956

Of Apes and Monkies

All the kinde of these Apes approch neerest of all beasts to the resemblance of a mans shape: but they differ one from another in the taile. Marvellous crafty and subtill they be to beguile themselves: for by report, as they see hunters doe before them, they will imitate them in every point, even to besmeare themselves with glew & birdlime, & shoo their feet within gins and snares, and by that means are caught. *Mucianus* saith, that he hath seene Apes play at chesse and table: and that at first sight they could know nuts made of waxe from others. He affirmes also, that when the moon is in the wain, the monkies & Marmosets (which in this kinde have tailes) are sad and heavy, but the new moone they adore and joy at, which they testifie by hopping and dancing. As for the eclipse of Sun or Moone, all other foure footed beasts also do greatly dread and feare. The she Apes of all sorts are wondrous fond of their little ones: and such as are made tame within house will carry them in their armes all about so soone as they have brought them into the world, keepe a shewing of them to every bodie, and they take pleasure to have them dandled by others, as if thereby they tooke knowledge that folke joyed for their safe deliverance: but such a culling and hugging of them they keep, that in the end with very clasping and clipping they kill them many times.

PLINY THE ELDER (AD 23–79), Natural History (tr. Philemon Holland, 1601)

Hamster Cage

Quiet, the children look on
As the small mammal
Nesting in chips and lettuce
Gives birth, bloody and natural.
They see how it's done,

Watch her licking them clean—
But more than licking, the teeth
Working on the diminutive head,
Back, haunch, one then both,
Till blood and a tuft of down

Are the only sign.
Drawn by cries, parents disbelieve,
Then, believing, go silent,
Send children off, remove
The unspeakable mother whose calm

Jaw mocked their bargain:
Treadmill, breadcrumbs, suet
In exchange for a clean bit
Of wilderness, a pet,
A cage of instruction.

CONRAD HILBERRY (b. 1928)

On the last house in a village was a stork's nest. The stork-mother sat in the nest with her four little ones, which stretched out their heads with the little black beaks, for they had not yet become red. A little way off, on the ridge of the roof, stood the stork-father, quite stiff and rigid, with one leg drawn up under him, so that, at any rate, he might have some trouble in standing as he kept watch. It seemed almost as if he were carved in wood, he stood so still. 'It must certainly look quite grand that my wife should have a guard near the nest,' he thought, 'for no one can know that I am her husband, but they will surely think that I have been ordered to stand here. It looks well!' and he continued to stand on one leg.

In the street below a troop of children were playing; and when they saw the storks, first one of the boldest of them, and afterwards all together, sang the old rhyme about the storks, but they sang it just as it came into the first singer's head:—

Stork, stork, fly home, I beg,
And don't stay idling on one leg.
There's your wife sits in her nest,
Rocking all her young to rest;
The first he will be hung,
The second roasted young,
They'll come and shoot the third,
And stab the fourth, I've heard.

'Just listen to what the boys are singing,' said the little storks; 'they say we shall be hanged and roasted.'

'You need not mind that!' said the mother; 'don't listen to them, and it matters not what they say.'

On the following day, when the children met together again to play, and saw the storks, they sang their rhyme,—

The first he will be hung,
The second roasted young.

'Must we be hanged and roasted?' the young storks asked.

'No, certainly not!' said the mother; 'you shall learn to fly, which I'll teach you, and then we'll fly out into the meadows and pay the frogs a visit as they sing "croak, croak!" then we'll eat them up, and that will be fun.'

'And what next?' asked the little ones.

'Then all the storks of the whole country will meet together, and the autumn manœuvring begins, when you must be able to fly well. That is of the greatest importance; for whichever of you does not fly properly, the general will pierce through with his beak, and kill;—so take care that you attend to the exercising when it begins.'

'So we shall be stabbed after all, as the boy said; and there! listen!—they are singing it again.'

'Attend to me, and not to them,' said the stork-mother: 'after the grand manœuvre we fly away to a warmer country, far, far from here, over mountains and forests. To Egypt we fly, where there are three-cornered stone houses, which rise up into a point above the clouds; these are called pyramids, and are older than a stork has any notion of. In that country is a river, which, overflowing its banks, turns the whole land into slime, and all one has to do is to pick up the frogs.'

Some time had now passed by, and the young ones had grown so big that they could stand up in the nest, and watch their father from afar, as he brought them beautiful frogs and small snakes, and such-like delicacies. Then what fun it was to watch his tricks! His head he would bend right back, laying it upon his tail, and with his beak he made a noise like a rattle, and told them besides such stories, all about the swamps.

'Listen to me: you must now learn to fly,' said the stork-mother one day; and then all the four young-ones had to get out of the nest on to the ridge of the roof. Oh, how they waddled, how they balanced themselves with their wings, and yet were near falling down!

'Now watch me,' said their mother, 'this is the way you must hold your head, and place your feet thus! One, two; one, two; that's the way to get on in the world.' Then she flew a little way, and the young ones gave an awkward jump, when, plump, down they went, for their bodies were too heavy.

'I'll not fly,' said one of them, and crept back into the nest; 'what do I care about going into a warmer country?'

'Do you wish to freeze to death when winter comes? And shall the boys come to hang and to roast you? Well, then, I'll call them.'

'No, no!' cried the young stork, and hopped out of the nest again to the others.

On the third day they began to be able to fly a little, and then thought they could float in the air; but, when they tried that, over they went, and were obliged to move their wings again pretty quickly. Then came the boys again, down below in the street, and sang,—

Stork, stork, fly home, I beg.

'Shall we not fly down and peck out their eyes?' said the young storks.

'No, leave that alone,' said the mother. 'Attend to me, which is much more important. One, two, three; now we'll fly to the right. One, two, three; and now to the left, round the chimney. Now, that was very well done, particularly the last turn, so that to-morrow you may be allowed to fly with me to the marsh. There we shall find several nice stork families; and mind you show that my children are the best. You may strut about as proudly as you like, for that creates respect. . . .

We must first see how you get on at the great manœuvre. If you come off badly, so that the general runs you through with his beak, then the boys are right, at least in one respect. Now let us see how you get on.'

'Yes, that you shall,' they answered, and took particular pains. They practised so diligently every day, and flew so straight and lightly, that it was a pleasure to look at them.

Now came autumn; and the storks began to meet together, preparatory to migrating to a warmer climate during our winter. Then there was a grand manœuvre. They had to fly over forests and villages, in order to see how they got on, for it was a serious journey that was before them. The young storks managed so well, that they received a reward of a frog and snake, which they lost no time in eating.

'Now we ought to take our revenge,' said they.

'Yes, certainly,' said their mother; 'and what I have planned is just the very best thing to do. I know where the pond is, in which the children lie till the stork comes and takes them to their parents. The dear little children sleep, and have such delightful dreams as they never have in after-life. All parents are anxious to have such a child, and all children wish to have a brother or a sister. Now, we will fly off to the pond, and fetch a child for each of those that did not sing that naughty song about the storks.'

'But what are we to do to him,—to that bad, ugly boy, who began the song?' cried out the young ones.

'In the pond there lies a dead child, which has dreamed itself to death. That one we will fetch for him, and then he will have to cry, because we have brought him a dead brother; but for the good boy, whom I hope you have not forgotten,—the one who said it was wrong to make game of the birds—for him we will fetch a brother and a sister; and as his name is Peter, so shall all storks be called Peter.'

What she said was done, and all storks were called Peter, as they are up to this day.

HANS CHRISTIAN ANDERSEN (1805–75), 'The Storks' (tr. Alfred Wehnert, 1866)

Swans Mating

Even now I wish that you had been there
Sitting beside me on the riverbank:
The cob and his pen sailing in rhythm
Until their small heads met and the final
Heraldic moment dissolved in ripples.

This was a marriage and a baptism,
A holding of breath, nearly a drowning,
Wings spread wide for balance where he trod,
Her feathers full of water and her neck
Under the water like a bar of light.

MICHAEL LONGLEY (b. 1939)

We are also rather concerned about our moorhen who went mad while we were in Italy and began to build a nest in a tree. No reasoning of ours, of course, could stop her. She finished the nest, laid her eggs, in [it] and now has hatched out two small balls of black fluff. These fall out, at intervals, and have to be sat on by their protective Mum. We daren't put them back, and heaven knows how she manages to. But apparently she does, for when she isn't being a black umbrella on the path, she walks about in the tree, looking as uneasy yet persevering as a district visitor in a brothel. Her feet flap as she staggers from branch to branch, you never saw a moorhen look so silly and so disconsolate. Though they often look both, poor bodies! Did you know that trout tease moorhens? They swim up from below and bite their feet.

SYLVIA TOWNSEND WARNER, letter of 20 May 1962 to George Planck

I was experimenting at one time with young mallards to find out why artificially incubated and freshly hatched ducklings of this species, in contrast to similarly treated greylag goslings, are unapproachable and shy. Greylag goslings unquestioningly accept the first living being whom they meet as their mother, and run confidently after him. Mallards, on the contrary, always refused to do this. If I took from the incubator freshly hatched mallards, they invariably ran away from me and pressed themselves in the nearest dark corner. Why? I remembered that I had once let a muscovy duck hatch a clutch of mallard eggs and that the tiny mallards had also failed to accept this foster-mother. As soon as they were dry, they had simply run away from her and I had trouble enough to catch these crying, erring children. On the other hand, I once let a fat white farmyard duck hatch out mallards and the little wild things ran just as happily after her as if she had been their real mother. The secret must have lain in her call note, for, in external appearance, the domestic duck was quite as different from a mallard as was the muscovy; but what she had in common with the mallard (which, of course, is the wild progenitor of our farmyard duck) were her vocal expressions. Though, in the process of domestication, the duck has altered considerably in colour pattern and body form, its voice has remained practically the same. The inference was clear: I must quack like a mother mallard in order to make the little ducks run after me. No sooner said than done. When, one Whit-Saturday, a brood of pure-bred young mallards was due to hatch, I put the eggs in the incubator, took the babies, as soon as they were dry, under my personal care, and quacked for them the mother's call-note in my best Mallardese. For hours on end I kept it up, for half the day. The quacking was successful. The little ducks lifted their gaze confidently towards me, obviously had no fear of me this time, and as, still quacking, I drew slowly away from them, they also set themselves obediently in motion and scuttled after me in a tightly huddled group, just as ducklings follow their mother. My theory was indisputably proved. The freshly hatched ducklings have an inborn reaction to the call-note, but not to the optical picture of the mother. Anything that emits the right quack note will be considered as mother, whether it is a fat white Pekin duck or a still fatter man. However, the substituted object must not exceed a certain height. At the beginning of these experiments, I had sat myself down in the grass amongst the ducklings and, in order to make them follow me, had dragged myself, sitting, away from them. As soon, however, as I stood up and tried, in a standing posture, to lead them on, they gave up, peered searchingly on all sides, but not upwards towards me and it was not long before they began that penetrating piping of abandoned ducklings that we are accustomed simply to call 'crying'. They were unable to adapt themselves to the fact that their foster-mother had become so tall. So I was forced to move along, squatting low, if I wished them to follow me. This was not very comfortable; still less comfortable was the fact that the mallard mother quacks unintermittently. If I ceased for even the space of half a minute from my melodious 'Quahg, gegegegeg, Quahg, gegegegeg', the necks of the ducklings became longer and longer corresponding exactly to 'long faces' in human children—and did I then not immediately recommence quacking, the shrill weeping began anew. As soon as I was silent, they seemed to think that I had died, or perhaps that I loved them no more: cause enough for crying! The ducklings, in contrast to the greylag goslings, were most demanding and tiring charges, for, imagine a two-hour walk with such children, all the time squatting low and quacking without interruption! In the interests of science I submitted myself literally for hours on end to this ordeal. So it came about, on a certain Whit-Sunday, that, in company with my ducklings, I was wandering about, squatting and quacking, in a May-green meadow at the upper part of our garden. I was congratulating myself on the obedience and exactitude with which my ducklings came waddling after me, when I suddenly looked up and saw the garden fence framed by a row of dead-white faces: a group of tourists was standing at the fence and staring horrified in my direction. Forgivable! For all they could see was a big man with a beard dragging himself, crouching, round the meadow, in figures of eight, glancing constantly over his shoulder and quacking—but the ducklings, the all-revealing and all-explaining ducklings were hidden in the tall spring grass from the view of the astonished crowd.

KONRAD LORENZ, *King Solomon's Ring*, 1952

Pigeons are able to retain their eggs even in the act of parturition. If they are disturbed by anything occurring in the neighbourhood of their nest, or a feather be plucked out, or if anything else troubles or disturbs them, they retain the egg they were about to lay.

. . . This is peculiar to pigeons, and so is the following: for they kiss each other when the male is about to mount, or else they will not endure it. The older bird first gives a kiss, but afterwards he mounts without kissing, but younger birds always kiss before copulation. This also is peculiar to these birds. The females kiss and mount upon each other like the males, when there is no male present. They do not project anything into each other, but

produce more eggs than those which produce fertile ones; from these eggs
nothing is hatched, but they are all barren.

ARISTOTLE (384–322 BC), *History of Animals* (tr. Richard Cresswell, 1897)

Reverie of the Termite Queen

Sealed with my consort in the royal room
Under the hill that I have never seen
But made the makers of, I lie in state
While minions ply me with both food and drink

To cosset Majesty while I factor forth
The hundred million children whom I must
Outlive a hundred times before I may
Collapse the shrivelled whistle of my womb

At last effete and do what distinguished thing
One does to die. My proles, my infantry,
Parade on their endless errands hither and yon
Above my mystery, the soul of state,

Where I lie pulsing full with the ignorant host
That I dismiss into the world without,
Concerning which I am both dark and blind
As to what it may be, and why it is.

HOWARD NEMEROV (1920–91)

Hence, when the Morus in Italia's lands
To spring's warm beam its timid leaf expands;
The Silk-Worm broods in countless tribes above
Crop the green treasure, uninform'd of love;
Erewhile the changeful Worm with circling head
Weaves the nice curtains of his silken bed;
Web within web involves his larva form,
Alike secured from sunshine and from storm;
For twelve long days He dreams of blossom'd groves,
Untasted honey, and ideal loves;
Wakes from his trance, alarmed with young Desire,
Finds his new sex, and feels ecstatic fire;
From flower to flower with honey'd lip he springs,
And seeks his velvet loves on silver wings.

ERASMUS DARWIN (1731–1802)

I peered at the butterfly he was holding. The white wings were set off not only by the dusky black edges but also by brilliant red spots. The wings were darker near the body, helping to keep the butterfly's ovaries warm. 'You very seldom find a virgin female *Parnassius*,' Bob explained. 'The males mate with them very soon after pupation. Most butterflies have to be dissected to find out if the females are virgins, but parnassian females mate only once, because after the mating the male secretes a fluid that solidifies and forms a structure called the sphragis around the female's reproductive opening.' He pointed to a neat little cap that fitted over the end of her abdomen. 'This assures that only this particular male's genes will be passed on. Parnassians copulate for three hours or more, during which time the liquid molds exactly to the female's shape and hardens. If the male lets go of her too soon, the sphragis will not be formed and will fall away. On the other hand, if he holds on too long it's *coitus perpetuus!*'

Sue Hubbell, Broadsides from the Other Orders: A Book of Bugs, 1993

When the buck rabbit first claps eyes on the doe the temperature of his ears rises precipitately, sometimes by as much as 14°F. The excitement is quickly transmitted to the doe and a similar rise in her ear temperature occurs almost simultaneously. The ears not only become warmer but there is a noticeable dilatation of the vessels and a blushing of the *pinnae* and no doubt an increased blood supply reaches the fleas feeding on these sites. They in turn are stimulated and can be seen hopping about on the surface of the fur and swapping from buck to doe and back again. Their feeding rate and blood intake is also increased precipitately—which can be gauged by the sudden reduction in the interval between defecations. Under ordinary circumstances a flea feeding on the ears of a rabbit will pass out bloody faecal pellets on an average once every twenty-six minutes. During mating of the rabbits this may rise to one pellet passed every six minutes. Within twenty-four hours of pairing the defecation rate of fleas feeding on the doe falls to an unusually low level—and they pass only one pellet every hour. This is a reaction due to a change of level in the hormones in the host's blood. The female rabbits respond to copulation by ovulation. This is associated with the release of luteinizing hormones (from the pituitary gland) into the circulation, which in turn stimulates the release of certain sex hormones—the progestins—from the *corpus luteum* in the rabbit's ovaries. The effect of the progestins is to reduce the feeding rate and defecation rate of the fleas and check the growth of their ovaries. The steady rise in progestins during the first twenty days of the rabbit's pregnancy is sufficient, despite the presence of oestrogens, to hold down the fleas' maturation and egg development, which only begins about the twenty-first day.

MIRIAM ROTHSCHILD, 'The Rabbit Flea and Hormones', 1967

The Flea

Marke but this flea, and marke in this,
How little that which thou deny'st me is;
It suck'd me first, and now sucks thee,
And in this flea, our two bloods mingled bee;
Thou know'st that this cannot be said
A sinne, nor shame, nor losse of maidenhead,
   Yet this enjoyes before it wooe,
    And pamper'd swells with one blood made of two,
    And this, alas, is more then wee would doe.

Oh stay, three lives in one flea spare,
Where wee almost, yea more then maryed are,
This flea is you and I, and this
Our mariage bed, and mariage temple is;
Though parents grudge, and you, w'are met,
And cloysterd in these living walls of Jet.
   Though use make you apt to kill mee,
    Let not to that, selfe murder added bee,
    And sacrilege, three sinnes in killing three.

Cruell and sodaine, hast thou since
Purpled thy naile, in blood of innocence?
Wherein could this flea guilty bee,
Except in that drop which it suckt from thee?
Yet thou triumph'st, and saist that thou
Find'st not thy selfe, nor mee the weaker now;
   'Tis true, then learne how false, feares bee;
    Just so much honor, when thou yeeld'st to mee,
    Will wast, as this flea's death tooke life from thee.

JOHN DONNE (1572–1631)

HABITAT

The sixth, and of creation last, arose
With ev'ning harps and matin, when God said,
'Let th' earth bring forth soul living in her kind,
Cattle and creeping things, and beast of the earth,
Each in their kind.' The earth obeyed, and straight
Op'ning her fertile womb teemed at a birth
Innumerous living creatures, perfect forms,
Limbed and full grown. Out of the ground up rose
As from his lair the wild beast where he wons
In forest wild, in thicket, brake, or den;
Among the trees in pairs they rose, they walked;
The cattle in the fields and meadows green:
Those rare and solitary, these in flocks
Pasturing at once, and in broad herds upsprung.
The grassy clods now calved, now half appeared
The tawny lion, pawing to get free
His hinder parts, then springs as broke from bonds,
And rampant shakes his brinded mane; the ounce,
The libbard, and the tiger, as the mole

Rising, the crumbled earth above them threw
In hillocks; the swift stag from under ground
Bore up his branching head; scarce from his mold
Behemoth, biggest born of earth, upheaved
His vastness; fleeced the flocks and bleating rose,
As plants; ambiguous between sea and land,
The river-horse and scaly crocodile.
At once came forth whatever creeps the ground,
Insect or worm: those waved their limber fans
For wings, and smallest lineaments exact
In all the liveries decked of summer's pride
With spots of gold and purple, azure and green;
These as a line their long dimension drew,
Streaking the ground with sinuous trace; not all
Minims of nature; some of serpent kind,
Wondrous in length and corpulence, involved
Their snaky folds, and added wings. First crept
The parsimonious emmet, provident
Of future, in small room large heart enclosed,
Pattern of just equality perhaps
Hereafter, joined in her popular tribes
Of commonalty; swarming next appeared
The female bee that feeds her husband drone
Deliciously, and builds her waxen cells
With honey stored. The rest are numberless,
And thou their natures know'st, and gav'st them names,
Needless to thee repeated; nor unknown
The serpent, subtlest beast of all the field,
Of huge extent sometimes, with brazen eyes
And hairy mane terrific, though to thee
Not noxious, but obedient at thy call.

JOHN MILTON, *Paradise Lost*, Book VII, 1667

Then Thel astonish'd view'd the Worm upon its dewy bed.

'Art thou a Worm? Image of weakness, art thou but a Worm?
I see thee like an infant wrapped in the Lilly's leaf.
Ah! weep not, little voice, thou canst not speak, but thou canst weep.
Is this a Worm? I see thee lay helpless & naked, weeping,
And none to answer, none to cherish thee with mother's smiles.'

WILLIAM BLAKE, *The Book of Thel*, 1789

And now to return to our swarming hive, where the bees have already given the signal for departure . . . At the moment this signal is given, it is as though one sudden mad impulse had simultaneously flung open wide every single gate in the city; and the black throng issues, or rather pours forth, in a double, or treble, or quadruple jet, as the number of exits may be—in a tense, direct, vibrating, uninterrupted stream that at once dissolves and melts into space, where the myriad transparent furious wings weave a tissue throbbing with sound. And this for some moments will quiver right over the hive, with prodigious rustle of gossamer silks that countless electrified hands might be ceaselessly rending and stitching; it floats undulating, it trembles and flutters, like a veil of gladness invisible fingers support in the sky, and wave to and fro, from the flowers to the blue, expecting sublime advent or departure. And at last one angle declines, another is lifted; the radiant mantle unites its four sunlit corners; and, like the wonderful carpet the fairy-tale speaks of that flits across space to obey its master's command, it steers its straight course, bending forward a little as though to hide in its folds the sacred presence of the future, towards the willow, the pear-tree, or lime whereon the queen has alighted; and round her each rhythmical wave comes to rest, as though on a nail of gold, and suspends its fabric of pearls and of luminous wings.

And then there is silence once more; and, in an instant, this mighty tumult, this awful curtain apparently laden with unspeakable menace and anger, this bewildering golden hail that streamed upon every object near— all these become merely a great, inoffensive, peaceful cluster of bees, composed of thousands of little motionless groups, that patiently wait, as they hang from the branch of a tree, for the scouts to return who have gone in search of a place of shelter.

MAURICE MAETERLINCK (1862–1949), *The Life of the Bee* (tr. Alfred Sutro, 1901)

The Minimal

I study the lives on a leaf: the little
Sleepers, numb nudgers in cold dimensions,
Beetles in caves, newts, stone-deaf fishes,
Lice tethered to long limp subterranean weeds,
Squirmers in bogs,
And bacterial creepers
Wriggling through wounds
Like elvers in ponds,
Their wan mouths kissing the warm sutures,
Cleaning and caressing,
Creeping and healing.

THEODORE ROETHKE (1908–63)

A Cranefly in September

She is struggling through grass-mesh—not flying,
Her wide-winged, stiff, weightless basket-work of limbs
Rocking, like an antique wain, a top-heavy ceremonial cart
Across mountain summits
(Not planing over water, dipping her tail)
But blundering with long strides, long reachings, reelings
And ginger-glistening wings
From collision to collision.
Aimless in no particular direction,
Just exerting her last to escape out of the overwhelming
Of whatever it is, legs, grass,
The garden, the county, the country, the world—

Sometimes she rests long minutes in the grass forest
Like a fairytale hero, only a marvel can help her.
She cannot fathom the mystery of this forest
In which, for instance, this giant watches—
The giant who knows she cannot be helped in any way.

Her jointed bamboo fuselage,
Her lobster shoulders, and her face
Like a pinhead dragon, with its tender moustache,
And the simple colourless church windows of her wings
Will come to an end, in mid-search, quite soon.
Everything about her, every perfected vestment
Is already superfluous.
The monstrous excess of her legs and curly feet
Are a problem beyond her.
The calculus of glucose and chitin inadequate
To plot her through the infinities of the stems.

The frayed apple leaves, the grunting raven, the defunct tractor
Sunk in nettles, wait with their multiplications
Like other galaxies.
The sky's Northward September procession, the vast soft armistice,
Like an Empire on the move,
Abandons her, tinily embattled
With her cumbering limbs and cumbered brain.

TED HUGHES (b. 1930)

Clock a Clay

In the cowslips peeps I lye
Hidden from the buzzing fly
While green grass beneath me lies
Pearled wi' dew like fishes eyes
Here I lye a Clock a clay
Waiting for the time o' day

While grassy forests quake surprise
And the wild wind sobs and sighs
My gold home rocks as like to fall
On its pillars green and tall
When the pattering rain drives bye
Clock a Clay keeps warm and dry

Day by day and night by night
All the week I hide from sight
In the cowslips peeps I lye
In rain and dew still warm and dry
Day and night and night and day
Red black spotted clock a clay

My home it shakes in wind and showers
Pale green pillar top't wi' flowers
Bending at the wild winds breath
Till I touch the grass beneath
Here still I live lone clock a clay
Watching for the time of day

JOHN CLARE (1793–1864)

Autobiography of a Lungworm

My normal dwelling is the lungs of swine,
    My normal shape a worm,
But other dwellings, other shapes, are mine
    Within my natural term.
Dimly I see my life, of all, the sign,
    Of better lives the germ.

clock a clay: ladybird

The pig, though I am inoffensive, coughs,
    Finding me irritant:
My eggs go with the contents of the troughs
    From mouth to excrement—
The pig thus thinks, perhaps, he forever doffs
    His niggling resident.

The eggs lie unconsidered in the dung
    Upon the farmyard floor,
Far from the scarlet and sustaining lung:
    But happily a poor
And humble denizen provides a rung
    To make ascension sure.

The earthworm eats the eggs; inside the warm
    Cylinder larvae hatch:
For years, if necessary, in this form
    I wait the lucky match
That will return me to my cherished norm,
    My ugly pelt dispatch.

Strangely, it is the pig himself becomes
    The god inside the car:
His greed devours the earthworms; so the slums
    Of his intestines are
The setting for the act when clay succumbs
    And force steers for its star.

The larvae burrow through the bowel wall
    And, having to the dregs
Drained ignominy, gain the lung's great hall.
    They change. Once more, like pegs,
Lungworms are anchored to the rise and fall
    —And start to lay their eggs.

What does this mean? The individual,
    Nature, mutation, strife?
I feel, though I am simple, still the whole
    Is complex; and that life—
A huge, doomed throbbing—has a wiry soul
    That must escape the knife.

ROY FULLER (1912–91)

The destructive habits of [*ptinus fur*] in museums are well-known. I have, however, had more reason, in my own case, to lament its ravages in my library; and I do not remember to have ever heard book collectors in general complain of its attacks in this way. A large number of my books, however, have suffered, principally in their bindings; and I do not find Russia leather any security, though its strong smell is thought by some to be prejudicial, or at least disagreeable, to insects in general. The leather of the bindings, however, is not the only part they devour: they often attack the paper and pasteboard of which the covers are made; and also the little cylindrical rolls, fastened down with thread, which appear at the top and bottom of most bound books. In this last part particularly, the maggots may often be found secreted. I find no effectual means of checking this annoyance, except that of often taking the books down and thoroughly brushing them.

REVD LEONARD JENYNS, *Observations in Natural History*, 1846

Song of the Death-Watch Beetle

Here come I, the death-watch beetle
Chewing away at the great cathedral;

Gnawing the mediaeval beams
And the magnificent carved rood screen

Gorging on gospels and epistles
From the illuminated missals;

As once I ate the odes of Sappho
And the histories of Manetho,

The lost plays of Euripides
And all the thought of Parmenides.

The Sibyl's leaves which the wind scattered,
And great aunt Delia's love letters.

Turn down the lamp in the cooling room:
There stand I with my little drum.

Death. Watch. You are watching death.
Blow out the lamp with your last breath.

JOHN HEATH-STUBBS (b. 1918)

Diary of a Church Mouse

*(Lines, written to order on a set subject, to be
spoken on the wireless.)*

Here among long-discarded cassocks,
Damp stools, and half-split open hassocks,
Here where the Vicar never looks
I nibble through old service books.
Lean and alone I spend my days
Behind this Church of England baize.
I share my dark forgotten room
With two oil-lamps and half a broom.
The cleaner never bothers me,
So here I eat my frugal tea.
My bread is sawdust mixed with straw;
My jam is polish for the floor.

   Christmas and Easter may be feasts
For congregations and for priests,
And so may Whitsun. All the same,
They do not fill my meagre frame.
For me the only feast at all
Is Autumn's Harvest Festival,
When I can satisfy my want
With ears of corn around the font.
I climb the eagle's brazen head
To burrow through a loaf of bread.
I scramble up the pulpit stair
And gnaw the marrows hanging there.

   It is enjoyable to taste
These items ere they go to waste,
But how annoying when one finds
That other mice with pagan minds
Come into church my food to share
Who have no proper business there.
Two field mice who have no desire
To be baptized, invade the choir.
A large and most unfriendly rat
Comes in to see what we are at.
He says he thinks there is no God
And yet he comes . . . it's rather odd.
This year he stole a sheaf of wheat
(It screened our special preacher's seat),

And prosperous mice from fields away
Come in to hear the organ play,
And under cover of its notes
Ate through the altar's sheaf of oats.
A Low Church mouse, who thinks that I
Am too papistical, and High,
Yet somehow doesn't think it wrong
To munch through Harvest Evensong,
While I, who starve the whole year through,
Must share my food with rodents who
Except at this time of the year
Not once inside the church appear.
   Within the human world I know
Such goings-on could not be so,
For human beings only do
What their religion tells them to.
They read the Bible every day
And always, night and morning, pray,
And just like me, the good church mouse,
Worship each week in God's own house.
   But all the same it's strange to me
How very full the church can be
With people I don't see at all
Except at Harvest Festival.

JOHN BETJEMAN (1906–84)

November 4, 1767.
I have procured some of the mice mentioned in my former letters, a young one and a female with young, both of which I have preserved in brandy. From the colour, shape, size, and manner of nesting, I make no doubt but that the species is nondescript. They are much smaller and more slender than the *mus domesticus medius* of Ray; and have more of the squirrel or dormouse colour: their belly is white, a straight line along their sides divides the shades of their back and belly. They never enter into houses; are carried into ricks and barns with the sheaves; abound in harvest, and build their nests amidst the straws of the corn above the ground, and sometimes in thistles. They breed as many as eight at a litter, in a little round nest composed of the blades of grass or wheat.

One of these nests I procured this autumn, most artificially platted, and composed of the blades of wheat; perfectly round, and about the size of a cricket-ball; with the aperture so ingeniously closed, that there was no discovering to what part it belonged. It was so compact and well filled, that

species: the harvest mouse, one of White's original discoveries

it would roll across the table without being discomposed, though it contained eight little mice that were naked and blind. As this nest was perfectly full, how could the dam come at her litter respectively so as to administer a teat to each? perhaps she opens different places for that purpose, adjusting them again when the business is over: but she could not possibly be contained herself in the ball with her young, which moreover would be daily increasing in bulk. This wonderful procreant cradle, an elegant instance of the efforts of instinct, was found in a wheat-field, suspended in the head of a thistle.

GILBERT WHITE (1720–93), *The Natural History of Selborne*

A New Year Greeting

After an Article by Mary J. Marples in
Scientific American, *January, 1969*

for Vassily Yanowsky

On this day tradition allots
    to taking stock of our lives,
my greetings to all of you, Yeasts,
    Bacteria, Viruses,
Aerobics and Anaerobics:
    A Very Happy New Year
to all for whom my ectoderm
    is as Middle Earth to me.

For creatures your size I offer
    a free choice of habitat,
so settle yourselves in the zone
    that suits you best, in the pools
of my pores or the tropical
    forests of arm-pit and crotch,
in the deserts of my fore-arms,
    or the cool woods of my scalp

Build colonies: I will supply
    adequate warmth and moisture,
the sebum and lipids you need,
    on condition you never
do me annoy with your presence,
    but behave as good guests should,
not rioting into acne
    or athlete's-foot or a boil.

Does my inner weather affect
   the surfaces where you live?
Do unpredictable changes
   record my rocketing plunge
from fairs when the mind is in tift
   and relevant thoughts occur
to fouls when nothing will happen
   and no one calls and it rains.

I should like to think that I make
   a not impossible world,
but an Eden it cannot be:
   my games, my purposive acts,
may turn to catastrophes there.
   If you were religious folk,
how would your dramas justify
   unmerited suffering?

By what myths would your priests account
   for the hurricanes that come
twice every twenty-four hours,
   each time I dress or undress,
when, clinging to keratin rafts,
   whole cities are swept away
to perish in space, or the Flood
   that scalds to death when I bathe?

Then, sooner or later, will dawn
   a day of Apocalypse,
when my mantle suddenly turns
   too cold, too rancid, for you,
appetising to predators
   of a fiercer sort, and I
am stripped of excuse and nimbus,
   a Past, subject to Judgement.

W. H. AUDEN (1907–73)

Goannas

At dawn they'd hear it heave itself across
the ceiling; every heavy-footed thump
was greeted with a long approving hiss
as its whiplash tongue darted out to probe

where diving rafters ruled the darkness under
the roof. At first they were alarmed—no house-guest
had been mentioned—but heard then that a goanna
slept in their attic; just a jumped-up lizard,

so neighbours said: no more than seven foot
from head to tail, but fatter than a barrel.
Soon it was spotted skulking in the shade
of the gum tree; inscrutable, the reptile

stared back at them, and with its tongue shot down
a gaudy dragonfly. As merciless
swiping mosquitoes as when, one by one,
it picked off victims from a scuttling mass

of cockroaches, or mopped up frantic ants,
it did not spare the praying mantises;
no insect in its path stood any chance.
I said how good it was we weren't their size.

Once I'd been swimming in the water-hole
at Berry Springs when bearing down on me
I saw the domed eyes of a crocodile.
I could not move to get out of its way

(kept up an automatic stroke), transfixed
by those determined eyes—and let it come
at me, as if the thing controlled my fate
and knew my name just as a bomb that's plumb

on target does. This monster had my number
yet at the very last veered off, no croc
after all but a rather frightened goanna.
I laughed my head off in a state of shock.

NEIL ASTLEY (b. 1953)

One day, as we were crossing the Essequibo, I saw a large two-toed sloth
on the ground upon the bank; how he had got there nobody could tell: the
Indian said he had never surprised a sloth in such a situation before: he
would hardly have come there to drink, for both above and below the
place, the branches of the trees touched the water, and afforded him an easy
and safe access to it. Be this as it may, though the trees were not above

twenty yards from him, he could not make his way through the sand time enough to escape before we landed. As soon as we got up to him he threw himself upon his back, and defended himself in gallant style with his fore-legs. 'Come, poor fellow,' said I to him, 'if thou hast got into a hobble to-day, thou shalt not suffer for it: I'll take no advantage of thee in misfortune; the forest is large enough both for thee and me to rove in: go thy ways up above, and enjoy thyself in these endless wilds; it is more than probable thou wilt never have another interview with man. So fare thee well.' On saying this, I took a long stick which was lying there, held it for him to hook on, and then conveyed him to a high and stately mora. He ascended with wonderful rapidity, and in about a minute he was almost at the top of the tree. He now went off in a side direction, and caught hold of the branch of a neighbouring tree; he then proceeded towards the heart of the forest. I stood looking on, lost in amazement at his singular mode of progress. I followed him with my eye till the intervening branches closed in betwixt us; and then I lost sight for ever of the two-toed sloth. I was going to add, that I never saw a sloth take to his heels in such earnest; but the expression will not do, for the sloth has no heels.

CHARLES WATERTON, *Wanderings in South America*, 1839

Giant Tortoise

I am related to stones
The slow accretion of moss where dirt is wedged
Long waxy hair that can split boulders.
Events are not important.

I live in my bone
Recalling the hour of my death.
It takes more toughness than most have got.
Or a saintliness.

Strength of a certain kind, anyway.
Bald toothless clumsy perhaps
With all the indignity of old age
But age is not important.

There is nothing worth remembering
But the silver glint in the muck
The thickening of great trees
The hard crust getting harder.

ANTHONY HECHT (b. 1923)

The Snail

To grass, or leaf, or fruit, or wall,
The Snail sticks close, nor fears to fall,
As if he grew there, house and all
                    Together.

Within that house secure he hides,
When danger imminent betides
Of storm, or other harm besides
                    Of weather.

Give but his horns the slightest touch,
His self-collecting power is such,
He shrinks into his house with much
                    Displeasure.

Where'er he dwells, he dwells alone,
Except himself has chattels none,
Well satisfied to be his own
                    Whole treasure.

Thus, hermit-like, his life he leads,
Nor partner of his banquet needs,
And if he meets one, only feeds
                    The faster.

Who seeks him must be worse than blind,
He and his house are so combined,
If, finding it, he fails to find
                    Its master.

WILLIAM COWPER (1731–1800), tr. from the Latin of Vincent Bourne

Venator [Huntsman]. The earth is a solid, settled element: an element most universally beneficial both to man and beast: to men who have their several recreations upon it, as horse-races, hunting, sweet smells, pleasant walks: the earth feeds man, and all those several beasts that both feed him and afford him recreation. What pleasure doth man take in hunting the stately stag, the generous buck, the wild boar, the cunning otter, the crafty fox, and the fearful hare? And if I may descend to a lower game, what pleasure is it sometimes with gins to betray the very vermin of the earth? as, namely, the fitchet, the fulimart, the ferret, the polecat, the mould-warp, and the like creatures that live upon the face and within the bowels of the earth. How doth the earth bring forth herbs, flowers, and fruits, both for physic and the pleasure of mankind! and above all, to me at least, the fruitful vine, of which, when I drink moderately, it clears my brain, cheers my heart, and sharpens my wit. How could Cleopatra have feasted Mark Antony, with eight wild boars roasted whole at one supper, and other meat suitable, if the earth had not been a bountiful mother? But to pass by the mighty elephant, which the earth breeds and nourisheth, and descend to the least of creatures, how doth the earth afford us a doctrinal example in the little pismire, who in the summer provides and lays up her winter provision, and teaches man to do the like! The earth feeds and carries those horses that carry us. If I would be prodigal of my time and your patience, what might not I say in commendations of the earth? that puts limits to the proud and raging sea, and by that means preserves both man and beast, that it destroys them not, as we see it daily doth those that venture upon the sea, and are there shipwrecked, drowned, and left to feed haddocks; when we that are so wise as to keep ourselves on the earth, walk, and talk, and live, and eat, and drink, and go a-hunting.

IZAAK WALTON, *The Compleat Angler*, 1653

Ye Shepherds! if your labours hope success,
Be first your purpose to procure a breed
To soil and clime adapted. Every soil
And clime, ev'n every tree and herb, receives
Its habitant peculiar: each to each
The Great Invisible, and each to all,
Thro' earth, and sea, and air, harmonious suits.
Tempestuous regions, Darwent's naked Peaks,
Snowden and blue Plynlymmon, and the wide
Aërial sides of Cader-ydris huge;
These are bestow'd on goat-horned sheep, of Fleece
Hairy and coarse, of long and nimble shank,
Who rove o'er bog or heath, and graze or brouze
Alternate, to collect, with due dispatch,
O'er the bleak wild, the thinly-scatter'd meal:
But hills of milder air, that gently rise
O'er dewy dales, a fairer species boast,
Of shorter limb, and frontlet more ornate:
Such the Silurian. If thy farm extends
Near Cotswold Downs, or the delicious groves

Of Symmonds, honour'd thro' the sandy soil
Of elmy Ross, or Devon's myrtle vales,
That drink clear rivers near the glassy sea,
Regard this sort, and hence thy sire of lambs
Select: his tawny Fleece in ringlets curl;
Long swings his slender tail; his front is fenc'd
With horns Ammonian, circulating twice
Around each open ear, like those fair scrolls
That grace the columns of th' Iönic dome.

   Yet should thy fertile glebe be marly clay,
Like Melton pastures, or Tripontian fields,
Where ever-gliding Avon's limpid wave
Thwarts the long course of dusty Watling-street;
That larger sort, of head defenceless, seek,
Whose Fleece is deep and clammy, close and plain;
The ram short-limbed, whose form compact describes
One level line along his spacious back;
Of full and ruddy eye, large ears, stretch'd head,
Nostrils dilated, breast and shoulders broad,
And spacious haunches, and a lofty dock.

   Thus to their kindred soil and air induc'd,
Thy thriving herd will bless thy skilful care,
That copies Nature, who, in every change,
In each variety, with wisdom works,
And powers diversifi'd of air and soil,
Her rich materials.

JOHN DYER (1699–1757), *The Fleece*

A Dead Mole

Strong-shouldered mole,
That so much lived below the ground,
Dug, fought and loved, hunted and fed,
For you to raise a mound
Was as for us to make a hole;
What wonder now that being dead
Your body lies here stout and square
Buried within the blue vault of the air?

ANDREW YOUNG (1885–1971)

To Keep Away Moles

for Elspeth Barker

Avaunt, mouldywarp,
    Out of my acres;
Vacate, velvet-coat,
    Your oubliettes and galleries;
The glebe of my neighbour
    Be for your pioning,
And my sward undisturbed:
    His earthworms are more succulent,
    His wire-worms more esculent,
    His leatherjackets of more nutriment.

That is the score,
Insectivore!

JOHN HEATH-STUBBS (b. 1918)

The creature in the hollow was a bird—a big bird, nearly a foot long. Neither of them had ever seen a bird like it before. The white part of its back, which they had glimpsed through the grass, was in fact only the shoulders and neck. The lower back was light grey and so were the wings, which tapered to long, black-tipped primaries folded together over the tail. The head was very dark brown—almost black—in such sharp contrast to the white neck that the bird looked as though it were wearing a kind of hood. The one dark-red leg that they could see ended in a webbed foot and three powerful, taloned toes. The beak, hooked slightly downwards at the end, was strong and sharp. As they stared it opened, disclosing a red mouth and throat. The bird hissed savagely and tried to strike, but still it did not move.

'It's hurt,' said Bigwig.

'Yes, you can tell that,' replied Silver. 'But it's not wounded anywhere that I can see. I'll go round—'

'Look out!' said Bigwig. 'He'll have you!'

Silver, as he started to move round the hollow, had come closer to the bird's head. He jumped back just in time to avoid a quick, darting blow of the beak.

'That would have broken your foot,' said Bigwig.

As they squatted, looking at the bird—for they both sensed intuitively that it would not rise—it suddenly burst into loud, raucous cries—'Yark! Yark! Yark!'—a tremendous sound at close quarters—that split the morning and carried far across the down. Bigwig and Silver turned and ran.

[They] returned with Hazel. The three of them squatted outside the bird's reach as it looked sharply and desperately from one to the other.

Hazel orders the others to feed it, with worms and insects, and in the evening they encourage it to move to a safer hole

It got up with a good deal of difficulty, staggering on its strong, blood-red legs. Then it opened its wings high above its body and Hazel jumped back, startled by the great, arching span. But at once it closed them again, grimacing with pain.

'Ving no good. I come.'

It followed Hazel docilely enough across the grass, but he was careful to keep out of its reach. Their arrival outside the wood caused something of a sensation, which Hazel cut short with a peremptory sharpness quite unlike his usual manner.

'Come on, get busy,' he said to Dandelion and Buckthorn. 'This bird's hurt and we're going to shelter it until it's better. Ask Bigwig to show you how to get it some food. It eats worms and insects. Try grasshoppers, spiders—anything. Hawkbit! Acorn! Yes, and you too, Fiver—come out of that rapt trance, or whatever you're in. We need an open, wide hole, broader than it's deep, with a flat floor a little below the level of the entrance: by nightfall.'

Black-headed gulls are gregarious. They live in colonies where they forage and feed, chatter and fight all day long. Solitude and reticence are unnatural to them. They move southwards in the breeding-season and at such times a wounded one is only too likely to find itself deserted. The gull's savagery and suspicion had been due partly to pain and partly to the unnerving knowledge that it had no companions and could not fly. By the following morning its natural instincts to mix with a flock and to talk were beginning to return. Bigwig made himself its companion. He would not hear of the gull going out to forage. Before ni-Frith the rabbits had managed to produce as much as it could eat—for a time at all events—and were able to sleep through the heat of the day. Bigwig, however, remained with the gull, making no secret of his admiration, talking and listening to it for several hours. At the evening feed he joined Hazel and Holly near the bank where Bluebell had told his story of El-ahrairah.

'How's the bird now?' asked Hazel.

'A good deal better, I think,' replied Bigwig. 'He's very tough, you know. My goodness, what a life he's had! You don't know what you're missing! I could sit and listen to him all day.'

'How was it hurt?'

'A cat jumped on him in a farmyard. He never heard it until the last moment. It tore the muscle of one of his wings, but apparently he gave it something to remember before he made off. Then he got himself up here somehow or other and just collapsed. Think of standing up to a cat! I can see now that I haven't really started yet. Why shouldn't a rabbit stand up to a cat? Let's just suppose that—'

'But what is this bird?' interrupted Holly.

'Well, I can't quite make out,' answered Bigwig. 'But if I understand him properly—and I'm not at all sure that I do—he says that where he comes from there are thousands of his kind—more than we can possibly imagine. Their flocks make the whole air white and in the breeding season their nests are like leaves in a wood—so he says.'

'But where? I've never seen *one*, even.'

'He says,' said Bigwig, looking very straight at Holly, 'he says that a long way from here the earth stops and there isn't any more.'

'Well, obviously it stops somewhere. What is there beyond?'

'Water.'

'A river, you mean?'

'No,' said Bigwig, 'not a river. He says there's a vast place of water, going on and on. You can't see to the other side. There isn't another side. At least there is, because he's been there. Oh, I don't know—I must admit I can't altogether understand it.'

'Was it telling you that it's been outside the world and come back again? That must be untrue.'

'I don't know,' said Bigwig, 'but I'm sure he's not lying. This water, apparently, moves all the time and keeps breaking against the earth: and when he can't hear that, he misses it. That's his name—Kehaar. It's the noise the water makes.'

The quiet of the evening silflay, when the western sun shone straight along the ridge, the grass tussocks threw shadows twice as long as themselves and the cool air smelt of thyme and dog roses, was something which they had all come to enjoy even more than former evenings in the meadows of Sandleford. Although they could not know it, the down was more lonely than it had been for hundreds of years. There were no sheep, and villagers from Kingsclere and Sydmonton no longer had any occasion to walk over the hills, either for business or for pleasure. In the fields of Sandleford the rabbits had seen men almost every day. Here, since their arrival, they had seen one and him on a horse. Looking round the little group that gathered on the grass, Hazel saw that all of them—even Holly—were looking stronger, sleeker and in better shape than when they had first come to the down. Whatever might lie ahead, at least he could feel that he had not failed them so far.

'We're doing well here,' he began, 'or so it seems to me. We're certainly not a bunch of hlessil any more. But all the same, there's something on my mind. I'm surprised, as a matter of fact, that I should be the first one of us to start thinking about it. Unless we can find the answer, then this warren's as good as finished, in spite of all we've done.'

'Why, how can that be, Hazel?' said Bigwig.

'Do you remember Nildro-hain?' asked Hazel.

'She stopped running. Poor Strawberry.'

'I know. And we have no does—not one—and no does means no kittens and in a few years no warren.'

It may seem incredible that the rabbits had given no thought to so vital a matter. But men have made the same mistake more than once—left the whole business out of account, or been content to trust to luck and the fortune of war. Rabbits live close to death and when death comes closer than usual, thinking about survival leaves little room for anything else. But now, in the evening sunshine on the friendly, empty down, with a good burrow at his back and the grass turning to pellets in his belly, Hazel knew that he was lonely for a doe. The others were silent and he could tell that his words had sunk in.

The rabbits grazed or lay basking in the sun. A lark went twittering up into the brighter sunshine above, soared and sang and came slowly down, ending with a sideways, spread-wing glide and a wagtail's run through the grass. The sun dipped lower. At last Blackberry said, 'What's to be done? Set out again?'

'I hope not,' said Hazel. 'It all depends. What I'd like to do is get hold of some does and bring them here.'

'Where from?'

'Another warren.'

'But are there any on these hills? How do we find out? The wind never brings the least smell of rabbits.'

'I'll tell you how,' said Hazel. 'The bird. The bird will go and search for us.'

RICHARD ADAMS, 'Kehaar', *Watership Down*, 1992

Song—The Owl

When cats run home and light is come,
  And dew is cold upon the ground,
And the far-off stream is dumb,
  And the whirring sail goes round,
  And the whirring sail goes round;
    Alone and warming his five wits,
    The white owl in the belfry sits.

When merry milkmaids click the latch,
  And rarely smells the new-mown hay,

> And the cock hath sung beneath the thatch
>> Twice or thrice his roundelay,
>> Twice or thrice his roundelay;
>>> Alone and warming his five wits,
>>> The white owl in the belfry sits.

ALFRED, LORD TENNYSON (1809–92)

It was a cold still afternoon with a hard steely sky overhead, when [the Mole] slipped out of the warm parlour into the open air. The country lay bare and entirely leafless around him, and he thought that he had never seen so far and so intimately into the insides of things as on that winter day when Nature was deep in her annual slumber and seemed to have kicked the clothes off. Copses, dells, quarries and all hidden places, which had been mysterious mines for exploration in leafy summer, now exposed themselves and their secrets pathetically, and seemed to ask him to overlook their shabby poverty for a while, till they could riot in rich masquerade as before, and trick and entice him with the old deceptions. It was pitiful in a way, and yet cheering—even exhilarating. He was glad that he liked the country undecorated, hard, and stripped of its finery. He had got down to the bare bones of it, and they were fine and strong and simple. He did not want the warm clover and the play of seeding grasses; the screens of quickset, the billowy drapery of beech and elm seemed best away; and with great cheerfulness of spirit he pushed on towards the Wild Wood, which lay before him low and threatening, like a black reef in some still southern sea.

There was nothing to alarm him at first entry. Twigs crackled under his feet, logs tripped him, funguses on stumps resembled caricatures, and startled him for the moment by their likeness to something familiar and far away; but that was all fun, and exciting. It led him on, and he penetrated to where the light was less, and trees crouched nearer and nearer, and holes made ugly mouths at him on either side.

Everything was very still now. The dusk advanced on him steadily, rapidly, gathering in behind and before; and the light seemed to be draining away like flood-water.

Then the faces began.

It was over his shoulder, and indistinctly, that he first thought he saw a face: a little evil wedge-shaped face, looking out at him from a hole. When he turned and confronted it, the thing had vanished.

He quickened his pace, telling himself cheerfully not to begin imagining things, or there would be simply no end to it. He passed another hole, and another, and another; and then—yes!—no!—yes! certainly a little narrow face, with hard eyes, had flashed up for an instant from a hole, and was gone. He hesitated—braced himself up for an effort and strode on. Then suddenly, and as if it had been so all the time, every hole, far and near, and there were hundreds of them, seemed to possess its face, coming and going rapidly, all fixing on him glances of malice and hatred: all hard-eyed and evil and sharp.

If he could only get away from the holes in the banks, he thought, there would be no more faces. He swung off the path and plunged into the untrodden places of the wood.

Then the whistling began.

Very faint and shrill it was, and far behind him, when first he heard it; but somehow it made him hurry forward. Then, still very faint and shrill, it sounded far ahead of him, and made him hesitate and want to go back. As he halted in indecision it broke out on either side, and seemed to be caught up and passed on throughout the whole length of the wood to its furthest limit. They were up and alert and ready, evidently, whoever they were! And he—he was alone, and unarmed, and far from any help; and the night was closing in.

Then the pattering began.

He thought it was only falling leaves at first, so slight and delicate was the sound of it. Then as it grew it took a regular rhythm, and he knew it for nothing else but the pat-pat-pat of little feet, still a very long way off. Was it in front or behind? It seemed to be first one, then the other, then both. It grew and it multiplied, till from every quarter as he listened anxiously, leaning this way and that, it seemed to be closing in on him. As he stood still to hearken, a rabbit came running hard towards him through the trees. He waited, expecting it to slacken pace, or to swerve from him into a different course. Instead, the animal almost brushed him as it dashed past, his face set and hard, his eyes staring. 'Get out of this, you fool, get out!' the Mole heard him mutter as he swung round a stump and disappeared down a friendly burrow.

The pattering increased till it sounded like sudden hail on the dry-leaf carpet spread around him. The whole wood seemed running now, running hard, hunting, chasing, closing in round something or—somebody? In panic, he began to run too, aimlessly, he knew not whither. He ran up against things, he fell over things and into things, he darted under things and dodged round things. At last he took refuge in the dark deep hollow of an old beech tree, which offered shelter, concealment—perhaps even safety, but who could tell? Anyhow, he was too tired to run any further, and could only snuggle down into the dry leaves which had drifted into the hollow and hope he was safe for the time. And as he lay there panting and trembling, and listened to the whistlings and the patterings outside, he knew it at last, in all its fullness, that dread thing which other little dwellers in field and hedgerow had encountered here, and known as their darkest moment—that thing which the Rat had vainly tried to shield him from—the Terror of the Wild Wood!

KENNETH GRAHAME, 'The Wild Wood', *The Wind in the Willows*, 1908

The other day, as I was calling on the ornithologist whose collection of birds is, I suppose, altogether unrivalled in Europe,—(at once a monument of unwearied love of science, and an example, in its treatment, of the most delicate and patient art)—Mr Gould—he showed me the nest of a common English bird; a nest which, notwithstanding his knowledge of the dexterous building of birds in all the world, was not without interest even to him, and was altogether amazing and delightful to me. It was a bullfinch's nest, which had been set in the fork of a sapling tree, where it needed an extended foundation. And the bird had built this first story of her nest with withered stalks of clematis blossom; and with nothing else. These twigs it had interwoven lightly, leaving the branched heads all at the outside, producing an intricate Gothic boss of extreme grace and quaintness, apparently arranged both with triumphant pleasure in the art of basket-making, and with definite purpose of obtaining ornamental form.

I fear there is no occasion to tell you that the bird had no purpose of the kind. I say that I *fear* this, because I would much rather have to undeceive you in attributing too much intellect to the lower animals, than too little. But I suppose the only error which, in the present condition of natural history, you are likely to fall into, is that of supposing that a bullfinch is merely a mechanical arrangement of nervous fibre, covered with feathers by a chronic cutaneous eruption; and impelled by a galvanic stimulus to the collection of clematis.

You would be in much greater, as well as in a more shameful, error, in supposing this, than if you attributed to the bullfinch the most deliberate rivalship with Mr Street's prettiest Gothic designs. The bird has exactly the degree of emotion, the extent of science, and the command of art, which are necessary for its happiness; it had felt the clematis twigs to be lighter and tougher than any others within its reach, and probably found the forked branches of them convenient for reticulation. It had naturally placed these outside, because it wanted a smooth surface for the bottom of its nest; and the beauty of the result was much more dependent on the blossoms than the bird.

Nevertheless, I am sure that if you had seen the nest,—much more, if you had stood beside the architect at work upon it,—you would have greatly desired to express your admiration to her.

JOHN RUSKIN, 'Nest Building', *The Eagle's Nest*, 1872

The Wrynecks Nest

That summer bird its oft repeated note
Chirps from the dotterel ash and in the hole
The green woodpecker made in years remote
It makes its nest—where peeping idlers strole
In anxious plundering moods—and bye and bye
The wrynecks curious eggs as white as snow
While squinting in the hollow tree they spy
The sitting bird looks up with jetty eye
And waves her head in terror too and fro
Speckled and veined in various shades of brown
And then a hissing noise assails the clown
And quick with hasty terror in his breast
From the trees knotty trunk he sluthers down
And thinks the strange bird guards a serpents nest

JOHN CLARE (1793–1864)

The yellowhammer is a year-round resident of England. It is well-known and conspicuous, the male particularly, with his yellow head and his habit of sitting on fence-posts and gates by the country roads to sing a curious little song that goes 'a-little-bit-of-bread-and-NO-cheese.' In winter, yellow-hammers live in flocks: males, females, and other kinds of birds as well. But as spring approached, Howard noticed that the cock yellowhammer began to edge out of the flock a bit, to spend a while sitting on a post, and to experiment with snatches of song. Soon the cocks would spend longer away from the flocks on their posts, and the cry 'a-little-bit-of-bread-and-NO-cheese' became a common country sound. The cocks seemed impelled to their chosen perches by some obscure urge. Several times Howard, watching the flock through his binoculars, saw a yellowhammer suddenly leave and come plummeting back to his post, almost as if he had forgotten something. Once there he would sing 'a-little-bit-of-bread-and-NO-cheese.'

The purpose of this singing and the belligerent attitude of the cocks in the weeks before the hens arrived must surely be judged by the result. Nobody got hurt in most of the fights, which were essentially ritual. More-over the cock that had first taken up its position on the post invariably 'won', in that it was the intruder who flew away. So aggression itself was not a purpose of the behaviour. What really resulted from this spectacular play in the spring was that the cocks became nicely spaced out across the land, with each getting fixed into its brain that the neighbourhood of a certain post was where it should be. This spacing and learning of home is the prime result of the behaviour and so must be its evolutionary purpose.

PAUL COLINVAUX, *Why Big Fierce Animals are Rare*, 1980

Satin Bower-Birds

In summer they can afford their independence,
down in the gullies, in the folds of forest;
but with the early frosts they're here again—
hopping like big toy birds, as round as pullets,
handsomely green and speckled, but somehow comic—
begging their bread. A domestic,
quarrelling, amateur troupe.

Ordinary birds with ordinary manners,
uninteresting as pigeons;
but, like the toad, they have a secret.
Look—the young male bird—
see his eye's perfect mineral blaze of blue.
The winter sea's not purer
than that blue flash set in a bird's head.

Then I remember
how ritually they worship that one colour.
Blue chips of glass, blue rag, blue paper,
the heads of my grape-hyacinths,
I found in their secret bower; and there are dances
done in the proper season,
for birth, initiation, marriage and perhaps death.

Seven years, some say, those green-brown birds
elect blue for their colour
and dance for it, their eyes round as the sea's horizons,
blue as grape-hyacinths.

And when those seven years are served?
See, there he flies, the old one,
the male made perfect—
black in the shadow, but in the caressing sun
bluer, more royal than the ancient sea.

JUDITH WRIGHT (b. 1915)

Why the bird sustains itself upon the air

The atmosphere is an element capable of being compressed within itself when it is struck by something moving at a greater rate of speed than that of its own velocity and it then forms a cloud within the rest of the air. . . .

When the bird finds itself within the wind it can sustain itself without flapping its wings, because the function which they have to perform against the air requires no motion. The motion of the air against the motionless wings sustains them, while the movement of the wings sustains them when the air is motionless.

The wind in passing the summits of mountains becomes swift and dense and as it blows beyond the mountains it becomes thin and slow, like water that issues from a narrow channel into the wide sea.

When the bird passes from a slow to a swift current of the wind it lets itself be carried by the wind until it has devised a new assistance for itself. . . .

When the bird moves with impetus against the wind it makes long quick beats with its wings with a slanting movement, and after thus beating its wings it remains for a while with all its members contracted and low. The bird will be overturned by the wind when in less slanting position it is so placed as to receive beneath it the percussion of any lateral wind. But if the bird that is struck laterally by the wind on the point of being overturned folds its upper wing it immediately goes back to the position of having its body turned towards the ground, while if it folds its lower wing it will immediately be turned upside down by the wind.

Nature has so provided that all large birds can stay at so great an elevation, that the wind which increases their flight may be of straight course and powerful. For if their flight were low among mountains where the wind goes round and is perpetually full of eddies and whirls and where they cannot find any spot of shelter in the fury of the wind compressed in the hollows of the mountains, nor so guide themselves with their great wings as to avoid being dashed upon the cliffs and the high rocks and trees, would not this sometimes be the cause of their destruction? Whereas at great altitudes whenever through some accident the wind turns in any way, the bird has always time to redirect its course and in safety adjust its flight which will always proceed entirely free. . . . Inasmuch as all beginnings of things are often the cause of great results, so we may see a small almost imperceptible movement of the rudder to have power to turn a ship of marvellous size and loaded with a very heavy cargo, and that, too, amid such a weight of water as presses on its every beam, and in the teeth of the impetuous winds which are enveloping its mighty sails. Therefore we may be certain in the case of those birds which can support themselves above the course of the winds without beating their wings, that a slight movement of wing or tail which will serve them to enter either below or above the wind, will suffice to prevent the fall of the said birds.

LEONARDO DA VINCI, Notebooks, 1505 (tr. Jean Paul Richter, 1939)

Swifts

Spring comes little, a little. All April it rains.
The new leaves stick in their fists. New ferns, still fiddleheads.
But one day the swifts are back. Face to the sun like a child
You shout, 'The swifts are back!'

Sure enough, bolt nocks bow to carry one sky-scyther
Two hundred miles an hour across fullblown windfields.
Swreeeee. Swreeee. Another. And another.
It's the cut air falling in shrieks on our chimneys and roofs.

The next day, a fleet of high crosses cruises in ether.
These are the air pilgrims, pilots of air rivers . . .
But a shift of wing and they're earth-skimmers, daggers,
Skilful in guiding the throw of themselves away from themselves.

Quick flutter, a scimitar upsweep, out of danger of touch, for
Earth is forbidden to them, water's forbidden to them.
All air and fire, little owlish ascetics, they outfly storms.
They rush to the pillars of altitude, the thermal fountains.

Here is a legend of swifts, a parable—
When the great Raven bent over earth to create the birds
The swifts were ungrateful. They were small muddy things
Like shoes, with long legs and short wings, so

They took themselves off to the mountains to sulk.
And they stayed there. 'Well,' said the Raven, after years of this,
'I will give you the sky, you can have the whole sky
On condition that you give up rest.'

'Yes, yes,' screamed the swifts. 'We abhor rest.
We detest the filth of growth, the sweat of sleep,
Soft nests in the wet fields, slimehold of worms.
Let us be free, be air!'

So the Raven took their legs and bound them into their bodies.
He bent their wings like boomerangs, honed them like knives.
He streamlined their feathers and stripped them of velvet.
Then he released them, *Never to Return*

Inscribed on their feet and wings. And so
We have swifts, though in reality not parables but
Bolts in the world's need, swift
Swifts, not in punishment, not in ecstasy, simply

Sleepers over oceans in the mill of the world's breathing.
The grace to say they live in another firmament.
A way to say the miracle will not occur,
And watch the miracle.

ANNE STEVENSON (b. 1933)

On an Indian Tomineios, the Least of Birds

I'm made in sport by nature, when
    She's tired with the stupendious weight
Of forming elephants and beasts of state:
    Rhinoceros, that love the fen;
    The elks, that scale the hills of snow;
And lions couching in their awful den.
    These do work nature hard, and then
    Her wearied hand in me doth show
What she can for her own diversion do.

    Man is a little world ('tis said),
    And I in miniature am drawn,
A perfect creature, but in shorthand shown.
    The ruck, in Madagascar bred
    (If new discoveries truth do speak),
Whom greatest beasts and armèd horsemen dread,
    Both him and me one artist made:
    Nature in this delight doth take,
That can so great and little monsters make.

    The Indians me a sunbeam name,
    And I may be the child of one:

ruck: roc (mythical bird)

So small I am, my kind is hardly known.
　To some a sportive bird I seem,
　And some believe me but a fly;
Though me a feathered fowl the best esteem.
　Whate'er I am, I'm nature's gem,
　And, like a sunbeam from the sky,
I can't be followed by the quickest eye.

　I'm the true bird of paradise,
　And heavenly dew's my only meat:
My mouth so small, 'twill nothing else admit.
　No scales know how my weight to poise,
　So light, I seem condensèd air;
And did at the end of the creation rise,
　When nature wanted more supplies,
　When she could little matter spare,
But in return did make the work more rare.

THOMAS HEYRICK (1649–94)

20 May 1849

On my return to Larissa there is but just time to make one drawing of dark Olympus ere a frightful thunderstorm, with deluges of rain, breaks over the plain and pursues me to the city. It continues to pour all the afternoon, and I amuse myself, as best as I can, in Hassan Bey's house. It is a large mansion, in the best Turkish style, and betokening the riches of its master. It occupies three sides of a walled courtyard, and one of its wings is allotted to the harem, who live concealed by a veil of close lattice work when at home, though I see them pass to and fro dressed in the usual disguise worn out of doors. I watch two storks employed in building on the roof of that part of the building. These birds are immensely numerous in Thessaly, and there is a nest on nearly every house in Larissa. No one disturbs them; and they are considered so peculiarly in favour with the Prophet that the Vulgar believe the conversion of a Christian as being certain to follow their choice of his roof for their dwelling; formerly a Christian so honoured was forced to turn Mussulman or quit his dwelling—so at least they told me in Ioannina, where two pairs have selected the Vice-Consul's house for their abode. It is very amusing to watch them when at work, as they take infinite pains in the construction of what after all seems a very ill-built nest. I have seen them, after twisting and bending a long bit of grass or root for an hour in all directions, throw it away altogether. That will not do after all, they say; and then flying away they return with a second piece of material, in the choice of which they are very particular; and, according to my informants at

Ioannina, only make use of one sort of root. When they have arranged the twig or grass in a satisfactory manner they put up their heads on their shoulders and clatter in a mysterious manner with a sound like dice shaken in a box. This clattering at early morning or evening, in this season of the year, is one certain characteristic that these towns are under Turkish government, inasmuch as the storks have all abandoned Greece (modern), for the Greeks shoot and molest them; only they still frequent Larissa, and the plain of the Spercheius, as being so near the frontier of Turkey that they can easily escape thither if necessary. This is foolishness in the Greeks, for the stork is most useful in devouring insects, especially the larva of the locust, which I observed in myriads on the plains near the entrance of Tempe; and I counted as many as seventy storks in one society, eating them as fast as possible, and with great dignity of carriage.

That part of the roof of the harem which is not occupied by storks is covered with pigeons and jackdaws, a humane attention paid to the lower orders of creation being always one of the most striking traits of Turkish character.

> EDWARD LEAR (1812–88), 'In Arkady', *Edward Lear in the Levant*, 1988 (ed. Susan Hyman)

But that which experience teacheth sea-faring men, especially those that come into the seas of *Sicilie*, of the qualitie and condition of the Halcyon bird, or as some call it Alcedo or Kings-fisher, exceeds all mens conceit. In what kinde of creature did ever nature so much prefer both their hatching, sitting, brooding, and birth? Poets faine, that the Iland of *Delos*, being before wandring and fleeting up and downe, was for the delivery of *Latona* made firme and setled. But Gods decree hath been, that all the watrie wildernesse should be quiet and made calme, without raine, wind, or tempest, during the time the *Halcyon* sitteth and bringeth forth her young-ones, which is much about the Winter *Solstitium*, and shortest day in the yeare: By whose privilege even in the hart and deadest time of Winter we have seven calme daies, and as many nights to saile without any danger. Their Hens know no other Cocke but their owne: They never forsake him all the daies of their life; and if the Cocke chance to be weake and crazed, the Hen will take him upon her neck, and carrie him with her, wheresoever she goeth, and serve him even untill death. Mans wit could never yet attaine to the full knowledge of that admirable kind of building or structure, which the *Halcion* useth in contriving of her neast, no, nor devise what it is-of.

Plutarke, who hath seen and handled many of them, thinkes it to be made of certaine fish-bones, which she so compacts, and conjoyneth together, enterlacing some long, and some crosse-waies, adding some foldings and roundings to it, that in the end she frameth a round kind of vessel, readie to float and swim upon the water: which done, she carrieth the same where the Sea-waves beat most; there the Sea gently beating upon it, shewes her how to daube and patch up the parts not well closed, and how to strengthen those places, and fashion those ribs, that are not fast, but stir with the Sea-waves: And on the other side, that which is closely wrought, the Sea beating on it, doth so fasten and conjoyne together, that nothing, no, not stone or yron, can any way loosen, divide, or break the same, except with great violence; and what is most to be wondred at, is the proportion and figure of the concavitie within; for, it is so composed and proportioned, that it can receive or admit no manner of thing, but the Bird that built it; for, to all things else, it is so impenetrable, close and hard, that nothing can possiblie enter in: no, not so much as the Sea-water. Loe here a most plaine description of this building, or construction taken from a verie good Author: yet me thinks, it doth not fully and sufficiently resolve us of the difficultie in this kinde of Architecture.

MONTAIGNE, *An Apologie of Raymond Sebond* (tr. Florio, 1603)

The Osprey

To whom certain water talents—
Webbed feet, oils—do not occur,
Regulates his liquid acre
From the sky, his proper element.

There, already, his eye removes
The trout each fathom magnifies.
He lives, without compromise,
His unamphibious two lives—

An inextinguishable bird whom
No lake's waters waterlog.
He shakes his feathers like a dog.
It's all of air that ferries him.

MICHAEL LONGLEY (b. 1939)

At these non-human hours they could get quite close to the waterfowl. Herons came, with a great bold noise as of opening doors and shutters, out of the boughs of a plantation which they frequented at the side of the mead; or, if already on the spot, hardily maintained their standing in the water as the pair walked by, watching them by moving their heads round in a slow, horizontal, passionless wheel, like the turn of puppets by clock-work.

They could then see the faint summer fogs in layers, woolly, level, and apparently no thicker than counterpanes, spread about the meadows in detached remnants of small extent. On the gray moisture of the grass were marks where the cows had lain through the night—dark-green islands of dry herbage the size of their carcases, in the general sea of dew. From each island proceeded a serpentine trail, by which the cow had rambled away to feed after getting up, at the end of which trail they found her; the snoring puff from her nostrils, when she recognized them, making an intenser little fog of her own amid the prevailing one. Then they drove the animals back to the barton, or sat down to milk them on the spot, as the case might require.

Or perhaps the summer fog was more general, and the meadows lay like a white sea, out of which the scattered trees rose like dangerous rocks. Birds would soar through it into the upper radiance, and hang on the wing sunning themselves, or alight on the wet rails subdividing the mead, which now shone like glass rods. Minute diamonds of moisture from the mist hung, too, upon Tess's eyelashes, and drops upon her hair, like seed pearls. When the day grew quite strong and commonplace these dried off her; moreover, Tess then lost her strange and ethereal beauty; her teeth, lips, and eyes scintillated in the sunbeams, and she was again the dazzlingly fair dairymaid only, who had to hold her own against the other women of the world.

THOMAS HARDY, Tess of the D'Urbervilles, 1891

I think you should know about our Remarkable Cow.

She is a black & white Holstein, one of a herd that grazes in the opposite field. During the drought, when there was nothing to graze on, she took to wading in what was left of the river, & grazing on brooklime; and developed this into long solitary walks up the river.

The weather changed; the river rose; she went on walking. When the river was in spate she went on imperturbably walking, with the water over her back. It is her daily routine: she sets out in the morning, climbs the other bank, grazes in a field she has no right to graze in . . . — comes back about an hour before sundown—looking ineffably calm and righteous.

I have grown very fond of her—and use her as a river-gauge. I used to know the river's level by how far it rose up a stake. I now go by how far it goes up the cow.

SYLVIA TOWNSEND WARNER, letter of 21 October 1976 to Joy Chute

The River Trent is speaking:

I throw my Christall Armes along the Flowry Vallies,
Which lying sleeke, and smooth, as any Garden-Allies,
Doe give me leave to play, whilst they doe Court my Streame,
And crowne my winding banks with many an *Anademe*:
My Silver-scaled Skuls about my Streames doe sweepe,
Now in the shallow foords, now in the falling Deepe:
So that of every kind, the new-spawn'd numerous Frie
Seeme in me as the Sands that on my Shore doe lye.
The *Barbell*, then which Fish, a braver doth not swimme,
Nor greater for the Ford within my spacious brimme,
Nor (newly taken) more the curious taste doth please;
The *Greling*, whose great Spawne is big as any Pease;
The *Pearch* with pricking Finnes, against the *Pike* prepar'd,
As Nature had thereon bestow'd this stronger guard,
His daintinesse to keepe, (each curious pallats proofe)
From his vile ravenous foe: next him I name the *Ruffe*,
His very neere Ally, and both for scale and Fin,
In taste, and for his Bayte (indeed) his next of kin;
The pretty slender *Dare*, of many cald the *Dace*,
Within my liquid glasse, when *Phœbus* lookes his face,
Oft swiftly as he swimmes, his silver belly showes,
But with such nimble slight, that ere yee can disclose
His shape, out of your sight like lightning he is shot.
The *Trout* by Nature markt with many a Crimson spot,
As though shee curious were in him above the rest,
And of fresh-water Fish, did note him for the best;
The *Roche*, whose common kind to every Flood doth fall;
The *Chub*, (whose neater name) which some a *Chevin* call,
Food to the Tyrant *Pyke*, (most being in his power)
Who for their numerous store he most doth them devoure;
The lustie *Salmon* then, from *Neptunes* watry Realme,
When as his season serves, stemming my tydeful Streame,
Then being in his kind, in me his pleasure takes,
(For whom the Fisher then all other Game forsakes)
Which bending of himselfe to th' fashion of a Ring,
Above the forced Weares, himselfe doth nimbly fling,
And often when the Net hath dragd him safe to land,
Is seene by naturall force to scape his murderers hand;

Anademe: garland

Whose graine doth rise in flakes, with fatnesse interlarded,
Of many a liquorish lip, that highly is regarded.

MICHAEL DRAYTON (1563–1631), *Poly-Olbion*, Song XXVI

Heaven

Fish (fly-replete, in depth of June,
Dawdling away their wat'ry noon)
Ponder deep wisdom, dark or clear,
Each secret fishy hope or fear.
Fish say, they have their Stream and Pond;
But is there anything Beyond?
This life cannot be All, they swear,
For how unpleasant, if it were!
One may not doubt that, somehow, Good
Shall come of Water and of Mud;
And, sure, the reverent eye must see
A Purpose in Liquidity.
We darkly know, by Faith we cry,
The future is not Wholly Dry.
Mud unto mud!—Death eddies near—
Not here the appointed End, not here!
But somewhere, beyond Space and Time,
Is wetter water, slimier slime!
And there (they trust) there swimmeth One
Who swam ere rivers were begun,
Immense, of fishy form and mind,
Squamous, omnipotent, and kind;
And under that Almighty Fin,
The littlest fish may enter in.
Oh! never fly conceals a hook,
Fish say, in the Eternal Brook,
But more than mundane weeds are there,
And mud, celestially fair;
Fat caterpillars drift around,
And Paradisal grubs are found;
Unfading moths, immortal flies,
And the worm that never dies.
And in that Heaven of all their wish,
There shall be no more land, say fish.

RUPERT BROOKE (1887–1915)

The second night [after his arrival] Mijbil came on to my bed in the small hours and remained asleep in the crook of my knees until the servant brought tea in the morning, and during that day he began to lose his apathy and take a keen, much too keen, interest in his surroundings. I fashioned a collar, or rather a body-belt, for him, and took him on a lead to the bathroom, where for half an hour he went wild with joy in the water, plunging and rolling in it, shooting up and down the length of the bath underwater, and making enough slosh and splash for a hippo. This, I was to learn, is a characteristic of otters; every drop of water must be, so to speak, extended and spread about the place; a bowl must at once be overturned, or, if it will not overturn, be sat in and sploshed in until it overflows. Water must be kept on the move and made to do things; when static it is as wasted and provoking as a buried talent.

It was only two days later that he escaped from my bedroom as I entered it, and I turned to see his tail disappearing round the bend of the corridor that led to the bathroom. By the time I had caught up with him he was up on the end of the bath and fumbling at the chromium taps with his paws. I watched, amazed by this early exhibition of an intelligence I had not yet guessed; in less than a minute he had turned the tap far enough to produce a dribble of water, and, after a moment or two of distraction at his success, achieved the full flow. (He had, in fact, been fortunate to turn the tap the right way; on subsequent occasions he would as often as not try with great violence to screw it up still tighter, chittering with irritation and disappointment at its failure to co-operate.)

GAVIN MAXWELL, Ring of Bright Water, 1960

And God created the great whales, and each
Soul living, each that crept, which plenteously
The waters generated by their kinds,
And every bird of wing after his kind;
And saw that it was good, and blessed them, saying,
'Be fruitful, multiply, and in the seas
And lakes and running streams the waters fill;
And let the fowl be multiplied on the earth.'
Forthwith the sounds and seas, each creek and bay,
With fry innumerable swarm, and shoals
Of fish that with their fins and shining scales
Glide under the green wave, in sculls that oft
Bank the mid-sea. Part single or with mate
Graze the seaweed their pasture, and through groves
Of coral stray, or sporting with quick glance
Show to the sun their waved coats dropped with gold,

Or in their pearly shells at ease, attend
Moist nutriment, or under rocks their food
In jointed armor watch; on smooth the seal
And bended dolphins play; part huge of bulk,
Wallowing unwieldy, enormous in their gait,
Tempest the ocean. There leviathan,
Hugest of living creatures, on the deep
Stretched like a promontory sleeps or swims,
And seems a moving land, and at his gills
Draws in, and at his trunk spouts out a sea.

JOHN MILTON, *Paradise Lost*, Book VII, 1667

Lying spread-eagled in the silky water, gazing into the sky, only moving my hands and feet slightly to keep afloat, I was looking at the Milky Way stretched like a chiffon scarf across the sky and wondering how many stars it contained. I could hear the voices of the others, laughing and talking on the beach, echoing over the water, and by lifting my head I could see their position on the shore by the pulsing lights of their cigarettes. Drifting there, relaxed and dreamy, I was suddenly startled to hear, quite close to me, a clop and gurgle of water, followed by a long, deep sigh, and a series of gentle ripples rocked me up and down. Hastily I righted myself and trod water, looking to see how far from the beach I had drifted. To my alarm I found that not only was I some considerable distance from the shore, but from the *Sea Cow* as well, and I was not at all sure what sort of creature it was swimming around in the dark waters beneath me. I could hear the others laughing on the shore at some joke or other, and I saw someone flip a cigarette-end high into the sky like a red star that curved over and extinguished itself at the rim of the sea. I was feeling more and more uncomfortable, and I was just about to call for assistance when, some twenty feet away from me, the sea seemed to part with a gentle swish and gurgle, a gleaming back appeared, gave a deep, satisfied sigh, and sank below the surface again. I had hardly time to recognise it as a porpoise before I found I was right in the midst of them. They rose all around me, sighing luxuriously, their black backs shining as they humped in the moonlight. There must have been about eight of them, and one rose so close that I could have swum forward three strokes and touched his ebony head. Heaving and sighing heavily, they played across the bay, and I swam with them, watching fascinated as they rose to the surface, crumpling the water, breathed deeply, and then dived beneath the surface again, leaving only an expanding hoop of foam to mark the spot. Presently, as if obeying a signal, they turned and headed out of the bay towards the distant coast of Albania, and I trod water and watched them go, swimming up the white chain of moonlight, backs agleam as they rose and plunged with heavy ecstasy in the water as warm as fresh milk. Behind them they left a trail of great bubbles that rocked and shone briefly like miniature moons before vanishing under the ripples.

One evening [the porpoises] put on an illuminated show for our benefit, aided by one of the most attractive insects that inhabited the island. We had discovered that in the hot months of the year the sea became full of phosphorescence. When there was moonlight this was not so noticeable— a faint greenish flicker round the bows of the boat, a brief flash as someone dived into the water. We found that the best time for the phosphorescence was when there was no moon at all. Another illuminated inhabitant of the summer months was the firefly. These slender brown beetles would fly as soon as it got dark, floating through the olive-groves by the score, their tails flashing on and off, giving a light that was greenish-white, not golden-green, as the sea was. Again, however, the fireflies were at their best when there was no bright moonlight to detract from their lights.

[One night] the phosphorescence was particularly good. . . . By plunging your hand into the water and dragging it along you could draw a wide golden-green ribbon of cold fire across the sea, and when you dived as you hit the surface it seemed as though you had plunged into a frosty furnace of glinting light. When we were tired we waded out of the sea, the water running off our bodies so that we seemed to be on fire, and lay on the sand to eat. Then, as the wine was opened at the end of the meal, as if by arrangement, a few fireflies appeared in the olives behind us—a sort of overture to the show.

First of all there were just two or three green specks, sliding smoothly through the trees, winking regularly. But gradually more and more appeared, until parts of the olive-grove were lit with a weird green glow. Never had we seen so many fireflies congregated in one spot; they flicked through the trees in swarms, they crawled on the grass, the bushes and the olive-trunks, they drifted in swarms over our heads and landed on the rugs, like green embers. Glittering streams of them flew out over the bay, swirling over the water, and then, right on cue, the porpoises appeared, swimming in line into the bay, rocking rhythmically through the water, their backs as if painted with phosphorus. In the centre of the bay they swam round, diving and rolling, occasionally leaping high in the air and falling back into a conflagration of light. With the fireflies above and the illuminated porpoises below it was a fantastic sight. We could even see the luminous trails beneath the surface where the porpoises swam in fiery patterns across the sandy bottom, and when they leapt high in the air the drops of emerald glowing water flicked from them, and you could not tell

if it was phosphorescence or fireflies you were looking at. For an hour or so
we watched this pageant, and then slowly the fireflies drifted back inland
and farther down the coast. Then the porpoises lined up and sped out to
sea, leaving a flaming path behind them that flickered and glowed, and then
died slowly, like a glowing branch laid across the bay.

GERALD DURRELL, *My Family and Other Animals*, 1956

Plankton

The great un-living energies
Tug at the earth's
Fluid overcoat,
Shake it like a blanket.
The moon applies brakes
And the volts spark off.
The battering wet
Battery of waves
Flashes sheet lightning
And the tides thunder
Under a ninety-
Million-mile-off sun.

But inches below
The enveloping film
Between brine and vapour,
The lesser energies
Explode into self-propulsion—
Single cells
Developing fins,
Tentacles, tails;
A tiny octopus,
Rayed like the sun,
That moves as the sun can't.

The earth turns its neck
And the sun exits;
And, dead on the dark,
The sea's cuticle
Phosphoresces with life,
Glows with the fry
And minutiae
That build up the body of the whale.

Dawn
Hatches out a spawn of glitter.
A bacterium
Becomes aware of itself,
Hears its own echo.
As the white day
Climbs up the sky,
The lesser energies,
From a billion billion
Microscopic eyes,
Look back at a blind sun.

NORMAN NICHOLSON (1910–87)

Beyond the shadow of the ship,
I watched the water-snakes:
They moved in tracks of shining white,
And when they reared, the elfish light
Fell off in hoary flakes.

Within the shadow of the ship
I watched their rich attire:
Blue, glossy green, and velvet black,
They coiled and swam; and every track
Was a flash of golden fire.

O happy living things! no tongue
Their beauty might declare:
A spring of love gushed from my heart,
And I blessed them unaware:
Sure my kind saint took pity on me,
And I blessed them unaware.

The self-same moment I could pray;
And from my neck so free
The Albatross fell off, and sank
Like lead into the sea.

SAMUEL TAYLOR COLERIDGE (1772–1834), *The Rime of the Ancient Mariner*

[*Maldonado, 1832–3*]
The largest gnawing animal in the world, the *Hydrocharus Capybara*
(the water-hog), is here also common. One which I shot at Monte Video

weighed 98 pounds: its length, from the end of the snout to the stump-like tail, was 3 feet 2 inches; and its girth, 3 feet 8. These great Rodents are generally called *carpinchos*: they occasionally frequent the islands in the mouth of the Plata, where the water is quite salt, but are far more abundant on the borders of fresh-water lakes and rivers. Near Maldonado three or four generally live together. In the daytime they either lie among the aquatic plants, or openly feed on the turf plain. When viewed at a distance, from their manner of walking and colour, they resemble pigs: but when seated on their haunches, and attentively watching any object with one eye, they reassume the appearance of their congeners, the cavies. Both the front and side view of their head has quite a ludicrous aspect, from the great depth of their jaw. These animals, at Maldonado, were very tame; by cautiously walking, I approached within 3 yards of four old ones. This tameness may probably be accounted for, by the Jaguar having been banished for some years, and by the Gaucho not thinking it worth his while to hunt them. As I approached nearer and nearer they frequently made their peculiar noise, which is a low abrupt grunt; not having much actual sound, but rather arising from the sudden expulsion of air: the only noise I know at all like it, is the first hoarse bark of a large dog. Having watched the four from almost within arm's length (and they me) for several minutes, they rushed into the water at full gallop, with the greatest impetuosity, and emitted, at the same time, their bark. After diving a short distance they came again to the surface, but only just showed the upper part of their heads. When the female is swimming in the water and has young ones, they are said to sit on her back.

CHARLES DARWIN, *Journal of Researches* (*Voyage of the Beagle*), 1839

Manatee

Just the same, the poem of the manatee
will not go away. It keeps inshore,
keeps disappearing in the tale
of sightings, encounters, caresses;
massive habitué, mortally
ready to be flesh, of the lull
and shallows of your Floridian sea-board.

There, daylight balances
in a cup, the manatee imperturbably
forages the river-mouth. Sweet passes
to salt, the measure of sun

and distance to the skim of water,
weed loses count and clouds
the pools, straggling herds-wide;

whose people, sinking slowly
to pasture, improbable as Zeppelins,
have never been told what happened
to Steller's sea-cow, two centuries
and an ocean away. Nor asked, what
survives here? Things that lie still,
things that have cover, the armour-clads,

what man lets be. This surely, this
interval, no-man's-land, weed-crammed
sand-bottoms, weed-streams, weed-seasons
and the calm exemplary nation
of lump-faced eaters of weed
browsing, suckling, circling
weedways of visionary twilight.

Poem, boulders that drift,
submarine idyll, silences
incomprehensibly large!
Here come the divers, bubbling
their little quick land-words, working
the frog-feet they learned to reach you,
juggling weed-trails and historic emotions;

they goggle—the mermaid bears
into focus. The death of sailormen's
an undesigning body, after all:
huge-pored, hare-lipped and bald,
the stare one weed-thought, the hide
an aged impervious tolerance
of weed, hide, hands . . .

What did they see in her, those press-ganged
years of pemmican and the lash?
Fresh meat in parting foam—
good men jumped in and the wake
unrolled to tent their feast;
man-eater for sure. The creature's
researched now, re-conceived,

civilised and cast in a cattle-part
for our old crepuscular dream
of man and the peaceable monsters.
Only, men hardly learn
undersea purposes, and course
circuits of deluded will
dandling the enigma; to end

with utility, Midlands farmers
in a Stubbs, dwarfed by their stud
uncaring bulls. The manatee
ignore curious glass,
move against the little limbs
assured of their region, torpidly
hand-feed, and never think to bite.

JUDITH RODRIGUEZ (b. 1936)

Seahorses

When we were children
We would cheer to find a seahorse
Among the wrack the breakers lifted
On to the beach. Sometimes two or three were together,
A team to pull a chariot of cuttle,
Or like a suicide wreathed in fine
Sea ivy and bleached sea roses
One stiff but apologetic in its trance.
Seahorses were vikings;
Somewhere they impassively
Launched on garrulous currents
Seeking a far grave: wherever
That was, they set their stallion
Noses to it, ready to be garnered
In the sea's time at the sea's pleasure.
If we wondered why we loved them
We might have thought
They were the only creatures which had to die
Before we could see them—
In this early rule of death we'd recognise
The armorial pride of head, the unbending
Seriousness of small creatures,
Credit them with the sea's rare love
Which threw them to us in their beauty,

Unlike the vast and pitiable whale
Which must be quickly buried for its smell.

PETER PORTER (b. 1929)

Lobster

What are you doing here
Samurai
In the west, in the sunset streams of the west?

How you lord it over those peasants,
The whelks
The mussels and the shrimps and scallops.

There you clank, in dark blue armour
Along the ocean floor,
With the shadows flowing over you,
Haddock, mackerel,
And the sun the shadow of a big yellow whale.

Nothing stands in your way, swashbuckler.

The orchards where you wander
Drop sufficient plunder,
Mercenary in the dark blue coat of mail.

Be content, be content far out
With the tides' bounty,
Going from smithy to smithy, in your season
For an ampler riveting.

Fold your big thumbs,
Under the trembling silver-blue scales of the moon.

GEORGE MACKAY BROWN (b. 1921)

Sea Mouse

The orphanage of possibility
has had to be expanded to
admit the sea mouse. No one
had asked for such a thing,
or prophesied its advent,

sheltering under ruching
edges of sea lettuce—
a wet thing but pettable
as, seen in the distance,
the tops of copses,

sun-honeyed, needle-pelted
pine trees, bearded barley,
or anything newborn not bald
but furred. No rodent this
scabrous, this unlooked-for

foundling, no catnip plaything
for a cat to worry, not even
an echinoderm, the creature
seems to be a worm. Silk-spiny,
baby-mummy-swaddled, it's

at home where every corridor
is mop-and-bucket scrubbed
and aired from wall to wall
twice daily by the inde-
fatigable tidal head nurse.

AMY CLAMPITT (1920–94)

Some Beasts

From the Spanish of Pablo Neruda

It was the twilight of the iguana.
From the rainbow-arch of the battlements,
his long tongue like a lance
sank down in the green leaves,
and a swarm of ants, monks with feet chanting,
crawled off into the jungle;
the guanaco, thin as oxygen
in the wide peaks of cloud,
went along, wearing his shoes of gold,
while the llama opened his honest eyes
on the breakable neatness
of a world full of dew.
The monkeys braided a sexual
thread that went on and on

along the shores of the dawn,
demolishing walls of pollen
and startling the butterflies of Muzo
into flying violets.
It was the night of the alligators,
the pure night, crawling
with snouts emerging from ooze,
and out of the sleepy marshes
the confused noise of scaly plates
returned to the ground where they began.

The jaguar brushes the leaves
with a luminous absence,
the puma runs through the branches
like a forest fire,
while the jungle's drunken eyes
burn from inside him.
The badgers scratch the river's
feet, scenting the nest
whose throbbing delicacy
they attack with red teeth.

And deep in the huge waters
the enormous anaconda lies
like the circle around the earth,
covered with ceremonies of mud,
devouring, religious.

JAMES WRIGHT (1927–80)

Once an Indian went hunting with his young brother-in-law Botoque. Near a tall cliff they noticed some macaws flying about and when they looked up saw the nest there. 'There'll be nestlings,' the elder man said. 'Climb up and get them, boy, and we'll have a treat tonight.' So Botoque climbed the cliff by a ladder his brother-in-law had made but found no nestlings in the nest, only two eggs. 'Take them; throw them down to me,' the man shouted to him. And Botoque threw them down. But these were magic eggs, they changed into stones while they were falling and hurt the man's hands quite badly. He thought Botoque had done it on purpose and in his fury he broke the ladder and left Botoque sitting on the cliff with no means of getting down to the ground again. 'May you starve; may you rot,' said the man as he went away.

For several days Botoque remained there alone. He grew thinner and thinner and hungrier and hungrier, for there was nothing in the nest but excrement, nor did the macaws return to it, though he expected them daily and was afraid because he had thrown down their eggs. One day however he saw a spotted jaguar out hunting, a bow and arrows slung across his back. The boy shrank back afraid, but the jaguar saw his shadow move across the ground below; he thought it some beast at first and tried to catch it, all in vain. Then he looked up and noticed the boy above him on the cliff and the broken ladder hanging down.

'I'll mend it for you,' he called up, and so he did, but Botoque was much too afraid at first to climb down it to meet him. In the end hunger and loneliness overcame the boy. When he had descended the ladder the jaguar put him on his back and carried him home to supper.

'It will be a good one too,' he said. 'Meat roasted on my fire, you'll have never tasted anything so good.' Botoque could not imagine what this roasted meat could be. Men had no fire in those days, so they did not know how to cook. And at first sight of the tree-trunk burning in a hearth made of stones, he could not imagine what he was seeing. The meat was delicious however, he ate and ate and ate, and when the jaguar offered to adopt him as his son he accepted gladly.

Unfortunately the jaguar was not alone in his village. He had a wife and she did not like Botoque at all. When her husband was away hunting she treated him very badly, scratching his face and giving him only dried-up remnants of meat to eat. The jaguar was angry and scolded her, but still she went on ill-treating the boy, sometimes feeding him nothing but leaves, and at last the jaguar said to Botoque,

'It is time you came hunting with me.' And once they were in the forest he gave the boy a new bow and arrows of his own and taught him how to use them as he did.

'Next time she ill-treats you, you have my permission to shoot an arrow into her,' he said.

The jaguar's wife would not heed any warnings. Next day she scratched Botoque's face again. So he shot an arrow into her breast and she fell down dead, and at once Botoque seized his bow and a piece of roasted meat and fled away back to his own village because he was afraid of the jaguar's anger.

No one recognised him there at first. Nor could Botoque make the other Indians believe his story. But then he offered them some of his roasted meat and as soon as they had tasted it they wanted to know how to cook meat for themselves.

'You need fire,' Botoque told them. 'Only the jaguar has fire.'

'Then we will have to take it away from him,' they said. Botoque showed the men the way to the jaguar's village and when they reached it they found no one at home and the meat raw, the jaguar's wife being dead. The Indians roasted the meat then and there and ate it, then they crept away from the village carrying the fire, and from that time on they had light to see by when night fell, they could warm themselves when it was cold and no longer must they eat their meat uncooked.

The jaguar on the other hand became their enemy for ever. Ever since men stole his weapon and his fire he has used only his claws for hunting, he rends his prey with his teeth as soon as he has caught it, eats it raw just as it is; and the only fire that remains to him is the fire that shines reflected in his eyes.

> South American fire myth, told by Claude Lévi-Strauss, 1964 (tr. John and Doreen Weightman, 1969)

To the Glow-Worm

Tastefull Illuminations of the night
Bright scatter'd twinkling stars o' spangl'd earth
Hail to the nameless colour'd dark-&-light
The watching nurse o' thy illumin'd birth
In thy still hour how dearly I delight
To rest my weary bones—from labour free
In lone spots out o' hearing & o' sight
To sigh days smother'd pains & pause on thee
Bedecking dangling brier & ivied tree
Or diamonds tipping on the grassy spear
Thy pale fac'd glimmering light I love to see
Gilding & glistering i' the dew drop near—
O still hours mate—my easing heart sobs free
While tiny bents low bend wi' many a added tear

JOHN CLARE (1793–1864)

The Mower to the Glowworms

Ye living lamps, by whose dear light
The nightingale does sit so late,
And studying all the summer night,
Her matchless songs does meditate;

Ye country comets, that portend
No war, nor prince's funeral,
Shining unto no higher end
Than to presage the grass's fall;

> Ye glowworms, whose officious flame
> To wandering mowers shows the way,
> That in the night have lost their aim,
> And after foolish fires do stray;
>
> Your courteous lights in vain you waste,
> Since Juliana here is come,
> For she my mind hath so displaced
> That I shall never find my home.

ANDREW MARVELL (1621–78)

[Rio de Janeiro, May–June 1832]

The climate, during the months of May and June, or the beginning of winter, was delightful. The mean temperature, from observations taken at nine o'clock, both morning and evening, was only 72°. It often rained heavily, but the drying southerly winds soon again rendered the walks pleasant. One morning, in the course of six hours, 1.6 inches of rain fell. As this storm passed over the forests, which surround the Corcovado, the sound produced by the drops pattering on the countless multitude of leaves, was very remarkable; it could be heard at the distance of a quarter of a mile, and was like the rushing of a great body of water. After the hotter days, it was delicious to sit quietly in the garden and watch the evening pass into night. . . .

At these times the fireflies are seen flitting about from hedge to hedge. All that I caught belonged to the family of Lampyridæ, or glowworms, and the greater number were *Lampyris occidentalis*. I found that this insect emitted the most brilliant flashes when irritated: in the intervals the abdominal rings were obscured. The flash was almost co-instantaneous in the two rings, but it was first just perceptible in the anterior one. The shining matter was fluid and very adhesive: little spots, where the skin had been torn, continued bright with a slight scintillation, whilst the uninjured parts were obscured. When the insect was decapitated the rings remained uninterruptedly bright, but not so brilliant as before: local irritation with a needle always increased the vividness of the light. The rings in one instance retained their luminous property nearly twenty-four hours after the death of the insect. From these facts it would appear probable, that the animal has only the power of concealing or extinguishing the light for short intervals, and that at other times the display is involuntary. On the muddy and wet gravel-walks I found the larvæ of this lampyris in great numbers: they resembled in general form the female of the English glowworm. These larvæ possessed but feeble luminous powers; very differently from their parents, on the slightest touch they feigned death, and ceased to shine.

CHARLES DARWIN, *Journal of Researches (Voyage of the Beagle)*, 1839

A number of animals spring from some hidden and secret source, even in the quadruped class, for instance salamanders, a creature shaped like a lizard, covered with spots, never appearing except in great rains and disappearing in fine weather. It is so chilly that it puts out fire by its contact, in the same way as ice does.

PLINY THE ELDER (AD 23–79), *Natural History* (tr. H. Rackham, 1937)

One day when I was about five years old, my father was sitting in a ground-floor room of ours in which washing had been going on, and where a large fire of oak logs had been left. Giovanni, his viola on his arm, was playing and singing by himself near the fire—for it was very cold. Looking into the fire he chanced to see in the middle of the most ardent flames a little creature like a lizard disporting itself in the midst of the intensest heat. Suddenly aware of what it was, he called my sister and me and pointed it out to us children. Then he gave me a sound box on the ears, which made me cry bitterly, on which he soothed me with kind words, saying, 'My dear little fellow, I did not hurt you for any harm you had done, but only that you might remember that the lizard in the fire there is a salamander, which never has been seen for a certainty by any one before.' Then he kissed me and gave me some farthings.

BENVENUTO CELLINI (1500–71), *The Life . . . written by himself* (tr. Anne MacDonell, 1907)

COMPANIONSHIP

To Mrs Reynolds's Cat

Cat! who hast passed thy grand climacteric,
  How many mice and rats hast in thy days
  Destroyed? How many tit-bits stolen? Gaze
With those bright languid segments green, and prick
Those velvet ears—but prithee do not stick
  Thy latent talons in me, and up-raise
  Thy gentle mew, and tell me all thy frays
Of fish and mice, and rats and tender chick.
Nay, look not down, nor lick thy dainty wrists—
  For all the wheezy asthma, and for all
Thy tail's tip is nicked off, and though the fists
  Of many a maid have given thee many a maul,
Still is that fur as soft as when the lists
  In youth thou enteredst on glass-bottled wall.

JOHN KEATS (1795–1821)

Nor would it be just, under this head, to omit the fondness which he shewed for animals which he had taken under his protection. I shall never forget the indulgence with which he treated Hodge, his cat; for whom he himself used to go out and buy oysters, lest his servants having that trouble should take a dislike to the poor creature. I am, unluckily, one of those who have an antipathy to a cat, so that I am uneasy when in the room with one; and I own, I frequently suffered a good deal from the presence of this same Hodge. I recollect him one day scrambling up Dr Johnson's breast, apparently with much satisfaction, while my friend smiling and half-whistling, rubbed down his back, and pulled him by the tail; and when I observed he was a fine cat, saying, 'Why yes, Sir, but I have had cats whom I liked better than this,' and then as if perceiving Hodge to be out of countenance, adding, 'but he is a very fine cat, a very fine cat indeed.'

JAMES BOSWELL, *Life of Johnson*, 1791

The Meadow Mouse

1

In a shoe box stuffed in an old nylon stocking
Sleeps the baby mouse I found in the meadow,
Where he trembled and shook beneath a stick
Till I caught him up by the tail and brought him in,
Cradled in my hand,
A little quaker, the whole body of him trembling,
His absurd whiskers sticking out like a cartoon-mouse,
His feet like small leaves,
Little lizard-feet,
Whitish and spread wide when he tried to struggle away,
Wriggling like a miniscule puppy.

Now he's eaten his three kinds of cheese and drunk from his
        bottle-cap watering-trough—
So much he just lies in one corner,
His tail curled under him, his belly big
As his head; his bat-like ears
Twitching, tilting toward the least sound.

Do I imagine he no longer trembles
When I come close to him?
He seems no longer to tremble.

2

But this morning the shoe-box house on the back porch is empty.
Where has he gone, my meadow mouse,
My thumb of a child that nuzzled in my palm?—
To run under the hawk's wing,
Under the eye of the great owl watching from the elm-tree,
To live by courtesy of the shrike, the snake, the tom-cat.

I think of the nestling fallen into the deep grass,
The turtle gasping in the dusty rubble of the highway,
The paralytic stunned in the tub, and the water rising,—
All things innocent, hapless, forsaken.

SoO THEODORE ROETHKE (1908–63)

To a Mouse, On turning her up in her Nest,
with the Plough, November, 1785.

Wee, sleeket, cowran, tim'rous *beastie*,
O, what a panic's in thy breastie!
Thou need na start awa sae hasty,
    Wi' bickering brattle!
I wad be laith to rin an' chase thee,
    Wi' murd'ring *pattle*!

I'm truly sorry Man's dominion
Has broken Nature's social union,
An' justifies that ill opinion,
    Which makes thee startle,
At me, thy poor, earth-born companion,
    An' *fellow-mortal*!

I doubt na, whyles, but thou may *thieve*;
What then? poor beastie, thou maun live!
A *daimen-icker* in a *thrave*
    'S a sma' request:
I'll get a blessin wi' the lave,
    An' never miss't!

brattle: scamper   *pattle*: plough-staff   *daimen*: odd   *icker*: ear
of corn   *thrave*: twenty-four sheaves

Thy wee-bit *housie*, too, in ruin!
It's silly wa's the win's are strewin!
An' naething, now, to big a new ane,
    O' foggage green!
An' bleak *December's winds* ensuin,
    Baith snell an' keen!

Thou saw the fields laid bare an' wast,
An' weary *Winter* comin fast,
An' cozie here, beneath the blast,
    Thou thought to dwell,
Till crash! the cruel *coulter* past
    Out thro' thy cell.

That wee-bit heap o' leaves an' stibble,
Has cost thee monie a weary nibble!
Now thou's turn'd out, for a' thy trouble,
    But house or hald,
To thole the Winter's *sleety dribble*,
    An' *cranreuch* cauld!

But Mousie, thou art no thy-lane,
In proving *foresight* may be vain:
The best laid schemes o' *Mice* an' *Men*,
    Gang aft agley,
An' lea'e us nought but grief an' pain,
    For promis'd joy!

Still, thou art blest, compar'd wi' *me*!
The *present* only toucheth thee:
But Och! I *backward* cast my e'e,
    On prospects drear!
An' *forward*, tho' I canna *see*,
    I *guess* an' *fear*!

ROBERT BURNS (1759–96)

---

big: build   *foggage*: coarse grass   *snell*: biting   *but*: without   *thole*: endure
cranreuch: hoar-frost   *thy-lane*: by thyself   *agley*: askew

'Look at rats,' went on William eloquently. 'No one makes a fuss of rats. Jus' 'cause they've not got feathers an' can't fly an' sing an' carry on like birds. Why shun't they have rat baths an' rat tables in their gardens same as they have bird baths an' bird tables? It's not fair, an' I've a jolly good mind to start on rats myself, jus' to show 'em. They're as good as birds any day.'

'She's goin' to have a bird week, she says,' said Ginger gloomily.

'A what?' said William.

'A bird week.'

'What's that?'

'Dunno. A lot more fuss. I believe she's goin' to have medals for children what do axe of kindness to birds that week. An' she's sayin' people oughtn't to have cats 'cause they eat birds.'

'And why shouldn't they?' demanded William, rising indignantly to the defence of an animal for which he had usually little affection or sympathy. 'Why shun't they eat birds? They've got to live, haven't they, same as her? What about birds eating worms? I guess worms have got feelin's same as anyone else. An' what about ole Miss Chesterfield eatin' cows an' pigs an' suchlike? Haven't *they* got any feelin's?'

'She doesn't,' said Ginger. 'She only eats vegetables.'

'Well, how does she know that cabbages and suchlike haven't got feelings? Just 'cause they haven't got feathers an' don't sing an' carry on like birds no one takes any notice of them. I'm jus' about sick of all the fuss people make of birds, jus' as if there wasn't anything else in the world what'd got any feelings.'

[Miss Chesterfield] soon had her bird week arrangements well in train. [She] held 'bird receptions' at the cottage and took favoured parties into the wood to watch the half-witted pigeon and the pompous robin perch on her finger and eat cake out of her hand. She gave prizes for the best arranged bird tables in the village. She gave medals for acts of kindness to birds (Ginger applied for one on the strength of having once accidentally left the cage of his aunt's parrot open, but was refused). . . .

William's disgust and despondency increased.

'Birds!' he ejaculated bitterly. 'I'm jus' about sick of 'em. She'll expect us givin' up our houses for 'em next an' goin' to live in trees to save birds the trouble of doin' it.'

He was considerably interested and cheered to hear a mention of 'rat week'. His father and the Vicar were discussing the subject and he heard the Vicar say: 'We really must make a special effort for rat week this year. The matter's absolutely urgent.'

'Rat week?' said William, pricking up his ears.

'Yes, rat week,' said his father shortly.

'Well, I'm jolly glad to hear of somethin' bein' done for rats at last,' said William fervently. 'I don't mind helpin' to give rats a good time. It's everyone fussin' over birds I'm so sick of.'

'What do you mean, give rats a good time?' said his father irritably. 'No one wants to give rats a good time. All we want is to get rid of them.'

'Get rid of them?' said William indignantly. 'Why?'

'Why? Because they're destructive vermin.'

'So are birds,' said William. 'Eatin' jolly well everything in the garden they can get hold of. Well, if you want to get rid of 'em, why're you having a rat week for them?'

'During rat week, William,' explained his father patiently, 'everyone does their best to exterminate as many of the pests as possible.'

'Exter—does that mean kill?' said William.

'It does.'

William gave a gasp of incredulous horror.

'*Gosh!* All that fuss about birds, an' then killin' poor rats! Jus' 'cause they've not got feathers an' can't sing. Well, it's jolly well the unfairest thing I ever heard of.'

But his father was not interested in William's views on rats. He waved him aside and continued his conversation with the Vicar.

William, still full of righteous indignation, went in search of his Outlaws.

'Makin' all that fuss over birds an' killin' rats,' he said when he had found them and laid the situation before them. 'There ought to be a lor against treatin' 'em different. If people make a fuss over birds they oughter be made to make a fuss over rats, too. I bet I'd feel *mad* about it if I was a rat. Well, I jolly well votes we *do* something to help the poor rats.'

'What can we do?' said Henry.

William considered for a few moments, then his face lightened.

'*Tell* you what we can do,' he said. 'We can have a rat week. A proper rat week. The same sort she had for birds. That'll help 'em a bit, anyway.'

The idea appealed to the Outlaws. It was original. It would give them plenty of outlet for their energy. It would compensate in some way for the humiliation their spirits had endured from Miss Chesterfield's cult of her feathered friends.

'An' we'll have a sanctu'ry for them same as she has,' went on William, 'an' we'll have rat baths an' rat tables same as she has, an' we'll make it a rat fortnight 'stead of a rat week, an' that'll be jolly well sucks for *her*.'

They set to work upon the plan with enthusiasm. The old barn was chosen as the sanctuary, and in it were placed low packing-cases for the rat tables, and bowls of water for the rat baths. William thoughtfully brought some straw and old sacking to serve as beds for their guests. All of them brought scraps from home and soon the 'rat tables' held an appetising array of bread, cheese, cold meat, cold potatoes, odd bits of pastry and many other such dainties salvaged from larder or dustbin.

The rat baths were filled with water, the beds of sacking and straw arranged comfortably along the wall. The only thing that remained was to find guests for the sanctuary. It was just when they were turning their thoughts to this problem that Ginger made a discovery. He discovered that his gardener was setting rat traps in the disused stables that ran at the bottom of his garden. They were rat traps of the old-fashioned kind—simple baited cages, which caught their victims alive, to be drowned by the gardener on his rounds in the morning. Here was the supply of guests for the sanctuary already to hand. Every morning Ginger rose early, took the trap down to the sanctuary, released its occupant and returned the trap to the stables. Later the gardener would come round, scratch his head in bewilderment over the empty baitless trap, and wonder how the 'cunning little devils' had managed it.

News of the sanctuary seemed to have spread through the rat population of the neighbourhood. Dark forms emerged from dark corners and swarmed each morning upon the laden food tables. William watched them with proud gratification. 'Jolly nice to see 'em having a good time same as birds,' he said. 'They've waited for it long enough, poor things.'

As the news spread rats from far and wide joined the happy family. Householders in the neighbourhood of the old barn consulted together anxiously on the sudden and alarming influx of rats, for, though faithful to their meal times in the sanctuary, the rats were not slow to discover the larders of all the houses near.

The attitude of the householders taught William that he must for the present keep his activities secret. The public was not yet educated up to them.

'We've gotter do it gradual,' he said to the Outlaws. . . . 'We gotter get 'em fond of rats. There's no reason why they shouldn't be. They're jolly well as sweet as those ole birds any day. We'll have a rat fortnight every year an' we'll do it gradual. This year we'll jus' get to know the rats, an' gettem to know us. An' next year we'll start gettin' people fond of them. We've jus' got to go gradual . . .'

Certainly the rats were getting to know William. They were on the look-out for him when he appeared. They clustered about his feet as he approached the table. They accepted him as their friend and protector and showed no fear when he came up to their table and watched them at their meals. On the whole he considered that his rat fortnight had been a great success. He had worked hard, and he was not sorry that it had come to an end. The families of all the Outlaws were becoming suspicious about the amount of 'scraps' that were disappearing from their larders, Miss Chesterfield's occupancy of the cottage was drawing to a close, and William felt that both birds and rats might now well take a less prominent place in the scheme of things.

Miss Chesterfield had decided to celebrate her departure by what she called a 'Children's Animal Fête.' Every child in the village was to come to it in fancy dress, and the fancy dress was to have some connection with an animal. The committee of mesmerised helpers was to provide the tea, and Sir Gerald Markham from Marleigh Manor had been hypnotised into acting as chairman and giving the prize. Sir Gerald was a man who did things, if he did them at all, on a large scale, and, though he could not understand why he had consented to have anything to do with an affair of which he thoroughly disapproved, still, having promised to provide a prize, he was going to provide a good one, and so he sent to London for a cinema-camera of the latest design.

William, disguised as Dick Whittington, comes to the fête.

He walked very slowly, still hoping that a deluge would come on, drenching every character so thoroughly that not even the hostess or Sir Gerald Markham himself could see how much inferior his Dick Whittington was to Hubert Lane's. It was certainly growing darker. He passed the door of the old barn without noticing it or looking in. He had quite forgotten his rat fortnight. It had ended yesterday. It now belonged quite definitely to the past, and William's thoughts were always too busy with the present to have time for the past. But his late friends and protégés did not know that their fortnight was over. They hung about the empty tables waiting for him to visit them as usual with delicious fragments of bread and cheese and pastry and cold pudding. They could not understand his sudden failure to provide for them.

Suddenly he appeared. They knew him even under his Dick Whittington disguise. They followed him trustingly, hopefully—dim black shapes sliding along in his shadow. William, sunk in his gloomy thoughts, was not aware of them. They loped silently behind him, taking courage from the gathering darkness, not believing that this universal provider could fail to provide for them at the last.

The participants . . . had assembled on Miss Chesterfield's lawn. The mesmerised helpers were helping in mesmerised fashion. Sir Gerald stood behind a table surveying dejectedly a motley crowd of children dressed as Red Riding Hoods with attendant wolves, or Pusses in Boots, or Goldylocks with one or more bears. The best costume there was certainly Hubert Lane's Dick Whittington. He stood in the front, eyeing with a confident and possessive swagger the cinema-camera that reposed on the table. The helpers looked anxiously at the darkening sky.

'Hadn't you better present the prize before it begins to rain?' they suggested to the chairman.

'But to whom?' he said.

'Hubert Lane's costume is the best.'

'But there's no originality about it,' he objected. 'There isn't a spark of originality in the whole bunch of them. If a single one of them had a single spark of originality——'

Suddenly another figure appeared walking round the house on to the lawn. And it was not alone. A little procession of black creeping forms followed it. With screams of terror the helpers fled, taking refuge in house, summer-house, greenhouse, tool shed. The guests fled also, Hubert Lane making ignominious and ineffectual attempts to climb a tree. Sir Gerald advanced upon William. William was now alone, his companions having modestly retired as soon as they saw the large company assembled on the lawn.

'Were they real?' said Sir Gerald Markham, much impressed.

'Were what real?' said William, who was still unaware of his escort.

'Well, whatever they were it was a marvellous effect. I've never seen anything better done. Original and impressive. What's your name?'

'William Brown,' said William, now completely bewildered.

The others were returning from their hiding-places to the lawn, looking round them timorously.

Sir Gerald Markham knocked on his desk for silence and announced:

'Ladies and gentlemen, I now have the pleasant duty of presenting the prize.' Hubert Lane smirked and stepped forward. 'The prize goes to William Brown for his excellent impersonation of the Pied Piper of Hamelin. How he got his scenic effects I'm not quite sure, but it was a clever idea brilliantly carried out . . . William Brown.'

William stepped forward to receive the prize.

RICHMAL CROMPTON, 'William the Rat Lover', William the Detective, 1935

In the daies of *Augustus Caesar* the Emperour, there was a Dolphin entred the gulfe or poole Lucrinus, which loved wondrous well a certain boy a poore mans son: who using to go every day to schoole from Baianum to Puteoli, was woont also about noone-tide to stay at the water side, and to call unto the Dolphin, *Simo, Simo,* and many times would give him fragments of bread, which of purpose he ever brought with him, and by this meanes allured the Dolphin to come ordinarily unto him at his call.

Well in processe of time, at what houre soever of the day, this boy lured for him and called *Simo*, were the Dolphin never so close hidden in any secret

Simo: Snubnose

and blind corner, out he would and come abroad, yea and skud amaine to this lad: and taking bread and other victuals at his hand, would gently offer him his back to mount upon, and then downe went the sharpe pointed prickles of his fins, which he would put up as it were within a sheath for fear of hurting the boy. Thus when he had him once on his back, he would carry him over the broad arme of the sea as farre as Puteoli to schoole; and in like manner convey him backe again home: and thus he continued for many yeeres together, so long as the child lived. But when the boy was fallen sicke & dead, yet the Dolphin gave not over his haunt, but usually came to the wonted place, & missing the lad, seemed to be heavie and mourne againe, untill for very griefe & sorrow (as it is doubtles to be presumed) he also was found dead upon the shore.

PLINY THE ELDER (AD 23–79), *Natural History* (tr. Philemon Holland, 1601)

A Crocodile

Hard by the lilied Nile I saw
A duskish river-dragon stretched along,
The brown habergeon of his limbs enamelled
With sanguine almandines and rainy pearl:
And on his back there lay a young one sleeping,
No bigger than a mouse; with eyes like beads,
And a small fragment of its speckled egg
Remaining on its harmless, pulpy snout;
A thing to laugh at, as it gaped to catch
The baulking, merry flies. In the iron jaws
Of the great devil-beast, like a pale soul
Fluttering in rocky hell, lightsomely flew
A snowy troculus, with roseate beak
Tearing the hairy leeches from his throat.

THOMAS LOVELL BEDDOES (1803–49)

The Turtle

(For My Grandson)

Not because of his eyes,
          the eyes of a bird,
                    but because he is beaked,
birdlike, to do an injury,
          has the turtle attracted you.
                    He is your only pet.

When we are together
        you talk of nothing else
                ascribing all sorts
of murderous motives
        to his least action.
                You ask me
to write a poem,
        should I have poems to write,
                about a turtle.

The turtle lives in the mud
        but is not mud-like,
                you can tell it by his eyes
which are clear.
        When he shall escape
                his present confinement
he will stride about the world
        destroying all
                with his sharp beak.
Whatever opposes him
        in the streets of the city
                shall go down.
Cars will be overturned.
        And upon his back
                shall ride,
to his conquests,
        my Lord,
                you!

You shall be master!
        In the beginning
                there was a great tortoise
who supported the world.
        Upon him
                all ultimately
rests.
        Without him
                nothing will stand.
He is all wise
        and can outrun the hare.
                In the night

his eyes carry him
    to unknown places.
        He is your friend.

            WILLIAM CARLOS WILLIAMS (1883–1963)

Cowper's Tame Hare

She came to him in dreams—her ears
Diddering like antennae, and her eyes
Wide as dark flowers where the dew
Holds and dissolves a purple hoard of shadow.
The thunder clouds crouched back, and the world opened
Tiny and bright as a celandine after rain.
A gentle light was on her, so that he
Who saw the talons in the vetch
Remembered now how buttercup and daisy
Would bounce like springs when a child's foot stepped off them.
Oh, but never dared he touch—
Her fur was still electric to the fingers.

Yet of all the beasts blazoned in gilt and blood
In the black-bound scriptures of his mind,
Pentecostal dove and paschal lamb,
Eagle, lion, serpent, she alone
Lived also in the noon of ducks and sparrows;
And the cleft-mouthed kiss which plugged the night with fever
Was sweetened by a lunch of docks and lettuce.

            NORMAN NICHOLSON (1910–87)

Well,—one at least is safe. One sheltered hare
Has never heard the sanguinary yell
Of cruel man exulting in her woes.
Innocent partner of my peaceful home,
Whom ten long years' experience of my care
Has made at last familiar, she has lost
Much of her vigilant instinctive dread,
Not needful here, beneath a roof like mine.
Yes,—thou mayst eat thy bread, and lick the hand
That feeds thee; thou mayst frolic on the floor
At evening, and at night retire secure
To thy straw couch, and slumber unalarmed:

For I have gained thy confidence, have pledged
All that is human in me to protect
Thine unsuspecting gratitude and love.
If I survive thee I will dig thy grave;
And, when I place thee in it, sighing say,
I knew at least one hare that had a friend.

WILLIAM COWPER (1731–1800), *The Task*

[*May, 1890*]
My first act was to give Bounce (what an investment that rabbit has been in spite of the hutches), a cupful of hemp seeds, the consequence being that when I wanted to draw him next morning he was partially intoxicated and wholly unmanageable.

Then I retired to bed, and lay awake chuckling till 2 in the morning, and afterwards had an impression that Bunny came to my bedside in a white cotton night cap and tickled me with his whiskers.

Sunday, October 30th [1892]
When I was walking out Benjamin I saw Miss Hutton's black cat jumping on something up the wood. I thought it was too far off to interfere, but as it seemed leisurely I went up in time to rescue a poor little rabbit, fast in a snare.

The cat had not hurt it, but I had great difficulty in slackening the noose round its neck. I warmed it at the fire, relieved it from a number of fleas, and it came round. It was such a little poor creature compared to mine. They are regular vermin, but one cannot stand by to see a thing mauled about from one's friendship for the race. Papa in his indignation pulled up the snare. I fancy our actions were much more illegal than Miss Hutton's.

After dinner I was half amused, half shocked, to see her little niece Maggie hunting everywhere for the wire. I just had enough sense not to show the stranger to Benjamin Bounce, but the smell of its fur on my dress was quite enough to upset the ill-regulated passions of that excitable buck rabbit.

Whether he thought I had a rival in my pocket, or like a Princess in a Fairy Tale was myself metamorphosed into a white rabbit I cannot say, but I had to lock him up.

Rabbits are creatures of warm volatile temperament but shallow and absurdly transparent. It is this naturalness, one touch of nature, that I find so delightful in Mr Benjamin Bunny, though I frankly admit his vulgarity. At one moment amiably sentimental to the verge of silliness, at the next, the upsetting of a jug or tea-cup which he immediately takes upon himself, will convert him into a demon, throwing himself on his back, scratching and spluttering. If I can lay hold of him without being bitten, within half a minute he is licking my hands as though nothing has happened.

He is an abject coward, but believes in bluster, could stare our old dog out of countenance, chase a cat that has turned tail.

Benjamin once fell into an Aquarium head first, and sat in the water which he could not get out of, pretending to eat a piece of string. Nothing like putting a face upon circumstances.

BEATRIX POTTER, *The Journal . . . from 1881–1897*

At the edge of the wood, not far from the smoking mound, there was a hut shaped like a round tent, but made not of canvas but of larch poles set up on end and all sloping together so that the longer poles crossed each other at the top. On the side of it nearest to the mound there was a doorway covered with a hanging flap made of an old sack. The sack was pulled aside from within and a little, bent old man, as wrinkled as a walnut and as brown, with long, bare arms covered with muscles, came out. He blinked at the explorers in the sunlight.

The 'Swallows' introduce themselves, and are invited to look inside the hut.

Gradually their eyes grew accustomed to the darkness, and they saw that on each side of the hut a stout log divided off a place where there were rugs and blankets. Between the two logs there was an open space, where it looked as if there had been a small fire. The open light came through the door-hole. Not a speck of light came from between the poles of which the wigwam was made. Every chink had been well stuffed with moss. Overhead there hung a lantern, like their own camp lantern, from a hook at the end of a bit of wire. But it was not lit. High above them was pitch darkness, where the poles met each other at the pointed top of the hut. The old man was squatting on the log that shut off one of the bed-places. The Swallows sat in a row along the other.

'Do you live here always?' asked Susan.

'While we're burning,' replied the old man.

'While you're burning the charcoal,' said Susan.

'Aye,' said the old man. 'Someone has to be with the fire night and day, to keep him down like.'

'Have you really got a serpent?' asked Titty.

'An adder? Aye,' said the old man. 'Like to see him?'

'Oh yes, please,' said all the Swallows.

'Well, you're sitting on him,' said the old man.

All the Swallows, even Captain John, jumped up as if they had sat on a pin. The old man laughed. He came across the hut and rummaged under the blankets and pulled out an old cigar-box.

'It's young Billy's adder,' he said; 'we'll take it out to him. Hi, Billy,' he shouted from the doorhole, 'let them have a look at your adder.'

He carried the little box out of the hut and the Swallows followed. Young Billy gave a last pat or two to the smoking mound, and came to them. He was another old man, but not quite so old as the first. . . . 'Let's have the box, dad,' he said, and Old Billy gave him the cigar-box. He put the box on the ground and knelt beside it. He undid the catch and lifted the lid. There was nothing to be seen but a lump of greenish moss. He took a twig and gently stirred the lump. There was a loud hiss, and the brown head of a snake shot out of the moss and over the side of the box. Its forked tongue darted in and out. Young Billy touched it gently with his twig. It hissed again and suddenly seemed to pour itself in a long brown stream over the edge of the box. Young Billy dropped his twig and took a stick and picked the snake up on the stick and lifted it off the ground. Its tail hung down on one side of the stick and its head on the other. Its head swayed from side to side as it swung there, hissing and darting out its tongue. The Swallows shrank back from it but could not look away. Suddenly it began sliding over the stick. Young Billy was ready for it, and before it dropped on the ground he caught it on another stick.

'Is it safe to touch it?' asked Susan.

'Look,' said Young Billy. He lowered the snake to the ground and put the stick in front of it. Instantly the snake struck at it open-mouthed.

'Never you go near an adder,' said Young Billy. 'There's plenty of them about. And you mind where you're stepping in the woods or up on the fell. They'll get out of your way if they see you, but if you happen to step on one, he'll bite, just as he did that stick. A bad bite it is too. There's many a one has died of it.'

'What do you keep him for?' asked John.

'Luck,' said Young Billy. 'Always had one in the hut, ever since I can remember, and dad, that's Old Billy here, can remember longer than me.'

'Aye, we've always had an adder,' said Old Billy, 'and so had my dad, when he was at the burning, and he was burning on these fells a hundred years ago.'

Young Billy neatly dropped the snake in its box and shut the lid of it. He held the box for the children to listen. They could hear the snake hissing inside. Then he gave the box back to Old Billy, who went off with it back into the hut.

A big puff of smoke rolled from the burning mound.

'Look there,' said Young Billy. 'Can't leave him a minute but he's out. Like the adder is fire. Just a bit of a hole and out he comes.'

ARTHUR RANSOME, *Swallows and Amazons*, 1930

It is to poetry, alas, that we have to trust for our most detailed description of Flush himself as a young dog. He was of that particular shade of dark brown which in sunshine flashes 'all over into gold'. His eyes were 'startled eyes of hazel bland'. His ears were 'tasselled'; his 'slender feet' were 'canopied in fringes' and his tail was broad. Making allowance for the exigencies of rhyme and the inaccuracies of poetic diction, there is nothing here but what would meet with the approval of the Spaniel Club. We cannot doubt that Flush was a pure-bred Cocker of the red variety marked by all the characteristic excellences of his kind.

Spaniels are by nature sympathetic; Flush, as his story proves, had an even excessive appreciation of human emotions.

He changes owner.

A voice said 'Flush'. He did not hear it. 'Flush', it repeated a second time. He started. He had thought himself alone. He turned. Was there something alive in the room with him? Was there something on the sofa? In the wild hope that this being, whatever it was, might open the door, that he might still rush after Miss Mitford and find her—that this was some game of hide-and-seek such as they used to play in the greenhouse at home—Flush darted to the sofa.

'Oh, Flush!' said Miss Barrett. For the first time she looked him in the face. For the first time Flush looked at the lady lying on the sofa.

Each was surprised. Heavy curls hung down on either side of Miss Barrett's face; large bright eyes shone out; a large mouth smiled. Heavy ears hung down on either side of Flush's face; his eyes, too, were large and bright: his mouth was wide. There was a likeness between them. As they gazed at each other each felt: Here am I—and then each felt: But how different! Hers was the pale worn face of an invalid, cut off from air, light, freedom. His was the warm ruddy face of a young animal; instinct with health and energy. Broken asunder, yet made in the same mould, could it be that each completed what was dormant in the other? She might have been—all that; and he— But no. Between them lay the widest gulf that can separate one being from another. She spoke. He was dumb. She was woman; he was dog. Thus closely united, thus immensely divided, they gazed at each other. Then with one bound Flush sprang on to the sofa and laid himself where he was to lie for ever after—on the rug at Miss Barrett's feet.

In spite of their astonishing blindness, even Miss Barrett's family began to notice, as the weeks passed, a change in Miss Barrett. She left her room and went down to sit in the drawing-room. Then she did what she had not done for many a long day—she actually walked on her own feet as far as the gate at Devonshire Place with her sister. Her friends, her family, were amazed at her improvement. But only Flush knew where her strength came from—it came from the dark man in the armchair. He came again and again and again. First it was once a week; then it was twice a week. He came always in the afternoon and left in the afternoon. Miss Barrett always saw him alone. And on the days when he did not come, his letters came. And when he himself was gone, his flowers were there. And in the mornings when she was alone, Miss Barrett wrote to him. That dark, taut, abrupt, vigorous man, with his black hair, his red cheeks and his yellow gloves, was everywhere. Naturally, Miss Barrett was better; of course she could walk. Flush himself felt that it was impossible to lie still. Old longings revived; a new restlessness possessed him. Even his sleep was full of dreams. He dreamt as he had not dreamt since the old days at Three Mile Cross—of hares starting from the long grass; of pheasants rocketing up with long tails streaming, of partridges rising with a whirr from the stubble. He dreamt that he was hunting, that he was chasing some spotted spaniel, who fled, who escaped him. He was in Spain; he was in Wales; he was in Berkshire; he was flying before park-keepers' truncheons in Regent's Park. Then he opened his eyes. There were no hares, and no partridges; no whips cracking and no black men crying 'Span! Span!' There was only Mr Browning in the armchair talking to Miss Barrett on the sofa.

Sleep became impossible while that man was there. Flush lay with his eyes wide open, listening. Though he could make no sense of the little words that hurtled over his head from two-thirty to four-thirty sometimes three times a week, he could detect with terrible accuracy that the tone of the words was changing. Miss Barrett's voice had been forced and unnaturally lively at first. Now it had gained a warmth and an ease that he had never heard in it before. And every time the man came, some new sound came into their voices—now they made a grotesque chattering; now they skimmed over him like birds flying widely; now they cooed and clucked, as if they were two birds settled in a nest; and then Miss Barrett's voice, rising again, went soaring and circling in the air; and then Mr Browning's voice barked out its sharp, harsh clapper of laughter; and then there was only a murmur, a quiet humming sound as the two voices joined together. But as the summer turned to autumn Flush noted, with horrid apprehension, another note. There was a new urgency, a new pressure and energy in the man's voice, at which Miss Barrett, Flush felt, took fright. Her voice fluttered; hesitated; seemed to falter and fade and plead and gasp, as if she were begging for a rest, for a pause, as if she were afraid. Then the man was silent.

Of him they took but little notice. He might have been a log of wood lying there at Miss Barrett's feet for all the attention Mr Browning paid him. Sometimes he scrubbed his head in a brisk, spasmodic way, energetically, without sentiment, as he passed him. Whatever that scrub might mean, Flush felt nothing but an intense dislike for Mr Browning. The very sight of him, so well tailored, so tight, so muscular, screwing his yellow gloves in his hand, set his teeth on edge. Oh! to let them meet sharply, completely in the stuff of his trousers! And yet he dared not. Taking it all in all, that winter—1845–6—was the most distressing that Flush had ever known.

VIRGINIA WOOLF, *Flush: A Biography*, 1933

To Flush, My Dog

Loving friend, the gift of one
Who her own true faith has run
    Through thy lower nature,
Be my benediction said
With my hand upon thy head,
    Gentle fellow creature!

Like a lady's ringlets brown,
Flow thy silken ears adown
    Either side demurely
Of thy silver-suited breast,
Shining out from all the rest
    Of thy body purely.

Darkly brown thy body is,
Till the sunshine striking this
    Alchemize its dullness,
When the sleek curls manifold
Flash all over into gold,
    With a burnished fullness.

Underneath my stroking hand,
Startled eyes of hazel bland
    Kindling, growing larger,
Up thou leapest with a spring,
Full of prank and curveting,
    Leaping like a charger.

gift of one: Mary Russell Mitford

Leap! thy broad tail waves a light,
Leap! thy slender feet are bright,
    Canopied in fringes;
Leap—those tasselled ears of thine
Flicker strangely, fair and fine,
    Down their golden inches.

Yet, my pretty, sportive friend,
Little is 't to such an end
    That I praise thy rareness!
Other dogs may be thy peers
Haply in these drooping ears,
    And this glossy fairness.

But of *thee* it shall be said,
This dog watched beside a bed
    Day and night unweary,—
Watched within a curtained room,
Where no sunbeam brake the gloom
    Round the sick and dreary.

Roses, gathered for a vase,
In that chamber died apace,
    Beam and breeze resigning;
This dog only, waited on,
Knowing that when light is gone
    Love remains for shining.

            .   .   .   .   .

Other dogs of loyal cheer
Bounded at the whistle clear,
    Up the woodside hieing;
This dog only, watched in reach
Of a faintly uttered speech,
    Or a louder sighing.

And if one or two quick tears
Dropped upon his glossy ears,
    Or a sigh came double,—
Up he sprang in eager haste,
Fawning, fondling, breathing fast,
    In a tender trouble.

            .   .   .   .   .

Therefore to this dog will I,
Tenderly not scornfully,
　　Render praise and favour:
With my hand upon his head,
Is my benediction said
　　Therefore, and for ever.

　　　·　　·　　·　　·

Blessings on thee, dog of mine,
Pretty collars make thee fine,
　　Sugared milk make fat thee!
Pleasures wag on in thy tail,
Hands of gentle motion fail
　　Nevermore, to pat thee!

Downy pillow take thy head,
Silken coverlid bestead,
　　Sunshine help thy sleeping!
No fly's buzzing wake thee up,
No man break thy purple cup,
　　Set for drinking deep in.

　　　·　　·　　·　　·

Mock I thee, in wishing weal?—
Tears are in my eyes to feel
　　Thou art made so straitly,
Blessing needs must straiten too,—
Little canst thou joy or do,
　　Thou who lovest *greatly*.

Yet be blessèd to the height
Of all good and all delight
　　Pervious to thy nature;
Only *loved* beyond that line,
With a love that answers thine,
　　Loving fellow creature!

ELIZABETH BARRETT BROWNING (1806–61)

In those tranquil, pre-puppy days no sound could be heard [in the greenhouse] except my pen scratching, for Ingulf, stretched out on a rug, was the last dog to make a sound, and, thankful not to have to walk anywhere or eat anything, lay motionless as a stone. Complete peace, accordingly, prevailed. Undisturbed I wrote. Nobody could look in at me from outside, because the windows were bleared over by the dust of ages, and no servant, driven by an uncontrollable itch to be given some more orders, if he or she came after me could be sure I was there, because Ingulf, convenient dog, averse from the smallest exertion, was to be relied on not to growl, whatever knockings there might be at the locked door. So that all I had to do, when would-be interrupters arrived, was to sit without moving, and pretend I was somewhere else.

Admirable conditions for work. They were put an end to by Ingo and Ivo. Wherever I went for the first week or two after their arrival, whatever cover I took, everybody knew exactly where I was. I was encompassed by a cloud of witnesses, all legs and tails, and neither they nor I could be hid. The corner where the greenhouse was, instead of being the quietest in the garden, became the noisiest. Out of it proceeded almost continual cries of *couche* and *pfui*. Inside it an uproar of enraptured barks, while havoc was being made of the simple furnishings, prevented any possibility of work.

We all calmed down, though, after a bit, though the puppies' first introduction to the greenhouse was a disaster. Some ancient flower-pots, piled forgotten in a corner, and never so much as glanced at by the indifferent Ingulf, were pounced on at once, and routed out and sent flying in pieces by huge puppies drunk with the delight of destruction. The rug on which Ingulf—surely, after all, an admirable dog?—had lain with such quiet dignity, was seized at each end, and tugged exultingly asunder. Short work was made of a cushion which was so unfortunate as to slip off my chair; and finally, leaping up in a paroxysm of high spirits to lick my distracted face, Ivo knocked the table over, and there was a most frightful mix-up on the floor of *Fräulein Schmidt and Mr Anstruther*—a story I was just then trying to write,—and ink, and broken glass. Could Shakespeare, could Kipling, have worked under such circumstances?

ELIZABETH VON ARNIM, *All the Dogs of My Life*, 1936

Enter Launce *with his dog* [Crab]

Launce. When a man's servant shall play the cur with him, look you, it goes hard: one that I brought up of a puppy; one that I saved from drowning, when three or four of his blind brothers and sisters went to it. I have taught him, even as one would say precisely, Thus I would teach a dog. I was sent to deliver him as a present to mistress Silvia from my master; and I came no sooner into the dining-chamber, but he steps me to her trencher, and steals her capon's leg. O, 'tis a foul thing, when a cur cannot keep himself in all companies! I would have, as one should say, one that takes upon him to be a dog indeed, to be, as it were, a dog at all things. If I had not had more wit than he, to take a fault upon me that he did, I think verily he had been hanged for't: sure as I live, he had suffer'd for't: you shall judge. He thrusts me himself into the company of three or four gentleman-like dogs under the duke's table: he had not been there (bless the mark) a pissing while, but all the chamber smelt him. 'Out with the dog!' says one; 'What cur is that?' says another; 'Whip him out,' says the third; 'Hang him up,' says the duke. I, having been ac- quainted with the smell before, knew it was Crab; and goes me to the fellow that whips the dogs: 'Friend,' quoth I, 'you mean to whip the dog?' 'Ay, marry, do I,' quoth he. 'You do him the more wrong,' quoth I; ''twas I did the thing you wot of.' He makes me no more ado, but whips me out of the chamber. How many masters would do this for his servant? Nay, I'll be sworn, I have sat in the stocks for puddings he hath stolen, otherwise he had been executed: I have stood on the pillory for geese he hath killed, otherwise he had suffer'd for't: thou thinkest not of this now!—Nay, I remember the trick you served me, when I took my leave of Madam Silvia: did not I bid thee still mark me, and do as I do? When didst thou see me heave up my leg, and make water against a gentlewoman's farthingale? Didst thou ever see me do such a trick?

Enter Proteus *and* Julia.

Pro. Sebastian is thy name? I like thee well,
And will employ thee in some service presently.

Jul. In what you please: I will do what I can.

Pro. I hope thou wilt.—[*To* Launce.]
How now, you whoreson peasant!
Where have you been these two days loitering?

Launce. Marry, sir, I carried mistress Silvia the dog you bade me.

Pro. And what says she to my little jewel?

Launce. Marry, she says, your dog was a cur; and tells you, currish thanks is good enough for such a present.

Pro. But she received my dog?

Launce. No, indeed, did she not: here have I brought him back again.

Pro. What! didst thou offer her this from me?

Launce. Ay, sir: the other squirrel was stolen from me by the hangman boys in the market-place; and then I offered her mine own, who is a dog as big as ten of yours, and therefore the gift the greater.

Pro. Go, get thee hence, and find my dog again,
Or ne'er return again into my sight.

WILLIAM SHAKESPEARE, *The Two Gentlemen of Verona*, IV. iv, ? 1594

Charlotte [Brontë] was more than commonly tender in her treatment of all dumb creatures, and they, with that fine instinct so often noticed, were invariably attracted towards her.

The feeling, which in Charlotte partook of something of the nature of an affection, was, with Emily, more of a passion. Some one speaking of her to

me, in a careless kind of strength of expression, said, 'she never showed
regard to any human creature; all her love was reserved for animals'. The
helplessness of an animal was its passport to Charlotte's heart; the fierce,
wild, intractability of its nature was what often recommended it to Emily.
Speaking of her dead sister, the former told me that from her many traits in
Shirley's character were taken; her way of sitting on the rug reading, with
her arm round her rough bull-dog's neck; her calling to a strange dog,
running past, with hanging head and lolling tongue, to give it a merciful
draught of water, its maddened snap at her, her nobly stern presence of
mind, going right into the kitchen, and taking up one of Tabby's red-hot
Italian irons to sear the bitten place, and telling no one, till the danger was
well-nigh over, for fear of the terrors that might beset their weaker minds.
All this, looked upon as a well-invented fiction in *Shirley*, was written down
by Charlotte with streaming eyes; it was the literal true account of what
Emily had done. The same tawny bull-dog (with his 'strangled whistle'),
called 'Tartar' in *Shirley*, was 'Keeper' in Haworth parsonage; a gift to
Emily. With the gift came a warning. Keeper was faithful to the depths of
his nature as long as he was with friends; but he who struck him with a stick
or whip, roused the relentless nature of the brute, who flew at his throat
forthwith, and held him there till one or the other was at the point of death.
Now Keeper's household fault was this. He loved to steal up-stairs, and
stretch his square, tawny limbs, on the comfortable beds, covered over with
delicate white counterpanes. But the cleanliness of the parsonage arrangements was perfect; and this habit of Keeper's was so objectionable, that
Emily, in reply to Tabby's remonstrances, declared that, if he was found
again transgressing, she herself, in defiance of warning and his well-known
ferocity of nature, would beat him so severely that he would never offend
again. In the gathering dusk of an autumn evening, Tabby came, half
triumphant, half trembling, but in great wrath, to tell Emily that Keeper
was lying on the best bed, in drowsy voluptuousness. Charlotte saw Emily's
whitening face, and set mouth, but dared not speak to interfere; no one
dared when Emily's eyes glowed in that manner out of the paleness of her
face, and when her lips were so compressed into stone. She went upstairs,
and Tabby and Charlotte stood in the gloomy passage below, full of the
dark shadows of coming night. Down-stairs came Emily, dragging after her
the unwilling Keeper, his hind legs set in a heavy attitude of resistance, held
by the 'scuft of his neck', but growling low and savagely all the time. The
watchers would fain have spoken, but durst not, for fear of taking off
Emily's attention, and causing her to avert her head for a moment from the
enraged brute. She let him go, planted in a dark corner at the bottom of the
stairs; no time was there to fetch stick or rod, for fear of the strangling
clutch at her throat—her bare clenched fist struck against his red fierce eyes,
before he had time to make his spring, and, in the language of the turf, she

'punished him' till his eyes were swelled up, and the half-blind stupefied beast was led to his accustomed lair, to have his swelled head fomented and cared for by the very Emily herself. The generous dog owed her no grudge; he loved her dearly ever after; he walked first among the mourners to her funeral; he slept moaning for nights at the door of her empty room, and never, so to speak, rejoiced, dog fashion, after her death. He, in his turn, was mourned over by the surviving sister. Let us somehow hope, in half Red Indian creed, that he follows Emily now; and, when he rests, sleeps on some soft white bed of dreams, unpunished when he awakens to the life of the land of shadows.

ELIZABETH C. GASKELL, *The Life of Charlotte Brontë*, 1857

On the way home from Silverstone I drove with my arm round Brownie, calling her: red setter, sorrel, Indian red, royal sovereign, red-hot poker, sanguine, nut-brown maid, goldfish, marmalade, conker, vixen, crust of bread, 18 carat, carrots, mahogany, chrysanthemum, bloom of rust and blue of shade. In fact, she is my Pocahontas, my nonpareil.

T. H. WHITE (1906–64) (quoted in Sylvia Townsend Warner, *A Biography*, 1967)

The Nymph Complaining for the Death of Her Fawn

The wanton troopers riding by
Have shot my fawn, and it will die.
Ungentle men! They cannot thrive—
To kill thee! Thou ne'er didst alive
Them any harm: alas, nor could
Thy death yet do them any good.
I'm sure I never wished them ill;
Nor do I for all this; nor will:
But if my simple prayers may yet
Prevail with heaven to forget
Thy murder, I will join my tears
Rather than fail. But, O my fears!

   .   .   .   .   .

With sweetest milk, and sugar, first
I it at mine own fingers nursed.
And as it grew, so every day
It waxed more white and sweet than they.
It had so sweet a breath! And oft

I blushed to see its foot more soft,
And white (shall I say than my hand?)
Nay, any lady's of the land.
    It is a wondrous thing, how fleet
'Twas on those little silver feet.
With what a pretty skipping grace,
It oft would challenge me the race:
And when 't had left me far away,
'Twould stay, and run again, and stay.
For it was nimbler much than hinds;
And trod, as on the foúr winds.
    I have a garden of my own
But so with roses overgrown,
And lilies, that you would it guess
To be a little wilderness.
And all the springtime of the year
It only lovèd to be there.
Among the beds of lilies, I
Have sought it oft, where it should lie;
Yet could not, till itself would rise,
Find it, although before mine eyes.
For, in the flaxen lilies' shade,
It like a bank of lilies laid.
Upon the roses it would feed,
Until its lips e'en seemed to bleed:
And then to me 'twould boldly trip,
And print those roses on my lip.
But all its chief delight was still
On roses thus itself to fill:
And its pure virgin limbs to fold
In whitest sheets of lilies cold.
Had it lived long, it would have been
Lilies without, roses within.

ANDREW MARVELL (1621–78)

Three days later we all went to Chapala for the Blessing of the Animals.
Every beast from round the lake, in festive garb, had been taken to receive
this annual benediction. I still felt uneasy in large gatherings, and the crush,
the noise, the smells, were overwhelming. A crowd of mules and bullocks
in garlands and fine hats was pressing in the square outside the church. The
smaller animals had a difficult time of it. There were new-born calves
carried on donkeys' backs, pigs clasped to bosoms, chickens clutched by

clumsy children, canaries in cages, a huge, angry parrot on a stick, guinea-pigs in apron pockets, ducks in baskets, cats immune on roofs, mongrel puppies led by strings, Don Otavio's Maltese terrier and Doña Anna's griffon carried in the arms of chauffeurs, and smelly rabbits carried by their ears; between them wandered straying geese, shuddering horses and a superb white angora goat who was made way for by the bullocks. The church bells went like mad, the priest held up the sacrament, outlined a blessing, people knelt in the dust raising their screeching beasts towards the holy monstrance—*Mamacita del cielo, Madrecita María, Virgen*, howling, braying, yelping, cackling, squeaking . . .

> SYBILLE BEDFORD, 'The End of a Visit', *A Visit to Don Otavio: A Traveller's Tale from Mexico*, 1953

In Egypt an ox is even worshipped in place of a god; its name is Apis. Its distinguishing mark is a bright white spot in the shape of a crescent on the right flank, and it has a knob under the tongue which they call a beetle. It is not lawful for it to exceed a certain number of years of life, and they kill it by drowning it in the fountain of the priests, proceeding with lamentation to look for another to put in its place, and they go on mourning till they have found one, actually shaving the hair off their heads. Nevertheless the search never continues long. When the successor is found it is led by 100 priests to Memphis. It has a pair of shrines, which they call its bedchambers, that supply the nations with auguries: when it enters one this is a joyful sign, but in the other one it portends terrible events. It gives answers to private individuals by taking food out of the hand of those who consult it; it turned away from the hand of Germanicus Caesar, who was made away with not long after. Usually living in retirement, when it sallies forth into assemblies it proceeds with lictors to clear the way, and companies of boys escort it singing a song in its honour; it seems to understand.

> PLINY THE ELDER (AD 23–79), *Natural History* (tr. H. Rackham, 1937)

Recognition

> On the Town Moor the butchers keep their cows,
> A healthy hospice near the abattoirs.
> Something is strange here, but they calmly browse,
> Flicking flies with the nameplate in their ears,
> And ruminate without conclusion, till
> I cross the skyline.
>   In my grey and blue
> They recognise me on the man-made hill

And give a low, surprised, ancestral moo,
Wildly start up on high-heeled feminine feet,
And run to kiss me with a clumsy joy.
Their eyes, like goddesses', sadden when we meet:
I'm not their farmer, nor his bovine boy.

But still they stare, incredulous, in a trance:
Something has come again . . . A second chance . . .

ALISTAIR ELLIOT (b. 1932)

The Lambs of Grasmere (1860)

The upland flocks grew starved and thinned:
   Their shepherds scarce could feed the lambs
Whose milkless mothers butted them,
   Or who were orphaned of their dams.
The lambs athirst for mother's milk
   Filled all the place with piteous sounds:
Their mothers' bones made white for miles
   The pastureless wet pasture grounds.

Day after day, night after night,
   From lamb to lamb the shepherds went,
With teapots for the bleating mouths,
   Instead of nature's nourishment.
The little shivering gaping things
   Soon knew the step that brought them aid,
And fondled the protecting hand,
   And rubbed it with a woolly head.

Then as the days waxed on to weeks,
   It was a pretty sight to see
These lambs with frisky heads and tails
   Skipping and leaping on the lea,
Bleating in tender trustful tones,
   Resting on rocky crag or mound,
And following the beloved feet
   That once had sought for them and found.

These very shepherds of their flocks,
   These loving lambs so meek to please,
Are worthy of recording words
   And honour in their due degrees:

So I might live a hundred years,
    And roam from strand to foreign strand,
Yet not forget this flooded spring
    And scarce-saved lambs of Westmoreland.

                              CHRISTINA ROSSETTI (1830–94)

Lalus. Sweet Lirope I have a lambe
    Newly wayned from the damme,
    Of the right kinde, it is notted,
    Naturally with purple spotted,
    Into laughter it will put you,
    To see how prettily 'twill but you;
    When on sporting it is set,
    It will beate you a corvet,
    And at every nimble bound
    Turne it selfe above the ground;
    When tis hungry it will bleate,
    From your hand to have its meate,
    And when it hath fully fed,
    It will fetch jumpes above your head,
    As innocently to expresse
    Its silly sheepish thankfullnesse,
    When you bid it, it will play,
    Be it either night or day,
    This Lirope I have for thee,
    So thou alone wilt live with me.

Cleon. From him O turne thine eare away,
    And heare me my lov'd Lirope,
    I have a kid as white as milke,
    His skin as soft as Naples silke,
    His hornes in length are wondrous even,
    And curiously by nature writhen;
    It is of th'Arcadian kinde,
    Ther's not the like twixt either Inde;
    If you walke, 'twill walke you by,
    If you sit downe, it downe will lye,
    It with gesture will you wooe,
    And counterfeit those things you doe;
    Ore each hillock it will vault,
    And nimbly doe the summer-sault,
    Upon the hinder legs 'twill goe,

And follow you a furlong so,
And if by chance a tune you roate,
'Twill foote it finely to your note,
Seeke the world and you may misse
To finde out such a thing as this;
This my love I have for thee
So thou'lt leave him and goe with me.

Lirope. Beleeve me youths your gifts are rare,
    And you offer wondrous faire;
    Lalus for lambe, Cleon for kyd,
    'Tis hard to judge which most doth bid,
    And have you two such things in store,
    And I n'er knew of them before?
    Well yet I dare a wager lay
    That Brag my litle dog shall play,
    As dainty tricks when I shall bid,
    As Lalus lambe, or Cleons kid.
    But t'may fall out that I may need them
    Till when yee may doe well to feed them;
    Your goate and mutton pretty be
    But youths these are noe bayts for me,
    Alasse good men, in vaine ye wooe,
    'Tis not your lambe nor kid will doe.

        MICHAEL DRAYTON (1563–1631), *The Muses Elizium*

The Shepherd Boy

The fly or beetle on their track
Are things that know no sin
And when they whemble on their back
What terror they seem in
The shepherd boy wi' bits o' bents
Will turn them up again
And start them where they nimbly went
Along the grassy plain
And such the shepherd boy is found
While lying on the sun crackt ground

The lady-bird that seldom stops
From climbing all the day
Climbs up the rushes tassle tops

Spreads wings and flies away
He sees them—lying on the grass
Musing the whole day long
And clears the way to let them pass
And sings a nameless song
He watches pismires on the hill
Always busy never still

He sees the traveller beetle run
Where thick the grass wood weaves
To hide the black-snail from the sun
He props up plantain leaves
The lady-cows have got a house
Within the cowslip pip
The spider weaving for his spouse
On threads will often slip
So looks and lyes the shepherd boy
The summer long his whole employ—

JOHN CLARE (1793–1864)

A Flye that Flew into my Mistris her Eye

While this Flye liv'd, she us'd to play
In the bright sunshine all the day;
Till, comming neere my Celia's sight,
She found a new and unknowne light,
So full of glory, that it made
The noone-day sun a gloomy shade;
At last this amorous Fly became
My rivall, and did court my flame.
She did from hand to bosome skip,
And from her breasts, her cheeke, and lip,
Suckt all the incense and the spice,
And grew a Bird of Paradise:
At last into her eye she flew;
There scorcht in heate and drown'd in dew,
Like Phaeton, from the sun's spheare
She fell, and with her dropt a teare,
Of which a pearle was straight compos'd,
Wherein her ashes lye enclos'd.
Thus she receiv'd from Celia's eye
Funerall flame, tombe, obsequie.

THOMAS CAREW (1594/5–1640)

Spiders

She played the piano sometimes in summer,
when westering sunlight through the open window
gave tarnished candlesticks and dusty curtains
a gentle elegance, so that not to age,
not to fade, would have seemed a lapse of taste.
The hesitant arpeggios, broken trills,
brought great shy listeners from the creepered trellis.
Scuttle, and pause, scuttle and pause, came spiders
on tentative delicate legs, to hear the music;
and I, a child, stayed with them, unafraid—
till turning from the yellow keys, one day
she told me of a room where long ago
it had been she who saw the spiders drawn
helpless by threads of music, and listened with them.
Then I felt shut with her into that dream
of endless corridors, rooms within rooms,
mirrors on mirrors compulsively reflected;
while down the corridors, nearer and nearer,
came the great spiders delicately walking.

RUTH BIDGOOD (b. 1922)

Among the numerous afflictions which the Europeans have entailed upon
some of the natives of the South Seas, is the accidental introduction among
them of that enemy of all repose and ruffler of even tempers—the Mosquito.
At the Sandwich Islands and at two or three of the Society group there are
now thriving colonies of these insects, who promise ere long to supplant
altogether the aboriginal sand-flies. They sting, buzz, and torment, from
one end of the year to the other, and by incessantly exasperating the natives
materially obstruct the benevolent labours of the missionaries.

From this grievous visitation, however, the Typees are as yet wholly
exempt; but its place is unfortunately in some degree supplied by the
occasional presence of a minute species of fly, which, without stinging, is
nevertheless productive of no little annoyance. The tameness of the birds
and lizards is as nothing when compared to the fearless confidence of this
insect. He will perch upon one of your eyelashes, and go to roost there, if
you do not disturb him, or force his way through your hair, or along the
cavity of the nostril, till you almost fancy he is resolved to explore the very
brain itself. On one occasion I was so inconsiderate as to yawn while a
number of them were hovering around me. I never repeated the act. Some
half-dozen darted into the open apartment, and began walking about its

ceiling; the sensation was dreadful. I involuntarily closed my mouth, and the poor creatures being enveloped in inner darkness, must in their consternation have stumbled over my palate, and been precipitated into the gulf beneath. At any rate, though I afterwards charitably held my mouth open for at least five minutes, with a view of affording egress to the stragglers, none of them ever availed themselves of the opportunity.

HERMAN MELVILLE, *Typee*, 1846

Serious Readers

All the flies are reading microscopic books;
They hold themselves quite tense and silent
With shoulders hunched, legs splayed out
On the white formica table-top, reading.
With my book I slide into the diner-booth;
They rise and circle and settle again, reading
With hunched corselets. They do not attempt to taste
Before me my fat hamburger-plate, but wait,
Like courteous readers until I put it to one side,
Then taste briefly and resume their tomes
Like reading-stands with horny specs. I
Read as I eat, one fly
Alights on my book, the size of print;
I let it be. Read and let read.

PETER REDGROVE (b. 1932)

To a Louse, On Seeing one on a Lady's Bonnet at Church

Ha! whare ye gaun, ye crowlan ferlie!
Your impudence protects you sairly:
I canna say but ye strunt rarely,
            Owre *gawze* and *lace*;
Tho' faith, I fear ye dine but sparely,
            On sic a place.

Ye ugly, creepan, blastet wonner,
Detested, shunn'd, by saunt an' sinner,

ferlie: 'term of contempt'   *strunt*: move with assurance   *wonner*: wonder, marvel

How daur ye set your fit upon her,
    Sae fine a *Lady*!
Gae somewhere else and seek your dinner,
    On some poor body.

Swith, in some beggar's haffet squattle;
There ye may creep, and sprawl, and sprattle,
Wi' ither kindred, jumping cattle,
    In shoals and nations;
Whare *horn* nor *bane* ne'er daur unsettle,
    Your thick plantations.

Now haud you there, ye're out o' sight,
Below the fatt'rels, snug and tight,
Na faith ye yet! ye'll no be right,
    Till ye've got on it,
The vera tapmost, towrin height
    O' *Miss's bonnet*.

My sooth! right bauld ye set your nose out,
As plump an' gray as onie grozet:
O for some rank, mercurial rozet,
    Or fell, red smeddum,
I'd gie you sic a hearty dose o't,
    Wad dress your droddum!

I wad na been surpriz'd to spy
You on an auld wife's *flainen toy*;
Or aiblins some bit duddie boy,
    On 's *wylecoat*;
But Miss's fine *Lunardi*, fye!
    How daur ye do't?

O *Jenny* dinna toss your head,
An' set your beauties a' abroad!
Ye little ken what cursed speed
    The blastie's makin!

---

haffet: lock of hair growing on the temple   *squattle*: squat, nestle   *sprattle*: struggle, clamber   *fatt'rels*: ribbon ends   *grozet*: gooseberry   *rozet*: resin   *smeddum*: fine powder used as insecticide   *droddum*: backside   *flainen toy*: flannel cap   *aiblins*: perhaps   *duddie*: ragged, tattered   *wylecoat*: flannel vest   *Lunardi*: a kind of bonnet named after the Italian balloonist   *blastie*: ill-tempered creature

Thae *winks* and *finger-ends*, I dread,
Are notice takin!

O wad some Pow'r the giftie gie us
To see oursels as others see us!
It wad frae monie a blunder free us
An' foolish notion:
What airs in dress an' gait wad lea'e us,
And ev'n Devotion!

Robert Burns (1759–96), *Poems*, 1786

How soft a Caterpillar steps—
I find one on my Hand
From such a velvet world it comes
Such plushes at command
Its soundless travels just arrest
My slow—terrestrial eye
Intent upon its own career
What use has it for me—

Emily Dickinson (1830–86)

After the death of his parents, the narrator finds his childhood books in an attic.

Well, as I told you, though it may for some people not be an earth-shattering event to remember themselves, it was for me as if my life had been turned upside down. I also discovered a room that thirty and some odd years ago had been my nursery; later it was used to store linen and the like, but the room had essentially been left the way it was when I sat there at my pinewood table beneath the kerosene lamp whose chain was decorated with three dolphins. There I sat once again for many hours a day, and read like a child whose legs are too short to touch the floor. For you see, we are accustomed to an unbounded head, reaching out into the empty ether, because we have solid ground beneath our feet. But childhood means to be as yet ungrounded at both ends, to still have soft flannel hands, instead of adult pincers, to sit before a book as though perched on a little leaf soaring over bottomless abysses through the room. And at that table, I tell you, I really couldn't reach the floor.

I also set myself a bed in this room and slept there. And then the blackbird came again. Once after midnight I was awakened by a wonderful, beautiful singing. I didn't wake up right away, but listened first for a long time in my sleep. It was the song of the nightingale; she wasn't perched in the garden bushes, but sat instead on the rooftop of a neighbor's house. Then I slept on a while with my eyes open. And I thought to myself: there are no nightingales here, it's a blackbird.

But don't think this is the same story I already told you today! No—because just as I was thinking: there are no nightingales here, it's a blackbird—at that very moment, I woke up. It was four in the morning, daylight streamed into my eyes, sleep sank away as quickly as the last trace of a wave is soaked up by the dry sand at the beach. And there, veiled in daylight as in a soft woolen scarf, a blackbird sat in the open window! It sat there just as sure as I sit here now.

I am your blackbird—it said—don't you remember me?

I really didn't remember right away, but I felt happy all over while the bird spoke to me.

I sat on this window sill once before, don't you remember?—it continued, and then I answered: yes, one day you sat there just where you now sit, and I quickly closed the window, shutting it in.

I am your mother—it said.

This part, I admit, I may very well have dreamed. But the bird itself I didn't dream up; she sat there, flew into my room, and I quickly shut the window. I went up to the attic and looked for a large wooden bird cage that I seemed to remember, for the blackbird had visited me once before—in my childhood, like I just told you. She sat on my window-sill and then flew into my room, and I needed a cage. But she soon grew tame, and I didn't keep her locked up anymore, she lived free in my room and flew in and out. And one day she didn't come back again, and now she had returned. I had no desire to worry about whether it was the same blackbird; I found the cage and a new box of books to boot, and all I can tell you is that I had never before been such a good person as from that day on: the day I had my blackbird back again—but how can I explain to you what I mean by being a good person?

Did she often speak again?—Aone asked craftily.

No—said Atwo—she didn't speak. But I had to find birdfood for her and worms. You can imagine that it was rather difficult for me: I mean the fact that she ate worms, and I was supposed to think of her as my mother—but it's possible to get used to anything, I tell you, it's just a matter of time—and don't most everyday matters likewise take getting used to! Since then I've never let her leave me, and that's about all I have to tell; this is the third story, and I don't know how it's going to end.

Robert Musil, 'The Blackbird', Posthumous Papers of a Living Author, 1936
(tr. Peter Wortsman, 1987)

A friend of mine has sent me the following particulars respecting a tame white owl, which was taken, when young, from a nest in the woods at Dilstone, near Hexham in Northumberland, and given by a lady to her children, who brought it up. Great pains appear to have been taken to domesticate this owl, in consequence of which it became very familiar. In imitation of its own call, it received the name of *Keevie*, to which it would readily answer when within hearing, following the sound from whatever part of the premises it might happen to be in. Its usual place of repose during the day was under the branches of an old Scotch fir, which grew down a steep inaccessible bank, where it would sit apparently asleep, but sufficiently awake to endeavour to attract the notice of any one who passed, by its usual cry of *keevie, keevie*. If the passenger stopped and answered it, it immediately scrambled up the boughs of the fir, till it brought itself to a level with the walk above, in hopes of being fed; but if he went on again, unheeding its solicitations, it returned to its former place, and resumed its slumbers. One of the most striking peculiarities in this tame owl is said to have been its fondness for music. It would often come into the drawing-room of an evening, on the shoulder of one of the children, and, on hearing the tones of the piano, would sit with its eyes gravely fixed on the instrument, and its head on one side in an attitude of attention; when, suddenly spreading his wings, he would alight on the keys, and making a dart at the performer's fingers with its beak, would continue hopping about, as if pleased with the execution.

After a while the flights of this owl into the woods became longer, and he only returned at dusk to receive his usual supper from the person who was in the habit of feeding him, and whom he readily permitted at such times to take him up, and carry him into the house for this purpose. Bye-and-bye it was observed that he did not devour his meal in the kitchen as formerly, but fled along the passage, dragging the meat after him, till he reached the garden-door, when he flew with it to a part of the shrubbery: on being followed, it was discovered that he had brought with him a companion, who, not having courage to accompany him the whole way, remained at a respectful distance to receive his bounty. After having served his visitor in this manner, he returned to the kitchen, and leisurely devoured his own portion. This practice was continued for some months, till at length one evening he was missed, and nowhere to be found: his companion, it is said, continued to visit the spot alone for several weeks uttering doleful cries, but could never be persuaded to come nearer to be fed. It proved, in the end, that the favourite had been killed; and its stuffed skin was one day recognized, alas! in a woodman's hut, by the children, who had so assiduously nurtured it and brought it up.

REVD LEONARD JENYNS, *Observations in Natural History*, 1846

The robin's relation with mankind seems unique. Most birds avoid mankind, usually with too good cause. That this is an artificial and quite unnecessary state of affairs is shown by the well-known fact that the birds of regions uninhabited by man show no such fear. On Bear Island I have picked guillemots off their eggs, and in the Galapagos flycatchers have tried to remove the hair of my head as nesting material, a habit also accredited to the kite in London in the second century A.D.

In winter in Britain garden birds of many kinds will come to food when it is put out for them, but all of these except the robin tend to retain their habitual shyness and at most come to ignore their benefactor. The robin, on the other hand, is not only remarkably tame but actively seeks out man's habitations at this season, and though this seems entirely inspired by the search for food, there is no other British bird which regularly enters into so domestic a relationship.

H. Coxeter told me of a robin which he had tamed to take food from him. There came a time when he had to shut up his house for half a year. On his return to the garden for the first time in six months he felt a sudden fluttering at his shoulder, and there was his robin. Lord Grey describes a similar incident, so it is clear that a robin can remember back for at least six months.

Much more remarkable is a case related by Renier. He had tamed a cock Robin to take food from him during the winter and it continued to do so during the spring. He eventually saw this cock and its mate visiting their nest, so he approached to look, at which the cock robin perched within a foot of his head and postured violently at him, *i.e.*, it treated Renier just as it would treat another robin. No tamer of robins could wish for a greater compliment, even though such treatment must be unfriendly. Renier also once observed threat display from his tamed robin when the supply of mealworms temporarily gave out, and M. K. Colquhoun records putting out food in Kew Gardens for a tame robin, which then postured at him. But further data are needed before these two latter instances can be satisfactorily interpreted.

Though so tame in taking food, the robin will not make a pet. Trusting it often becomes, but friendly never. In contrast, a tame raven, parrot, goose or gull will follow its human owner about with evident friendliness. The reason for the difference is to be found in the natural behaviour of these birds. The birds which make friendly pets are naturally social outside the breeding season; on seeing a fellow member of their own kind they normally associate with it, and their friendliness to mankind is rightly so-called, since it is simply their natural social behaviour directed towards man instead of towards their own kind. The robin, on the other hand, is solitary all the year round, and on meeting a fellow member of its species it normally fights it, hence almost the only part of its behaviour available for transfer to man is hostility. That the latter is occasionally transferred is shown by Renier's tame robin.

DAVID LACK, *The Life of the Robin*, 1943

Mary . . . went down the path and through the second green door. There she found more walls and winter vegetables and glass frames, but in the second wall there was another green door and it was not open. Perhaps it led into the garden which no one had seen for ten years.

She could see the tops of trees above the wall, and when she stood still she saw a bird with a bright red breast sitting on the topmost branch of one of them, and suddenly he burst into his winter song—almost as if he had caught sight of her and was calling to her.

She stopped and listened to him, and somehow his cheerful, friendly little whistle gave her a pleased feeling—even a disagreeable little girl may be lonely, and the big closed house and big bare moor and big bare gardens had made this one feel as if there was no one left in the world but herself. If she had been an affectionate child, who had been used to being loved, she would have broken her heart, but even though she was 'Mistress Mary Quite Contrary' she was desolate, and the bright-breasted little bird brought a look into her sour little face which was almost a smile. She listened to him until he flew away. He was not like an Indian bird, and she liked him and wondered if she should ever see him again. Perhaps he lived in the mysterious garden and knew all about it.

Perhaps it was because she had nothing whatever to do that she thought so much of the deserted garden.

She thought of the robin and of the way he seemed to sing his song at her, and as she remembered the tree-top he perched on she stopped rather suddenly on the path.

'I believe that tree was in the secret garden—I feel sure it was,' she said. 'There was a wall round the place and there was no door.'

She walked back into the first kitchen-garden she had entered and found the old man digging there. She went and stood beside him and watched him a few moments in her cold little way. He took no notice of her, and so at last she spoke to him.

'I have been into the other gardens,' she said.

'There was nothin' to prevent thee,' he answered crustily.

'I went into the orchard.'

'There was no dog at th' door to bite thee,' he answered.

'There was no door there into the other garden,' said Mary.

'What garden?' he said in a rough voice, stopping his digging for a moment.

'The one on the other side of the wall,' answered Mistress Mary. 'There are trees there—I saw the tops of them. A bird with a red breast was sitting on one of them, and he sang.'

To her surprise the surly old weather-beaten face actually changed its expression. A slow smile spread over it and the gardener looked quite different. It made her think that it was curious how much nicer a person looked when he smiled. She had not thought of it before.

He turned about to the orchard side of his garden and began to whistle—a low soft whistle. She could not understand how such a surly man could make such a coaxing sound.

Almost the next moment a wonderful thing happened. She heard a soft little rushing flight through the air—and it was the bird with the red breast flying to them, and he actually alighted on the big clod of earth quite near to the gardener's foot.

'Here he is,' chuckled the old man, and then he spoke to the bird as if he were speaking to a child.

'Where has tha' been, tha' cheeky little beggar?' he said. 'I've not seen thee before to-day. Has tha' begun tha' courtin' this early in th' season? Tha'rt too forrad.'

The bird put his tiny head on one side and looked up at him with his soft bright eye which was like a black dewdrop. He seemed quite familiar and not the least afraid. He hopped about and pecked the earth briskly, looking for seeds and insects. It actually gave Mary a queer feeling in her heart, because he was so pretty and cheerful and seemed so like a person. He had a tiny plump body and a delicate beak, and slender delicate legs.

'Will he always come when you call him?' she asked almost in a whisper.

'Aye, that he will. I've knowed him ever since he was a fledgling. He come out of th' nest in th' other garden, an' when first he flew over th' wall he was too weak to fly back for a few days an' we got friendly. When he went over th' wall again th' rest of th' brood was gone an' he was lonely an' he come back to me.'

'What kind of a bird is he?' Mary asked.

'Doesn't tha' know? He's a robin redbreast, an' they're th' friendliest, curiousest birds alive. They're almost as friendly as dogs—if you know how to get on with 'em. Watch him peckin' about there an' lookin' round at us now an' again. He knows we're talkin' about him.'

It was the queerest thing in the world to see the old fellow. He looked at the plump little scarlet-waistcoated bird as if he were both proud and fond of him.

'He's a conceited one,' he chuckled. 'He likes to hear folk talk about him. An' curious—bless me, there never was his like for curiosity an' meddlin.' He's always comin' to see what I'm plantin'. He knows all th' things Mester Craven never troubles hissel' to find out. He's th' head gardener, he is.'

The robin hopped about busily pecking the soil, and now and then stopped and looked at them a little. Mary thought his black dewdrop eyes gazed at her with great curiosity. It really seemed as if he were finding out all about her. The queer feeling in her heart increased.

'Where did the rest of the brood fly to?' she asked.

'There's no knowin'. The old ones turn 'em out o' their nest an' make 'em fly, an' they're scattered before you know it. This one was a knowin' one an' he knew he was lonely.'

Mistress Mary went a step nearer to the robin and looked at him very hard.

'I'm lonely,' she said.

She had not known before that this was one of the things which made her feel sour and cross. She seemed to find it out when the robin looked at her and she looked at the robin.

The old gardener pushed his cap back on his bald head and stared at her a minute.

'Art tha' th' little wench from India?' he asked.

Mary nodded.

'Then no wonder tha'rt lonely. Tha'lt be lonelier before tha's done,' he said.

He began to dig again, driving his spade deep into the rich black garden soil while the robin hopped about very busily employed.

'What is your name?' Mary inquired.

He stood up to answer her.

'Ben Weatherstaff,' he answered, and then he added with a surly chuckle, 'I'm lonely mysel' except when he's with me,' and he jerked his thumb toward the robin. 'He's th' only friend I've got.'

Suddenly a clear rippling little sound broke out near her and she turned round. She was standing a few feet from a young apple-tree, and the robin had flown on to one of its branches and had burst out into a scrap of a song. Ben Weatherstaff laughed outright.

'What did he do that for?' asked Mary.

'He's made up his mind to make friends with thee,' replied Ben. 'Dang me if he hasn't took a fancy to thee.'

Frances Hodgson Burnett, The Secret Garden, 1911

Friday June 25th.

When I rose I went just before tea into the Garden, I looked up at my Swallow's nest & it was gone. It had fallen down. Poor little creatures they could not themselves be more distressed than I was I went upstairs to look at the Ruins. They lay in a large heap upon the window ledge; these

Swallows had been ten days employed in building this nest, & it seemed to be almost finished—I had watched them early in the morning, in the day many & many a time & in the evenings when it was almost dark I had seen them sitting together side by side in their unfinished nest both morning & night. When they first came about the window they used to hang against the panes, with their white Bellies & their forked tails looking like fish, but then they fluttered & sang their own little twittering song. As soon as the nest was broad enough, a sort of ledge for them they sate both mornings & evenings, but they did not pass the night there. I watched them one morning when William was at Eusemere, for more than an hour. Every now & then there was a feeling motion in their wings a sort of tremulousness & they sang a low song to one another.

[*Tuesday 29th June.*] . . .

It is now 8 o'clock I will go & see if my swallows are on their nest. Yes! there they are side by side both looking down into the garden. I have been out on purpose to see their faces. I knew by looking at the window that they were there.

DOROTHY WORDSWORTH, *The Grasmere Journals*, 1802

He was called Loulou. His body was green, the tips of his wings were pink, his brow was blue, and his breast golden.

But he had a tiresome passion for chewing his perch, he plucked his feathers out, scattered his droppings, spilt his bath-water. Much annoyed, Mme Aubain gave him to Félicité for good.

Félicité undertook his education. Soon he was repeating, 'Charming boy! At your service, sir! Hail Mary!' He was placed near the door, and people were surprised that he didn't answer to the name of Jacquot, since all parrots were called Jacquot. They compared him to a turkey, to a block of wood: so many daggers piercing Félicité's heart! Strangely obstinate of Loulou, to stop talking the moment anyone looked at him!

All the same, he was keen on company, for on Sundays, when the Rochefeuille sisters, M. Houppeville and some new acquaintances—the apothecary Onfroy, M. Varin and Captain Mathieu—were at their game of cards, he would rap on the window-panes with his wings, and agitate so furiously that they couldn't hear themselves speak.

Certainly Bourais's face struck him as very funny. As soon as he caught sight of it, he burst into laughter, laughing with all his might. His shrieks bounced around the yard, followed by their echoes; the neighbours gathered at their windows and laughed too. So that the parrot shouldn't see him, M. Bourais would creep along the wall, hiding his face behind his hat, until he reached the river, and then come in through the garden gate. The looks he gave the parrot lacked tenderness.

Once the butcher's boy had flicked Loulou for having made so free as to poke his nose into the basket; and from that day he was always trying to nip the boy through his shirt. Fabu threatened to wring his neck, but he was not cruel, despite the tattoos on his arms and his thick sideburns. On the contrary, he was rather fond of the bird, to the point of wanting to teach him a few swear-words for fun. Alarmed by these carrying-ons, Félicité installed the bird in the kitchen. His little chain was removed, and he could move freely about the house.

Three years later Félicité became deaf . . . The small circle of her ideas grew still narrower, and the pealing of the bells and the lowing of the cattle ceased to exist for her. All living creatures went about their business as silently as ghosts. Only one sound reached her ears now, the voice of the parrot.

As if to entertain her, he would copy the tick-tock of the turnspit, the shrill cry of a fishmonger, the joiner's saw across the way; and when the bell rang, he would imitate Mme Aubain: 'Félicité! The door! The door!'

They held conversations, he spouting the three phrases of his repertoire *ad nauseam*, and she answering them in words equally disjointed, in which she poured out her heart. In her isolation, Loulou was almost a son, a lover. He climbed up her fingers, nibbled at her lips, clinging to her shawl, and as she bent over him, wagging her head as nannies do, the wide wings of her bonnet and the wings of the bird quivered in unison.

When the clouds gathered and the thunder rumbled, he would let out shrieks, perhaps remembering the showers of his native forests. The streaming water sent him into a frenzy; he fluttered around frantically, mounted to the ceiling, knocking everything over, and then flew through the window to splash about in the garden. But he soon came back in, to perch on one of the firedogs, hopping around to dry his feathers, now showing his tail, now his beak.

One morning during the terrible winter of 1837, when Félicité had put him in front of the fire because of the cold, she found him dead in the middle of his cage, his head hanging down, his claws between the bars. Probably congestion of the lungs had killed him; she believed he had been poisoned by parsley and, despite the absence of any proof, her suspicions fell on Fabu.

She cried so much that her mistress told her: 'Well, have him stuffed!'

At last Loulou arrived—splendidly erect on a branch of tree screwed to a mahogany stand, one foot raised, the head cocked to the side, and biting on a nut which the taxidermist, out of love of the grandiose, had gilded.

Félicité shut him up in her room.

This place, to which she admitted very few people, contained so many religious objects and miscellaneous knick-knacks that it looked at the same time like a chapel and a bazaar . . . By means of a small bracket, Loulou was lodged on a chimney-piece jutting out into the room. Every morning when Félicité awoke, she could see him in the first light of dawn, and she remembered bygone days, and insignificant happenings in the smallest detail, without sorrow, in all tranquillity . . .

In church she constantly gazed at the Holy Ghost, observing that it had something of the parrot about it. The likeness appeared even more obvious in a popular colour-print representing the baptism of Our Lord. With its purple wings and emerald body, it was the very image of Loulou.

Having bought the print, she hung it so that at one glance she could see the two together. They were linked in her mind, the parrot finding himself sanctified by this relationship with the Holy Ghost, while the latter became more alive in her eyes and more intelligible. To speak to us, God the Father couldn't have chosen a dove, since those creatures have no voice, but rather one of Loulou's ancestors. Félicité said her prayers with her eyes on the picture, but from time to time she turned a little towards the bird.

Her last agony began. A rattle, coming faster and faster, lifted her ribs. Bubbles of froth gathered at the corners of her mouth, and her whole body shook . . . Then she closed her eyes. Her lips were smiling. Her heart-beats grew slower one by one, and softer, like a fountain running out, an echo dying away. And as she breathed her last, she thought she was seeing, in the half-open heavens, an immense parrot hovering over her head.

GUSTAVE FLAUBERT, 'Un coeur simple', 1877 (tr. D. J. Enright and Madeleine Enright, 1994)

An old German proverb says that one crow will not peck out the eye of another and for once the proverb is right. A tame crow or raven will no more think of pecking at your eye than he will at that of one of his own kind. Often when Roah, my tame raven, was sitting on my arm, I purposely put my face so near to his bill that my open eye came close to its wickedly curved point. Then Roah did something positively touching. With a nervous, worried movement he withdrew his beak from my eye, just as a father who is shaving will hold back his razor blade from the inquisitive fingers of his tiny daughter. Only in one particular connection did Roah ever approach my eye with his bill during this facial grooming. Many of the higher, social birds and mammals, above all monkeys, will groom the skin of a fellow-member of their species in those parts of his body to which he himself cannot obtain access. In birds, it is particularly the head and the region of the eyes which are dependent on the attentions of a fellow. In my description of the jackdaw I have already spoken of the gestures with which these birds invite one another to preen their head feathers. When, with half-shut eyes, I held my head sideways towards Roah, just as corvine birds do to each other, he understood this movement in spite of the fact that I have no head feathers to ruffle, and at once began to groom me. While doing so, he never pinched my skin, for the epidermis of birds is delicate and would not stand such rough treatment. With wonderful precision, he submitted every attainable hair to a dry-cleaning process by drawing it separately through his bill. He worked with the same intensive concentration that distinguishes the 'lousing' monkey and the operating surgeon. This is not meant as a joke: the social grooming of monkeys, and particularly of anthropoid apes, has not the object of catching vermin—these animals usually have none—and is not limited to the cleaning of the skin, but serves also more remarkable operations, for instance the dexterous removal of thorns and even the squeezing-out of small carbuncles.

KONRAD LORENZ, *King Solomon's Ring*, 1952

At that time I had a marmoset called Mitz which accompanied me almost everywhere, sitting on my shoulder or inside my waistcoat. . . .

Mitz was a curious character. I kept her alive for five years, which was a year longer . . . than the Zoo had ever been able to keep a marmoset. She was eventually killed by a terrible cold snap at Christmas when the electricity failed for the whole of a bitter cold night at Rodmell. During the day she was always with me, but the moment it became dark in the evening she left me, scuttled across the room into a large birdcage which I kept full of scraps of silk. She rolled herself into a ball in the middle of the silk and slept until the next morning—the moment the sun rose, she left the cage and came over to me. She was extremely jealous, a trait which I on occasions took advantage of to outwit her. She was always quite free in the house, but I had to be careful not to let her get out into the garden at Rodmell by herself, for, if she did, she would climb up a tree and refuse to come down. When this happened, I usually succeeded in getting her back by climbing a ladder and holding out to her a butterfly net in which I had put the lid of a tin with a little honey on it. She was so fond of honey that usually she could not resist it and then I caught her in the net.

Late one summer afternoon on a Sunday, when we were just going to get into the car to drive back to London, she escaped into the garden at Rodmell and climbed about 30 foot up a lime-tree at the gate. When I called to her to come down, I could see her small head among the leaves watching me, but she would not budge. I tried the butterfly net trick, but not even the honey would tempt her. So I got Virginia to stand with me under the tree and I kissed her. Mitz came down as fast as she could and jumped on my shoulder chattering with anger. We successfully played the same trick on her another time when she got away into a large fig-tree and I could not dislodge her. She was rather fond of a spaniel which I had at the time and in cold weather liked to snuggle up against the dog in front of a hot fire. She would eat almost anything. Meal-worms and fruit were regular articles of her diet. She once caught and ate a lizard and the Zoo keeper told me that in the open-air cage their marmosets would sometimes catch and eat sparrows. Mitz had a passion for macaroons and tapioca pudding. When given tapioca, she seized it in both hands and stuffed her mouth so full that large blobs of tapioca oozed out at both sides of her face.

LEONARD WOOLF, *Downhill all the Way* (vol. iv of his autobiography), 1919–39

Selborne, September 9, 1767.
I was much entertained last summer with a tame bat, which would take flies out of a person's hand. If you gave it anything to eat, it brought its wings round before the mouth, hovering and hiding its head in the manner of birds of prey when they feed. The adroitness it showed in shearing off the wings of the flies, which were always rejected, was worthy of observation, and pleased me much. Insects seem to be most acceptable, though it did not refuse raw flesh when offered: so that the notion that bats go down chimnies and gnaw men's bacon, seems no improbable story. While I amused myself with this wonderful quadruped, I saw it several times confute the vulgar opinion, that bats when down on a flat surface cannot get on the wing again, by rising with great ease from the floor. It ran, I observed, with more dispatch than I was aware of; but in a most ridiculous and grotesque manner.

GILBERT WHITE (1720–93), *The Natural History of Selborne*

The Badgers

When the badger glimmered away
into another garden
you stood, half-lit with whiskey,
sensing you had disturbed
some soft returning.

The murdered dead,
you thought.
But could it not have been
some violent shattered boy

nosing out what got mislaid
between the cradle and the explosion,
evenings when windows stood open
and the compost smoked down the backs?

Visitations are taken for signs.
At a second house I listened
for duntings under the laurels
and heard intimations whispered
about being vaguely honoured.

And to read even by carcasses
the badgers have come back.
One that grew notorious
lay untouched in the roadside.
Last night one had me braking
but more in fear than in honour.

Cool from the sett and redolent
of his runs under the night,
the bogey of fern country
broke cover in me
for what he is:
pig family
and not at all what he's painted.

How perilous is it to choose
not to love the life we're shown?
His sturdy dirty body
and interloping grovel.
The intelligence in his bone.
The unquestionable houseboy's shoulders
that could have been my own.

SEAMUS HEANEY (b. 1939)

Enter Groom of the Stable.
Groom. Hail, royal prince!
K. Rich.   Thanks, noble peer;
    The cheapest of us is ten groats too dear.
    What art thou? and how comest thou hither, man,
    Where no man never comes but that sad dog
    That brings me food to make misfortune live?

Groom. I was a poor groom of thy stable, king,
   When thou wert king; who, travelling towards York,
   With much ado at length have gotten leave
   To look upon my sometimes royal master's face.
   O! how it yearn'd my heart when I beheld
   In London streets, that coronation day
   When Bolingbroke rode on roan Barbary,
   That horse that thou so often hast bestrid,
   That horse that I so carefully have dress'd.
K. Rich. Rode he on Barbary? Tell me, gentle friend,
   How went he under him?
Groom. So proudly as if he disdain'd the ground.
K. Rich. So proud that Bolingbroke was on his back!
   That jade hath eat bread from my royal hand;
   This hand hath made him proud with clapping him.
   Would he not stumble? Would he not fall down,—
   Since pride must have a fall,—and break the neck
   Of that proud man that did usurp his back?
   Forgiveness, horse! why do I rail on thee,
   Since thou, created to be aw'd by man,
   Wast born to bear? I was not made a horse;
   And yet I bear a burden like an ass,
   Spur-gall'd and tir'd by jauncing Bolingbroke.

                    WILLIAM SHAKESPEARE, *Richard II*, v. v, 1597

The Horses

Barely a twelvemonth after
The seven days war that put the world to sleep,
Late in the evening the strange horses came.
By then we had made our covenant with silence,
But in the first few days it was so still
We listened to our breathing and were afraid.
On the second day
The radios failed; we turned the knobs; no answer.
On the third day a warship passed us, heading north,
Dead bodies piled on the deck. On the sixth day
A plane plunged over us into the sea. Thereafter
Nothing. The radios dumb;
And still they stand in corners of our kitchens,
And stand, perhaps, turned on, in a million rooms

All over the world. But now if they should speak,
If on a sudden they should speak again,
If on the stroke of noon a voice should speak,
We would not listen, we would not let it bring
That old bad world that swallowed its children quick
At one great gulp. We would not have it again.
Sometimes we think of the nations lying asleep,
Curled blindly in impenetrable sorrow,
And then the thought confounds us with its strangeness.
The tractors lie about our fields; at evening
They look like dank sea-monsters couched and waiting.
We leave them where they are and let them rust:
'They'll moulder away and be like other loam'.
We make our oxen drag our rusty ploughs,
Long laid aside. We have gone back
Far past our fathers' land.
                              And then, that evening
Late in the summer the strange horses came.
We heard a distant tapping on the road,
A deepening drumming; it stopped, went on again
And at the corner changed to hollow thunder.
We saw the heads
Like a wild wave charging and were afraid.
We had sold our horses in our fathers' time
To buy new tractors. Now they were strange to us
As fabulous steeds set on an ancient shield
Or illustrations in a book of knights.
We did not dare go near them. Yet they waited,
Stubborn and shy, as if they had been sent
By an old command to find our whereabouts
And that long-lost archaic companionship.
In the first moment we had never a thought
That they were creatures to be owned and used.
Among them were some half-a-dozen colts
Dropped in some wilderness of the broken world,
Yet new as if they had come from their own Eden.
Since then they have pulled our ploughs and borne our loads,
But that free servitude still can pierce our hearts.
Our life is changed; their coming our beginning.

EDWIN MUIR (1887–1959)

[*Banda Oriental, Nov. 1833*]

November 14th

In the morning we rose early in the hopes of being able to ride a good distance; but it was a vain attempt, for all the rivers were flooded. We passed in boats the streams of Canelones, St Lucia, and San José, and thus lost much time. On a former excursion I crossed the Lucia, near its mouth, and I was surprised to observe how easily our horses, although not used to swim, passed over a width of at least 600 yards. On mentioning this at Monte Video I was told that a vessel containing some mountebanks and their horses, being wrecked in the Plata, one horse swam seven miles to the shore. In the course of the day I was amused by the dexterity with which a Gaucho forced a restive horse to swim a river. He stripped off his clothes, and jumping on its back, rode into the water till it was out of its depth; then slipping off over the crupper, he caught hold of the tail, and as often as the horse turned round, the man frightened it back, by splashing water in its face. As soon as the horse touched the bottom on the other side, the man pulled himself on, and was firmly seated, bridle in hand, before the horse gained the bank. A naked man, on a naked horse, is a fine spectacle; I had no idea how well the two animals suited each other. The tail of a horse is a very useful appendage; I have passed a river in a boat with four people in it, which was ferried across in the same way as the Gaucho. If a man and horse have to cross a broad river, the best plan is for the man to catch hold of the pummel or mane, and help himself with the other arm.

CHARLES DARWIN, *Journal of Researches* (*Voyage of the Beagle*), 1839

Nicholas Nye

Thistle and darnel and dock grew there,
    And a bush, in the corner, of may,
On the orchard wall I used to sprawl
    In the blazing heat of the day;
Half asleep and half awake,
    While the birds went twittering by,
And nobody there my lone to share
    But Nicholas Nye.

Nicholas Nye was lean and grey,
    Lame of a leg and old,
More than a score of donkey's years
    He had seen since he was foaled;

He munched the thistles, purple and spiked,
    Would sometimes stoop and sigh,
And turn his head, as if he said,
    'Poor Nicholas Nye!'

Alone with his shadow he'd drowse in the meadow,
    Lazily swinging his tail,
At break of day he used to bray,—
    Not much too hearty and hale;
But a wonderful gumption was under his skin,
    And a clear calm light in his eye,
And once in a while: he'd smile . . .
    Would Nicholas Nye.

Seem to be smiling at me, he would,
    From his bush in the corner, of may,—
Bony and ownerless, widowed and worn,
    Knobble-kneed, lonely and grey;
And over the grass would seem to pass
    'Neath the deep dark blue of the sky,
Something much better than words between me
    And Nicholas Nye.

But dusk would come in the apple boughs,
    The green of the glow-worm shine,
The birds in nest would crouch to rest,
    And home I'd trudge to mine;
And there, in the moonlight, dark with dew,
    Asking not wherefore nor why,
Would brood like a ghost, and as still as a post,
    Old Nicholas Nye.

WALTER DE LA MARE (1873–1956)

At Loyongalane we established our base camp and spent the next three days in repairing saddlery and packing donkey loads. Each load weighed approximately fifty pounds, two to each donkey. At last all was ready. There were eighteen donkeys loaded with food and camping gear, four with water containers, one riding mule for anyone who went weak or lame, and five spare donkeys. I was worried about what Elsa's attitude towards the donkeys was going to be. She watched all our repacking with restrained interest, then when we started loading she had to be chained up, for the sight of so much lovely meat braying and kicking and rolling in the sand in an endeavour to throw off unwanted burdens, with shouting Africans rushing about trying to bring order into the chaos, made her tense with excitement. The main cavalcade started off in the morning and we followed with Elsa later in the day when it was cooler. Our march was northwards along the shore line. Elsa was very excited and rushed like a puppy from one to the other of us, then she dashed in among the flocks of flamingoes, retrieved a duck we had shot, and finally went swimming in the lake, where one of us had to cover her with a rifle on account of the crocodiles. Later, when we passed a herd of camels, I was obliged to put her on the chain; this made her furious and her efforts to meet these new friends nearly pulled my arms off. I, however, had no wish to see a stampeding, panic-stricken herd of camels falling over each other, bellowing, gurgling, legs intertwined, and Elsa in their midst. Fortunately these were the last livestock we met along the shore.

When night fell, we saw the fires of the camp by the lake. Again I put Elsa on the chain for fear that she might have enough energy left to chase our donkeys. . . . While we had a belated sundowner we decided that at dawn each morning the lion party . . . and Elsa would start off, while camp was being struck and the animals saddled and loaded. In this way, we would benefit by the cooler hours and the pack animals would follow at a safe distance, dispensing us from any need to keep Elsa on the chain. Then about nine-thirty, we would look for a shady place where we could rest during the heat of the day and where the donkeys could get some grazing. As soon as these were sighted, we would put Elsa on the chain. In the afternoon we would reverse our routine, the donkey party leaving two hours before the lion party and pitching camp before dark. We kept to this routine during the whole safari and it worked out very well, for it kept Elsa and the donkeys apart, except during the midday rest, when she was chained up and very sleepy. As it turned out, both parties soon learned to take each other for granted and to accept that everything which formed part of the safari must be tolerated.

We found that Elsa marched well until about nine in the morning, then she began to feel the heat and kept stopping wherever a rock or bush gave shade. In the afternoon, she was reluctant to move before five; after that, once her pads had hardened, she could have gone on all night. On an average she trotted from seven to eight hours daily, and kept in wonderful condition. She dipped herself in the lake and swam as often as possible, often only six or eight feet from the crocodiles; no shouting or waving on my part would bring her back till she felt like doing so. Usually we reached camp between eight and nine in the evening; often the donkey party would fire Very lights to guide us.

To keep Elsa's paws in good condition, I had often to grease them, an act which she seemed to understand and to like. During the midday rest, I usually lay on my camp bed so as to be able to relax in more comfort than the hard pebbles provided. Elsa saw the point of this, adopted my idea and joined me. Soon I could consider myself fortunate if she left me a small corner, and sometimes I was unlucky and had to sit on the ground while she stretched herself full-length on the bed. But as a rule we curled up together on the bed, I hoping that it might not break beneath our combined weight. During our long marches Nuru always carried drinking-water and a bowl for Elsa; she had her evening meal towards nine o'clock and afterwards slept heavily, tied up near my bed.

The route up Kulal was steep and the climate became arctic as we reached the higher slopes. We walked over saddles, crossed deep ravines and struggled along precipices. Here the bush was lower and then it changed into beautiful alpine flora.

Next morning we reached the top of Kulal; it was a relief to be walking on more or less even ground. Camp was pitched in a beautiful little glade, close to a rather muddy spring, fouled by the cattle of the Samburu tribesmen. Their astonishment was great at finding a nearly fully grown lion in our camp.

In the dense forest belt near the top on most mornings there was heavy mist, so we made a blazing cedar-log fire to keep us warm. At night it was so cold that I kept Elsa in my small tent, made her a nest of lichen and covered her with my warmest blanket. Most of my night was usually spent replacing it as it fell off continually and Elsa would begin to shiver. When I did this, she always licked my arm. She never made any attempt to tear the tent and get out; on the contrary she remained in it long after her usual waking hour, snuggling in her nest, where she was warm and cosy, whereas outside there was a blasting gale and wet mist. But as soon as the sun had cleared the fog away, she came to life and enjoyed the invigorating mountain air. Indeed she loved the place, for the ground was soft and cool, the forest gave thick shade and there were plenty of buffalo droppings to roll in.

Because of the shade and altitude, walking during the heat of the day was no effort in this region, and she was able to explore the mountain with us. She watched the eagles circling high in the air and was annoyed by the crows who followed her and dived low to tease her, and on one occasion woke a buffalo out of his sleep and chased him. She had excellent scent, hearing and eyesight and never lost herself in the thick undergrowth. One afternoon we were following the advance party, which had gone well ahead through the forest, and Elsa was ambushing us in a playful way from behind every bush, when suddenly, from the direction in which she had just disappeared, we heard a panic-stricken bray. A moment later a donkey broke through the wood with Elsa clinging to it and mauling it. Fortunately the forest was so thick that they could not go very fast, so we quickly reached the struggling pair and gave Elsa the beating we thought she deserved; she had never done anything of this sort before, and I was very much alarmed, for I had prided myself on the fact that she always obeyed my call instead of chasing an animal unduly. But again I could only blame myself for not putting Elsa on the lead, and the donkey herdsman who had let the animal stray behind the others.

JOY ADAMSON, Born Free: A Lioness of Two Worlds, 1961

Androcles and the lion

Touching gratitude and thankfulnesse, (for me thinks we have need to further this word greatly) this onely example shall suffice, of which *Appion* reporteth to have been a spectator himselfe. One day (saith he) that the Senate of *Rome*, (to please and recreate the common people) caused a great number of wilde beasts to be baited, namely huge great Lions, it so fortuned, that there was one amongst the rest, who by reason of his furious and stately carriage, of his unmatched strength, of his great limbs, and of his loud, and terror-causing roaring, drew all by-standers eyes to gaze upon him. Amongst other slaves, that in sight of all the people were presented to encounter with these beasts, there chanced to be one *Androdus of Dacia*, who belonged unto a Roman Lord, who had been Consull. This huge Lion, having eyed him afar off, first made a suddaine stop, as strucken into a kind of admiration, then with a milde and gentle contenance, as if he would willingly have taken acquaintance of him, faire and softly approached unto him: Which done, and resting assured he was the man he tooke him for, begun fawningly to wagge his taile, as dogges doe that fawne upon their new-found masters, and licke the poore and miserable slaves hands and thighes, who through feare was almost out of his wits and halfe dead. *Androdus* at last taking hart of grace; and by reason of the Lions mildnesse having rouzed up his spirits, and wishly fixing his eies upon him, to see whether he could call him to remembrance; it was to all beholders a singular pleasure to observe the love, the joy, and blandishments, each endevored to enter-shew one another. Whereat the people raising a loud crie, and by their shouting and clapping of hands seeming to be much pleased; the Emperour willed the slave to be brought before him, as desirous to understand of him the cause of so strange and seeld-seene an accident: Who related this new, and wonderfull storie unto him.

My Master (said he) being Proconsull in *Affrica*, forsomuch as he caused me every day to be most cruelly beaten, and held me in so rigorous bondage, I was constrained, as being wearie of my life, to run away . . . to the desart, and most unfrequented wildernesses of that region, with a full resolution, if I could not compasse the meanes to sustaine my selfe, to finde one way or other, with violence to make my selfe away.

One day, the Sunne about noonetide being extreamly hote, and the scorching heat thereof intolerable, I fortuned to come unto a wilde-unhanted cave, hidden amongst crags, and almost inaccessible, and where I imagined no footing had ever been; therein I hid my selfe: I had not long been there, but in comes this Lion, with one of his pawes sore hurt, and bloody-goared, wailing for the smart, and groaning for the paine he felt; at whose arrivall, I was much dismaied, but he seeing me lie close-cowring in a corner of his den, gently made his approaches unto me, holding forth his goared paw toward me, and seemed with shewing the same humbly to sue, and suppliantly to beg for help at my hands. I, moved with ruth, taking it into my hand, pulled out a great splint, which was gotten into it, and shaking-off all feare, first I wrung and crusht his sore, and caused the filth and matter, which therein was gathered, to come forth; than, as gently as for my heart I could, I cleansed, wiped, and dried the same. He feeling some ease in his griefe, and his paine to cease, still holding his foot betweene my hands, began to sleep and take some rest. Thence forward he and I lived together, the full space of three yeares in his den, with such meat as he shifted-for: For, what beasts he killed, or what prey soever he tooke, he ever brought home the better part, and shared it with me . . . But at last wearied with this kinde of brutish life, the Lion being one day gone to purchase his wonted prey, I left the place, hoping to mend my fortunes, and having wandred up and downe three dayes, I was at last taken by certaine Souldiers, which from *Africa* brought me into this Citie to my Master againe, who immediately condemned me to death, and to be devoured by wilde beasts. And as I now perceive, the same Lion was also shortly after taken, who as you see hath now requited me of the good turne I did him, and the health which by my meanes he recovered.

MONTAIGNE, *An Apologie of Raymond Sebond* (tr. Florio, 1603)

TALKERS

On the Grasshopper and Cricket

The poetry of earth is never dead:
   When all the birds are faint with the hot sun,
   And hide in cooling trees, a voice will run
From hedge to hedge about the new-mown mead—
That is the Grasshopper's. He takes the lead
   In summer luxury; he has never done
   With his delights, for when tired out with fun
He rests at ease beneath some pleasant weed.
The poetry of earth is ceasing never:
   On a lone winter evening, when the frost
    Has wrought a silence, from the stove there shrills
The Cricket's song, in warmth increasing ever,
   And seems to one in drowsiness half lost,
    The Grasshopper's among some grassy hills.

JOHN KEATS (1795–1821)

[In 1897] twelve varieties of musical insects are sold in Tōkyō. Nine can be artificially bred—namely the suzumushi, matsumushi, kirigirisu, kantan, kutsuwamushi, Emma-kōrogi, kin-hibari, kusa-hibari (also called Asa-suzu), and the Yamato-suzu, or Yoshino-suzu. Three varieties, I am told, are not bred for sale, but captured for the market: these are the kanétataki, umaoi or hataori, and kuro-hibari. But a considerable number of all the insects annually offered for sale are caught in their native haunts.

The night-singers are, with few exceptions, easily taken. They are captured with the help of lanterns. Being quickly attracted by light, they approach the lanterns; and when near enough to be observed, they can readily be covered with nets or little baskets. Males and females are usually secured at the same time, for the creatures move about in couples. Only the males sing; but a certain number of females are always taken for breeding purposes. Males and females are kept in the same vessel only for breeding: they are never left together in a cage, because the male ceases to sing when thus mated, and will die in a short time after pairing.

The breeding pairs are kept in jars or other earthen vessels half-filled with moistened clay, and are supplied every day with fresh food. They do not live long: the male dies first, and the female survives only until her eggs have been laid. The young insects hatched from them shed their skin in about forty days from birth, after which they grow more rapidly, and soon attain their full development. In their natural state these creatures are hatched a little before the Doyō, or Period of Greatest Heat by the old calendar—that is to say, about the middle of July—and they begin to sing in October. But when bred in a warm room, they are hatched early in April; and, with careful feeding, they can be offered for sale before the end of May. When very young, their food is triturated and spread for them upon a smooth piece of wood; but the adults are usually furnished with unprepared food, consisting of parings of eggplant, melon rind, cucumber rind, or the soft interior parts of the white onion. Some insects, however, are specially nourished—the abura-kirigirisu, for example, being fed with sugar-water and slices of musk-melon.

Kutsuwamushi

There are several varieties of this extraordinary creature—also called onomatopoetically gatcha-gatcha—which is most provokingly described in dictionaries as 'a kind of noisy cricket'! The variety commonly sold in Tōkyō has a green back, and a yellowish-white abdomen; but there are also brown and reddish varieties. The kutsuwamushi is difficult to capture, but easy to breed. As the tsuku-tsuku-bōshi is the most wonderful musician among the sun-loving cicadae, or semi, so the kutsuwamushi is the most wonderful of night-crickets. It owes its name, which means 'The Bridle-bit-Insect,' to its noise, which resembles the jingling and ringing of the old-fashioned

Japanese bridle-bit (kutsuwa). But the sound is really much louder and much more complicated than ever was the jingling of a single kutsuwa; and the accuracy of the comparison is not easily discerned while the creature is storming beside you. Without the evidence of one's own eyes, it were hard to believe that so small a life could make so prodigious a noise. Certainly the vibratory apparatus in this insect must be very complicated. The sound begins with a thin sharp whizzing, as of leaking steam, and slowly strengthens; then to the whizzing is suddenly added a quick dry clatter, as of castanets; and then, as the whole machinery rushes into operation, you hear, high above the whizzing and the clatter, a torrent of rapid ringing tones like the tapping of a gong. These, the last to begin, are also the first to cease; then the castanets stop; and finally the whizzing dies; but the full orchestra may remain in operation for several hours at a time, without a pause. Heard from far away at night the sound is pleasant, and is really so much like the ringing of a bridle-bit that when you first listen to it you cannot but feel how much real poetry belongs to the name of this insect, celebrated from of old as 'playing at ghostly escort in ways where no man can pass'.

LAFCADIO HEARN, Exotics and Retrospectives, 1898

Cicadas

You know those windless summer evenings, swollen to stasis
by too-substantial melodies, rich as a
running-down record, ground round
to full quiet. Even the leaves
have thick tongues.

And if the first crickets quicken then,
other inhabitants, at window or door
or rising from table, feel in the lungs
a slim false-freshness, by this
trick of the ear.

Chanters of miracles took for a simple sign
the Latin cicada, because of his long waiting
and sweet change in daylight, and his singing
all his life, pinched on the ash leaf,
heedless of ants.

Others made morals; all were puzzled and joyed
by this gratuitous song. Such a plain thing

morals could not surround, nor listening:
not 'chirr' nor 'cri-cri.' There is no straight
way of approaching it.

This thin uncomprehended song it is
springs healing questions into binding air.
Fabre, by firing all the municipal cannon
under a piping tree, found out
cicadas cannot hear.

RICHARD WILBUR (b. 1921)

Stonechat on Cul Beg

A flint-on-flint ticking—and there he is,
Trim and dandy—in square miles of bracken
And bogs and boulders a tiny work of art,
Bright as an illumination on a monkish parchment.

I queue up to watch him. He makes me a group
Of solemn connoisseurs trying to see the brushstrokes.
I want to thumb the air in their knowing way.
I murmur *Chinese black*, I murmur *alizarin*.

But the little picture with four flirts and a delicate
Up-swinging's landed on another boulder.
He gives me a stained-glass look and keeps
Chick-chacking at me. I suppose he's swearing.

You'd expect something like oboes or piccolos
(Though other birds, too, have pebbles in their throats—
And of them I love best the airy skylark
Twittering like marbles squeezed in your fist).

Cul Beg looks away—his show's been stolen.
And the up-staged loch would yawn if it could.
Only the benign sun in his fatherly way
Beams on his bright child throwing a tantrum.

NORMAN MacCAIG (b. 1910)

Last night I heard a screech-owl in the garden, taking her little owls for a moonlight flit. Her maternal voice was extraordinarily gentle and solicitous, and they expressed themselves in brief tinny exclamations, very much as if they were striking small cheap triangles.

> SYLVIA TOWNSEND WARNER, letter of 7 September 1973 to William Maxwell

The Butter Bump

This is a thing that makes a very odd noise morning & evening among the flags & large reedshaws in the fens some describe the noise as something like the bellowing of bulls but I have often heard it & cannot liken it to that sound at all in fact it is difficult to describe what it is like its noise had procurd it the above name by the common people the first part of its noise is an indistinct sort of muttering sound very like the word butter utterd in a hurried manner & bump comes very quick after & bumps a sound on the ear as if eccho had mocked the bump of a gun just as the mutter ceasd nay this [is] not like I have often thought the putting ones mouth to the hole of an empty large cask & uttering the word 'butter bump' sharply woud imitate the sound exactly after its first call that imitates the word 'butter bump' it repeats the word bump singly several times in a more determind & louder manner—thus butter bump bump bump butter bump' it strikes people at first as something like the coopers mallet hitting on empty casks when I was a boy this was one of the fen wonders I usd often to go with my mother to see my aunt at Peakirk when I often wanderd in the fen with the boys birdnesting & when I enquired what the strange noise was they describd it as coming from a bird larger than an ox that coud kill all the cattle in the fen if it chose & destroy the village likewise but that it was very harmless & all the harm it did was the drinking so much water as to nearly empty the dykes in summer & spoil the rest so that the stock coud scarcely drink what it left this was not only a story among children but their parents believd the same thing such is the power of superstition over ignorant people who have no desire to go beyond hearsay & enquire for themselves but the 'world gets wiser every day' tis not believd now nor heard as a wonder any longer they say that it is a small bird that makes the noise not unlike the quail

> JOHN CLARE, 'Nature Notes', 1825–37

The meadows lead down to the shores of the mere, and the nearest fields melt almost insensibly into the green margin of the water, for at the edge it is so full of flags, and rushes, and weeds as at a distance to be barely distinguishable there from the sward. As we approach, the cuckoo sings passing over head; 'she cries as she flies' is the common country saying.

I used to imagine that the cuckoo was fond of an echo, having noticed that a particular clump of trees overhanging some water, the opposite bank of which sent back a clear reply, was a specially favourite resort of that bird. The reduplication of the liquid notes, as they travelled to and fro, was peculiarly pleasant: the water, perhaps, lending, like a sounding-board, a fulness and roundness to her song. She might possibly have fancied that another bird was answering; certainly she 'cried' much longer there than in other places. Morning after morning, and about the same time—eleven o'clock—a cuckoo sang in that group of trees, from noting which I was led to think that perhaps the cuckoo, though apparently wandering aimlessly about, really has more method and regularity in her habits than would seem.

Country people will have it that cuckoos are growing scarcer every year, and do not come in the numbers they formerly did; and, whether it be the chance of unfavourable seasons or other causes, it is certainly the fact in some localities. I recollect seeing as many as four at once in a tall elm—a tree they love—all crying and gurgling, as it were, in the throat together; this was some years since, and that district is now much less frequented by these birds.

There was a superstition that where or in whatever condition you happened to be when you heard the cuckoo the first time in the spring, so you would remain for the next twelvemonth; for which reason it was a misfortune to hear her first in bed, since it might mean a long illness. This, by-the-by, may have been a pleasant fable invented to get milkmaids up early of a morning.

RICHARD JEFFERIES, The Gamekeeper at Home, 1890

Selborne, Aug. 1, 1771.

Dear Sir,

From what follows, it will appear that neither owls nor cuckoos keep to one note. A friend remarks that many (most) of his owls hoot in B flat: but that one went almost half a note below A. The pipe he tried their notes by was a common half-crown pitch-pipe, such as masters use for tuning of harpsichords; it was the common London pitch.

A neighbour of mine, who is said to have a nice ear, remarks that the owls about this village hoot in three different keys, in G flat, or F sharp, in B flat and A flat. He heard two hooting to each other, the one in A flat, and the other in B flat. *Query*: Do these different notes proceed from different species, or only from various individuals? The same person finds upon trial that the note of the cuckoo (of which we have but one species) varies in different individuals; for, about Selborne wood, he found they were mostly in D: he heard two sing together, the one in D, the other in D sharp, who made a disagreeable concert: he afterwards heard one in D sharp, and about Wolmer-forest some in C. As to nightingales, he says that their notes are so short, and their transitions so rapid, that he cannot well ascertain their key. Perhaps in a cage, and in a room, their notes may be more distinguishable. This person has tried to settle the notes of a swift, and of several other small birds, but cannot bring them to any criterion.

GILBERT WHITE (1720–93), *The Natural History of Selborne*

The Darkling Thrush

I leant upon a coppice gate
    When Frost was spectre-gray,
And Winter's dregs made desolate
    The weakening eye of day.
The tangled bine-stems scored the sky
    Like strings of broken lyres,
And all mankind that haunted nigh
    Had sought their household fires.

The land's sharp features seemed to be
    The Century's corpse outleant,
His crypt the cloudy canopy,
    The wind his death-lament.
The ancient pulse of germ and birth
    Was shrunken hard and dry,
And every spirit upon earth
    Seemed fervourless as I.

At once a voice arose among
    The bleak twigs overhead
In a full-hearted evensong
    Of joy illimited;
An aged thrush, frail, gaunt, and small,
    In blast-beruffled plume,
Had chosen thus to fling his soul
    Upon the growing gloom.

So little cause for carolings
    Of such ecstatic sound
Was written on terrestrial things
    Afar or nigh around,

That I could think there trembled through
   His happy good-night air
Some blessed Hope, whereof he knew
   And I was unaware.

THOMAS HARDY (1840–1928)

from *Philip Sparrow*

Pla ce bo!
Who is there, who?
Di le xi!
Dame Margery.
Fa, re, my, my.
Wherefore and why, why?
For the soul of Philip Sparrow
That was late slain at Carrow,
Among the Nunnes Black.
For that sweet soules sake,
And for all sparrows' souls
Set in our bead-rolls,
Pater noster qui,
With an *Ave Mari,*
And with the corner of a Creed,
The more shall be your meed.

   When I remember again
How my Philip was slain,
Never half the pain
Was between you twain,
Pyramus and Thisbe,
As then befell to me.
I wept and I wailed,
The teares down hailed,
But nothing it availed
To call Philip again,
Whom Gib, our cat, hath slain.

   .   .   .   .   .

   It was so pretty a fool,
It would sit on a stool,

Pla ce bo: beginning of the Office for the Dead   *Carrow*: Carrow Abbey, near
Norwich

And learned after my school
For to keep his cut,
With 'Philip, keep your cut!'

   It had a velvet cap,
And would sit upon my lap,
And seek after small wormes,
And sometime white bread-crumbes;
And many times and oft
Between my breastes soft
It woulde lie and rest;
It was proper and prest.

   Sometime he would gasp
When he saw a wasp;
A fly or a gnat,
He would fly at that;
And prettily he would pant
When he saw an ant.
Lord, how he would pry
After the butterfly!
Lord, how he would hop
After the gressop!
And when I said, 'Phip, Phip!'
Then he would leap and skip,
And take me by the lip.
Alas, it will me slo
That Philip is gone me fro! . . .

   Lauda, anima mea, Dominum!
To weep with me look that ye come
All manner of birdes in your kind;
See none be left behind.
To mourning looke that ye fall
With dolorous songes funerall,
Some to sing, and some to say,
Some to weep, and some to pray,
Every birde in his lay.
The goldfinch, the wagtail;
The jangling jay to rail,

---

keep his cut: behave properly   *prest*: quick, sprightly   *gressop*: grasshopper
slo: slay   *Lauda . . . Dominum*: 'Praise the Lord, O my soul' (Ps. 145: 1)

The flecked pie to chatter
Of this dolorous matter;
And Robin Redbreast,
He shall be the priest
The requiem mass to sing,
Softly warbeling,
With help of the red sparrow
And the chattering swallow,
This hearse for to hallow.

·   ·   ·   ·   ·

The lusty chanting nightingale;
The popinjay to tell her tale,
That tooteth oft in a glass,
Shall read the Gospel at mass;
The mavis with her whistle
Shall read there the Epistle.
But with a large and a long
To keepe just plain-song,
Our chanters shall be the cuckoo,
The culver, the stockdoo.
With 'peewit' the lapwing,
The Versicles shall sing.

The bittern with his bumpe,
The crane with his trumpe,
The swan of Maeander,
The goose and the gander,
The duck and the drake,
Shall watch at this wake;
The peacock so proud,
Because his voice is loud,
And hath a glorious tail,
He shall sing the Grail;

·   ·   ·   ·   ·

The ostrich, that will eat
An horseshoe so great,
In the stead of meat,
Such fervent heat
His stomach doth frete;

---

pie: magpie   *popinjay*: parrot   *tooteth*: peers   *mavis*: song-thrush
culver: dove   *stockdoo*: wild pigeon   *bumpe*: booming voice   *Grail*:
gradual   *frete*: consume

He cannot well fly,
Nor sing tunably,
Yet at a brayd
He hath well assayed
To sol-fa above E-la.
Fa, lorell, fa, fa!
Ne quando
Male contando,
The best that we can,
To make him our bell-man,
And let him ring the bells.
He can do nothing else.

    .   .   .   .

The goshawk shall have a roll
The choristers to control;
The lanners and the marlions
Shall stand in their mourning-gowns;
The hobby and the musket
The censers and the cross shall fet;
The kestrel in all this wark
Shall be holy water clerk.

    And now the dark cloudy night
Chaseth away Phoebus bright,
Taking his course toward the west,
God send my sparrow's soul good rest!
Requiem aeternum dona eis, Domine!
Fa, fa, fa, mi, re, re,
A por ta in fe ri,
Fa, fa, fa, mi, mi.

    Credo videre bona Domini,
I pray God, Philip to heaven may fly:
Domine, exaudi orationem meam
To heaven he shall, from heaven he came:

---

at a brayd: suddenly   *Ne . . . cantando*: lest ever by singing badly   *lanners*: species of falcon   *marlions*: merlins, small swift falcons   *hobby*: small falcon   *musket*: male of the sparrowhawk   *fet*: fetch   *Requiem . . . Domine*: 'Grant them eternal rest, O Lord!'   *A por ta in fe ri*: 'From the gates of hell . . .'   *Credo . . . Domini*: 'I had thought to see the goodness of the Lord' (Ps. 26: 13)   *Domine . . . meam*: 'Lord, hear my prayer' (Ps. 102: 2)

Do mi nus vo bis cum!
Of all good prayers God send him some!
Oremus,
Deus, cui proprium est misereri et parcere,
On Philip's soul have pity!

JOHN SKELTON (*c.*1460–1529)

Love's agent

The courting of a girl and boy
who love and sigh and touch and toy
inflames the nightingale with joy:
    she has to trill and coo it.

She's love's announcer and town-crier;
she lights the spark and stokes the fire;
she swells the lover with desire,
    then boasts that he'll pursue it.

I've heard her in a leafy glade
encouraging some heated blade
to pierce a girl who was a maid—
    and countless times will rue it.

A lady may be made of stone,
her heart encased in bronze, not bone;
but when she hears this melting tone
    her body burns to do it.

The nightingale takes Cupid's part:
when he's installed the teasing dart
she makes the inflammation start
    by wanton warblings to it.

ANON., 12th cent. Latin, tr. Fleur Adcock

Currawong

The currawong has shallow eyes.—
bold shallow buttons of yellow glass
that see all round his sleek black skull.

Deus . . . parcere: 'O God, whose nature it is to be merciful and to spare'

Small birds sit quiet when he flies;
mothers of nestlings cry *Alas!*
He is a gangster, his wife's a moll.

But I remember long ago
(a child beside the seldom sea)
the currawongs as wild as night
quarrelling, talking, crying so,
in the scarlet-tufted coral-tree;
and past them that blue stretch of light,

the ocean with its dangerous song.
Robber then and robber still,
he cries now with the same strange word
(*currawong—currawong*)
that from those coxcomb trees I heard.
Take my bread and eat your fill,
bold, cruel and melodious bird.

JUDITH WRIGHT (b. 1915)

The Pelican Chorus

King and Queen of the Pelicans we;
No other Birds so grand we see!
None but we have feet like fins!
With lovely leathery throats and chins!
  Ploffskin, Pluffskin, Pelican jee!
  We think no Birds so happy as we!
  Plumpskin, Ploshkin, Pelican jill!
  We think so then, and we thought so still!

We live on the Nile. The Nile we love.
By night we sleep on the cliffs above;
By day we fish, and at eve we stand
On long bare islands of yellow sand.
And when the sun sinks slowly down
And the great rock walls grow dark and brown,
Where the purple river rolls fast and dim
And the Ivory Ibis starlike skim,
Wing to wing we dance around,—
Stamping our feet with a flumpy sound,—
Opening our mouths as Pelicans ought,

And this is the song we nightly snort;—
   Ploffskin, Pluffskin, Pelican jee,—
   We think no Birds so happy as we!
   Plumpskin, Ploshkin, Pelican jill,—
   We think so then, and we thought so still.

Last year came out our Daughter, Dell;
And all the Birds received her well.
To do her honour, a feast we made
For every bird that can swim or wade.
Herons and Gulls, and Cormorants black,
Cranes, and Flamingoes with scarlet back,
Plovers and Storks, and Geese in clouds,
Swans and Dilberry Ducks in crowds.
Thousands of Birds in wondrous flight!
They ate and drank and danced all night,
And echoing back from the rocks you heard
Multitude-echoes from Bird and Bird,—
   Ploffskin, Pluffskin, Pelican jee,
   We think no Birds so happy as we!
   Plumpskin, Ploshkin, Pelican jill,
   We think so then, and we thought so still!

Yes, they came; and among the rest,
The King of the Cranes all grandly dressed.
Such a lovely tail! Its feathers float
Between the ends of his blue dress-coat;
With pea-green trowsers all so neat,
And a delicate frill to hide his feet,—
(For though no one speaks of it, every one knows,
He has got no webs between his toes!)

As soon as he saw our Daughter Dell,
In violent love that Crane King fell,—
On seeing her waddling form so fair,
With a wreath of shrimps in her short white hair.
And before the end of the next long day,
Our Dell had given her heart away;
For the King of the Cranes had won that heart,
With a Crocodile's egg and a large fish-tart.
She vowed to marry the King of the Cranes,
Leaving the Nile for stranger plains;
And away they flew in a gathering crowd

Of endless birds in a lengthening cloud.
   Ploffskin, Pluffskin, Pelican jee,
   We think no Birds so happy as we!
   Plumpskin, Ploshkin, Pelican jill,
   We think so then, and we thought so still!

And far away in the twilight sky,
We heard them singing a lessening cry,—
Farther and farther till out of sight,
And we stood alone in the silent night!
Often since, in the nights of June,
We sit on the sand and watch the moon;—
She has gone to the great Gromboolian plain,
And we probably never shall meet again!
Oft, in the long still nights of June,
We sit on the rocks and watch the moon;—
—She dwells by the streams of the Chankly Bore,
And we probably never shall see her more.
   Ploffskin, Pluffskin, Pelican jee,
   We think no Birds so happy as we!
   Plumpskin, Ploshkin, Pelican jill,
   We think so then, and we thought so still!

EDWARD LEAR (1812–88), *Nonsense Songs*

The raven, Grip, who through thick and thin remains loyal to his master, Barnaby, plays a large part in Dickens's primarily historical novel, set in the period of the anti-Popery riots of 1780.

'Halloa!' cried a hoarse voice in his ear. 'Halloa, halloa, halloa! Bow wow wow. What's the matter here! Hal-loa!'

The speaker . . . was a large raven, who had perched upon the top of the easy-chair, . . . and listened with a polite attention and a most extraordinary appearance of comprehending every word, to all they had said up to this point; turning his head from one to the other, as if his office were to judge between them, and it were of the very last importance that he should not lose a word.

'Look at him!' said Varden, divided between admiration of the bird and a kind of fear of him. 'Was there ever such a knowing imp as that! Oh he's a dreadful fellow!'

The raven, with his head very much on one side, and his bright eye shining like a diamond, preserved a thoughtful silence for a few seconds, and then replied in a voice so hoarse and distant, that it seemed to come through his thick feathers rather than out of his mouth.

'Halloa, halloa, halloa! What's the matter here! Keep up your spirits. Never say die. Bow wow wow. I'm a devil, I'm a devil, I'm a devil. Hurrah!'—And then, as if exulting in his infernal character, he began to whistle.

'I more than half believe he speaks the truth. Upon my word I do,' said Varden. 'Do you see how he looks at me, as if he knew what I was saying?'

To which the bird, balancing himself on tiptoe, as it were, and moving his body up and down in a sort of grave dance, rejoined, 'I'm a devil, I'm a devil, I'm a devil,' and flapped his wings against his sides as if he were bursting with laughter. Barnaby clapped his hands, and fairly rolled upon the ground in an ecstasy of delight.

'Strange companions, sir,' said the locksmith, shaking his head, and looking from one to the other. 'The bird has all the wit.'

'Strange indeed!' said Edward, holding out his forefinger to the raven, who, in acknowledgment of the attention, made a dive at it immediately with his iron bill. 'Is he old?'

'A mere boy, sir,' replied the locksmith. 'A hundred and twenty, or thereabouts. Call him down, Barnaby, my man.'

'Call him!' echoed Barnaby, sitting upright upon the floor, and staring vacantly at Gabriel, as he thrust his hair back from his face. 'But who can make him come! He calls me, and makes me go where he will. He goes on before, and I follow. He's the master, and I'm the man. Is that the truth, Grip?'

The raven gave a short, comfortable, confidential kind of croak;—a most expressive croak, which seemed to say, 'You needn't let these fellows into our secrets. We understand each other. It's all right.'

'*I* make *him* come?' cried Barnaby, pointing to the bird. 'Him, who never goes to sleep, or so much as winks!—Why, any time of night, you may see his eyes in my dark room, shining like two sparks. And every night, and all night too, he's broad awake, talking to himself, thinking what he shall do to-morrow, where we shall go, and what he shall steal, and hide, and bury. *I* make *him* come. Ha ha ha!'

On second thoughts, the bird appeared disposed to come of himself. After a short survey of the ground, and a few sidelong looks at the ceiling and at everybody present in turn, he fluttered to the floor, and went to Barnaby—not in a hop, or walk, or run, but in a pace like that of a very particular gentleman with exceedingly tight boots on, trying to walk fast over loose pebbles. Then, stepping into his extended hand, and condescending to be held out at arm's length, he gave vent to a succession of sounds, not unlike the drawing of some eight or ten dozen of long corks, and again asserted his brimstone birth and parentage with great distinctness.

Grip was by no means an idle or unprofitable member of the humble household. Partly by dint of Barnaby's tuition, and partly by pursuing a species of self-instruction common to his tribe, and exerting his powers of observation to the utmost, he had acquired a degree of sagacity which rendered him famous for miles round. His conversational powers and surprising performances were the universal theme: and as many persons came to see the wonderful raven, and none left his exertions unrewarded—when he condescended to exhibit, which was not always, for genius is capricious—his earnings formed an important item in the common stock. Indeed, the bird himself appeared to know his value well; for though he was perfectly free and unrestrained in the presence of Barnaby and his mother, he maintained in public an amazing gravity, and never stooped to any other gratuitous performances than biting the ankles of vagabond boys (an exercise in which he much delighted), killing a fowl or two occasionally, and swallowing the dinners of various neighbouring dogs, of whom the boldest held him in great awe and dread.

When Barnaby is innocently caught up in the riots, and arrested, Grip follows him.

'Go to the guard-house, and see [said the serjeant]. You'll find a bird there, that's got their cry as pat as any of 'em, and bawls "No Popery," like a man—or like a devil, as he says he is. I shouldn't wonder. The devil's loose in London somewhere. Damme if I wouldn't twist his neck round, on the chance, if I had *my* way.'

The young man had taken two or three steps away, as if to go and see this creature, when he was arrested by the voice of Barnaby.

'It's mine,' he called out, half laughing and half weeping—'my pet, my friend Grip. Ha ha ha! Don't hurt him, he has done no harm. I taught him; it's my fault. Let me have him, if you please. He's the only friend I have left now. He'll not dance, or talk, or whistle for you, I know; but he will for me, because he knows me and loves me—though you wouldn't think it—very well. You wouldn't hurt a bird, I'm sure. You're a brave soldier, sir, and wouldn't harm a woman or a child—no, no, nor a poor bird, I'm certain.'

This latter adjuration was addressed to the serjeant, whom Barnaby judged from his red coat to be high in office, and able to seal Grip's destiny by a word. But that gentleman, in reply, surlily damned him for a thief and rebel as he was, and with many disinterested imprecations on his own eyes, liver, blood, and body, assured him that if it rested with him to decide, he would put a final stopper on the bird, and his master too.

'You talk boldly to a caged man,' said Barnaby, in anger. 'If I was on the other side of the door and there were none to part us, you'd change your note—ay, you may toss your head—you would! Kill the bird—do. Kill anything you can, and so revenge yourself on those who with their bare hands untied could do as much to you!'

Having vented his defiance, he flung himself into the furthest corner of his prison, and muttering, 'Good-bye, Grip—good-bye, dear old Grip!' shed tears for the first time since he had been taken captive; and hid his face in the straw.

CHARLES DICKENS, *Barnaby Rudge*, 1841

The Mockingbird

Look one way and the sun is going down,
Look the other and the moon is rising.
The sparrow's shadow's longer than the lawn.
The bats squeak: 'Night is here'; the birds cheep: 'Day is gone.'
On the willow's highest branch, monopolizing
Day and night, cheeping, squeaking, soaring,
The mockingbird is imitating life.

All day the mockingbird has owned the yard.
As light first woke the world, the sparrows trooped
Onto the seedy lawn: the mockingbird
Chased them off shrieking. Hour by hour, fighting hard
To make the world his own, he swooped
On thrushes, thrashers, jays, and chickadees—
At noon he drove away a big black cat.

Now, in the moonlight, he sits here and sings.
A thrush is singing, then a thrasher, then a jay—
Then, all at once, a cat begins meowing.
A mockingbird can sound like anything.
He imitates the world he drove away
So well that for a minute, in the moonlight,
Which one's the mockingbird? which one's the world?

RANDALL JARRELL (1914–65)

Bats' Ultrasound

Sleeping-bagged in a duplex wing
with fleas, in rock-cleft or building
radar bats are darkness in miniature,
their whole face one tufty crinkled ear
with weak eyes, fine teeth bared to sing.

Few are vampires. None flit through the mirror.
Where they flutter at evening's a queer
tonal hunting zone above highest C.
Insect prey at the peak of our hearing
drone re to their detailing tee:

ah, eyrie-ire; aero hour, eh?
O'er our ur-area (our era aye
ere your raw row) we air our array,
err, yaw, row wry—aura our orrery,
our eerie ü our ray, our arrow.

A rare ear, our aery Yahweh.

LES MURRAY (b. 1938)

Another parrot [that] interested me . . . was a member of the same numerous genus, a double-fronted amazon, *Chrysotis lavalainte*, a larger bird, green, with face and fore-part of head pure yellow, and some crimson colour in the wings and tail. I came upon it at an inn, the Lamb, at Hindon, a village in the South Wiltshire downs. One could plainly see that it was a very old bird, and, judging from the ragged state of its plumage, that it had long fallen into the period of irregular or imperfect moult—'the sere, the yellow leaf' in the bird's life. It also had the tremor of the very aged—man or bird. But its eyes were still as bright as polished yellow gems and full of the almost uncanny parrot intelligence. The voice, too, was loud and cheerful; its call to its mistress—'Mother, mother!' would ring through the whole rambling old house. He talked and laughed heartily and uttered a variety of powerful notes as round and full and modulated as those of any grey parrot. Now, all that would not have attracted me much to the bird if I had not heard its singular history, told to me by its mistress, the landlady. She had had it in her possession fifty years, and its story was as follows:

Her father-in-law, the landlord of the Lamb, had a beloved son who went off to sea and was seen and heard of no more for a space of fourteen years, when one day he turned up in the possession of a sailor's usual fortune, acquired in distant barbarous lands—a parrot in a cage! This he left with his parents, charging them to take the greatest care of it, as it was really a very wonderful bird, as they would soon know if they could only understand its language, and he then began to make ready to set off again, promising his mother to write this time and not to stay away more than five or at most ten years.

Meanwhile, his father, who was anxious to keep him, succeeded in bringing about a meeting between him and a girl of his acquaintance, one who, he believed, would make his son the best wife in the world. The young wanderer saw and loved, and as the feeling was returned he soon married and endowed her with all his worldly possessions, which consisted of the parrot and cage. Eventually he succeeded his father as tenant of the Lamb, where he died many years ago: the widow was grey when I first knew her and old like her parrot; and she was like the bird too in her youthful spirit and the brilliance of her eyes.

Her young sailor had picked up the bird at Vera Cruz in Mexico. He saw a girl standing in the market place with the parrot on her shoulder. She was talking and singing to the bird, and the bird was talking, whistling, and singing back to her—singing snatches of songs in Spanish. It was a wonderful bird, and he was enchanted and bought it, and brought it all the way back to England and Wiltshire. It was, the girl had told him, just five years old, and as fifty years had gone by it was, when I first knew it, or was supposed to be, fifty-five. In its Wiltshire home it continued to talk and sing in Spanish, and had two favourite songs, which delighted everybody, although no one could understand the words. By and by it took to learning words and sentences in English, and spoke less in Spanish year after year until in about ten to twelve years that language had been completely forgotten.

Nevertheless, I thought it would be worth while trying a little Spanish on old Polly of the Lamb, and thought it best to begin by making friends. It was of little use to offer her something to eat. Poll was a person who rather despised sweeties and kickshaws. It had been the custom of the house for half a century to allow Polly to eat what she liked and when she liked, and as she—it was really a he—was of a social disposition she preferred taking her meals with the family and eating the same food. At breakfast she would come to the table and partake of bacon and fried eggs, also toast and butter and jam and marmalade, at dinner it was a cut off the joint with (usually) two vegetables, then pudding or tart with pippins and cheese to follow. Between meals she amused herself with bird seed, but preferred a meaty mutton-bone, which she would hold in one hand or foot and feed on with great satisfaction. It was not strange that when I held out food for her she took it as an insult, and when I changed my tactics and offered to scratch her head she lost her temper altogether, and when I persisted in my advances she grew dangerous and succeeded in getting in several nips with her huge beak, which drew blood from my fingers.

It was only then, after all my best blandishments had been exhausted, and when our relations were at their worst, that I began talking to her in Spanish in a sort of caressing falsetto like a 'native' girl, calling her 'Lorito' instead of Polly, coupled with all the endearing epithets commonly used by the women of the green continent in addressing their green pets. Polly instantly became attentive. She listened and listened, coming down nearer to listen better, the one eye she fixed on me shining like a fiery gem. But she spoke no word, Spanish or English, only from time to time little low inarticulate sounds came from her. It was evident after two or three days that she was powerless to recall the old lore, but to me it also appeared evident that some vague memory of a vanished time had been evoked—that she was conscious of a past and was trying to recall it. At all events the effect of the experiment was that her hostility vanished, and we became friends at once. She would come down to me, step on to my hand, climb to my shoulder, and allow me to walk about with her.

W. H. Hudson, *Birds and Man*, 1915

'Now listen, Doctor, and I'll tell you something. Did you know that animals can talk?' [said Polynesia].

'I knew that parrots can talk,' said the Doctor.

'Oh, we parrots can talk in two languages—people's language and bird language,' said Polynesia proudly. 'If I say "Polly wants a cracker," you understand me. But hear this: *Ka-ka oi-ee, fee-fee?*'

'Good gracious!' cried the Doctor. 'What does that mean?'

'That means, "Is the porridge hot yet?" in bird language.'

'My! You don't say so!' said the Doctor. 'You never talked that way to me before.'

'What would have been the good?' said Polynesia, dusting some biscuit crumbs off her left wing. 'You wouldn't have understood me if I had.'

'Tell me some more,' said the Doctor, all excited, and he rushed over to the dresser drawer and came back with the butcher's book and a pencil. 'Now, don't go too fast and I'll write it down. This is interesting, very interesting—something quite new. Give me the Birds' ABC first—slowly, now.'

So that was the way the Doctor came to know that animals had a language of their own and could talk to one another. And all that afternoon, while it was raining, Polynesia sat on the kitchen table giving him bird words to put down in the book.

At tea-time, when the dog, Jip, came in, the parrot said to the Doctor, 'See, *he's* talking to you.'

'Looks to me as though he were scratching his ear,' said the Doctor.

'But animals don't always speak with their mouths,' said the parrot in a high voice, raising her eyebrows. 'They talk with their ears, with their feet, with their tails—with everything. Sometimes they don't *want* to make a noise. Do you see now the way he's twitching up one side of his nose?'

'What's that mean?' asked the Doctor.

'That means, "Can't you see that it has stopped raining?" ' Polynesia answered. 'He is asking you a question. Dogs nearly always use their noses for asking questions.'

After a while, with the parrot's help, the Doctor got to learn the language of the animals so well that he could talk to them himself and understand everything they said. Then he gave up being a people's doctor altogether.

HUGH LOFTING, 'Animal Language', *The Story of Doctor Doolittle*, 1920

The mid-sixties saw the start of a project that, along with other similar research, was to teach us a great deal about the chimpanzee mind. This was Project Washoe, conceived by Trixie and Allen Gardner. They purchased an infant chimpanzee and began to teach her the signs of ASL, the American Sign Language used by the deaf. Twenty years earlier another husband and wife team, Richard and Cathy Hayes, had tried, with an almost total lack of success, to teach a young chimp, Vikki, to talk. The Hayes's undertaking taught us a lot about the chimpanzee mind, but Vikki, although she did well in IQ tests, and was clearly an intelligent youngster, could not learn human speech. The Gardners, however, achieved spectacular success with their pupil, Washoe. Not only did she learn signs easily, but she quickly began to string them together in meaningful ways. It was clear that each sign evoked, in her mind, a mental image of the object it represented. If, for example, she was asked, in sign language, to fetch an apple, she would go and locate an apple that was out of sight in another room.

Other chimps entered the project, some starting their lives in deaf signing families before joining Washoe. And finally Washoe adopted an infant, Loulis. He came from a lab where no thought of teaching signs had ever penetrated. When he was with Washoe he was given no lessons in language acquisition—not by humans, anyway. Yet by the time he was eight years old he had made fifty-eight signs in their correct contexts. How did he learn them? Mostly, it seems, by imitating the behaviour of Washoe and the other three signing chimps, Dar, Moja and Tatu. Sometimes, though, he received tuition from Washoe herself. One day, for example, she began to swagger about bipedally, hair bristling, signing *food! food! food!* in great excitement. She had seen a human approaching with a bar of chocolate. Loulis, only eighteen months old, watched passively. Suddenly Washoe stopped her swaggering, went over to him, took his hand, and moulded the sign for *food* (fingers pointing towards mouth). Another time, in a similar context, she made the sign for *chewing gum*—but with *her* hand on *his* body. On a third occasion Washoe, apropos of nothing, picked up a small chair, took it over to Loulis, set it down in front of him, and very distinctly made the *chair* sign three times, watching him closely as she did so. The two food signs became incorporated into Loulis's vocabulary but the sign for chair did not. Obviously the priorities of a young chimp are similar to those of a human child!

Chimpanzees who have been taught a language can combine signs creatively in order to describe objects for which they have no symbol. Washoe, for example, puzzled her caretakers by asking, repeatedly, for a *rock berry*. Eventually it transpired that she was referring to brazil nuts which she had encountered for the first time a while before. Another language-trained chimp described a cucumber as a *green banana*, and another referred to an Alka-Seltzer as a *listen drink*. They can even invent signs. Lucy, as she got older, had to be put on a leash for her outings. One day, eager to set off but having no sign for *leash*, she signalled her wishes by holding a crooked index finger to the ring on her collar. This sign became part of her vocabulary.

> JANE GOODALL, *Through a Window: Thirty Years with the Chimpanzees of Gombe*, 1990

The wolf's howl is the social signal perhaps most familiar to everyone. It typically consists of a single note, rising sharply at the beginning or breaking abruptly at the end as the animal strains for volume. It can contain as many as twelve related harmonics. When wolves howl together they harmonize, rather than chorus on the same note, creating an impression of more animals howling than there actually are.

There has been more speculation about the nature and function of the wolf's howl than the music, probably, of any other animal. It is a rich, captivating sound, a seductive echo that can moan on eerily and raise the hair on your head. Wolves apparently howl to assemble the pack, especially before and after the hunt; to pass on an alarm, especially at the den site; to locate each other in a storm or in unfamiliar territory; and to communicate across great distances. Some Eskimos, according to writer / naturalist Farley Mowat, claim to be able to understand what wolves are howling about and to take advantage of it when the howling reveals the approach of migrating caribou. The howl may carry six miles or more in still arctic air.

There is little evidence that wolves howl during a chase, but they may do so afterward, perhaps to celebrate a successful hunt (the presence of food), their prowess, or the fact that they are all together again, that no one has been injured. Adolph Murie, who had an eye for such things, reported a lone wolf howling while hunting mice.

There has never been any evidence that wolves howl at the moon, or howl more frequently during a full moon, though howling may be more frequent in the evening or early morning. Howling reaches a seasonal peak in the winter months, during the time of courtship and breeding; it is easy to see how the idea that wolves howl at the moon might have gained credence and played well on the imagination during these cold, clear nights when the sound carried far and a full moon lent an eerie aspect to a snowscape.

What emotions prompt a howl remain unknown, though field and laboratory researchers both suggest that solo howls and group howling alike are brought on by restlessness and anxiety. Loneliness is the emotion most often mentioned, but group howling has a quality of celebration and camaraderie about it, what wildlife biologist Durward Allen called 'the jubilation of wolves.' Murie writes of four wolves assembled on a skyline, wagging their tails and frisking together. They began to howl, and while they did so a gray female ran up from the den a hundred yards away and joined them. She was greeted with energetic tail wagging and general good feeling, then they all threw back their heads and howled. The howling, wrote Murie, floated softly across the tundra. Then, abruptly, the assembly broke up. The mother returned to the den and the pups; the others departed on the evening hunt.

The wolf's other vocalizations have received less attention, though wolves seem to use these other sounds more often, to communicate more information. They are commonly divided into three categories: growls, barks, and whines or squeaks. Howls have been recorded and studied in the wild. Growls, squeaks, and barks have only rarely been heard in the field, so we must proceed here solely on the basis of information from captive animals.

Wolves only infrequently bark, and then it is a quiet 'woof' more often than a dog-type bark. They do not bark continuously like dogs but woof a few times and then retreat, as for example when a stranger approaches the pen. Barks reported from the field are associated with a pack's being surprised at its den and an animal, usually the female, rising to bark a warning.

Growling is heard during food challenges and, like the bark, is associated with threat behavior or an assertion of rights in some social context. To the human ear this is perhaps the most doglike wolf sound in terms of its association with other behaviors, such as a squabble over a bone. Growling is common among pups when they're playing. Pups also growl when they jerk at the ruff of a reclining adult and comically will even try to growl adults off a piece of food. Another type of growl is a higher-pitched one that begins to sound like a whine and often precedes a snapping lunge at another wolf.

Perhaps the most interesting sounds are the whines and high-pitched social squeaks associated with greeting, feeding the pups, play, pen pacing, and other situations of anxiety, curiosity, and inquiry. They are the sounds of intimacy. . . .

Some squeaks were repeated often enough to be recognized; these were associated with certain specific behaviors, leading one to think of them as bits of true communication.

BARRY HOLSTUN LOPEZ, *Of Wolves and Men*, 1978

We immediately loved. At sight we loved. . . . She whimpered round me, in delighted recognition that here at last was a playmate and friend. Her whole body was one great wag of welcome. She showed off. She did all her tricks. She flung herself on her back, so that I might see for myself how beautiful her stomach was—

'Do not,' interrupted my husband, 'kiss the dog. No dog should be kissed. I have provided you, for kissing purposes, with myself.'

That first year of marriage, Cornelia and I were everything to each other. Alone all day from directly after breakfast till evening, because my husband went off early to inspect his remoter farms and didn't come back till dark, if I wished to talk I had to talk to Cornelia.

Dogs being great linguists, she quickly picked up English, far more quickly than I picked up German, so we understood each other very well, and *couche, schönmachen*, and *pfui* continued for a long time to be my whole vocabulary.

Fortunately, we liked the same things. She only wanted to be out of doors in the sun, and so did I. Expeditions to the nearer woods soon became our daily business, and the instant my husband, in his high cart, had lurched off round the first corner, we were off round the opposite one, disappearing as quickly as we could, almost scuttling, in our eagerness to be gone beyond reach and sight of the servants.

I would make for the open; and once in it, once safe, how happy Cornelia and I were! We frisked across the unreproachful fields, laughing and talking—I swear she laughed and talked,—to the cover of the nearest wood. The world was all before us, and my pockets bulged with biscuits and bones which, when sorted out, would be our several luncheons. What could be more perfect? Nothing, out there, minded what we did. Nothing wanted to be given orders. The March wind, blowing my skirt all anyhow, and causing Cornelia's ears to stream out behind her, didn't care a fig that I was a fleeing *Hausfrau*.

ELIZABETH VON ARNIM, *All the Dogs of My Life*, 1936

A human hand . . . pulled me out of the container and tossed me aside, and I immediately felt two violent blows on both sides of my face, where majestic whiskers, I may well say, now flourish. The hand, as I can now judge, injured by the muscular play of my paws, boxed my ears, and I experienced for the first time moral cause and effect, and a similar moral instinct persuaded me to draw in my claws just as quickly as I had extended them. Later, retracting my claws was recognized quite rightly as a sign of the greatest friendliness and graciousness and was designated by the phrase 'velvet paws'.

As I already mentioned, the hand tossed me onto the ground. Soon after, it picked me up again by the head and pressed it down so that my mouth was placed in a liquid, which—I do not know how it occurred to me, it must have been physical instinct—I began to lap and which aroused in me a feeling of strange inner comfort. It was, I now know, sweet milk that I enjoyed; I had been hungry and became sated by drinking. Thus my physical education followed my moral one.

Two hands picked me up again, but more gently than before, and placed me on a warm, soft bed. I felt better and better, and I began to express my inner happiness with those sounds that are peculiar to my kind and which are designated by the rather apt expression 'purring'. Thus my worldly education made giant strides. What an advantage, what a precious gift of heaven it is to be able to express physical happiness with sound and gesture! First I learned to growl, then I acquired the inimitable talent of twisting my tail in the most charming circles, and then I developed the wonderful gift of expressing with the one little word *meow* joy, sorrow, rapture and delight, fear and despair—in brief, all emotions and passions in all their most manifold degrees. What is the language of man in comparison to the simplest of all simple means of making oneself comprehensible!

E. T. A. HOFFMAN, *Kater Murr*, 1819–21, *Selected Writings* (tr. Leonard J. Kent and Elizabeth C. Knight, 1969)

And Bā'laam rose up in the morning, and saddled his ass, and went with the princes of Mō'ab.

And God's anger was kindled because he went: and the angel of the LORD stood in the way for an adversary against him. Now he was riding upon his ass, and his two servants were with him.

And the ass saw the angel of the LORD standing in the way, and his sword drawn in his hand: and the ass turned aside out of the way, and went into the field: and Bā'laam smote the ass, to turn her into the way.

But the angel of the LORD stood in a path of the vineyards, a wall being on this side, and a wall on that side.

And when the ass saw the angel of the LORD, she thrust herself unto the wall, and crushed Bā'laam's foot against the wall: and he smote her again.

And the angel of the LORD went further, and stood in a narrow place, where was no way to turn either to the right hand or to the left.

And when the ass saw the angel of the LORD, she fell down under Bā'laam: and Bā'laam's anger was kindled, and he smote the ass with a staff.

And the LORD opened the mouth of the ass, and she said unto Bā'laam, What have I done unto thee, that thou hast smitten me these three times?

And Bā'laam said unto the ass, Because thou hast mocked me: I would
there were a sword in mine hand, for now would I kill thee.

And the ass said unto Bā'laam, Am not I thine ass, upon which thou hast
ridden ever since I was thine unto this day? was I ever wont to do so unto
thee? And he said, Nay.

Then the LORD opened the eyes of Bā'laam, and he saw the angel of the
LORD standing in the way, and his sword drawn in his hand: and he bowed
down his head, and fell flat on his face.

And the angel of the LORD said unto him, Wherefore hast thou smitten
thine ass these three times? behold, I went out to withstand thee, because
thy way is perverse before me:

And the ass saw me, and turned from me these three times: unless she
had turned from me, surely now also I had slain thee, and saved her alive.

And Bā'laam said unto the angel of the LORD, I have sinned; for I knew
not that thou stoodest in the way against me: now therefore, if it displease
thee, I will get me back again.

Numbers 22: 21–34

'Twas by a poor ass, who had just turned in with a couple of large panniers
upon his back, to collect eleemosunary turnip-tops and cabbage-leaves; and
stood dubious, with his two fore-feet on the inside of the threshold, and
with his two hinder feet towards the street, as not knowing very well
whether he was to go in, or no.

Now, 'tis an animal (be in what hurry I may) I cannot bear to strike—
there is a patient endurance of sufferings, wrote so unaffectedly in his looks
and carriage, which pleads so mightily for him, that it always disarms me;
and to that degree, that I do not like to speak unkindly to him: on the
contrary, meet him where I will—whether in town or country—in cart or
under panniers—whether in liberty or bondage—I have ever something
civil to say to him on my part; and as one word begets another (if he has as
little to do as I)—I generally fall into conversation with him; and surely
never is my imagination so busy as in framing his responses from the
etchings of his countenance—and where those carry me not deep
enough—in flying from my own heart into his, and seeing what is natural
for an ass to think—as well as a man, upon the occasion. In truth, it is the
only creature of all the classes of beings below me, with whom I can do this:
for parrots, jackdaws, &c.—I never exchange a word with them—nor with
the apes, &c. for pretty near the same reason; they act by rote, as the others
speak by it, and equally make me silent: nay my dog and my cat, though I
value them both—(and for my dog he would speak if he could)—yet
somehow or other, they neither of them possess the talents for conversation—I can make nothing of a discourse with them, beyond the *proposition*,

the *reply*, and *rejoinder*, which terminated my father's and my mother's conversations, in his beds of justice—and those uttered—there's an end of the dialogue—

—But with an ass, I can commune for ever.

Come, *Honesty!* said I,—seeing it was impracticable to pass betwixt him and the gate—art thou for coming in, or going out?

The ass twisted his head round to look up the street—

Well—replied I—we'll wait a minute for thy driver:

—He turned his head thoughtful about, and looked wistfully the opposite way—

I understand thee perfectly, answered I—if thou takest a wrong step in this affair, he will cudgel thee to death—Well! a minute is but a minute, and if it saves a fellow-creature a drubbing, it shall not be set down as ill spent.

He was eating the stem of an artichoke as this discourse went on, and in the little peevish contentions of nature betwixt hunger and unsavouriness, had dropt it out of his mouth half a dozen times, and picked it up again—God help thee, Jack! said I, thou hast a bitter breakfast on't—and many a bitter day's labour,—and many a bitter blow, I fear, for its wages—'tis all—all bitterness to thee, whatever life is to others.—And now thy mouth, if one knew the truth of it, is as bitter, I dare say, as soot—(for he had cast aside the stem) and thou hast not a friend perhaps in all this world, that will give thee a macaroon.—In saying this, I pulled out a paper of 'em, which I had just purchased, and gave him one—and at this moment that I am telling it, my heart smites me, that there was more of pleasantry in the conceit, of seeing *how* an ass would eat a macaroon—than of benevolence in giving him one, which presided in the act.

When the ass had eaten his macaroon, I pressed him to come in—the poor beast was heavy loaded—his legs seemed to tremble under him—he hung rather backwards, and as I pulled at his halter, it broke short in my hand—he looked up pensive in my face—'Don't thrash me with it—but if you will, you may'—If I do, said I, I'll be d—d.

The word was but one-half of it pronounced, like the abbess of Andoüillets'—(so there was no sin in it)—when a person coming in, let fall a thundering bastinado upon the poor devil's crupper, which put an end to the ceremony.

   Out upon it!

cried I—but the interjection was equivocal—and, I think, wrong placed too—for the end of an osier which had started out from the contexture of the ass's pannier, had caught hold of my breeches pocket, as he rushed by me, and rent it in the most disastrous direction you can imagine—so that the

Out upon it! in my opinion, should have come in here—but this I leave to be settled by

The

REVIEWERS

of

MY BREECHES

which I have brought over along with me for that purpose.

LAURENCE STERNE, *The Life and Opinions of Tristram Shandy*, 1759–67

The Loch Ness Monster's Song

Sssnnnwhufffll?
Hnwhuffl hhnnwfl hnfl hfl?
Gdroblboblhobngbl gbl gl g g g g glbgl.
Drublhaflablhaflubhafgabhaflhafl fl fl—
gm grawwwww grf grawf awfgm graw gm.
Hovoplodok-doplodovok-plovodokot-doplodokosh?
Splgraw fok fok splgrafhatchgabrlgabrl fok splfok!
Zgra kra gka fok!
Grof grawff gahf?
Gombl mbl bl—
blm plm,
blm plm,
blm plm,
blp.

EDWIN MORGAN (b. 1920)

WORKERS

For here at work are the scavenger beetles to whom is entrusted the high office of clearing the ground of impurities. . . .

As compensation for their unpleasant work, more than one gives out a strong scent of musk, and its ventral parts gleam like polished metal. Geotrupes hypocrita has the under part of its body bright with metallic lights of copper and gold, and G. stercorarius with amethystine violet. But the usual colour is black. It is in tropical regions that we find dung beetles in gorgeous array—absolutely living jewels. Under camel droppings in Upper Egypt is found a beetle rivalling the dazzling green of an emerald; Guiana, Brazil, Senegal, can show Copridæ of a metallic red, rich as the red of copper, bright as that of a ruby. If such a jewelled race be wanting to our country, still its dung beetles are not less remarkable for their habits.

What eagerness is displayed around a dropping! Never did adventurers from the four corners of the world show such eagerness in working a Californian claim! Before the sun grows too hot there they are by hundreds, large and small, pell-mell, of every kind and form and shape, hastening to secure a slice of the cake! Some work in the open air and rake the surface, some open galleries in the thickest part, seeking choice morsels, others toil in the under part and bury their treasure as soon as possible in the adjacent ground, and the smallest crumble some scrap fallen from the excavations of their strong fellow-workers. Some again—newcomers, and doubtless the hungriest—eat then and there, but the aim of the greater number is to lay up a store which will allow them to pass long days of plenty down in some sure retreat. A fresh dropping is not to be found just when wanted in a plain where no thyme grows; such a gift is indeed a piece of good fortune, and only comes to the lucky. So when found, the wealth is prudently stored. The smell has carried the good news a couple of miles round, and all have rushed to gather up provender. Some laggards are still coming in on the wing or on foot.

What is the one now trotting towards the heap, fearing to arrive too late? His long legs work with a brusque, awkward action, as if moved by some machine inside him; his little red antennæ spread their fans—sure sign of anxious greediness. He is coming, has arrived, not without upsetting some of the guests. It is the Sacred Beetle, all in black, the largest and most celebrated of our dung beetles.

Here he is at table, beside his fellow-guests, who are giving last touches to their balls with the flat of their large front legs, or enriching them with a last layer before retiring to enjoy the fruit of their labours in peace.

Let us follow this famous ball in each stage of construction.

The edge of the beetle's head is large and flat, and armed with six angular teeth arranged in a semicircle. It is the tool for digging and dividing, the rake to lift or reject such vegetable fibres as are not nutritious, to seek out what is best and rake it together. A choice is thus made, for these keen connoisseurs like one thing better than another—a somewhat careless choice, indeed, if the beetle alone be concerned, but one which is rigorously scrupulous if the maternal ball be in question, with its central hollow where the egg will hatch. Then every scrap of fibre is rejected, and only the quintessence of the stercorous matter is used to build the inner layer of the cell. Then, as soon as it is hatched, the young larva finds in the walls of its dwelling a dainty food which strengthens digestion and enables it later to attack the coarse outer layers. For its own needs the beetle is less fastidious, contenting itself with a general selection. The toothed head hollows and seeks, rejects and gathers, somewhat at haphazard. The forelegs aid mightily. They are flattened, bent into the arc of a circle, are furnished with strong nerves and armed with five stout teeth. If an effort has to be made, an obstacle overthrown, a path forced through the thickest part of the heap, the dung beetle elbows its way; in other words, throws its toothed legs right and left, and clears a half circle with a vigorous sweep of its rake. Room being made, these same feet have a new task; they collect bundles of the material raked up by the head, and pass it under the insect to the four hind-feet. These are planned for the turner's trade. The legs, especially the

last pair, are long and slender, slightly bent in an arc, and ending in a very
sharp spur or talon. A glance shows that they form a spherical compass,
capable of holding a globe in the bent legs to verify and correct its shape. In
fact, their mission is to shape the ball. Bundle after bundle the material
accumulates under the insect, held between the four legs which by a slight
pressure lend it their own curve and something of shape. Then from time
to time the rough hewn ball is set in motion between the legs of the double
spherical compass, turned underneath the beetle, and rolled into a perfect
sphere. Should the outer layer fail in plasticity and threaten to scale off, or
if some part be too fibrous, and refuse to be shaped by rotation, the faulty
part is retouched by the forefeet; little taps of their broad surface give
consistency to the new layer and imbed the recalcitrant fibre in the general
mass. When the sun shines and work is urgent, one is amazed by the
feverish activity with which the turner labours. Work goes on fast; first
there was a pellet, now it is as large as a nut, by and by it will be of the size
of an apple. I have seen some greedy beetles make up a ball as large as an
apple. Assuredly there is food in the larder for some days to come!

Provender being gathered, the next thing is to retire from the *mêlée*, and
carry it to a fitting place. Now we see some of the most characteristic habits
of the Scarabæus. He sets out at once, embracing the ball with the long hind
legs, whose talons, planted in the mass, serve as pivots—leans on the
intermediary legs as pivots, and using as levers the flat of the toothed
forefeet, which press the ground alternately, journeys backward with his
load, the body bent, the head low, and the hinder part upraised. The hind
feet, which are the chief organs in the mechanism, move continually, going
and coming and changing the place where the talons are stuck in, to alter
the axis of rotation, to keep the load balanced and advance by an alternate
push right and left. Thus the ball comes in contact with the ground in every
part of it, which gives it a perfect shape and lends consistency to the outer
layer by a uniform pressure. Courage! it moves, it rolls, and the journey's
end will be reached, though not without trouble. Here is a first difficulty.
The beetle has to cross a slope, and the heavy ball would naturally follow
the incline, but for reasons best known to itself, the insect prefers to cross
this natural slope—an audacious plan, which one false step or a grain of
sand to upset the balance will defeat. The false step is made, the ball rolls to
the bottom of the valley, and the insect, upset by the impetus of its load,
staggers, gets again on its legs, and hastens to harness itself afresh. The
mechanism works capitally. But look out, scatterbrain! follow the hollow of
the valley, it will spare labour and misadventure. The road is good and quite
level, and your ball will roll along with no exertion. Not a bit of it. The
insect has made up its mind to remount the slope already so fatal to it.
Perhaps it suits it to return to the heights. Against that I have nothing to say,
the Scarabæus knows better than I do whether it be advisable to dwell in

lofty regions. At all events, take this path which will lead you up by a gentle incline. Not at all. If there be near at hand some very stiff slope impossible to climb, then that slope this wrong-headed insect prefers. Then begins the labour of Sisyphus. With endless precautions the monstrous load is pain-fully hoisted, step by step to a certain height, the beetle always going tail first. One asks one's self by what miracle of statics such a mass can be kept on the slope. Ah! a clumsy movement brings all this toil to naught. Down goes the ball, dragging the beetle with it. The escalade is repeated, soon followed by a fresh fall. The attempt is renewed, and better managed at the difficult points; a nasty grass-root, which occasioned the previous tumbles, is prudently turned; we have almost got to the top. But gently! gently! the ascent is perilous, and a mere nothing may ruin all. A leg slips on a bit of smooth gravel, and ball and scavenger roll down together. The beetle begins all over again, with tireless obstinacy. Ten times, twenty times, will it attempt that further ascent, until persistency vanquishes all obstacles, or until, better advised, it takes the level road.

The scavenger does not always roll his ball single-handed, but frequently takes a partner, or rather, a partner takes him. The affair is usually managed thus: the ball being prepared, a beetle comes out of the throng, pushing it backwards. One of the newcomers, whose own work is hardly begun, leaves its task and runs to the ball, now in motion, to lend a hand to the lucky proprietor, who appears to accept the proffered aid in an amiable spirit. The two work as partners, each doing its best to convey the ball to a place of safety. Was a treaty made in the workshop, a tacit agreement to share the cake? While one kneaded and shaped, was the other tapping rich veins whence to extract choice material for their common use? I have never observed such collaboration, but have always seen every beetle exclusively occupied by his own affairs on the field of labour, so that the last comer has no acquired rights.

JEAN HENRI FABRE, *La Vie des Insectes*, 'The Sacred Beetle' (tr. 'the author of Mademoiselle Mori' *c.*1901)

Of all the Race of Animals, alone
The Bees have common Cities of their own:
And common Sons, beneath one Law they live,
And with one common Stock their Traffick drive.
Each has a certain home, a sev'ral Stall:
All is the States, the State provides for all.
Mindful of coming Cold, they share the Pain:
And hoard, for Winter's use, the Summer's gain.
Some o're the Publick Magazines preside,

And some are sent new Forrage to provide:
These drudge in Fields abroad, and those at home
Lay deep Foundations for the labour'd Comb,
With dew, *Narcissus* Leaves, and clammy Gum.
To pitch the waxen Flooring some contrive:
Some nurse the future Nation of the Hive:
Sweet Honey some condense, some purge the Grout;
The rest, in Cells apart, the liquid *Nectar* shut.
All, with united Force, combine to drive
The lazy Drones from the laborious Hive.
With Envy stung, they view each others Deeds:
With Diligence the fragrant Work proceeds.
As when the *Cyclops*, at th' Almighty Nod,
New Thunder hasten for their angry God:
Subdu'd in Fire the Stubborn Mettal lyes,
One brawny Smith the puffing Bellows plyes;
And draws, and blows reciprocating Air:
Others to quench the hissing Mass prepare:
With lifted Arms they order ev'ry Blow,
And chime their sounding Hammers in a Row;
With labour'd Anvils *Ætna* groans below.
Strongly they strike, huge Flakes of Flames expire,
With Tongs they turn the Steel, and vex it in the Fire.
If little things with great we may compare,
Such are the Bees, and such their busie Care:
Studious of Honey, each in his Degree,
The youthful Swain, the grave experienc'd Bee:
That in the Field; this in Affairs of State,
Employ'd at home, abides within the Gate:
To fortify the Combs, to build the Wall,
To prop the Ruins lest the Fabrick fall:
But late at Night, with weary Pinions come
The lab'ring Youth, and heavy laden home.
Plains, Meads, and Orchards all the day he plies,
The gleans of yellow Thime distend his Thighs:
He spoils the Saffron Flow'rs, he sips the blues
Of Vi'lets, wilding Blooms, and Willow Dews.
Their Toyl is common, common is their Sleep;
They shake their Wings when Morn begins to peep;
Rush through the City Gates without delay,
Nor ends their Work, but with declining Day:
Then having spent the last remains of Light,
They give thir Bodies due repose at Night:

When hollow Murmurs of their Ev'ning Bells,
Dismiss the sleepy Swains, and toll 'em to their Cells.
When once in Beds their weary Limbs they steep,
No buzzing Sounds disturb thir Golden Sleep.
'Tis sacred Silence all. Nor dare they stray,
When Rain is promis'd, or a stormy Day:
But near the city Walls their Watring take,
Nor Forrage far, but short Excursions make.
    And as when empty Barks on Billows float,
With sandy Ballast Sailors trim the Boat;
So Bees bear Gravel Stones, whose poising Weight
Steers thro' the whistling Winds their steddy Flight.
    But what's more strange, their modest Appetites,
Averse from *Venus*, fly the nuptial Rites.
No lust enervates their Heroic Mind,
Nor wasts their Strength on wanton Woman-Kind.
But in their Mouths reside their Genial Pow'rs,
They gather Children from the Leaves and Flow'rs.
Thus make they Kings to fill the Regal Seat;
And thus their little Citizens create:
And waxen Cities build, and Palaces of State.
And oft on Rocks their tender Wings they tear,
And sink beneath the Burthens which they bear.
Such Rage of Honey in their Bosom beats:
And such a Zeal they have for flow'ry Sweets.
    Thus tho' the race of Life they quickly run,
Which in the space of sev'n short Years is done;
Th' immortal Line in sure Succession reigns,
The Fortune of the Family remains:
And Grandsires Grandsons the long List contains.

VIRGIL (70–19 BC), *Georgics*, book IV, tr. JOHN DRYDEN (1631–1700)

The Spider holds a Silver Ball
In unperceived Hands—
And dancing softly to Himself
His Yarn of Pearl—unwinds—

He plies from Nought to Nought—
In unsubstantial Trade—
Supplants our Tapestries with His—
In half the period—

An Hour to rear supreme
His Continents of Light—
Then dangle from the Housewife's Broom—
His Boundaries—forgot—

EMILY DICKINSON (1830–86)

In Niimi's neighborhood, where there are plenty of mulberry-trees, many families keep silkworms;—the tending and feeding being mostly done by women and children. The worms are kept in large oblong trays, elevated upon light wooden stands about three feet high. It is curious to see hundreds of caterpillars feeding all together in one tray, and to hear the soft papery noise which they make while gnawing their mulberry-leaves. As they approach maturity, the creatures need almost constant attention. At brief intervals some expert visits each tray to inspect progress, picks up the plumpest feeders, and decides, by gently rolling them between forefinger and thumb, which are ready to spin. These are dropped into covered boxes, where they soon swathe themselves out of sight in white floss. A few only of the best are suffered to emerge from their silky sleep,—the selected breeders. They have beautiful wings, but cannot use them. They have mouths, but do not eat. They only pair, lay eggs, and die. For thousands of years their race has been so well-cared for, that it can no longer take any care of itself.

LAFCADIO HEARN, 'Silkworms', In Ghostly Japan, 1899

Friday 3rd October [1800].
When Wm & I returned from accompanying Jones we met an old man almost double, he had on a coat thrown over his shoulders above his waistcoat & coat. Under this he carried a bundle & had an apron on & a night cap. His face was interesting. He had Dark eyes & a long nose—John who afterwards met him at Wythburn took him for a Jew. He was of Scotch parents but had been born in the army. He had had a wife '& a good woman & it pleased God to bless us with ten children'—all these were dead but one of whom he had not heard for many years, a Sailor—his trade was to gather leeches but now leeches are scarce & he had not strength for it—he lived by begging & was making his way to Carlisle where he should buy a few godly books to sell. He said leeches were very scarce partly owing to this dry season, but many years they have been scarce—he supposed it owing to their being much sought after, that they did not breed fast, & were of slow growth. Leeches were formerly 2/6 100; they are now 30/.

DOROTHY WORDSWORTH (1771–1855), The Grasmere Journals

[At the end of July 1936, White] fetched the goshawk from Buckingham railway station, a light weight, bumping and screaming in a canvas-covered basket. Taken from its nest in Germany it had travelled to England by air, then on by rail to Scotland; thence, swopped for a female, to the falconer in Shropshire from whom he bought it.

'I picked up the clothes basket in a gingerly way and carried it into the barn. I had only just escaped from humanity, and the poor gos had only just been caught by it.'

The bird's jesses had been knotted into the basket. He untied them, and left it alone to recover. After an interval he put on his falconer's glove, went back to the barn, took the bird on his wrist and momentarily looked at it by the light of the hanging oil lamp. Then, correctly, he looked away: hawks must not be eyed. It gave a leap of rebellion, fell off his wrist and hung upside down on its jesses, flailing its wings. He was prepared for this too. It is called bating and would happen a thousand times.

He was impatient to begin—too impatient to consult the Shropshire falconer or to find out if there were any contemporary manuals on falconry. Unwittingly, he achieved the distinction of being perhaps the only twentieth-century falconer to man a bird by methods Shakespeare would have accepted as traditional. Nowadays a hawk is acclimatized to man by a process analogous to running-in a car. It is moved, little by little, from entire seclusion to a background of daily life. It associates its keeper with the food he leaves with it, it comes to think of him as an appurtenance and finally consents to be handled by him. It is then manned and ready for training.

The old method of 'watching' the bird is based on the fact that birds, like men, sleep by night. White, standing in the barn with Gos on his fist, patiently replacing him when he bated, whistling to him or repeating poems or stroking his talons with a feather or offering a bit of fresh-killed rabbit, always attentive to him yet always scrupulously aloof, patiently and unyieldingly and sleeplessly keeping him awake for three nights running until the wild bird abdicated from its feral state and fell asleep on the gloved hand, was as much a figure out of the past as the ghost of a ballad falconer would have been. 'It is strangely like some of the eighteenth-century stories of seduction,' David Garnett said of the resulting book. But seduction is only half the story. Eighteenth-century seducers knew their business: in the story of White and Gos, two virginities met together.

For six weeks White kept a day-book, entering, sometimes barely able to keep his eyes open, the uncertain progress of Gos's training. Sandwiched among these are his own domestic works: cleaning grates, scrubbing floors, shooting rabbits and pigeons for Gos's victuals, making bookshelves and a kitchen table, house-painting. He was putting a coat of blue paint on the front door when Gos escaped. With the kindest motives he had lengthened the bird's tether by six yards of tarred twine, a twine which he knew to be defective, since it had broken before.

'I saw the end of the twine lying loose, with no leash tied to it. It had snapped quite clean. Gos was gone.'

SYLVIA TOWNSEND WARNER, *T. H. White: A Biography*, 1967

When making for the Brooke, the Falkoner doth espie
On River, Plash, or Mere, where store of Fowle doth lye:
Whence forced over land, by skilfull Falconers trade:
A faire convenient flight, may easily be made.
He whistleth off his Hawkes, whose nimble pineons streight,
Doe worke themselves by turnes, into a stately height:
And if that after check, the one or both doe goe,
Sometimes he them the Lure, sometimes doth water show;
The trembling Fowle that heare the Jigging Hawk-bels ring,
And find it is too late, to trust then to their wing,
Lye flat upon the flood, whilst the high-mounted Hawks,
Then being lords alone, in their etheriall walkes,
Aloft so bravely stirre, their bells so thicke that shake;
Which when the Falkoner sees, that scarce one plane they make
The gallant'st Birds saith he, that ever flew on wing,
And sweares there is a Flight, were worthy of a King.
    Then making to the Flood, to force the Fowles to rise,
The fierce and eager Hawkes, downe thrilling from the Skies,
Make sundry Canceleers e'r they the Fowle can reach,
Which then to save their lives, their wings doe lively stretch.
But when the whizzing Bels the silent ayre doe cleave,
And that their greatest speed, them vainly doe deceive;
And the sharpe cruell Hawkes, they at their backs doe view,
Themselves for very feare they instantly ineawe.
    The Hawkes get up againe into their former place;
And ranging here and there, in that their ayery race:
Still as the fearefull Fowle attempt to scape away,
With many a stouping brave, them in againe they lay.
But when the Falkoners take their Hawking-poles in hand,
And crossing of the Brooke, doe put it over land:
The Hawke gives it a souse, that makes it to rebound,
Well neere the height of man, sometime above the ground;

ineawe: plunge into the water

Oft takes a leg, or wing, oft takes away the head,
And oft from necke to tayle, the backe in two doth shread.
With many a Wo ho ho, and jocond Lure againe,
When he his quarry makes upon the grassy plaine.

MICHAEL DRAYTON (1563–1631), *Poly-Olbion*, Song xx

Cormorant

Men speak lightly of frustration,
As if they'd invented it.

As if like the cormorant
Of Gifu, thick leg roped, a ring

Cutting into the neck, they dived
All night to the fish-swelled water

And flapped up with the catch lodged
In the throat, only to have

The fisher yank it out and toss
It gasping on a breathless heap.

Then to dive again, hunger
Churning in the craw, air just

Slipping by the throat-ring
To spray against the lungs.

And once more to be jerked back in
And have the fisher grab the spoil.

Men speak lightly of frustration,
And dim in the lantern light

The cormorant makes out the flash
Of fins and, just beyond,

The streamered boats of tourists
Rocking under *saké* fumes.

LUCIEN STRYK (b. 1924)

The community of fowls to which Tess had been appointed as supervisor, purveyor, nurse, surgeon, and friend, made its headquarters in an old thatched cottage standing in an enclosure that had once been a garden, but was now a trampled and sanded square. The house was overrun with ivy, its chimney being enlarged by the boughs of the parasite to the aspect of a ruined tower. The lower rooms were entirely given over to the birds, who walked about them with a proprietary air, as though the place had been built by themselves, and not by certain dusty copyholders who now lay east and west in the churchyard.

The rooms wherein dozens of infants had wailed at their nursing now resounded with the tapping of nascent chicks. Distracted hens in coops occupied spots where formerly stood chairs supporting sedate agriculturists. The chimney-corner and once blazing hearth was now filled with inverted beehives, in which the hens laid their eggs; while out of doors the plots that each succeeding householder had carefully shaped with his spade were torn by the cocks in wildest fashion.

When Tess had occupied herself about an hour the next morning in altering and improving the arrangements, according to her skilled ideas as the daughter of a professed poulterer, the door in the wall opened and a servant in white cap and apron entered. She had come from the manor-house.

'Mrs d'Urberville wants the fowls as usual,' she said; but perceiving that Tess did not quite understand, she explained, 'Mis'ess is a old lady, and blind.'

'Blind!' said Tess.

Almost before her misgiving at the news could find time to shape itself she took, under her companion's direction, two of the most beautiful of the Hamburghs in her arms, and followed the maid-servant, who had likewise taken two, to the adjacent mansion, which, though ornate and imposing, showed traces everywhere on this side that some occupant of its chambers could bend to the love of dumb creatures—feathers floating within view of the front, and hen-coops standing on the grass.

'Ah, you are the young woman come to look after my birds?' said Mrs d'Urberville, recognizing a new footstep. 'I hope you will be kind to them. My bailiff tells me you are quite the proper person. Well, where are they? Ah, this is Strut! But he is hardly so lively to-day, is he? He is alarmed at being handled by a stranger, I suppose. And Phena too—yes, they are a little frightened—aren't you, dears? But they will soon get used to you.'

While the old lady had been speaking Tess and the other maid, in obedience to her gestures, had placed the fowls severally in her lap, and she had felt them over from head to tail, examining their beaks, their combs, the manes of the cocks, their wings, and their claws. Her touch enabled her to recognize them in a moment, and to discover if a single feather were crippled or draggled. She handled their crops, and knew what they had eaten, and if too little or too much; her face enacting a vivid pantomime of the criticisms passing in her mind.

The birds that the two girls had brought in were duly returned to the yard, and the process was repeated till all the pet cocks and hens had been submitted to the old woman—Hamburghs, Bantams, Cochins, Brahmas, Dorkings, and such other sorts as were in fashion just then—her perception of each visitor being seldom at fault as she received the bird upon her knees.

It reminded Tess of a Confirmation, in which Mrs d'Urberville was the bishop, the fowls the young people presented, and herself and the maidservant the parson and curate of the parish bringing them up.

THOMAS HARDY, *Tess of the D'Urbervilles*, 1891

Winkie

'We also serve'

GIVE ME GOOD PIGEONS!
You pose in your glass case
Putting a brave face on your taxidermed
Municipal afterlife.
Close by you, Winkie, is a photograph,
A bomber's aircrew snapped in the Second War.
You were their mascot and survival kit.
    Click-click went their tongues;
    And *Winkie-Winkie* they sang
Pressing titbits through the wooden bars
On leather and vibrating fingers.
Winkie-Winkie chirped the goggled men.

Over Norway, its fuselage and wings on fire,
The bomber droned down to the sea,
    Flames sizzling in sleet
    As frantic signals pinged
Against deaf radio ears in nowhere.

Cupped hands released you from a rubber boat.
    Miniature of instinct,
    Dedicated one, your stuffed breast swells
With pride in your only nature!

GIVE ME GOOD PIGEONS!
Their *chuck-chuck-chuck's*
A thwarted cooing from the woods
Haunting city squares
Named for dimwits and dignitaries
With old bucolic neighbourhoods,
Fife, Gowrie and the Mearns.
Whether as spy-birds on a sneaky errand
Bearing a snip of microfilm for eyes
Devoted to secrecy, released by a hand
Clandestinely over a window-sill in Warsaw,
Or with the gentler mail of love, birth and death
Winged over the suburbs and snipers from
The besieged city—see the rifle, the Prussian eye
Point through the foliage round the gardened villas—
    You are liberty's bird,
    Unstreamlined and civilian,
    With the guts and stamina of a taxpayer
And behind you the solidarity of your species,
    The Universal Union of Pigeons.

    Your mission doesn't matter
    Nor what unvisa'd coasts
    You cross on your postal expeditions,
Nor the direction you take, or whatever
Nationality is claimed for the forests below
Or who pretends to own the air and seasons
And the pronunciation of rivers and mountains.
    The blame is not yours—
    Docile legionary,
    Warrior bearing words,
    Beloved of the Intelligence Services'
    Eccentric dogsbodies,
In the obscurest ministerial spires
With their bowls and jugs, their bags of maize
For kept cushats, *pigeons voyageurs*, homers,
Birds of the cloak-and-dagger cryptography.

An imprisoned lover turns on his stinking straw
And a dove at the window chortles.
A letter is read to the sound of cooing.

I do not like the big brave boasts of war.
    GIVE ME GOOD PIGEONS!—

A very large number of Great Commoners
Built like Nye Bevan or Gambetta.

  Winkie read his charts
On his table of instinct, and found the Tay's dent
    On the planet of places.
    A perfect rescue—saved by a bird
    Homing down to Carnoustie.

Bird of X-marks-the-spot
Bird of the ringed foot, married to the miles
Bird of human purpose but immune to guilt
Bearer of tidings and long-distance billet-doux
Reports of troop movements, the planned assassination
Scorner of moats, guard towers and jammed radio
Dove that to a hand in Babylon
Brought more news of the strange horsemen
And bird that to Chaucerian casements brought
Melodious greetings to the heartsick Lady
Bird of the allotments, bird of the long race
Hand-held bird, heartbeat in gentle hands
Olympic bird, love-bird, bird of the peace
Dove of the Annunciation, forerunner of Christ
Bird of the strange beam and the beautiful lily
Mendicant bird, begging around footwear
With your jabbing head, your hungry, urban strut

FLY, WINKIE, FLY!

DOUGLAS DUNN (b. 1942)

'Get to your places!' shouted the Queen in a voice of thunder, and people began running about in all directions, tumbling up against each other; however, they got settled down in a minute or two, and the game began. Alice thought she had never seen such a curious croquet-ground in all her life; it was all ridges and furrows; the balls were live hedgehogs, the mallets live flamingoes, and the soldiers had to double themselves up and to stand upon their hands and feet, to make the arches.

The chief difficulty Alice found at first was in managing her flamingo: she succeeded in getting its body tucked away, comfortably enough, under her arm, with its legs hanging down, but generally, just as she had got its neck nicely straightened out, and was going to give the hedgehog a blow with its head, it *would* twist itself round and look up in her face, with such a puzzled expression that she could not help bursting out laughing: and when she had got its head down, and was going to begin again, it was very provoking to find that the hedgehog had unrolled itself, and was in the act of crawling away: besides all this, there was generally a ridge or a furrow in the way wherever she wanted to send the hedgehog to, and, as the doubled-up soldiers were always getting up and walking off to other parts of the ground, Alice soon came to the conclusion that it was a very difficult game indeed.

LEWIS CARROLL, *Alice's Adventures in Wonderland*, 1865

The magic circle was now occupied by Lamarck's Educated Apes. A dozen chimpanzees, six of either sex, all in sailor suits, were seated in pairs at little wooden double desks, each with a slate and slate pencil clutched in their leathery hands. A chimp in a sober black suit with a watch-chain looped athwart his bosom, a mortarboard at a rakish angle on his head, stood at the blackboard armed with a cue. The pupils were hushed and attentive, in marked contrast to the young woman in a grubby print wrapper who sat on the plush-topped barrier of the ring idly filing her nails with an emery board. She yawned. She paid them no attention. The chimps put themselves through their own paces; the trainer's woman was no more than their keeper and Monsieur Lamarck, a feckless drunkard, left them to rehearse on their own.

Walser could make no sense of the diagram chalked on the blackboard yet the chimps appeared to be occupied in transcribing it to their slates. The partings in the centres of their glossy heads were white as honeycomb. The Professor made a few swift passes with his left hand and pointed to the lower right-hand corner of the diagram; a female towards the back of the class raised her arm eagerly. When the Professor pointed his cue at her, she performed a sequence of gestures that reminded Walser of the movements of the hands of Balinese dancers. The Professor considered, nodded and chalked in another arabesque on the diagram. The neat, shining heads at once bent in unison and the air shrilled with the scratching of a dozen slate pencils, a sound like a flock of starlings coming in to roost.

Walser smiled under his matte white; how irresistibly comic, these hirsute studies! Yet his curiosity was piqued by this mysterious scholarship. He squinted again at the diagram but could not tease a meaning out of it. Yet there seemed to be . . . could it be? Was it possible? . . . was there *writing* on the blackboard? If he crept round towards the Tsar's box, he might be able to see better . . . Stealing softly across the tiered benches in the clown's long shoes he had not yet learned to master, the clumsy toe knocked against an empty vodka bottle left in the angle of a step. The bottle skipped down the rest of the tiers and banged against the barrier.

At this unexpected noise, the silent group all turned and fixed the intruder with thirteen pairs of quick, dark eyes. Walser slipped on to a bench and tried to make himself inconspicuous, but he knew he had stumbled on a secret when the lesson immediately stopped.

The Professor whipped out a yellow duster and wiped off the diagram in a trice. The girl who'd asked the question solemnly stood on her head on the lid of her desk. Her desk-mate took a catapult from his pocket and struck the Professor full in the face with a juicy ink-pellet, inducing in him a farcical and gibbering outrage.

Their bored keeper went on filing her nails. It was only the 'apes at school' number.

Faced with this insurrection in the classroom, the Professor happily discovered a cache of dunces' caps stacked behind the blackboard. He bounced round the ring, disposing a cap on each capering head; then, on impulse, leapt lightly across the barrier and Walser got a dunce's cap, too. The Professor's face, grinning like a Cheshire cat, was not six inches from Walser's own as he popped it on. Their eyes met.

Walser never forgot this first, intimate exchange with one of these beings whose life ran parallel to his, this inhabitant of the magic circle of difference, unreachable . . . but not unknowable; this exchange with the speaking eyes of the dumb. It was like the clearing of a haze. Then the Professor, as if acknowledging their meeting across the gulf of strangeness, pressed his tough forefinger down on Walser's painted smile, bidding him be silent.

ANGELA CARTER, *Nights at the Circus*, 1984

We must not forget what *Plutarke* affirmeth to have seene a dog in *Rome* doe before the Emperour *Vespasian* the father, in the Theatre of *Marcellus*. This Dog served a jugler, who was to play a fiction of many faces, and sundry countenances, where he also was to act a part. Amongst other things, he was for a long while to counterfeit and faine himselfe dead, because he had eaten of a certaine drugge: having swallowed a peece of bread, which was supposed to be the drug, he began sodainly to stagger and shake, as if he had beene giddie, then stretching and laying himselfe along, as stiffe as if hee were starke-dead, suffered himselfe to be dragged and haled from one place to another, according to the subject and plot of the play, and when he knew his time, first he began faire and softly to stirre, as if he were rouzed out of a dead slumber, then lifting up his head, hee looked and stared so gastly, that all the bystanders were amazed.

Arrius protesteth to have seene an Elephant, who on every thigh having a Cimball hanging, and one fastned to his truncke, at the sound of which, all other Elephants danced in a round, now rising aloft, then lowting full low at certaine cadences, even as the instrument directed them, and was much delighted with the harmony. In the great shews of *Rome*, Elephants were ordinarily seene, taught to move and dance at the sound of a voice, certaine dances, wherein were many strange shifts, enterchanges, caprings, and cadences, very hard to be learned. Some have beene noted to konne and practise their lessons, using much study and care, as being loath to be chidden and beaten of their masters.

MONTAIGNE, An Apologie of Raymond Sebond (tr. Florio, 1603)

At the first camp we reached I found about twenty Burmans, including a carpenter of sorts, erecting a set of jungle buildings. It was explained to me that this camp was to be my headquarters during the coming monsoon months. I soon realised that the elephant was the backbone of the Burmese teak industry.

The history of the Bombay Burma Corporation went back to the time of King Theebaw, when a senior member of the firm, who visited Burma, appreciated the great possibilities of the teak trade and was able to obtain a lease of certain forest areas on agreeing to pay a fixed royalty per ton of teak extracted.

As a result, sawmills were established at the ports, and forests previously regarded as inaccessible were opened up, a system of rafting teak-logs down the creeks and rivers was organised and elephants were bought on a large scale. Teak is one of the world's best hardwoods, partly because of the silica it contains. In the mixed deciduous forests of Burma, teak grows best at heights between two thousand and three thousand feet in steep, precipitous country, though it is also found in the rich valleys. The trees often stand ten or twelve to the acre, but usually only one tree—the largest—is selected, and the remaining trees, which are immature or under the girth limit, are left for the next cycle of felling, which is probably twenty-five or thirty years later. Under this system the teak forests would never be exhausted. The tree chosen is killed by ringing the bark at the base, and the dead tree is left standing for three years before it is felled, by which time the timber is seasoned and has become light enough to float; for green teak will not float. As teak grows best in country which is inaccessible to tractors and machinery, elephant power is essential for hauling and pushing the logs from the stump to the nearest stream that will be capable of floating them during the flood-waters of the monsoon months.

Not only do the streams, creeks and rivers vary very much in size, but the degree of flooding during the monsoon spates varies with each, and depends on the size and situation of the catchment area feeding it. A great deal of experience is required to judge how high the flood will reach—or, in other words, below what level the logs must be hauled. There are all sorts of natural indications to enable one to judge this, that one learns in time.

Debris from last year's floods caught up in bushes is a good guide, but often does not last from one year to the next. Less obvious indications are that jungle weaver-birds, which build near the creeks, never let their pendulous nests hang low enough to touch flood-water, and that lower down, near the rivers, turtles lay their eggs only above the level of the highest flood.

A lot of clearance work is necessary in the jungle. Gorges have to be blasted clear of the huge boulders in their beds, which if left would trap the logs in jams when they were coming down on a spate. Dragging-paths have to be cut through the jungle for elephant haulage, and these have to circumvent natural obstacles such as cliffs, ravines and waterfalls. The Bombay Burma Corporation had to build up herds of elephants. Some were bought, mostly from Siam, but a few also from India. The majority were, however, obtained by capturing wild elephants in Burma and breaking them in. This process is known as 'kheddaring', and Burmans, Karens and Shans employ rather different methods in carrying it out.

When, however, the Bombay Burma Corporation had built up considerable herds of elephants, it realised the importance of the elephant calves born in captivity. These could be broken in and trained much more easily than captured wild elephants. Finally, when the Corporation's herds had nearly reached a strength of two thousand animals, it was found that births balanced the deaths, and that new supplies of elephants were required only on rare occasions. The kheddaring of wild elephants, on any extensive scale, thus came to an end, as it was unnecessary.

The health, management and handling of the elephants in this enormous organisation impressed me as the factor on which everything else depended. I well remember wondering how many people who had waltzed on the teak deck of a luxury liner had ever realised that the boards of which it was built had been hauled as logs from the stump by an elephant in the Burma jungles.

J. H. WILLIAMS, *Elephant Bill*, 1950

Ringwell cubbing days are among my happiest memories. Those mornings now reappear in my mind, lively and freshly painted by the sunshine of an autumn which made amends for the rainy weeks which had washed away the summer. Four days a week we were up before daylight. I had heard the snoring stable-hands roll out of bed with yawns and grumblings, and they were out and about before the reticent Henry came into my room with a candle and a jug of warm water. (How Henry managed to get up was a mystery.) Any old clothes were good enough for cubbing, and I was very soon downstairs in the stuffy little living-room, where Denis had an apparatus for boiling eggs. While they were bubbling he put the cocoa-powder in the cups, two careful spoonfuls each, and not a grain more. A third spoonful was unthinkable.

Not many minutes afterwards we were out by the range of loose-boxes under the rustling trees, with quiet stars overhead and scarcely a hint of morning. In the kennels the two packs were baying at one another from their separate yards, and as soon as Denis had got his horse from the gruff white-coated head-groom, a gate released the hounds—twenty-five or thirty couple of them, and all very much on their toes. Out they streamed like a flood of water, throwing their tongues and spreading away in all directions with waving sterns, as though they had never been out in the world before. Even then I used to feel the strangeness of the scene with its sharp exuberance of unkennelled energy. Will's hearty voice and the crack of his whip stood out above the clamour and commotion which surged around Denis and his horse. Then, without any apparent lull or interruption, the whirlpool became a well-regulated torrent flowing through the gateway into the road, along which the sound of hoofs receded with a purposeful clip-clopping. Whereupon I hoisted myself on to an unknown horse—usually an excited one—and set off higgledy-piggledy along the road to catch them up. Sometimes we had as many as twelve miles to go, but more often we were at the meet in less than an hour.

The mornings I remember most zestfully were those which took us up on to the chalk downs. To watch the day breaking from purple to dazzling gold while we trotted up a deep-rutted lane; to inhale the early freshness when we were on the sheep-cropped uplands; to stare back at the low country with its cock-crowing farms and mist-coiled waterways; thus to be riding out with a sense of spacious discovery—was it not something stolen from the lie-a-bed world and the luckless city workers—even though it ended in nothing more than the killing of a leash of fox-cubs? (for whom, to tell the truth, I felt an unconfessed sympathy). Up on the downs in fine September weather sixteen years ago.

SIEGFRIED SASSOON, *Memoirs of a Fox-Hunting Man*, 1928

Fetching Cows

The black one, last as usual, swings her head
And coils a black tongue round a grass-tuft. I
Watch her soft weight come down, her split feet spread.

In front, the others swing and slouch; they roll
Their great Greek eyes and breathe out milky gusts
From muzzles black and shiny as wet coal.

The collie trots, bored, at my heels, then plops
Into the ditch. The sea makes a tired sound
That's always stopping though it never stops.

A haycart squats prickeared against the sky.
Hay breath and milk breath. Far out in the West
The wrecked sun founders though its colours fly.

The collie's bored. There's nothing to control . . .
The black cow is two native carriers
Bringing its belly home, slung from a pole.

NORMAN MacCAIG (b. 1910)

Suddenly there arose from all parts of the lowland a prolonged and repeated call—

'Waow! waow! waow!'

From the furthest east to the furthest west the cries spread as if by contagion, accompanied in some cases by the barking of a dog. It was not the expression of the valley's consciousness that beautiful Tess had arrived, but the ordinary announcement of milking-time—half-past four o'clock, when the dairymen set about getting in the cows.

The red and white herd nearest at hand, which had been phlegmatically waiting for the call, now trooped towards the steading in the background, their great bags of milk swinging under them as they walked. Tess followed slowly in their rear, and entered the barton by the open gate through which they had entered before her. Long thatched sheds stretched round the enclosure, their slopes encrusted with vivid green moss, and their eaves supported by wooden posts rubbed to a glossy smoothness by the flanks of infinite cows and calves of bygone years, now passed to an oblivion almost inconceivable in its profundity. Between the posts were ranged the milchers, each exhibiting herself at the present moment to a whimsical eye in the rear as a circle on two stalks, down the centre of which a switch moved pendulum-wise; while the sun, lowering itself behind this patient row, threw their shadows accurately inwards upon the wall. Thus it threw shadows of these obscure and homely figures every evening with as much care over each contour as if it had been the profile of a Court beauty on a palace wall; copied them as diligently as it had copied Olympian shapes on marble *façades* long ago, or the outline of Alexander, Cæsar, and the Pharaohs.

They were the less restful cows that were stalled. Those that would stand still of their own will were milked in the middle of the yard, where many of such better behaved ones stood waiting now—all prime milchers, such as were seldom seen out of this valley, and not always within it; nourished by the succulent feed which the water-meads supplied at this prime season of the year. Those of them that were spotted with white reflected the sunshine in dazzling brilliancy, and the polished brass knobs on their horns glittered with something of military display. Their large-veined udders hung ponderous as sandbags, the teats sticking out like the legs of a gipsy's crock; and as each animal lingered for her turn to arrive the milk oozed forth and fell in drops to the ground.

The milkers formed quite a little battalion of men and maids, the men operating on the hard-teated animals, the maids on the kindlier natures. It was a large dairy. There were nearly a hundred milchers under Crick's management, all told; and of the herd the master-dairyman milked six or eight with his own hands, unless away from home. These were the cows that milked hardest of all; for his journey milkmen being more or less casually hired, he would not entrust this half-dozen to their treatment, lest, from indifference, they should not milk them fully; nor to the maids, lest they should fail in the same way for lack of finger-grip; with the result that in course of time the cows would 'go azew'—that is, dry up. It was not the loss for the moment that made slack milking so serious, but that with the decline of demand there came decline, and ultimately cessation, of supply.

After Tess had settled down to her cow there was for a time no talk in the barton, and not a sound interfered with the purr of the milk-jets into the numerous pails, except a momentary exclamation to one or other of the beasts requesting her to turn round or stand still. The only movements were those of the milkers' hands up and down, and the swing of the cows' tails. Thus they all worked on, encompassed by the vast flat mead which extended to either slope of the valley—a level landscape compounded of old landscapes long forgotten, and, no doubt, differing in character very greatly from the landscape they composed now.

THOMAS HARDY, *Tess of the D'Urbervilles*, 1891

There were railings along the road leading to [Silver Street] bridge, lovely Georgian railings, now improved away; and often people were glad to dodge behind them to escape from the terrified and terrifying herds of cattle, which were driven with bangs and shouts, through the streets to the Monday cattle-market. There had always been some sort of bridge, where the bridge is now, and Desiderius Erasmus himself must often have walked down our road when he went out from Queens' to take the air.

In the summer the thick white dust came powdering in at all the windows; rising in clouds from the horses' hooves, and whitening the grass and the trees across the road. And in the winter the oozy, jammy mud sloshed about, and the street-cleaners scraped it up in delicious soupy spoonfuls, and threw it into their carts. And everywhere and all the time there was the smell of horses; it came in at the windows with the dust; not very nice, but not nearly so nasty as the petrol and exhaust smells are now. And often we heard the clattering of the feet of the hansom-cab horses and the jingling of their bells, as they cantered by; for they were mostly retired Newmarket race-horses, and so they always had to pretend to gallop, to satisfy the undergraduates, however slowly they might really be going. My cousin Nora said she knew the faces of every one of those horses.

Then there was the rush and rattle of the butchers' traps and their furious little ponies, whom we believed to be fed on meat to make them fierce; and the yellow milk-carts, like Roman chariots, with their big brass-bound churns of milk and their little dippers hooked on at the side; and the hairy-footed shire horses, who drew the great corn-wagons in from the country. And on Saturdays, market days, the farmers came trotting by in their traps; and the carriers' carts plodded in with their slow horses from villages as much as fifteen miles away. Sometimes they were hooded carts, sometimes they were just open carts, with planks for seats, on which sat twelve cloaked and bonneted women, six a side, squeezed together, for the interminable journey. As late as 1914 I knew the carrier of Croydon-cum-Clopton, twelve miles from Cambridge; his cart started at 6.30 in the morning and got back about ten at night. Though he was not old, he could neither read nor write; but he took commissions all along the road—a packet of needles for Mrs This, and a new teapot for Mrs That—and delivered them all correctly on the way back.

All day long the slow four-wheelers used to go clip-clopping along to the station. And sometimes, even slower, even heavier, yet more dismal, there was the Plop, Plop, Plop, of the feet of the oldest horses in the world, as they plugged along, pulling the funereal Girton cabs out to Girton with four melancholy students in each; while the drab Newnham girls skurried to and fro to their lectures on foot. And all the time there were dons going 'to lecture, with the wind in their gowns'; and undergraduates in their Norfolk jackets, setting out in pairs to do the 'Grantchester Grind' for exercise.

Gwen Raverat, Period Piece: A Cambridge Childhood, 1952

Black Beauty grows up.

When I was four years old, Squire Gordon came to look at me. He examined my eyes, my mouth, and my legs; he felt them all down; and then I had to walk and trot and gallop before him; he seemed to like me, and said, 'When he has been well broken in, he will do very well.' My master said he would break me in himself, as he should not like me to be frightened or hurt, and he lost no time about it, for the next day he began.

Every one may not know what breaking in is, therefore I will describe it. It means to teach a horse to wear a saddle and bridle and to carry on his back a man, woman, or child; to go just the way they wish, and to go quietly. Besides this, he has to learn to wear a collar, a crupper, and a breeching, and to stand still whilst they are put on; then to have a cart or a chaise fixed behind him, so that he cannot walk or trot without dragging it after him: and he must go fast or slow, just as his driver wishes. He must never start at what he sees, nor speak to other horses, nor bite, nor kick, nor have any will of his own; but always do his master's will; even though he may be very tired or hungry; but the worst of all is, when his harness is once on, he may neither jump for joy nor lie down for weariness. So you see this breaking in is a great thing.

Later in his career, Black Beauty works for a London cabbie.

It is always difficult to drive fast in the city in the middle of the day, when the streets are full of traffic, but we did what could be done; and when a good driver and a good horse, who understand each other, are of one mind, it is wonderful what they can do. I had a very good mouth—that is, I could be guided by the slightest touch of the rein, and that is a great thing in London, amongst carriages, omnibuses, carts, vans, trucks, cabs, and great wagons creeping along at a walking pace; some going one way, some another, some going slowly, others wanting to pass them, omnibuses stopping short every few minutes to take up a passenger, obliging the horse that is coming behind to pull up too, or to pass, and get before them: perhaps you try to pass, but just then, something else comes dashing in through the narrow opening, and you have to keep in behind the omnibus again; presently you think you see a chance, and manage to get to the front, going so near the wheels on each side, that half an inch nearer and they would scrape. Well—you get along for a bit, but soon find yourself in a long train of carts and carriages all obliged to go at a walk; perhaps you come to a regular block-up, and have to stand still for minutes together, till something clears out into a side street, or the policeman interferes: you have to be ready for any chance—to dash forward if there be an opening, and be quick as a rat dog to see if there be room, and if there be time, lest you get your own wheels locked, or smashed, or the shaft of some other vehicle run into your chest or shoulder. All this is what you have to be ready for. If you want to get through London fast in the middle of the day, it wants a deal of practice.

ANNA SEWELL, Black Beauty, 1877

The old horse is not a common cart-horse; and though he has got down by degrees to 'odd jobber', yet he has seen very different days, and not so very long ago either. His is the simple history of so many horses that come down in the world as low as Dibdin's 'high-mettled racer', though they may not have started quite so well. His master used in better times to be a bit of a horse-breeder; and at four years old the colt looked so useful, and was so fond of jumping, that he kept him for his own riding in the days when a farmer thought that he had as good a right as anybody else to ride a good horse. He kept the horse, refusing a big offer for him, and rode him to hounds for some years. Without being a flyer he was honest and full of courage, and knew what was wanted of him almost as soon as his rider had made up his mind. When about six years old he was broken to harness, and for years took the farmer and his wife to market in the old four-wheel, ten miles there and back. By degrees he got more trapping and less hunting, and was slower at both than formerly. But it didn't matter much, for the time had come when there was very little hunting for farmers. You would have said one thing of him yet with certainty—that he never would fall. But the country roads were covered with loose stones one dry summer, and he fell and broke his knees. He was patched up for a bit, in hopes that he wouldn't fall again; but he did. Then his master got another horse, and the old fellow was gradually relegated to odd jobs. I have no doubt that he found this disagreeable enough at first; but he made the best of his lot. Perhaps he was thankful things were no worse.

The old man whose office it now became to harness and take him to the mill had a fellow-feeling for him. 'We're both on us has beens,' he used to remark with a grin. The old man had been a rare 'old sorted' waggoner, and no day, a few years ago, had been too long for him; but, like the old horse, he had gradually got less and less able to work, and of course as this happened his wages fell off. But, like his old equine friend, he subdued whatever bitter feelings he may have had and made the best of his lot. Two winters ago he got a thorough wetting; and when he went home at night the rheumatism took hold of him, and he was never good for much afterwards. He always facetiously alludes to that date as the time when he broke his knees.

When the snow began to fall about four o'clock in the afternoon, the old horse didn't bother his head about it, for he thought his friend Robin would be sure to fetch him in; but old Robin had been at home with the rheumat- ism since dinner-time. He had had little to eat all day, for the field he was turned into was as bare as your hand; and he was depending on the lock of hay which would be thrown into his shed at night. He looked forward to this supper with complacency, feeling, to use his own unspoken words, as if he could have eaten a manger if he had one. The field in which he was now to spend the night owing to the carter's forgetfulness, was on high ground; and, the hedge having been fleached last year, there was no shelter to be had. As draining has been overdone in some places, so in cold climates where the spring is late it is a great mistake to cut down all your high thick thorn hedges just that your farm may look a little neater than your neighbour's. So thinks the old horse as night comes on, and the south-west wind whistles past him, and he begins to understand the situation. The snow lies white on his back like a blanket. He knows of course every inch of the field, and when he finds he is forgotten he walks slowly to the lowest part of it, near the gate which he would so greatly like to see opened. The wind does not catch him so badly here, and what there is he turns his tail to; and when once he has taken up his position he stands as still as if carved out of wood or stone. Young horses will sometimes trot or canter about to keep themselves warm. An old horse knows that he cannot trot about for ever, and that when he stops he will be colder than before. So he stands perfectly still.

Late at night it came on to snow again, and the old horse was seen by a benighted villager still standing by the gate. The man said that as he went by the footpath across the fields he walked right up against the horse before he saw him, and that the poor old creature seemed to wake up and followed him slowly about twenty yards down the field. Then the man got over the stile, and there he left the horse; and there in the morning they found him. I shouldn't like to think that horses (and dogs) cannot think of anything in the long hours and days when they appear to have nothing to do. But if they do think, I am afraid their thoughts must be very painful ones sometimes. Who has not seen the best-natured old horse give a sudden stamp, with vexation—or a whisk of his tail, with disgust perhaps—at the foolish way which you persist in misunderstanding him.

The old horse's last thoughts must have been very bitter. From foaldom he had done his best to be an honest horse, and this was what he got by it in the end. 'Well, it's a good thing it's over.' Who can say that he did not give one last thought to old Robin who had cared for him so long? The old man is failing fast, and no one likes to be burdened with him. He has had something from the parish for some years, but not enough to find bread and cheese for him and his old missus when he is unable to work, which now happens sadly too often. The farmer is aware of a mild pang under his rough coat when the old horse is found laid out with his winding-sheet about him. He thinks for a minute or two of the days long ago when he carried him so well. Far happier days: he cannot afford to dwell on them. So he hardens his heart again for the work which is no longer a labour of love.

RICHARD JEFFERIES, *Field and Farm*, 1884

Retiring pit ponies end centuries of tradition

The last pit ponies employed by British Coal yesterday learnt that there really is light at the end of the tunnel. Their emergence into the grey light of Northumberland and an early retirement ended three centuries of mining tradition, much of it grim.

Flax, a 14-year-old grey Welsh mountain pony, was the last to pad out of Ellington Colliery, six days after the mine was mothballed. Ahead of him, also freshly released from stables four miles underground, came Alan, a dark bay Dartmoor pony, Carl, another grey Welsh mountain pony, and Tom, a Black Fell cob.

Tom Watson, Ellington's manager, said: 'It's the end of an era. Men and horses have worked together down mines for almost 300 years. They have been perfect partners.'

Ellington once employed more than 80 ponies and horses to haul coal, but the number dwindled as power systems were installed. These last four salvaged steel girders and wooden supports from areas beyond the reach of power lines, often miles under the North Sea.

In their heyday, before the First World War, nearly 70,000 ponies worked underground, often with backs rubbed raw by the low roofs and feet crippled by potholes. Flax, Alan, Carl and Tom spent their off-duty hours in well-lit loose boxes, were never tied up and were exercised regularly. Ellington's under-manager, Ian Bates, said the ponies worked the same shifts as their handlers and at the end of each shift they were washed down, groomed, fed and stabled. They had daily checks from the blacksmith and farrier and a vet gave them an annual medical.

Mr Bates said: 'The health record of every pony has been carefully documented. In short, the ponies had first-class attention because they did a first-class job.'

Keith Adams, a blacksmith and farrier for over 20 years, accompanied Flax to the surface. 'Most handlers say the horses do the work of three men,' he said, 'so it's hardly surprising they were so well looked after.'

To make sure that life stays sweet for the retirees, the RSPCA interviewed the 50 applicants from all over Britain who offered homes for the ponies to make sure that there would be adequate grazing and stabling for them. New owners will not be allowed to ride or work the ponies in retirement and the RSPCA will make regular checks.

JOE JOSEPH, The Times, 25 February 1994

[*Passage of Cordillera. 18 March 1835*]
Our manner of travelling was delightfully independent. In the inhabited parts we bought a little firewood, hired pasture for the animals, and biv-

ouacked in the corner of the same field with them. Carrying an iron pot, we cooked and ate our supper under the cloudless sky, and knew no trouble. My companions were Mariano Gonzales, who had formerly accompanied me, and an 'arriero', with his ten mules and a 'madrina'.

The madrina (or godmother) is a most important personage. She is an old steady mare, with a little bell round her neck; and wheresoever she goes, the mules, like good children, follow her. If several large troops are turned into one field to graze, in the morning the muleteer has only to lead the madrinas a little apart, and tinkle their bells; and, although there may be 200 or 300 mules together, each immediately knows its own bell, and separates itself from the rest. The affection of these animals for their madrinas saves infinite trouble. It is nearly impossible to lose an old mule; for if detained for several hours by force, she will, by the power of smell, like a dog, track out her companions, or rather the madrina; for, according to the muleteer, she is the chief object of affection. In a troop each animal carries, on a level road, a cargo weighing 416 pounds (more than 29 stone); but in a mountainous country 100 pounds less. Yet with what delicate slim limbs, without any proportional bulk of muscle, these animals support so great a burden! The mule always appears to me a most surprising animal. That a hybrid should possess more reason, memory, obstinacy, social affection, and powers of muscular endurance, than either of its parents, seems to indicate that art has here outmastered nature.

CHARLES DARWIN, *Journal of Researches* (*Voyage of the Beagle*), 1839

I had a common donkey pack-saddle—a *barde*, as they call it—fitted upon Modestine; and once more loaded her with my effects. The doubled sack, my pilot-coat (for it was warm, and I was to walk in my waistcoat), a great bar of black bread, and an open basket containing the white bread, the mutton, and the bottles, were all corded together in a very elaborate system of knots, and I looked on the result with fatuous content. In such a monstrous deck-cargo, all poised above the donkey's shoulders, with nothing below to balance, on a brand-new pack-saddle that had not yet been worn to fit the animal, and fastened with brand-new girths that might be expected to stretch and slacken by the way, even a very careless traveller should have seen disaster brewing. That elaborate system of knots, again, was the work of too many sympathisers to be very artfully designed. It is true they tightened the cords with a will; as many as three at a time would have a foot against Modestine's quarters, and be hauling with clenched teeth; but I learned afterwards that one thoughtful person, without any exercise of force, can make a more solid job than half a dozen heated and enthusiastic grooms. I was then but a novice; even after the misadventure of the pad nothing could disturb my security, and I went forth from the stable-door as an ox goeth to the slaughter.

The bell of Monastier was just striking nine as I got quit of these preliminary troubles and descended the hill through the common. As long as I was within sight of the windows, a secret shame and the fear of some laughable defeat withheld me from tampering with Modestine. She tripped along upon her four small hoofs with a sober daintiness of gait; from time to time she shook her ears or her tail; and she looked so small under the bundle that my mind misgave me. We got across the ford without difficulty—there was no doubt about the matter, she was docility itself—and once on the other bank, where the road begins to mount through pine-woods, I took in my right hand the unhallowed staff, and with a quaking spirit applied it to the donkey. Modestine brisked up her pace for perhaps three steps, and then relapsed into her former minuet. Another application had the same effect, and so with the third. I am worthy the name of an Englishman, and it goes against my conscience to lay my hand rudely on a female. I desisted, and looked her all over from head to foot; the poor brute's knees were trembling and her breathing was distressed; it was plain that she could go no faster on a hill. God forbid, thought I, that I should brutalise this innocent creature; let her go at her own pace, and let me patiently follow.

What that pace was, there is no word mean enough to describe; it was something as much slower than a walk as a walk is slower than a run; it kept me hanging on each foot for an incredible length of time; in five minutes it exhausted the spirit and set up a fever in all the muscles of the leg. And yet I had to keep close at hand and measure my advance exactly upon hers; for if I dropped a few yards into the rear, or went on a few yards ahead, Modestine came instantly to a halt and began to browse. The thought that this was to last from here to Alais nearly broke my heart. Of all conceivable journeys, this promised to be the most tedious. I tried to tell myself it was a lovely day; I tried to charm my foreboding spirit with tobacco; but I had a vision ever present to me of the long, long roads, up hill and down dale, and a pair of figures ever infinitesimally moving, foot by foot, a yard to the minute, and, like things enchanted in a nightmare, approaching no nearer to the goal.

In the meantime there came up behind us a tall peasant, perhaps forty years of age, of an ironical snuffy countenance, and arrayed in the green tail-coat of the country. He overtook us hand over hand, and stopped to consider our pitiful advance.

'Your donkey,' says he, 'is very old?'

I told him, I believed not.

Then, he supposed, we had come far.

I told him, we had but newly left Monastier.

'*Et vous marchez comme ça!*' cried he; and, throwing back his head, he laughed long and heartily. I watched him, half prepared to feel offended, until he had satisfied his mirth; and then, 'You must have no pity on these animals,' said he; and, plucking a switch out of a thicket, he began to lace Modestine about the stern-works, uttering a cry. The rogue pricked up her ears and broke into a good round pace, which she kept up without flagging, and without exhibiting the least symptom of distress, as long as the peasant kept beside us. Her former panting and shaking had been, I regret to say, a piece of comedy.

My *deus ex machina*, before he left me, supplied some excellent, if inhumane, advice; presented me with the switch, which he declared she would feel more tenderly than my cane; and finally taught me the true cry or masonic word of donkey-drivers, 'Proot!' All the time, he regarded me with a comical incredulous air, which was embarrassing to confront; and smiled over my donkey-driving, as I might have smiled over his orthography, or his green tail-coat.

ROBERT LOUIS STEVENSON, *Travels with a Donkey in the Cevennes*, 1879

Time Out

The donkey sat down on the roadside
Suddenly, as though tired of carrying
His cross. There was a varnish
Of sweat on his coat, and a fly
On his left ear. The tinker
Beating him finally gave in,
Sat on the grass himself, prying
His coat for his pipe. The donkey
(not beautiful but more fragile
than any swan, with his small
front hooves folded under him)
Gathered enough courage to raise
That fearsome head, lipping a daisy,
As if to say—slowly, contentedly—
Yes, there is a virtue in movement,
But only going so far, so fast,
Sucking the sweet grass of stubbornness.

JOHN MONTAGUE (b. 1929)

HABITS

I had known a great number of attractive and charming animals from mice to elephants, but I have never seen one to compare with Chumley for force and charm of personality, or for intelligence. After knowing him for a while you ceased to look upon him as an animal; you regarded him more as a wizard, mischievous, courtly old man, who had, for some reason best known to himself, disguised himself as a chimpanzee. His manners were perfect: he would never grab his food and start guzzling, as the other monkeys did, without first giving you a greeting, and thanking you with a series of his most expressive 'hoo hoos'. Then he would eat delicately and slowly, pushing those pieces he did not want to the side of his plate with his fingers. His only breach of table manners came at the end of a meal, for then he would seize his empty mug and plate and hurl them as far away as possible.

He had, of course, many habits which made him seem more human, and his smoking was one. He could light his cigarette with matches or a lighter with equal facility, and then he would lie down on the ground on his back, one arm under his head and his legs bent up and crossed, blowing great clouds of smoke into the sky, and occasionally examining the end of his cigarette professionally to see if the ash needed removing. If it did he would perform the operation carefully with one finger-nail. Give him a bottle of lemonade and a glass, and he would pour himself out a drink with all the care and concentration of a world-famous barman mixing a cocktail. He was the only animal I have met that would think of sharing things with you: on many occasions, if I gave him a bunch of bananas or two or three mangoes, he would choose one and hold it out to me with an inquiring expression on his face, and he would grunt with satisfaction if I accepted it and sat down beside him on the ground to eat it.

GERALD DURRELL, *The Overloaded Ark*, 1953

The *Bever* is a kind of *amphibious* Creature, but he lives mostly in the *Water*. His Stones, they say, are medicinal; and it is principally for their Sake, he knows that People seek his Life; and therefore when he finds himself hard pinch'd, he bites 'em off, and by leaving them to his Pursuers, he saves himself.

AESOP, 'A Hunted Be[a]ver', *Fables*, 1692

An enormous old timber wolf and a rather weaker, obviously younger one are the opposing champions and they are moving in circles round each other, exhibiting admirable 'footwork'. At the same time, the bared fangs flash in such a rapid exchange of snaps that the eye can scarcely follow them. So far, nothing has really happened. The jaws of one wolf close on the gleaming white teeth of the other, who is on the alert and wards off the attack. Only the lips have received one or two minor injuries. The younger wolf is gradually being forced backwards. It dawns upon us that the older one is purposely manoeuvring him towards the fence. We wait with breathless anticipation what will happen when he 'goes to the wall'. Now he strikes the wire netting, stumbles . . . and the old one is upon him. And now the incredible happens, just the opposite of what you would expect. The furious whirling of the grey bodies has come to a sudden standstill. Shoulder to shoulder they stand, pressed against each other in a stiff and strained attitude, both heads now facing in the same direction. Both wolves are growling angrily, the elder in a deep bass, the younger in higher tones, suggestive of the fear that underlies his threat. But notice carefully the position of the two opponents; the older wolf has his muzzle close, very close against the neck of the younger, and the latter holds away his head, offering unprotected to his enemy the bend of his neck, the most vulnerable part of his whole body! Less than an inch from the tensed neck-muscles, where the jugular vein lies immediately beneath the skin, gleam the fangs of his antagonist from beneath the wickedly retracted lips. Whereas, during the thick of the fight, both wolves were intent on keeping only their teeth, the one invulnerable part of the body, in opposition to each other, it now appears that the discomfited fighter proffers intentionally that part of his anatomy to which a bite must assuredly prove fatal. Appearances are notoriously deceptive, but in his case, surprisingly, they are not!

Since the fight is stopped so suddenly by this action, the victor frequently finds himself straddling his vanquished foe in anything but a comfortable position. So to remain, with his muzzle applied to the neck of the 'under-dog' soon becomes tedious for the champion, and, seeing that he cannot bite anyway, he soon withdraws. Upon this, the underdog may hastily attempt to put distance between himself and his superior. But he is not usually successful in this, for, as soon as he abandons his rigid attitude of submission, the other again falls upon him like a thunderbolt and the victim must again freeze into his former posture. It seems as if the victor is only waiting for the moment when the other will relinquish his submissive attitude, thereby enabling him to give vent to his urgent desire to bite. But, luckily for the 'underdog', the top-dog at the close of the fight is overcome by the pressing need to leave his trade-mark on the battlefield, to designate it as his personal property—in other words, he must lift his leg against the nearest upright object. This right-of-possession ceremony is usually taken advantage of by the underdog to make himself scarce.

KONRAD LORENZ, King Solomon's Ring, 1952

The Lemmings

Once in a hundred years the Lemmings come
Westward, in search of food, over the snow;
Westward, until the salt sea drowns them dumb;
Westward, till all are drowned, those Lemmings go.

Once, it is thought, there was a westward land
(Now drowned) where there was food for those starved things,
And memory of the place has burnt its brand
In the little brains of all the Lemming kings.

Perhaps, long since, there was a land beyond
Westward from death, some city, some calm place
Where one could taste God's quiet and be fond
With the little beauty of a human face;

But now the land is drowned. Yet still we press
Westward, in search, to death, to nothingness.

JOHN MASEFIELD (1878–1967)

The reproduction of mice is a most astonishing thing when compared with other animals both for the number of young produced and the speed of it. There is the case of a female mouse having got shut up in a jar of millet seed while pregnant, and after a short while when the jar was opened 120 mice came to light. The way in which mice appear in enormous numbers in the countryside and disappear is also a puzzle. In many places an innumerable multitude of field mice appears regularly, with the result that very little of the corn crop is left. They get to work with such speed that those in charge of smallish farms will on one day see that it is time for reaping to start, and the next day early in the morning they will go out with their reapers and discover the whole crop has been devoured. Their disappearance too is unaccountable: in a few days they will have completely disappeared. Yet before that the farm hands would have been fumigating and digging them out, hunting them down and turning pigs on to them (pigs root their holes up), without making any headway against them. Foxes, too, hunt them, and wild ferrets are particularly good at getting rid of them; but even these creatures are no match for the speed and volume of their reproduction. Rain is the only thing which can control their attacks—and then they disappear with speed. There is a place in Persia where when a female mouse is cut open the female embryos are seen to be pregnant. Some people say, indeed stoutly maintain, that, if they merely lick salt, mice become pregnant, without any copulation.

ARISTOTLE (384–322 BC), *History of Animals* (tr. A. L. Peck, 1965–70)

The Rats Underground

The rats underground are chewing
the telephone cables. They like
the weak shock they get
when their bite disconnects us.

The rats underground are addicted
to electricity. Their spit
is charged with it. Speak
to me quickly, before we're cut off.

VICKI RAYMOND (b. 1949)

Worms do not possess any sense of hearing. They took not the least notice of the shrill notes from a metal whistle, which was repeatedly sounded near them; nor did they of the deepest and loudest tones of a bassoon. They were indifferent to shouts, if care was taken that the breath did not strike them. When placed on a table close to the keys of a piano, which was played as loudly as possible, they remained perfectly quiet.

Although they are indifferent to undulations in the air audible by us, they are extremely sensitive to vibrations in any solid object. When the pots containing two worms which had remained quite indifferent to the sound of the piano, were placed on this instrument, and the note C in the bass clef was struck, both instantly retreated into their burrows. After a time they emerged, and when G above the line in the treble clef was struck they again retreated. Under similar circumstances on another night one worm dashed into its burrow on a very high note being struck only once, and the other worm when C in the treble clef was struck. On these occasions the worms were not touching the sides of the pots, which stood in saucers; so that the vibrations, before reaching their bodies, had to pass from the sounding board of the piano, through the saucer, the bottom of the pot and the damp, not very compact earth on which they lay with their tails in their burrows. They often showed their sensitiveness when the pot in which they lived, or the table on which the pot stood, was accidentally and lightly struck; but they appeared less sensitive to such jars than to the vibrations of the piano; and their sensitiveness to jars varied much at different times. It has often been said that if the ground is beaten or otherwise made to tremble, worms believe that they are pursued by a mole and leave their burrows. I beat the ground in many places where worms abounded, but not one emerged. When, however, the ground is dug with a fork and is violently disturbed beneath a worm, it will often crawl quickly out of its burrow.

CHARLES DARWIN, *The Formation of Vegetable Mould through the Action of Worms with Observations on their Habits*, 1881

April 12, 1772.

Dear Sir,

While I was in Sussex last autumn my residence was at the village near Lewes, from whence I had formerly the pleasure of writing to you. On the first of November I remarked that the old tortoise, formerly mentioned, began first to dig the ground in order to the forming its hybernaculum, which it had fixed on just beside a great tuft of hepaticas. It scrapes out the ground with its fore-feet, and throws it up over its back with its hind; but the motion of its legs is ridiculously slow, little exceeding the hour-hand of a clock; and suitable to the composure of an animal said to be a whole month in performing one feat of copulation. Nothing can be more assiduous than this creature night and day in scooping the earth, and forcing its great body into the cavity; but, as the noons of that season proved unusually warm and sunny, it was continually interrupted, and called forth by the heat in the middle of the day; and though I continued there till the thirteenth of November, yet the work remained unfinished. Harsher weather, and frosty mornings, would have quickened its operations. No part of its behaviour ever struck me more than the extreme timidity it always expresses with regard to rain; for though it has a shell that would secure it against the wheel of a loaded cart, yet does it discover as much solicitude about rain as a lady dressed in all her best attire, shuffling away on the first sprinklings, and running its head up in a corner.

I was much taken with its sagacity in discerning those that do it kind offices; for, as soon as the good old lady comes in sight who has waited on it for more than thirty years, it hobbles towards its benefactress with awkward alacrity; but remains inattentive to strangers. Thus not only '*the ox knoweth his owner, and the ass his master's crib,*' but the most abject reptile and torpid of beings distinguishes the hand that feeds it, and is touched with the feelings of gratitude!

Selborne, April 21, 1780.

Dear Sir,

The old Sussex tortoise, that I have mentioned to you so often, is become my property. I dug it out of its winter dormitory in March last, when it was enough awakened to express its resentments by hissing; and, packing it in a box with earth, carried it eighty miles in post-chaises. The rattle and hurry of the journey so perfectly roused it that, when I turned it out on a border, it walked twice down to the bottom of my garden; however, in the evening, the weather being cold, it buried itself in the loose mound, and continues still concealed.

As it will be under my eye, I shall now have an opportunity of enlarging my observations on its mode of life, and propensities; and perceive already that, towards the time of coming forth, it opens a breathing place in the ground near its head, requiring, I conclude, a freer respiration, as it becomes more alive. This creature not only goes under the earth from the middle of November to the middle of April, but sleeps great part of the summer; for it goes to bed in the longest days at four in the afternoon, and often does not stir in the morning till late. Besides, it retires to rest for every shower; and does not move at all in wet days.

When one reflects on the state of this strange being, it is a matter of wonder to find that Providence should bestow such a profusion of days, such a seeming waste of longevity, on a reptile that appears to relish it so little as to squander more than two-thirds of its existence in joyless stupor, and be lost to all sensation for months together in the profoundest of slumbers.

GILBERT WHITE (1720–93), *The Natural History of Selborne*

Bad Mouth

There are no leaf-eating snakes.
All are fanged and gorge on blood.
Each one is a hunter's hunter,
nothing more than an endless gullet
pulling itself on over the still-alive prey
like a sock gone ravenous, like an evil glove,
like sheer greed, lithe and devious.

Puff adder buried in hot sand
or poisoning the toes of boots,
for whom killing is easy and careless
as war, as digestion,
why should you be spared?

And you, *Constrictor constrictor*,
sinuous ribbon of true darkness,
one long muscle with eyes and an anus,
looping like thick tar out of the trees
to squeeze the voice from anything edible,
reducing it to scales and belly.

And you, pit viper
with your venomous pallid throat
and teeth like syringes
and your nasty radar
homing in on the deep red shadow
nothing else knows it casts . . .
Shall I concede these deaths?

Between us there is no fellow feeling,
as witness: a snake cannot scream.
Observe the alien
chainmail skin, straight out
of science fiction, pure
shiver, pure Saturn.

Those who can explain them
can explain anything.

Some say they're a snarled puzzle
only gasoline and a match can untangle.

Even their mating is barely sexual,
a romance between two lengths
of cyanide-colored string.
Despite their live births and squirming nests
it's hard to believe in snakes loving.

Alone among the animals
the snake does not sing.
The reason for them is the same
as the reason for stars, and not human.

MARGARET ATWOOD (b. 1939)

The keeper's wife has nothing to do with rabbits, but knows that their skins and fur are still bought in large quantities. She had heard that geese were once kept in large flocks almost entirely for their feathers, which were plucked twice a year, she thinks; but this is not practised now, at least not in the south. She has had snakes' skins, or more properly sloughs, for the curious. It is very difficult to get one entire; they are fragile, and so twisted in the grass where the snake leaves them as to be generally broken. Some country folk put them in their hats to cure headache, which is a very old superstition, but more in sport than earnest.

RICHARD JEFFERIES, *The Gamekeeper at Home*, 1890

One November evening, in the neighbourhood of Lyndhurst, I saw a flock of geese marching in a long procession, led, as their custom is, by a majestical gander; they were coming home from their feeding-ground in the forest, and when I spied them were approaching their owner's cottage. Arrived at the wooden gate of the garden in front of the cottage, the leading bird drew up square before it, and with repeated loud screams demanded admittance. Pretty soon, in response to the summons, a man came out of the cottage, walked briskly down the garden path and opened the gate, but only wide enough to put his right leg through; then, placing his foot and knee against the leading bird, he thrust him roughly back; as he did so three young geese pressed forward and were allowed to pass in; then the gate was slammed in the face of the gander and the rest of his followers, and the man went back to the cottage. The gander's indignation was fine to see, though he had most probably experienced the same rude treatment on many previous occasions. Drawing up to the gate again he called more loudly than before; then deliberately lifted a leg, and placing his broad webbed foot like an open hand against the gate actually tried to push it open! His strength was not sufficient; but he continued to push and to call until the man returned to open the gate and let the birds go in.

It was an amusing scene, and the behaviour of the bird struck me as characteristic. It was this lofty spirit of the goose and strict adhesion to his rights, as well as his noble appearance and the stately formality and deliberation of his conduct, that caused me very long ago to respect and admire him above all our domestic birds. Doubtless from the æsthetic point of view other domesticated species are his superiors in some things: the mute swan, 'floating double', graceful and majestical, with arched neck and ruffled scapulars; the oriental pea-fowl in his glittering mantle; the helmeted guinea-fowl, powdered with stars, and the red cock with his military bearing—a shining Elizabethan knight of the feathered world, singer, lover, and fighter. It is hardly to be doubted that, mentally, the goose is above all these; and to my mind his, too, is the nobler figure; but it is a very familiar figure, and we have not forgotten the reason of its presence among us. He satisfies a material want only too generously, and on this account is too much associated in the mind with mere flavours. We keep a swan or a peacock for ornament; a goose for the table—he is the Michaelmas and Christmas bird.

W. H. HUDSON, Birds and Man, 1915

A Bird came down the Walk—
He did not know I saw—
He bit an Angleworm in halves
And ate the fellow, raw,

And then he drank a Dew
From a convenient Grass—
And then hopped sidewise to the Wall
To let a Beetle pass—

He glanced with rapid eyes
That hurried all around—
They looked like frightened Beads, I thought—
He stirred his Velvet Head

Like one in danger, Cautious,
I offered him a Crumb
And he unrolled his feathers
And rowed him softer home—

Than Oars divide the Ocean,
Too silver for a seam—
Or Butterflies, off Banks of Noon
Leap, plashless as they swim.

Emily Dickinson (1830–86)

Sandpiper

The roaring alongside he takes for granted,
and that every so often the world is bound to shake.
He runs, he runs to the south, finical, awkward,
in a state of controlled panic, a student of Blake.

The beach hisses like fat. On his left, a sheet
of interrupting water comes and goes
and glazes over his dark and brittle feet.
He runs, he runs straight through it, watching his toes.

—Watching, rather, the spaces of sand between them,
where (no detail too small) the Atlantic drains
rapidly backwards and downwards. As he runs,
he stares at the dragging grains.

The world is a mist. And then the world is
minute and vast and clear. The tide
is higher or lower. He couldn't tell you which.
His beak is focussed; he is preoccupied,

looking for something, something, something.
Poor bird, he is obsessed!
The millions of grains are black, white, tan, and gray,
mixed with quartz grains, rose and amethyst.

Elizabeth Bishop (1911–79)

I take up one of the [pearl oyster] shells. With the point of a scalpel, I break off in little pieces the surface of the pearly band . . . and I soon discover that it forms a sort of shell, enwrapping something, upon which it applies itself and models itself exactly. Patiently and carefully, for it is fragile, I uncover the object thus surrounded, and I find that it is a small fish, dead, of course, and petrified, with a longish body, caught in the mother-of-pearl and so preserved. I can discern its head, the eyes sunken in their orbits, the snout through which the bones protrude, and I can also see the fins, all the rays of which are preserved, and the whole body, in which the vertebrae may be seen one behind the other. This object is the mummy of a fish, preserving its normal form. The thick band which protrudes in the inside of the shell is a tomb of mother-of-pearl in which the mummy is buried.

It is not difficult to reconstruct the phases of the extraordinary event which has turned this oyster shell into a sort of mausoleum, wherein is a tomb in which a corpse is buried. This corpse was first impregnated with calcareous matter, as we may easily see if we treat it with weak acid. Thus embalmed, it was covered with one layer of mother-of-pearl after another, until it was completely surrounded. Nature had built for it a tomb of rare and precious stone, a magnificent coffin: she had done for this little fish what the Egyptians used to do for the remains of their kings.

When alive, in their native waters, the pearl oysters, on the bottom where they live and where the fishermen gather them, leave their shell half open, and their valves allow the water from outside to penetrate freely into the large interior cavity. Two currents are set up, one going in and the other coming out, so that the water is continually renewed, bringing dissolved oxygen to the gills, and particles of food to the digestive tube. The thick, pleated edges of the mantle, which line those of the shell, have fluted contours so arranged as to direct these currents into channels and take them where they have to go. Although they are fixed to one place and cannot move from it, the oysters thus receive what they need, and live in due conformity with the requirements of their particular structure.

They live so well that they swarm, however little circumstances are in their favour. Side by side, and even one on top of another, they form extensive banks, with little ones beside the big ones, and all together form large heaps spread out over the sea bottom. These banks, made of compact and strong shells, themselves serve as supports and shelters to other creatures. On them, under them, between them, flourishes a rich vegetation of seaweed, mingled with the rocky arborescences of coral. Bright-hued sea-anemones, different kinds of molluscs and other creatures, settle wherever they can find a suitable place. A regular population, varied and highly coloured, swarms and develops to an extraordinary degree upon this solid support. Fishes are there too, profiting by the number of likely victims, especially since they are so easy to secure. Some of them are particularly common, among them one whose existence, even more than that of the rest, is bound up with the oysters to such an extent that it deserves the name of 'Pearl-fish' which has been given to it. It is this fish which becomes the hero whose end is to be a mummy encased in a coffin of pearl.

This fish belongs to the genus *Fierasfer*. Its specific name is *Fierasfer affinis*. In appearance it is like a very small eel, long and supple, undulating, slightly brownish in colour, with translucent tones and flashes of silver. The resemblance is only in form and appearance, for, in reality, *Fierasfer* belongs to a different group from that of the eels and congers, and has neither their structure nor their mode of life. In its ordinary state, it sometimes lodges, folded up on itself, in the interior of the pearl oyster, and makes its abode in the roomy cavity surrounded by the mantle. The oysters live well, and the pearl-fish, settling down with them, finds shelter, if not a livelihood. Situated beside the oyster's gills, taking advantage of the entering current which flows towards them, protected by the thick envelope of the shell which covers the mantle, it can enjoy, in peace, and remote from every risk, the charms of a life of complete repose. It takes cover in this shelter which it has chosen. It enters through the space left between the open valves, and goes out the same way when the need of food compels it to do so; it returns again when it has fed. The fish asks the oyster to allow it to share the shelter of its shell and the oyster agrees; both live together in complete harmony.

But things sometimes go wrong, and the agreement is occasionally broken. It may happen that the visitor, when young and not very big, mistakes the door. Instead of passing through the opening in the edges of the mantle and so into the cavity to which it is allowed access, it tries to find its way between the mantle and the shell, to enter thereby into the private quarters of its host. Then the oyster defends itself and punishes the intruder. When the fish has forced its way into this private ground, the mantle contracts, tightens round it, and imprisons it against the shell. The intruder is unable to move, cannot free itself, breathes with difficulty and finally dies, where it is in the narrow gaol in which it has imprisoned itself. Caught in a trap, it suffers there the punishment of death. Then the oyster, not being able to get rid of the corpse, sets to work to embalm it, to mummify and to immure it. Its secretion of calcareous matter begins by infiltrating the tissues of the fish, and then incrusts them. The secretion continues and the new deposits spread in little blades of pearl which surround the mummy and gradually totally enclose it. Thus the tomb of pearl is built.

LOUIS ROULE, *Fishes Their Ways of Life*, 1927 (tr. Conrad Elphinstone, 1935)

Among marine animals there are many instances reported of the mild, gentle disposition of the dolphin, . . . It is said that when a dolphin was captured and wounded on the coast of Caria, so great a number came up to the harbour, that the fishermen let him go, when they all went away together. And one large dolphin, it is said, always follows the young ones, to take care of them; and sometimes a herd of large and small dolphins has been seen together, and two of these having left appeared soon after, supporting and carrying on their back a small dead dolphin, that was ready to sink, as if in pity for it, that it might not be devoured by any other wild creature.

ARISTOTLE (384–322 BC), *History of Animals* (tr. Richard Cresswell, 1897)

The Whale

WHALE is the greatest beast   In all the ocean waste;
Whom if you ever espied   Sprawling upon the tide,
An isle he would seem to be   Built on the sands of the sea.

When this fierce fish would feed,   He spreads his great mouth wide,
And thence expels his breath,   The sweetest smell on earth.
The other fishes come,   Ravished by that perfume;
They dawdle within his jaws,   Unwary of the ruse.
He slams his jaw-gates then,   And drinks those fishes in . . .

This whale-fish dwells secure   Down near the ocean floor
Until that season arrives   When winter with summer strives
And storm stirs all the sea;   In such inclemency
His lair he cannot keep,   But up from the troubled deep
He rises, and lies still.   Then while the weather is ill,
Sailors driven and tossed   Who fear that they are lost,
Sighting the quiet whale,   Mistake him for an isle.
They view him with delight   And hasten with all their might
To make their vessels fast   And climb ashore at last;
With tinder, steel, and stone   They kindle a blaze thereon,
Warm them, and drink, and eat.   But, feeling the fire's heat,
The whale to sea-deep dives   And robs them of their lives.

tr. from *The Middle English Bestiary* by Richard Wilbur, 1952

Beasts, as well as wee, have choice in their loves, and are very nice in chusing of their mates. They are not altogether void of our extreme and unappesable jealousies. Lustfull desires are either naturall, and necessary, as eating and drinking; or else naturall and not necessary, as the acquaintance of males and females: or else neither necessary nor naturall: Of this last kinde are almost all mens: For, they are all superfluous and artificiall. It is wonderfull to see with how little nature will be satisfied, and how little she hath left for us to be desired. The preparations in our kitchins, doe nothing at all concerne her lawes. The Stoikes say, that a man might very well sustaine himselfe with one Olive a day. The delicacy of our wines, is no part of her lesson, no more is the surcharge and relishing, which we adde unto our letcherous appetites.

These strange lustfull longings, which the ignorance of good, and a false opinion have possest us with, are in number so infinite, that in a manner they expell all those which are naturall: even as if there were so many strangers in a City, that should either banish and expell all the naturall inhabitants thereof, or utterly suppresse their ancient power and authority, and absolutely usurping the same, take possession of it. Brute beasts are much more regulare than we; and with more moderation containe themselves within the compasse, which nature hath prescribed them: yet not so exactly, but that they have some coherency with our riotous licentiousnesse. And even as there have beene found certaine furious longings and unnaturall desires, which have provoked men unto the love of beasts, so have diverse times some of them been drawne to love us, and are possessed with monstrous affections from one kind to another: witnesse the Elephant, that in the love of an herb-wife, in the city of *Alexandria*, was co-rivall with *Aristophanes*, the Grammarian; who in all offices pertayning to an earnest wooer and passionate suiter, yeelded nothing unto him: For, walking thorow the Fruit-market, he would here and there snatch up some with his truncke, and carry them unto her: as neere as might be he would never loose the sight of her: and now and then over her band put his truncke into her bosome, and feele her breasts. They also report of a Dragon, that was exceedingly in love with a young maiden; and of a Goose in the City of *Asope*, which dearely loved a young childe: also of a Ram that belonged to the Musitian *Glausia*. Doe we not daily se Munkies ragingly in love with women, and furiously to pursue them? And certaine other beasts, given to love the males of their owne sex? *Oppianus* and others report some examples, to shew the reverence, and manifest the awe, some beasts in their marriages, beare unto their kindred: but experience makes us often see the contrary.

Montaigne, An Apologie of Raymond Sebond (tr. Florio, 1603)

In preparation for his expedition across the Sahara on a camel, Geoffrey Moorhouse visits London Zoo to meet some specimens of this creature.

They had three Arabians at the Zoo, and one of them was a heavily built bull named Fred. As we walked towards his pen for the first time, his keeper told me about the perversity of bulls. You had to be careful of them at all times, he said, but particularly during the rutting season. They were liable to attack without provocation, with necks outstretched, and they always went for a man's belly with their teeth. There were cases, he said, of natives having been disembowelled this way. I remembered Wilfred Thesiger writing about an old man and a child who had been savaged to death by a bull as they sat by a campfire in Arabia.

Fred was sitting down when we arrived at his pen. As we entered, he shambled to his feet and padded over towards us. A single pace away, and his neck arched high in the air. Then something half ridiculous, half revolting happened. There gradually emerged from the side of his mouth a pink bubble, a membrane which slowly expanded into a great drooling balloon that went slithering obscenely down the animal's neck, before it deflated and disappeared inside the maw again. From somewhere within there came the sound of slobbering, sucking turmoil. Down into our faces swept the sweet stench of decomposed vegetation, mixed with heaven knows what stomach juices. Thus the bull camel betrays his excitement when confronted with a cow on heat. I stood my ground, manfully, while Fred's keeper grinned at us both.

'He fancies you,' he said.

GEOFFREY MOORHOUSE, *The Fearful Void*, 1974

[*Patagonia, Dec. 1833*]

The characteristic quadruped of the plains of Patagonia is the Guanaco, which by some naturalists is considered as the same animal with the Llama, but in its wild state, is the South American representative of the camel of the East. In size it may be compared to an ass, mounted on taller legs, and with a very long neck.

Generally the guanacoes are wild and extremely wary. Mr Stokes told me, that he one day saw through a glass a herd of these beasts, which evidently had been frightened, running away at full speed, although their distance was so great that they could not be distinguished by the naked eye. The sportsman frequently receives the first intimation of their presence, by hearing, from a long distance, the peculiar shrill neighing note of alarm. If he then looks attentively, he will perhaps see the herd standing in a line on the side of some distant hill. On approaching them, a few more squeals are given, and then off they set at an apparently slow, but really quick canter, along some narrow beaten track to a neighbouring hill. If, however, by chance he should abruptly meet a single animal, or several together, they will generally stand motionless, and intently gaze at him; then perhaps move on a few yards, turn round, and look again. What is the cause of this difference in their shyness? Do they mistake a man in the distance for their chief enemy the puma? Or does curiosity overcome their timidity? That they are curious is certain; for if a person lies on the ground, and plays strange antics, such as throwing up his feet in the air, they will allmost always approach by degrees to reconnoitre him. It was an artifice that was repeatedly practised by our sportsmen with success, and it had moreover the advantage of allowing several shots to be fired, which were all taken as parts of the performance. On the mountains of Tierra del Fuego, and in other places, I have more than once seen a guanaco, on being approached, not only neigh and squeal, but prance and leap about in the most ridiculous manner, apparently in defiance as a challenge. These animals are very easily domesticated, and I have seen some thus kept near the houses, although at large on their native plains. They are in this state very bold, and readily attack a man, by striking him from behind with both knees. It is asserted, that the motive for these attacks is jealousy on account of their females. The wild guanacoes, however, have no idea of defence; even a single dog will secure one of these large animals, till the huntsman can come up. In many of their habits they are like sheep in a flock. Thus when they see men approaching in several directions on horseback, they soon became bewildered and know not which way to run. This greatly facilitates the Indian method of hunting, for they are thus easily driven to a central point, and are encompassed.

The guanacoes readily take to the water: several times at Port Valdes they were seen swimming from island to island. Byron, in his voyage, says he saw them drinking salt water.

They appear to have favourite spots for dying in. On the banks of the St Cruz, the ground was actually white with bones, in certain circumscribed spaces, which were generally bushy and all near the river. . . . The animals in most cases, must have crawled, before dying, beneath and amongst the bushes.

CHARLES DARWIN, *Journal of Researches* (*Voyage of the Beagle*), 1839

The Gecko

I don't know how many thousand years
Of evolution have not taught the gecko
You can't jump *up* downwards.

Blue-flecked, pink-flecked, semi-transparent,
Sucker-footed, he creeps
Across the ceiling. He sees
With his extraordinary protuberant eyes
A fly, just hovering below him . . . He
                                        jumps
                                                and
Flick!
        He falls to the floor:
Poor little half-dazed lizard!

How did this absurd, this innocent creature
Become a symbol of evil?

The Copts say:
'Saint Shenouda has commanded us to destroy you!'
Whereat the thing is supposed to curl up and die,
Or at least depart, embarrassed.

And everyone, Moslem or Christian, is agreed
It sneaks into houses, it spits
Into the salt-box, tabernacle of life,
Contagious of leprosy;
Like its own whiteness it fades to in the dark.

Shenouda, intransigently holy father,
Striding out of the desert with grit in your beard,
Do you concern yourself, then,
With such trivialities?

It could be so. In your day,
In those of Pachomius, Anthony,
The wastelands pullulated with dragons.
This is a parody, a miniature.

There is so much evil in the world
Anything can be a symbol of it.

JOHN HEATH-STUBBS (b. 1918)

Consider a wolf-spider as it hunts through the litter of leaves on the woodland floor. It must be a splendid hunter; that goes without saying for otherwise its line would long since have died out. But it must be proficient at other things too. Even as it hunts, it must keep some of its eight eyes on the look-out for the things that hunt it; and when it sees an enemy it must do the right thing to save itself. It must know what to do when it rains. It must have a life style that enables it to survive the winter. It must rest safely when the time is not apt for hunting. And there comes a season of the year when the spiders, as it were, feel the sap rising in their eight legs. The male must respond by going to look for a female spider, and when he finds her, he must convince her that he is not merely something to eat—yet. And she, in the fullness of time, must carry an egg-sack as she goes about her hunting, and later must let the babies ride on her back. They, in turn, must learn the various forms of fending for themselves as they go through the different moults of the spider's life until they, too, are swift-running, pouncing hunters of the woodland floor.

Wolf-spidering is a complex job, not something to be undertaken by an amateur. We might say that there is a profession of wolf-spidering. It is necessary to be good at all its manifold tasks to survive at it. What is more, the profession is possible only in very restricted circumstances. A woodland floor is necessary, for instance, and the right climate with a winter roughly like that your ancestors were used to; and enough of the right sorts of things to hunt; and the right shelter when you need it; and the numbers of natural enemies must be kept within reasonable bounds. For success, individual spiders must be superlatively good at their jobs and the right circumstances must prevail. Unless both the skills of spidering and the opportunity are present, there will not be any wolf-spiders. The 'niche' of wolf-spidering will not be filled.

PAUL COLINVAUX, *Why Big Fierce Animals are Rare*, 1980

Tom Kitten has been 'rolled up in a bundle, and tied with string in very hard knots' by the rats, Anna Maria and Samuel Whiskers.

While Tom Kitten was left alone under the floor of the attic, he wriggled about and tried to mew for help.

But his mouth was full of soot and cobwebs, and he was tied up in such very tight knots, he could not make anybody hear him.

Except a spider, which came out of a crack in the ceiling and examined the knots critically, from a safe distance.

It was a judge of knots because it had a habit of tying up unfortunate blue-bottles. It did not offer to assist him.

Tom Kitten wriggled and squirmed until he was quite exhausted.

BEATRIX POTTER, *The Tale of Samuel Whiskers, or, The Roly-Poly Pudding*, 1908

You must bear with a handwritten letter: I have a kitten who is learning to type. In the end no doubt he will type much better than I do, but we can't both do it at once; and his will is younger and stronger than mine. His name is Quiddity, he is four months, his eyes are like gentians, his voice is like a foghorn, he is good and intelligent and unbiddable as an angel; and Valentine gave him to me to heal the gash in my heart left by the death of my dearest and wisest Niou, who died last summer.

SYLVIA TOWNSEND WARNER, letter of 26 December 1963 to Marchette and Joy Chute

My grandfather, Andrea Cellini, was still alive when I was about three years old and he was more than a hundred. One day a cistern pipe was being moved, when out of it came a great scorpion. Unseen by the others, it slipped from the cistern to the ground and crept away under a bench. I saw it and ran and laid hold of it. So large was it that when I clenched it in my little fist the tail stuck out from one end and from the other its two claws. In high delight I ran, they tell me, to my grandfather, saying, 'Look, grandad, at my dear little crab.' When he saw it was a scorpion, he all but fell dead of fright and anxiety for me. With many caresses he begged me to give it to him; but I only clutched it the tighter, weeping and declaring I would not give it up to anybody. My father, who was also in the house, came running at the sound of my cries. Dazed with terror, he could for the moment think of no way of preventing the venomous animal from killing me. But suddenly his eyes fell on a pair of shears, and so, coaxing me the while, he cut off the tail and the claws. Then when the great danger was over, he took the happening for a good omen.

BENVENUTO CELLINI (1500–71), *The Life . . . written by himself* (tr. Anne MacDonell, 1907)

RED IN TOOTH
AND CLAW

The Mephitic Skunk

It might possibly give the reader some faint conception of the odious character of this creature (for adjectives are weak to describe it) when I say that, in talking to strangers from abroad, I have never thought it necessary to speak of sunstroke, jaguars, or the assassin's knife, but have never omitted to warn them of the skunk, minutely describing its habits and personal appearance.

I knew an Englishman who, on taking a first gallop across the pampas, saw one, and, quickly dismounting, hurled himself bodily on to it to effect its capture. Poor man! he did not know that the little animal is never unwilling to be caught. Men have been blinded for ever by a discharge of the fiery liquid full in their faces. On a mucous membrane it burns like sulphuric acid, say the unfortunates who have had the experience. How does nature protect the skunk itself from the injurious effects of its potent fluid? I have not unfrequently found individuals stone-blind, sometimes moving so briskly about that the blindness must have been of long stand-ing—very possibly in some cases an accidental drop discharged by the animal itself has caused the loss of sight. When coming to close quarters with a skunk, by covering up the face, one's clothes only are ruined. But this is not all one has to fear from an encounter; the worst is that effluvium, after which crushed garlic is lavender, which tortures the olfactory nerves, and appears to pervade the whole system like a pestilent ether, nauseating one until sea-sickness seems almost a pleasant sensation in comparison.

To those who know the skunk only from reputation, my words might seem too strong; many, however, who have come to close quarters with the little animal will think them ridiculously weak. And consider what must the feelings be of one who has had the following experience—not an uncommon experience on the pampas. There is to be a dance at a neighbouring house a few miles away; he has been looking forward to it, and, dressing himself with due care, mounts his horse and sets out full of joyous anticipations. It is a dark windy evening, but there is a convenient bridle-path through the dense thicket of giant thistles, and striking it he puts his horse into a swinging gallop. Unhappily the path is already occupied by a skunk, invisible in the darkness, that, in obedience to the promptings of its insane instinct, refuses to get out of it, until the flying hoofs hit it and send it like a well-kicked football into the thistles. But the forefeet of the horse, up as high as his knees perhaps, have been sprinkled, and the rider, after coming out into the open, dismounts and walks away twenty yards from his animal, and literally *smells* himself all over, and with a feeling of profound relief pronounces himself clean. Not the minutest drop of the diabolical spray has touched his dancing shoes! Springing into the saddle he proceeds to his journey's end, is warmly welcomed by his host, and speedily forgetting his slight misadventure, mingles with a happy crowd of friends. In a little while people begin exchanging whispers and significant glances; men are seen smiling at nothing in particular; the hostess wears a clouded face; the ladies cough and put their scented handkerchiefs to their noses, and presently they begin to feel faint and retire from the room. Our hero begins to notice that there is something wrong, and presently discovers its cause; he, unhappily, has been the last person in the room to remark that familiar but most abominable odour, rising like a deadly exhalation from the floor, conquering all other odours, and every moment becoming more powerful. A drop *has* touched his shoe after all; and fearing to be found out, and edging towards the door, he makes his escape, and is speedily riding home again; knowing full well that his sudden and early departure from the scene will be quickly discovered and set down to the right cause.

W. H. HUDSON (1841–1922), *The Naturalist in La Plata*, 1892

Centipede

Sat in my red room with a centipede,
I've no idea when he'll come out;
from the spine of which book,
from the entrails of which chair.
But he's there.

I flapped the slats of a plastic fly-swat
at his multitudinous crescent on the floor.
I had never seen a centipede before.
His fringe of oars surged on in clumps, he veered
and vanished.

Since then I have worn shoes to sit at my desk.
My study attends him, supine and suburban
to his glamour of fangs, his avenue of legs,
the spans of his back and his multiple head in procession.
What has happened

is that till the world's ribs unfasten we closet together,
he and I, eye to eye, prospecting our plaster crevice.
Though I looked up his Latin and habits, not niched in a book
nor tacking a threadbare lap of blue-matted floor
he shines now,

but steers all levels to the abominable fall
that is fear. A finger's length of segments rustling
with centipede intent, stirs in my head;
dark jewel, he has always festered there.
I scan my wall.

JUDITH RODRIGUEZ (b. 1936)

One day when I went out to my wood-pile, or rather my pile of stumps, I observed two large ants, the one red, the other much larger, nearly half an inch long, and black, fiercely contending with one another. Having once got hold they never let go, but struggled and wrestled and rolled on the chips incessantly. Looking farther, I was surprised to find that the chips were covered with such combatants, that it was not a *duellum*, but a *bellum*, a war between two races of ants, the red always pitted against the black, and frequently two red ones to one black. The legions of these Myrmidons covered all the hills and vales in my woodyard, and the ground was already strewn with the dead and dying, both red and black. It was the only battle which I have ever witnessed, the only battle-field I ever trod while the battle was raging; internecine war; the red republicans on the one hand, and the black imperialists on the other. On every side they were engaged in deadly combat, yet without any noise that I could hear, and human soldiers never fought so resolutely. I watched a couple that were fast locked in each other's embraces, in a little sunny valley amid the chips, now at noon-day prepared to fight till the sun went down, or life went out. The smaller red champion had fastened himself like a vice to his adversary's front, and through all the tumblings on that field never for an instant ceased to gnaw at one of his feelers near the root, having already caused the other to go by the board; while the stronger black one dashed him from side to side, and as I saw on looking nearer, had already divested him of several of his members. They fought with more pertinacity than bull-dogs. Neither manifested the least disposition to retreat. It was evident that their battle-cry was Conquer or die. In the meanwhile there came along a single red ant on the hill-side of this valley, evidently full of excitement, who either had despatched his foe, or had not yet taken part in the battle; probably the latter, for he had lost none of his limbs; whose mother had charged him to return with his shield or upon it. Or perchance he was some Achilles, who had nourished his wrath apart, and had now come to avenge or rescue his Patroclus. He saw this unequal combat from afar—for the blacks were nearly twice the size of the red—he drew near with rapid pace till he stood on his guard within half an inch of the combatants; then, watching his opportunity, he sprang upon the black warrior, and commenced his operations near the root of his right fore-leg, leaving the foe to select among his own members; and so there were three united for life, as if a new kind of attraction had been invented which put all other locks and cements to shame. I should not have wondered by this time to find that they had their respective musical bands stationed on some eminent chip, and playing their national airs the while, to excite the slow and cheer the dying combatants. I was myself excited somewhat even as if they had been men. The more you think of it, the less the difference. And certainly there is not a fight recorded in Concord history, at least, if in the history of America, that will bear a moment's comparison with this, whether for the numbers engaged in it, or for the patriotism and heroism displayed.

I took up the chip on which the three I have particularly described were struggling, carried it into my house, and placed it under a tumbler on my window sill, in order to see the issue. Holding a microscope to the first-mentioned red ant, I saw that, though he was assiduously gnawing at the near fore-leg of his enemy, having severed his remaining feeler, his own breast was all torn away, exposing what vitals he had there to the jaws of the black warrior, whose breast-plate was apparently too thick for him to pierce; and the dark carbuncles of the sufferer's eyes shone with ferocity such as war only could excite. They struggled half an hour longer under the tumbler, and when I looked again the black soldier had severed the heads of his foes from their bodies, and the still living heads were hanging on either side of him like ghastly trophies at his saddle-bow, still apparently as firmly fastened as ever, and he was endeavouring with feeble struggles, being without feelers and with only the remnant of a leg, and I know not how many other wounds, to divest himself of them; which at length, after half an hour more, he accomplished. I raised the glass, and he went off over the window-sill in that crippled state. Whether he finally survived that combat, and spent the remainder of his days in some Hôtel des Invalides, I do not know; but I thought that his industry would not be worth much thereafter. I never learned which party was victorious, nor the cause of the war; but I felt for the rest of that day as if I had had my feelings excited and harrowed by witnessing the struggle, the ferocity and carnage, of a human battle before my door.

HENRY DAVID THOREAU, *Walden, or Life in the Woods*, 1854

Stretched across the upper part of the doorway was a big spider's web, and hanging from the top of the web, head down, was a large grey spider. She was about the size of a gum-drop. She had eight legs, and she was waving one of them at Wilbur in friendly greeting.

'My name,' said the spider, 'is Charlotte.' . . . 'I wish I could see you, Wilbur, as clearly as you can see me.'

'Why can't you?' asked the pig. 'I'm right here.'

'Yes, but I'm near-sighted,' replied Charlotte. 'I've always been dreadfully near-sighted. It's good in some ways, not so good in others. Watch me wrap up this fly.'

A fly that had been crawling along Wilbur's trough had flown up and blundered into the lower part of Charlotte's web and was tangled in the sticky threads. The fly was beating its wings furiously, trying to break loose and free itself.

'First,' said Charlotte, 'I dive at him.' She plunged headfirst towards the fly. As she dropped, a tiny silken thread unwound from her rear end.

'Next, I wrap him up.' She grabbed the fly, threw a few jets of silk round it, and rolled it over and over, wrapping it so that it couldn't move. Wilbur watched in horror. He could hardly believe what he was seeing, and although he detested flies he was sorry for this one.

'There!' said Charlotte. 'Now I knock him out, so he'll be more comfortable.' She bit the fly. 'He can't feel a thing now,' she remarked. 'He'll make a perfect breakfast for me.'

'You mean you *eat* flies?' gasped Wilbur.

'Certainly. Flies, bugs, grasshoppers, choice beetles, moths, butterflies, tasty cockroaches, gnats, midges, daddy-long-legs, centipedes, mosquitoes, crickets—anything that is careless enough to get caught in my web. I have to live, don't I?'

'Why, yes, of course,' said Wilbur. 'Do they taste good?'

'Delicious. Of course, I don't really eat them. I drink them—drink their blood. I love blood,' said Charlotte, and her pleasant, thin voice grew even thinner and more pleasant.

E. B. WHITE, *Charlotte's Web*, 1952

A Mosquito

The lady whines, then dines; is slapped and killed;
Yet it's her killer's blood that has been spilled.

BRAD LEITHAUSER (b. 1953)

Tuesday, March 14th [1893]—We set off to Devonshire and Cornwall, the Osborne Hotel, Torquay. I didn't much want to go. I did not take to what I had seen of Torquay, and it is possible to see too much of Ada Smallfield.

I sniffed my bedroom on arrival, and for a few hours felt a certain grim satisfaction when my forebodings were maintained, but it is possible to have too much Natural History in a bed.

I did not undress after the first night, but I was obliged to lie on it because there were only two chairs and one of them was broken. It is very uncomfortable to sleep with Keating's powder in the hair. What is to be thought of people who recommend near relations to an Hotel where there are bugs?

BEATRIX POTTER, *The Journal . . . from 1881–1897*

Mosquito

When did you start your tricks
Monsieur?

What do you stand on such high legs for?
Why this length of shredded shank
You exaltation?

Is it so that you shall lift your centre of gravity upwards
And weigh no more than air as you alight upon me,
Stand upon me weightless, you phantom?

Queer, with your thin wings and your streaming legs
How you sail like a heron, or a dull clot of air,
A nothingness.

Yet what an aura surrounds you;
Your evil little aura, prowling, and casting a numbness on my mind.

That is your trick, your bit of filthy magic:
Invisibility, and the anæsthetic power
To deaden my attention in your direction.

But I know your game now, streaky sorcerer.

    .   .   .   .   .

It is your trump
It is your hateful little trump
You pointed fiend,
Which shakes my sudden blood to hatred of you:
It is your small, high, hateful bugle in my ear.

Why do you do it?
Surely it is bad policy.

They say you can't help it.

If that is so, then I believe a little in Providence protecting the innocent.
But it sounds so amazingly like a slogan,
A yell of triumph as you snatch my scalp.

Blood, red blood
Super-magical
Forbidden liquor.

I behold you stand
For a second enspasmed in oblivion,
Obscenely ecstasied
Sucking live blood,
My blood.

Such silence, such suspended transport,
Such gorging,
Such obscenity of trespass.

You stagger
As well as you may.

Only your accursed hairy frailty
Your own imponderable weightlessness
Saves you, wafts you away on the very draught my anger makes in its
      snatching.

Away with a pæan of derision
You winged blood-drop.

Can I not overtake you?
Are you one too many for me,
Winged Victory?
Am I not mosquito enough to out-mosquito you?

Queer, what a big stain my sucked blood makes
Beside the infinitesimal faint smear of you!
Queer, what a dim dark smudge you have disappeared into!

D. H. LAWRENCE (1885–1930)

IKARI, *June* 25 [1878]—Fujihara has forty-six farm-houses and a *yadoya*—all
dark, damp, dirty, and draughty, a combination of dwelling-house, barn,
and stable. The *yadoya* consisted of a *daidokoro*, or open kitchen, and stable
below, and a small loft above, capable of division, and I found on returning
from a walk six Japanese in extreme *déshabillé* occupying the part through
which I had to pass. On this being remedied I sat down to write, but was
soon driven upon the balcony, under the eaves, by myriads of fleas, which
hopped out of the mats as sandhoppers do out of the sea sand, and even in
the balcony hopped over my letter. There were two outer walls of hairy
mud with living creatures crawling in the cracks; cobwebs hung from the
uncovered rafters. The mats were brown with age and dirt, the rice was
musty, and only partially cleaned, the eggs had seen better days, and the tea
was musty.

I saw everything out of doors with Ito—the patient industry, the exquisitely situated village, the evening avocations, the quiet dulness—and then
contemplated it all from my balcony and read the sentence (from a paper in
the Transactions of the Asiatic Society) which had led me to devise this
journey, 'There is a most exquisitely picturesque, but difficult, route up the
course of the Kinugawa, which seems almost as unknown to Japanese as to
foreigners.' There was a pure lemon-coloured sky above, and slush a foot
deep below. A road, at this time a quagmire, intersected by a rapid stream,
crossed in many places by planks, runs through the village. This stream is at
once 'lavatory' and 'drinking fountain'. People come back from their work,
sit on the planks, take off their muddy clothes and wring them out, and

bathe their feet in the current. On either side are the dwellings, in front of which are much-decayed manure heaps, and the women were engaged in breaking them up and treading them into a pulp with their bare feet. All wear the vest and trousers at their work, but only the short petticoats in their houses, and I saw several respectable mothers of families cross the road and pay visits in this garment only, without any sense of impropriety. The younger children wear nothing but a string and an amulet. The persons, clothing, and houses are alive with vermin, and if the word squalor can be applied to independent and industrious people, they were squalid. Beetles, spiders, and wood-lice held a carnival in my room after dark, and the presence of horses in the same house brought a number of horse-flies. I sprinkled my stretcher with insect powder, but my blanket had been on the floor for one minute, and fleas rendered sleep impossible. The night was very long. The *andon* went out, leaving a strong smell of rancid oil. The primitive Japanese dog—a cream-coloured wolfish-looking animal, the size of a collie, very noisy and aggressive, but as cowardly as bullies usually are—was in great force in Fujihara, and the barking, growling, and quarrelling of these useless curs continued at intervals until daylight; and when they were not quarrelling, they were howling. Torrents of rain fell, obliging me to move my bed from place to place to get out of the drip. At five Ito came and entreated me to leave, whimpering, 'I've had no sleep; there are thousands and thousands of fleas!'

ISABELLA BIRD, *Unbeaten Tracks in Japan*, 1878

The Happiness of a Flea

How Happier is that Flea
Which in thy Brest doth playe,
Than that pied Butterflie
Which courtes the Flame, and in the same doth die?
That hath a light Delight
(Poore Foole) contented only with a Sight,
When this doth sporte, and swell with dearest Food,
And if hee die, hee Knight-like dies in Blood.

Of that Same

Thou diedst, yet hast thy Tombe
Betweene those Pappes, ô deare and stately Roome!
Flea, happier farre, more blest,
Than *Phœnix* burning in his spicie Nest.

WILLIAM DRUMMOND of Hawthornden (1585–1649)

'Did you sleep well last night, my dear?' [asked Sister Ovide] 'No,' [the novice] replied, 'I was bitten by fleas.' 'Are there any fleas in your cell? Well, you must get rid of them immediately. Do you know the manner in which the rules of our Order enjoin us to drive them out, so that a sister may never again see even the tail of one during the whole time of her conventual life?' 'No,' the novice replied. 'Very well, then, I will tell you. Do you see any fleas here? Do you perceive any vestiges of fleas? Do you smell an odour of fleas. Is there any appearance of a flea in my room? Just look.' 'I do not see any,' the novice said, who was Mademoiselle de Ficunes, 'and I smell no smell except my own!' 'Do as I am going to tell you, and you will be no longer bitten. Directly you feel the bite, my child, you must undress, lift up your chemise, but be careful not to sin whilst looking all over your body, you must think of nothing but the cursed flea, hunting for it in good faith, without paying attention to other things, only doing your best to discover the flea and how to catch it, which is in itself a difficult matter, as you may easily be deceived by the little natural black spots which appear on your skin, and are your inheritance. Have you any, my dear?'

'Yes,' she replied, 'I have two violet spots, one on my shoulder and another on my back, rather low down; but it is hidden in a fold of the flesh.' 'How did you see it?' asked Sister Perpetua. 'I did not know anything about it, Monsieur Montrezor discovered it.' 'Ha! ha!' the sister said, 'did he see nothing more than that?' 'He saw everything,' she replied. 'I was quite small. He was rather more than nine years of age, and we were playing together.' . . .

Then, as the nuns could hardly restrain their laughter, Sister Ovide continued: 'The above-mentioned flea will in vain jump from your legs to your eyes, try and hide in the hollows, in the forests, in the ditches, go up hill and down dale, determined to escape you; but the rules of our house order you to pursue it courageously, whilst repeating Aves. Generally by the time you get to the third Ave, you will capture the beast.'—'The flea?' the novice said.

'Certainly the flea!' Sister Ovide replied, 'but in order to avoid the dangers of that chase, you must be very careful in whatever spot you put your finger, to touch nothing but it. Then, without paying any heed to its cries, complaints, groans, efforts and contortions, if by chance it happens to rebel, as is often the case, you squeeze it under your thumb, or any other finger of the hand which holds it, and with the other hand you must take a veil to bind the said flea's eyes, and prevent it from hopping, as the creature will not know where to go, as it cannot see clearly. However, as it will still be able to bite you, and might have gone mad with rage, you must gently open its mouth and delicately insert a twig of the blessed box tree which is hanging over your bed by the side of the holy water basin, into its mouth, and then the flea will be obliged to remain quiet. But you must remember that the rules of our Order do not allow you to possess any property on earth, so that the beast cannot belong to you. You must, however, take into consideration that it is one of God's creatures, and you must try and make what you are doing more agreeable to it. Therefore, before everything else, you must verify three important things, namely: whether the flea is a male, or female, or if it be a virgin. Supposing it to be a virgin, which is very unlikely, because these creatures have no morals, are all very lascivious and give themselves up to the first comer, you must seize its hind legs, and drawing them under its little housing you must tie it with one of your hairs and carry it to the Superior, who will decide upon its fate, after consulting the Chapter. If it be a male'—'How can one know whether a flea is a virgin?' the curious novice asked. 'In the first place, she is sad and melancholy, and does not laugh like the others do, does not bite so sharply, her mouth is not so wide open, and she blushes when one touches her.' 'If that be so,' the novice replied, 'I have been bitten by male fleas.'

HONORÉ DE BALZAC (1799–1850), *Droll Stories* (tr. R. Whittling, 1896)

The majestic metal wire armature of a crinoline, which belonged to some lady of the Czarist court, is exhibited at the Kremlin Museum. From the waistband, or rather from the horrifying metal hoop that serves as a waist-band, hang two small tubes made of china, with the shape and size of specimen vials used by chemists; one reads on the description that they were traps for fleas. A teaspoon of honey was put at the bottom of the vial; the fleas, in their peregrinations between one fold of cloth and another, were attracted by the smell of the honey, entered the vial, slipped down its smooth sides, fell to the bottom and were stuck.

This is a chapter in a novel which describes the interminable struggle between two forms of cunning: the conscious, short-term cunning of man who must defend himself from parasites, invent his stratagems in the course of a few generations, and the evolutionary cunning of the parasite which required millions of years but attains results that astound us.

Among animals it is precisely the parasites whom we should admire most for the originality of the inventions inscribed in their anatomy, their physiology and their habits. We do not admire them because they are a nuisance or harmful, but once we have overcome this prejudice an area opens before us in which, and this is the truth, reality far surpasses the imagination. It is enough to think of intestinal worms: they feed themselves at our expense with a food so perfect that, unique in creation together perhaps with the angels, they have no anus; or think of the fleas on rabbits whose ovaries, thanks to a complicated play of hormonal messages, work in synchrony with the ovaries of the host: thus rabbit and guest give birth at the same time, so that at birth each small rabbit receives his portion of minuscule larvae and will leave the nest already provided with fleas which are his contemporaries.

These are necessary stratagems. It must be remembered that the trade of parasite ('he who eats alongside you') is not easy, neither in the animal nor the human world. A good parasite must exploit a host larger, stronger and faster (or, in the human version, richer and more powerful) than he, but it is indispensable that he should make him suffer as little as possible, or he risks being expelled: and he mustn't cause his death (in human terms: go bankrupt), because then he too would be ruined. Think of mosquitoes and vampire-bats, which though so different from each other, have invented anaesthesia and use it in order not to disturb too much the sleep of the host during their modest removal of blood. A human analogy for this kind of anaesthesia could be found in the flattery of a powerful dispenser of benefits, but the parallel between human and animal parasites cannot be taken much further: in our complex society the sponging table companion has definitely yielded the field to parasitic classes and incomes against which it is more difficult to defend oneself.

> Primo Levi, 'The Leap of the Flea', *Other People's Trades*, 1985 (tr. Raymond Rosenthal, 1989)

Fall River Parasite

It is done in the first weeks.
The blind elders, those with foresight
who manipulate the bones
and speak in tongues must confirm
the child well formed, reactions normal,
faculties functional. Then
with singing and exhortation
according to custom
the child is lowered to the water.
Women howl, drums beat, ram's horns
sound for initiation.

In the river of that land
the Worm is endemic.
He insinuates his generation
through sundry apertures
and the innocent, unguarded,
take in, digest, assimilate.

Reaching maturity
Worm, working the system,

issues finally through the eye
(sharp spines blinding the children
in the scars of his passage)
and returns to his origins.

And the old ones never say
avoid water. For they speak
with the Worm's voice
from the baptismal river.

Dorothy Nimmo (b. 1932)

Pharaoh and the Worm

Lord of Lower and Upper Egypt,
Lord of the Nile,
Lord of the World,
Keeper of the Keys of the Gates
Of Abydos through which the souls of all the dead
File down into the underworld.
Lord of all Life, Face of the Sun,
God of the Heavens, Scorpion God,
Amon Ra whose blood flies through
The heavens like the falling stars.

He lies: a cleft stick on his leg
Turns slowly, squeak by squeak,
As inch by inch,
Like the last curlings of the Nile
Through the yellow delta flats,
Like the turnings of gold wire
About the Pharaoh's neck,
Like the spiral of the rays
Circling the sun, the doctor twirls,
Inch by inch, the yard-long guinea worm
From its proud lodging in the Boy-God's thigh.

Mike Harding (b. 1944)

James looked very hot. He sat on the tree trunk next to Dana, held his head in his hand—and then bounded up with a yell. There was a leech on his left arm. He pulled it off with his right hand, but the leech looped over and sank its mouthparts into his palm. James began to dance, wriggling convulsively.

He made a curious yelping sound. The Iban lay down, and laughed. James pulled the leech out of his right palm with his left hand. The brown-black, tough, rubbery, segmented, inch-long Common ground leech, *Haemadipsa zeylanica*, then twisted over and began to take a drink at the base of James's thumb.

'Shit!' said James.

At this point, Leon obviously decided that the two had got to know each other well enough.

'Ah, my best friend,' he said to James, as he pulled the leech out, rubbed it on a tree and cut it in half with his parang, 'why you come so far to suffer so? Eh?'

James sat down, trembling a bit, and pulled out a cigarette.

I looked at my legs. And then I looked again. They were undulating with leeches. In fact James's leech suddenly seemed much less of a joke. They were edging up my trousers, looping up towards my knees with alternate placements of their anterior and posterior suckers, seeming, with each rear attachment, to wave their front ends in the air and take a sniff. They were all over my boots, too, and three particularly brave individuals were trying to make their way in via the air-holes. There were more on the way—in fact they were moving towards us across the jungle floor from every angle, their damp brown bodies half-camouflaged against the rotting leaves.

'Oh God,' said James, *'they are really pleased to see us.'*

The Iban were also suffering, and we spent the next few minutes pulling leeches off our persons and wiping them on the trees. The bite of *Haemadipsa zeylanica* is painless (although that of the Borneo tiger-leech is pungent), containing an anaesthetic in its saliva as well as an anti-coagulant, but nonetheless it was unpleasant to watch them fill with blood at great speed, distending, becoming globular and wobbly.

Now that I had become accustomed to leech-spotting I discovered that they were rearing up and sniffing at us from the trees, too, from leaves and creepers at face height. We covered ourselves with Autan jelly, socks and trousers, chests, arms and neck. Dana, Leon and Inghai put on their best (and only) pairs of long trousers, and I lent them pairs of socks (they were desperate). I took the opportunity to sidle off behind a bush and fill my boots and y-fronts with handfuls of zinc powder. Sitting down again, I was pleased to see that chemical warfare works: the leeches looped and flowed towards me and then stopped, in mid-sniff, as disgusted by me as I was by them. They waved their heads about, thought a bit, decided that they really were revolted, and reversed.

REDMOND O'HANLON, *Into the Heart of Borneo . . . with James Fenton,* 1984

We will now take a view of the Vampire [bat]. As there was a free entrance and exit to the vampire, in the loft where I slept, I had many a fine opportunity of paying attention to this nocturnal surgeon. He does not always live on blood. When the moon shone bright, and the fruit of the banana-tree was ripe, I could see him approach and eat it. He would also bring into the loft, from the forest, a green round fruit, something like the wild guava, and about the size of a nutmeg. There was something also, in the blossom of the sawarri nut-tree, which was grateful to him; for on coming up Waratilla creek, in a moonlight night, I saw several vampires fluttering round the top of the sawarri tree, and every now and then the blossoms, which they had broken off, fell into the water. They certainly did not drop off naturally, for on examining several of them, they appeared quite fresh and blooming. So I concluded the vampires pulled them from the tree, either to get at the incipient fruit, or to catch the insects which often take up their abode in flowers.

The vampire, in general, measures about twenty-six inches from wing to wing extended, though I once killed one which measured thirty-two inches. He frequents old abandoned houses and hollow trees; and sometimes a cluster of them may be seen in the forest hanging head downwards from the branch of a tree.

The vampire has a curious membrane, which rises from the nose, and gives it a very singular appearance. It has been remarked before, that there are two species of vampire in Guiana, a larger and a smaller. The larger sucks men and other animals; the smaller seems to confine himself chiefly to birds. I learnt from a gentleman, high up in the river Demerara, that he was completely unsuccessful with his fowls, on account of the small vampire. He showed me some that had been sucked the night before, and they were scarcely able to walk.

Some years ago I went to the river Paumaron with a Scotch gentleman, by name Tarbet. We hung our hammocks in the thatched loft of a planter's house. Next morning I heard this gentleman muttering in his hammock, and now and then letting fall an imprecation or two, just about the time he ought to have been saying his morning prayers. 'What is the matter, Sir,' said I, softly; 'is any thing amiss?' 'What's the matter!' answered he surlily; 'why, the vampires have been sucking me to death.' As soon as there was light enough, I went to his hammock, and saw it much stained with blood. 'There,' said he, thrusting his foot out of the hammock, 'see how these infernal imps have been drawing my life's blood.' On examining his foot, I found the vampire had tapped his great toe: there was a wound somewhat less than that made by a leech; the blood was still oozing from it; I conjectured he might have lost from ten to twelve ounces of blood. Whilst examining it, I think I put him into a worse humour by remarking, that an

European surgeon would not have been so generous as to have blooded him without making a charge. He looked up in my face, but did not say a word: I saw he was of opinion that I had better have spared this piece of ill-timed levity.

CHARLES WATERTON, Wanderings in South America, 1839

Cannibal

Shark, with your mouth tucked under
That severs like a knife,
You leave no time for wonder
In your swift thrusting life.

You taste blood. It's your brother's,
And at your side he flits.
But blood, like any other's.
You bite him into bits.

THOM GUNN (b. 1929)

There are some terrible robbers in the pond world, and, in our aquarium, we may witness all the cruelties of an embittered struggle for existence enacted before our very eyes. If you have introduced to your aquarium a mixed catch, you will soon be able to see an example of these conflicts, for, amongst the new arrivals, there will probably be a larva of the water-beetle Dytiscus. Considering their relative size, the voracity and cunning with which these animals destroy their prey eclipse the methods of even such notorious robbers as tigers, lions, wolves, or killer whales. These are all as lambs compared with the Dytiscus larva.

It is a slim, streamlined insect, rather more than two inches long. Its six legs are equipped with stout fringes of bristles which form broad oar-like blades that propel the animal with quick and sure movements through the water. The wide, flat head bears an enormous, pincer-shaped pair of jaws which are hollow and serve not only as syringes for injecting poison, but also as orifices of ingestion. The animal lies in ambush on some waterplant; suddenly it shoots at lightning speed towards its prey, darts underneath it, then quickly jerks up its head and grabs the victim in its jaws. 'Prey', for these creatures, is all that moves or that smells of 'animal' in any way. It has often happened to me that, while standing quietly in the water of a pond, I have been 'eaten' by a Dytiscus larva. Even for man, an injection of the poisonous digestive juice of this insect is extremely painful.

KONRAD LORENZ, King Solomon's Ring, 1952

The Crocodile or, Public Decency

Though some at my aversion smile,
I cannot love the crocodile.
Its conduct does not seem to me
Consistent with sincerity.

Where Nile, with beneficial flood,
Improves the desert sand to mud,
The infant child, its banks upon,
Will run about with nothing on.
The London County Council not
Being adjacent to the spot,
This is the consequence. Meanwhile,
What is that object in the Nile
Which swallows water, chokes and spits?
It is the crocodile in fits.

'Oh infant! oh my country's shame!
Suppose a European came!
Picture his feelings, on his pure
Personally conducted tour!
The British Peer's averted look,
The mantling blush of Messrs. Cook!
Come, awful infant, come and be
Dressed, if in nothing else, in me.'

Then disappears into the Nile
The infant, clad in crocodile,
And meekly yields his youthful breath
To darkness, decency, and death.
His mother, in the local dells,
Deplores him with Egyptian yells:
Her hieroglyphic howls are vain,
Nor will the lost return again.
The crocodile itself no less
Displays, but does not feel, distress,
And with its tears augments the Nile;
The false, amphibious crocodile.

'Is it that winds Etesian blow,
Or melts on Ethiop hills the snow?'
So, midst the inundated scene,
Inquire the floating fellaheen.

From Cairo's ramparts gazing far
The mild Khedive and stern Sirdar
Say, as they scan the watery plain,
'There goes that crocodile again.'
The copious tribute of its lids
Submerges half the pyramids,
And over all the Sphinx it flows,
Except her non-existent nose.

A. E. HOUSMAN (1859–1936)

Eighteen miles from our summer home in the Himalayas there is a long ridge running east and west, some 9,000 feet in height. On the upper slopes of the eastern end of this ridge there is a luxuriant growth of oat-grass; below this grass the hill falls steeply away in a series of rock cliffs to the Kosi River below.

One day a party of women and girls from the village on the north face of the ridge were cutting the oat-grass, when a tiger suddenly appeared in their midst. In the stampede that followed an elderly woman lost her footing, rolled down the steep slope, and disappeared over the cliff. The tiger, evidently alarmed by the screams of the women, vanished as mysteriously as it had appeared, and when the women had re-assembled and recovered from their fright, they went down the grassy slope and, looking over the cliff, saw their companion lying on a narrow ledge some distance below them.

The woman said she was badly injured—it was found later that she had broken a leg and fractured several ribs—and that she could not move. Ways and means of a rescue were discussed, and it was finally decided that it was a job for men; and as no one appeared to be willing to remain at the spot, they informed the injured woman that they were going back to the village for help. The woman begged not to be left alone, however, and at her entreaty a girl, sixteen years of age, volunteered to stay with her. So, while the rest of the party set off for the village, the girl made her way down to the right, where a rift in the cliff enabled her to get a foothold on the ledge.

This ledge extended only half-way across the face of the cliff and ended, a few yards from where the woman was lying, in a shallow depression. Fearing that she might fall off the ledge and be killed on the rocks hundreds of feet below, the woman asked the girl to move her to this depression, and this difficult and dangerous feat the girl successfully accomplished. There was only room for one in the depression, so the girl squatted, as only an Indian can squat, on the ledge facing the woman.

The village was four miles away, and once, and once again, the two on the ledge speculated as to the length of time it would take their companions to get back to the village; what men they were likely to find in the village at that time of day; how long it would take to explain what had happened, and finally, how long it would take the rescue party to arrive.

Conversation had been carried on in whispers for fear the tiger might be lurking in the vicinity and hear them, and then, suddenly, the woman gave a gasp and the girl, seeing the look of horror on her face and the direction in which she was looking, turned her head and over her shoulder saw the tiger, stepping out of the rift in the cliff on to the ledge.

Few of us, I imagine, have escaped that worst of all nightmares in which, while our limbs and vocal cords are paralysed with fear, some terrible beast in monstrous form approaches to destroy us; the nightmare from which, sweating fear in every pore, we waken with a cry of thankfulness to Heaven that it was only a dream. There was no such happy awakening from the nightmare of that unfortunate girl, and little imagination is needed to picture the scene. A rock cliff with a narrow ledge running partly across it and ending in a little depression in which an injured woman is lying; a young girl frozen with terror squatting on the ledge, and a tiger slowly creeping towards her; retreat in every direction cut off, and no help at hand.

Mothi Singh, an old friend of mine, was in the village visiting a sick daughter when the women arrived, and he headed the rescue party. When this party went down the grassy slope and looked over the cliff, they saw the woman lying in a swoon, and on the ledge they saw splashes of blood.

The injured woman was carried back to the village, and when she had been revived and had told her story, Mothi Singh set out on his eighteen-mile walk to me. He was an old man well over sixty, but he scouted the suggestion that he was tired and needed a rest, so we set off together to make investigations. But there was nothing that I could do, for twenty-four hours had elapsed, and all that the tiger had left of the brave young girl who had volunteered to stay with her injured companion were a few bits of bone and her torn and bloodstained clothes.

This was the first human being killed by the tiger which later received recognition in Government records as 'The Mohan Man-Eater'.

JIM CORBETT, Man-Eaters of Kumaon, 1944

Vultures

Hung there in the thermal
whiteout of noon, dark ash
in the chimney's updraft, turning
slowly like a thumb pressed down
on target; indolent V's; flies, until they drop.

Then they're hyenas, raucous
around the kill, flapping their black
umbrellas, the feathered red-eyed widows
whose pot bodies violate mourning,
the snigger at funerals,
the burp at the wake.

They cluster, like beetles
laying their eggs on carrion,
gluttonous for a space, a little
territory of murder: food
and children.

Frowzy old saint, bald-
headed and musty, scrawny-
necked recluse on your pillar
of blazing air which is not
heaven: what do you make
of death, which you do not
cause, which you eat daily?

I make life, which is a prayer.
I make clean bones.
I make a gray zinc noise
which to me is a song.

Well, heart, out of all this
carnage, could you do better?

MARGARET ATWOOD (b. 1939)

Ngong, 3rd January, 1928

Now I'm going to tell you about something really exciting that happened
on New Year's Day. Very early in the morning Denys and I made up our
minds to try to drive out along the new road from Ngong to Narok. . . .
It was the most beautiful clear morning, and it is a very fine road. . . . We
saw masses of game, eland, zebra and grant. Then, when we had driven
fifteen miles from the house, Kanuthia pointed to the right and whispered
'Simba,' and sure enough,—on top of a huge dark mass, which later on
proved to be a dead giraffe, a big lion was towering with its face straight
toward us. Now the Masai have been suffering a lot from lions, and Denys
had earlier been asked by the Game Department to try to shoot lions there,
so of course we felt it was a good *opportunity*. Denys shot it with two

shots, at about 250 yards—an old lion, not a particularly good mane, but how big and magnificent they are, and how interesting it was to see them again.—

Then we covered it up with thorn branches intending to skin it on the way home, and drove on to find, as I said, six miles further on that the road came to an abrupt end, so we had to turn round and drive back. I had to keep a lookout for the giraffe so that we did not drive past it, and when I caught sight of it I could hardly believe my eyes: another lion was standing on it looking toward us,—an absolutely splendid, big *black-maned* lion, I think the best I have seen. I think it must be one of the most beautiful sights in the world. We sat there for a while considering whether to shoot it or not, but came to the conclusion that we had to have it, so just as it was about to take itself off Denys shot it; it leaped high up into the air and fell straight down. Denys says it is the best skin he has ever had; the mane was completely black and grew right back over the shoulders.—We then skinned them both and then, very proud and happy, had a New Year's *breakfast* of bread and cheese, raisins and almonds, that we had with us, and a bottle of red wine, in the lovely clear air, with the Ngong Hills and the bright green plains around us; I don't think I have ever had a more delightful New Year's morning.

KAREN BLIXEN, to Ingeborg Dinesen, *Letters from Africa, 1914–1931*

Mountain Lion

Climbing through the January snow, into the Lobo canyon
Dark grow the spruce trees, blue is the balsam, water sounds still
    unfrozen, and the trail is still evident.

Men!
Two men!
Men! The only animal in the world to fear!

They hesitate.
We hesitate.
They have a gun.
We have no gun.

Then we all advance, to meet.

Two Mexicans, strangers, emerging out of the dark and snow and
    inwardness of the Lobo valley.
What are they doing here on this vanishing trail?

What is he carrying?
Something yellow.
A deer?

Qué tiene, amigo?—
León—

He smiles, foolishly, as if he were caught doing wrong.
And we smile, foolishly, as if we didn't know.
He is quite gentle and dark-faced.

It is a mountain lion,
A long, slim cat, yellow like a lioness.
Dead.

He trapped her this morning, he says, smiling foolishly.

Lift up her face,
Her round, bright face, bright as frost.
Her round, fine-fashioned head, with two dead ears:
And stripes in the brilliant frost of her face, sharp, fine dark rays,
Dark, keen, fine rays in the brilliant frost of her face.
Beautiful dead eyes.

Hermoso es!

They go out towards the open;
We go on into the gloom of Lobo.

And above the trees I found her lair,
A hole in the blood-orange brilliant rocks that stick up, a little cave.
And bones, and twigs, and a perilous ascent.

So, she will never leap up that way again, with the yellow flash of a
    mountain lion's long shoot!
And her bright striped frost-face will never watch any more, out of the
    shadow of the cave in the blood-orange rock,
Above the trees of the Lobo dark valley-mouth!

Instead, I look out.
And out to the dim of the desert, like a dream, never real;
To the snow of the Sangre de Cristo mountains, the ice of the mountains
    of Picoris,
And near across at the opposite steep of snow, green trees motionless
    standing in snow, like a Christmas toy.

And I think in this empty world there was room for me and a mountain
    lion.
And I think in the world beyond, how easily we might spare a million or
    two of humans
And never miss them.
Yet what a gap in the world, the missing white frost-face of that slim
    yellow mountain lion!

D. H. Lawrence (1885–1930)

[*The Badger*]

The badger grunting on his woodland track
With shaggy hide and sharp nose scrowed with black
Roots in the bushes and the woods and makes
A great hugh burrow in the ferns and brakes
With nose on ground he runs a awkard pace
And anything will beat him in the race
The shepherds dog will run him to his den
Followed and hooted by the dogs and men
The woodman when the hunting comes about
Go round at night to stop the foxes out
And hurrying through the bushes ferns and brakes
Nor sees the many hol[e]s the badger makes
And often through the bushes to the chin
Breaks the old holes and tumbles headlong in

When midnight comes a host of dogs and men
Go out and track the badger to his den
And put a sack within the hole and lye
Till the old grunting badger passes bye
He comes and hears they let the strongest loose
The old fox hears the noise and drops the goose
The poacher shoots and hurrys from the cry
And the old hare half wounded buzzes bye
They get a forked stick to bear him down
And clapt the dogs and bore him to the town
And bait him all the day with many dogs
And laugh and shout and fright the scampering hogs
He runs along and bites at all he meets
They shout and hollo down the noisey streets

He turns about to face the loud uproar
And drives the rebels to their very doors

The frequent stone is hurled where ere they go
When badgers fight and every ones a foe
The dogs are clapt and urged to join the fray
The badger turns and drives them all away
Though scar[c]ely half as big dimute and small
He fights with dogs for hours and beats them all
The heavy mastiff savage in the fray
Lies down and licks his feet and turns away
The bull dog knows his match and waxes cold
The badger grins and never leaves his hold
He drive[s] the crowd and follows at their heels
And bites them through the drunkard swears and reels

The frighted women takes the boys away
The blackguard laughs and hurrys on the fray
He trys to reach the woods a awkard race
But sticks and cudgels quickly stop the chace
He turns agen and drives the noisey crowd
And beats the many dogs in noises loud
He drives away and beats them every one
And then they loose them all and set them on
He falls as dead and kicked by boys and men
Then starts and grins and drives the crowd agen
Till kicked and torn and beaten out he lies
And leaves his hold and cackles groans and dies

JOHN CLARE (1793–1864)

A Night at Rat-Killing

Considering the immense number of rats which form an article of commerce with many of the lower orders, whose business it is to keep them for the purpose of rat matches, I thought it necessary, for the full elucidation of my subject, to visit the well-known public-house in London, where, on a certain night in the week, a pit is built up, and regular rat-killing matches take place, and where those who have sporting dogs, and are anxious to test their qualities, can, after such matches are finished, purchase half a dozen or a dozen rats for them to practise upon, and judge for themselves of their dogs' 'performances.'

I arrived at about eight o'clock at the tavern where the performances were to take place. I was too early, but there was plenty to occupy my leisure in looking at the curious scene around me, and taking notes of the habits and conversation of the customers who were flocking in.

The front of the long bar was crowded with men of every grade of society, all smoking, drinking, and talking about dogs. Many of them had brought with them their 'fancy' animals, so that a kind of 'canine exhibition' was going on; some carried under their arm small bull-dogs, whose flat pink noses rubbed against my arm as I passed; others had Skye-terriers, curled up like balls of hair, and sleeping like children, as they were nursed by their owners. The only animals that seemed awake, and under continual excitement, were the little brown English terriers, who, despite the neat black leathern collars by which they were held, struggled to get loose, as if they smelt the rats in the room above, and were impatient to begin the fray.

As the visitors poured in, they, at the request of the proprietor 'not to block up the bar,' took their seats in the parlour, and, accompanied by a waiter, who kept shouting, 'Give your orders, gentlemen,' I entered the room. . . . Over the fireplace were square glazed boxes, in which were the stuffed forms of dogs famous in their day. . . .

'That there *is* a dog,' [the proprietor's son told me], pointing to one represented with a rat in its mouth, 'it was as good as any in England, though it's so small. I've seen her kill a dozen rats almost as big as herself, though they killed *her* at last, for sewer-rats are dreadful for giving dogs canker in the mouth, and she wore herself out with continually killing them, though we always rinsed her mouth out well with peppermint and water while she were at work. When rats bite they are pisonous, and an ulcer is formed, which we are obleeged to lance; that's what killed her.'

There was no announcement that the room above was ready, though everybody seemed to understand it; for all rose at once, and mounting the broad wooden staircase, which led to what was once the 'drawing-room,' dropped their shillings into the hand of the proprietor, and entered the rat-killing apartment.

'The pit,' as it is called, consists of a small circus, some six feet in diameter. It is about as large as a centre flower-bed, and is fitted with a high wooden rim that reaches to elbow height. Over it the branches of a gas lamp are arranged, which light up the white painted floor, and every part of the little arena. On one side of the room is a recess, which the proprietor calls his 'private box,' and this apartment the Captain and his friend soon took possession of, whilst the audience generally clambered upon the tables and forms, or hung over the sides of the pit itself.

All the little dogs which the visitors had brought up with them were now squalling and barking, and struggling in their masters' arms, as if they were thoroughly acquainted with the uses of the pit; and when a rusty wire cage of rats, filled with the dark moving mass, was brought forward, the noise of the dogs was so great that the proprietor was obliged to shout out—'Now, you that have dogs *do* make 'em shut up.'

After several inexperienced dogs, the main match was due to start.

And true enough we shortly heard a wheezing and a screaming in the passage without, as if some strong-winded animal were being strangled, and presently a boy entered, carrying in his arms a bull-terrier in a perfect fit of excitement, foaming at the mouth and stretching its neck forward, so that the collar which held it back seemed to be cutting its throat in two.

When all the arrangements had been made the 'second' and the dog jumped into the pit, and after 'letting him see 'em a bit,' the terrier was let loose.

The moment the dog was 'free,' he became quiet in a most business-like manner, and rushed at the rats, burying his nose in the mound till he brought out one in his mouth. In a short time a dozen rats with wetted necks were lying bleeding on the floor, and the white paint of the pit became grained with blood.

In a little time the terrier had a rat hanging to his nose, which, despite his tossing, still held on. He dashed up against the sides, leaving a patch of blood as if a strawberry had been smashed there.

'He doesn't squeal, that's one good thing,' said one of the lookers-on.

As the rats fell on their sides after a bite they were collected together in the centre, where they lay quivering in their death-gasps!

'Hi, Butcher! hi, Butcher!' shouted the second, 'good dog! bur-r-r-r-h!' and he beat the sides of the pit like a drum till the dog flew about with new life.

The poor little wretches in this brief interval, as if forgetting their danger, again commenced cleaning themselves, some nibbling the ends of their tails, others hopping about, going now to the legs of the lad in the pit, and sniffing at his trousers, or, strange to say, advancing, smelling, to within a few paces of their enemy the dog.

It was nearly twelve o'clock before the evening's performance concluded.

HENRY MAYHEW, *London Labour and the London Poor*, 1861–2

The sixt of August we discovered land in 66 degrees 40 minuts of latitude, altogether void from the pester of ice: we ankered in a very faire rode under a brave mount, the cliffes whereof were as orient as golde. This mount was named Mount Raleigh. The rode where our ships lay at anker was called

Totnes rode. The sound which did compasse the mount was named Exeter sound. The foreland towards the North was called Diers cape. The foreland towards the South was named Cape Walsingham. So soone as we were come to an anker in Totnes rode under Mount Raleigh, we espied foure white beares at the foot of the mount: we supposing them to be goats or wolves, manned our boats and went towards them: but when we came neere the shore, we found them to be white beares of a monstrous bignesse: we being desirous of fresh victual and the sport, began to assault them, and I being on land, one of them came downe the hill right against me: my piece was charged with hailshot & a bullet: I discharged my piece and shot him in the necke; he roared a litle, and tooke the water straight, making small account of his hurt. Then we followed him with our boat, and killed him with boare-speares, & two more that night. We found nothing in their mawes; but we judged by their dung that they fed upon grasse, because it appeared in all respects like the dung of an horse, wherein we might very plainly see the very strawes.

The 7 we went on shore to another beare which lay all night upon the top of an Island under Mount Raleigh, and when we came up to him he lay fast asleep. I levelled at his head, and the stone of my piece gave no fire: with that he looked up, and layed downe his head againe: then I shot being charged with two bullets, and strooke him in the head: he being but amazed fell backwards: whereupon we ran all upon him with boare-speares, and thrust him in the body: yet for all that he gript away our boare-speares, and went towards the water; and as he was going downe, he came backe againe. Then our Master shot his boare-speare, and strooke him in the head, and made him to take the water, and swimme into a cove fast by, where we killed him, and brought him aboord. The breadth of his forefoot from one side to the other was foureteene inches over. They were very fat, so as we were constrained to cast the fat away.

> JOHN JANES, *The first voyage of M. John Davis, undertaken in June 1585. for the discoverie of the Northwest passage, written by M. John Janes . . .*, in *The Principal Navigations Voyages Traffiques & Discoveries of the English Nation . . .* by Richard Hakluyt (1552–1616)

The Idlers that sport only with inanimate nature may claim some indulgence; if they are useless they are still innocent: but there are others, whom I know not how to mention without more emotion than my love of quiet willingly admits. Among the inferiour professors of medical knowledge, is a race of wretches, whose lives are only varied by varieties of cruelty; whose favourite amusement is to nail dogs to tables and open them alive; to try how long life may be continued in various degrees of mutilation, or with the excision or laceration of the vital parts; to examine whether burning irons are felt more acutely by the bone or tendon; and whether the more lasting agonies are produced by poison forced into the mouth or injected into the veins.

It is not without reluctance that I offend the sensibility of the tender mind with images like these. If such cruelties were not practised it were to be desired that they should not be conceived, but since they are published every day with ostentation, let me be allowed once to mention them, since I mention them with abhorrence.

Mead has invidiously remarked of Woodward that he gathered shells and stones, and would pass for a philosopher. With pretensions much less reasonable, the anatomical novice tears out the living bowels of an animal, and stiles himself physician, prepares himself by familiar cruelty for that profession which he is to exercise upon the tender and the helpless, upon feeble bodies and broken minds, and by which he has opportunities to extend his arts of torture, and continue those experiments upon infancy and age, which he has hitherto tried upon cats and dogs.

What is alleged in defence of these hateful practices, every one knows; but the truth is, that by knives, fire, and poison, knowledge is not always sought, and is very seldom attained. The experiments that have been tried, are tried again; he that burned an animal with irons yesterday, will be willing to amuse himself with burning another to-morrow.

SAMUEL JOHNSON, *The Idler*, no. 17, 5 August 1758

The fox was strong, he was full of running,
He could run for an hour and then be cunning,
But the cry behind him made him chill,
They were nearer now and they meant to kill.
They meant to run him until his blood
Clogged on his heart as his brush with mud,
Till his back bent up and his tongue hung flagging,
And his belly and brush were filthed from dragging.
Till he crouched stone-still, dead-beat and dirty,
With nothing but teeth against the thirty.
And all the way to that blinding end
He would meet with men and have none his friend:
Men to holloa and men to run him,
With stones to stagger and yells to stun him;
Men to head him, with whips to beat him,
Teeth to mangle and mouths to eat him.
And all the way, that wild high crying.
To cold his blood with the thought of dying,

The horn and the cheer, and the drum-like thunder
Of the horsehooves stamping the meadows under.
He upped his brush and went with a will
For the Sarsen Stones on Wan Dyke Hill.

JOHN MASEFIELD, *Reynard the Fox*, 1919

The foxes caught the summer birds of the tundra—the ptarmigan, sandpipers, and buntings; and these birds were at once a size-jump smaller than
the foxes and much more numerous. The ptarmigan ate the fruit and leaves
of tundra plants, but the sandpipers and buntings ate insects and worms,
which were again a size-jump smaller as well as being more numerous. The
foxes also ate seagulls and eider ducks, smaller and more numerous than
the foxes, and these birds ate the tiny abundant life of the sea. Elton not only
saw all this but, as Sherlock Holmes often lectured Watson, he *observed* it
also. That small things were common and large things rare has been known
by everybody since the dawn of thought, but Elton pondered it as Newton
once pondered a falling apple, and knew he was watching something odd.
Why should large animals be so remarkably rare? And why should life come
in discrete sizes?

Elton's summer on Spitzbergen gave him the answer to the second of
these questions even as he posed it. The discrete sizes came about from the
mechanics of eating and being eaten. He had seen a fox eat a sandpiper and
a sandpiper eat a worm. These animals of different sizes were linked
together by invisible chains of eating and being eaten.

PAUL COLINVAUX, *Why Big Fierce Animals are Rare*, 1980

Owl

is my favourite. Who flies
like a nothing through the night,
who-whoing. Is a feather
duster in leafy corners ring-a-rosy-ing
boles of mice. Twice

you hear him call. Who
is he looking for? You hear
him hoovering over the floor
of the wood. O would you be gold
rings in the driving skull

if you could? Hooded and
vulnerable by the winter suns

owl looks. Is the grain of bark
in the dark. Round beaks are at
work in the pellety nest,

resting. Owl is an eye
in the barn. For a hole
in the trunk owl's blood
is to blame. Black talons in the
petrified fur! Cold walnut hands

on the case of the brain! In the reign
of the chicken owl comes like
a god. Is a goad in
the rain to the pink eyes,
dripping. For a meal in the day

flew, killed, on the moor. Six
mouths are the seed of his
arc in the season. Torn meat
from the sky. Owl lives
by the claws of his brain. On the branch

in the sever of the hand's
twigs owl is a backward look.
Flown wind in the skin. Fine
rain in the bones. Owl breaks
like the day. Am an owl, am an owl.

GEORGE MACBETH (1932–92)

Weasels frequently hunt in couples, and sometimes more than two will work together. I once saw five, and have heard of eight. The five I saw were working a sandy bank drilled with holes, from which the rabbits in wild alarm were darting in all directions. The weasels raced from hole to hole and along the sides of the bank exactly like a pack of hounds, and seemed intensely excited. Their manner of hunting resembles the motions of ants; these insects run a little way very swiftly, then stop, turn to the right or left, make a short *détour*, and afterwards on again in a straight line. So the pack of weasels darted forward, stopped, went from side to side, and then on a yard or two, and repeated the process. To see their reddish heads thrust for a moment from the holes, then withdrawn to reappear at another, would have been amusing had it not been for the reflection that their frisky tricks would assuredly end in death. They ran their quarry out of the bank and into a wood, where I lost sight of them. The pack of eight was seen by a labourer returning down a woodland lane from work one afternoon. He told me he got into the ditch, half from curiosity to watch them, and half from fear—laughable as that may seem—for he had heard the old people tell stories of men in the days when the corn was kept for years in barns, and so bred hundreds of rats, being attacked by those vicious brutes. He said they made a noise, crying to each other, short sharp snappy sounds; but the pack of five I myself saw hunted in silence.

RICHARD JEFFERIES, The Gamekeeper at Home, 1890

The Buzzard

The buzzard turns a circle in the sky,
making its ends meet.
When it completes the figure
a round blue segment drops out of the air,
leaving a black hole
through which the souls of many little birds
fly up to heaven.

ALASDAIR MACLEAN (b. 1926)

Sailing through the Straits of Magellan in 1578, Francis Drake's expedition discovers penguins.

30 leagues within the streights there be 3 islands. To the greatest our general gave the name of Elizabeth: to the 2 Bartholomew, because we found it on S. Bartholomews day: the 3 he named S. Georges island. Here we staied one day & victualled our selves with a kinde of foule which is plentifull in that isle, and whose flesh is not farre unlike a fat goose here in England: they have no wings, but short pineons which serve their turne in swimming. Their colour is somewhat blacke mixt with white spots under their belly, and about their necke. They walke so upright, that a farre off a man would take them to be litle children. If a man aproch any thing neere them, they run into holes in the ground (which be not very deepe) whereof the island is full. So that to take them we had staves with hookes fast to the ends, wherewith some of our men pulled them out and others being ready with cudgels did knocke them on the head, for they bite so cruellie with their crooked bils, that none of us was able to handle them alive.

EDWARD CLIFFE, The voyage of M. John Winter into the South sea by the Streight
of Magellan, in consort with M. Francis Drake, begun in the yeere 1577 . . . Written
by Edward Cliffe Mariner, in The Principal Navigations Voyages Traffiques &
Discoveries of the English Nation . . . by Richard Hakluyt (1552–1616)

Vulture

The vulture's very like a sack
    Set down and left there drooping.
His crooked neck and creaky back
    Look badly bent from stooping
Down to the ground to eat dead cows
    So they won't go to waste
Thus making up in usefulness
    For what he lacks in taste.

X. J. KENNEDY (b. 1929)

Sunt Leones

The lions who ate the Christians on the sands of the arena
By indulging native appetites played what has now been seen a
Not entirely negligible part
In consolidating at the very start
The position of the Early Christian Church.
Initiatory rites are always bloody
And the lions, it appears
From contemporary art, made a study
Of dyeing Coliseum sands a ruddy
Liturgically sacrificial hue
And if the Christians felt a little blue—
Well people being eaten often do.
Theirs was the death, and theirs the crown undying,
A state of things which must be satisfying.
My point which up to this has been obscured
Is that it was the lions who procured
By chewing up blood gristle flesh and bone
The martyrdoms on which the Church has grown.
I only write this poem because I thought it rather looked
As if the part the lions played was being overlooked.
By lions' jaws great benefits and blessings were begotten
And so our debt to Lionhood must never be forgotten.

STEVIE SMITH (1902–71)

I do not know of a more striking instance in the animal kingdom of adaptation of structure to habit than is afforded by the hairy armadillo— *Dasypus villosus*. He appears to us, roughly speaking, to resemble an ant-eater saddled with a dish cover; yet this creature, with the cunning which Nature has given it to supplement all deficiencies, has discovered in its bony encumbrance a highly efficient weapon of offence.

A friend of mine, a careful observer, who was engaged in cattle-breeding amongst the stony sierras near Cape Corrientes, described to me an encounter he witnessed between an armadillo and a poisonous snake. While seated on the hillside one day he observed a snake, about twenty inches in length, lying coiled up on a stone five or six yards beneath him. By-and-by, a hairy armadillo appeared trotting directly towards it. Apparently the snake perceived and feared its approach, for it quickly uncoiled itself and began gliding away. Instantly the armadillo rushed on to it, and, squatting close down, began swaying its body backward and forward with a regular sawing motion, thus lacerating its victim with the sharp, deep-cut edges of its bony covering. The snake struggled to free itself, biting savagely at its aggressor, for its head and neck were disengaged. Its bites made no impression, and very soon it dropped its head, and when its enemy drew off, it was dead and very much mangled. The armadillo at once began its meal, taking the tail in its mouth and slowly progressing towards the head; but when about a third of the snake still remained it seemed satisfied, and, leaving that portion, trotted away.

W. H. Hudson, The Naturalist in La Plata, 1892

Whiles Laocon, that chosen was by lot
Neptunus priest, did sacrifice a bull
Before the holy altar, sodenly
From Tenedon, behold! in circles great
By the calme seas come fletyng adders twaine,
Which plied towardes the shore—I lothe to tell—
With rered brest lift up above the seas;
Whose bloody crestes aloft the waves were seen.
The hinder part swame hidden in the flood;
Their grisly backes were linked manifold.
With sound of broken waves they gate the strand,
With gloing eyen, tainted with blood and fire;
Whoes waltring tongs did lick their hissing mouthes.
We fled away, our face the blood forsoke;
But they with gate direct to Lacon ran.
And first of all eche serpent doth enwrap
The bodies small of his two tender sonnes,
Whoes wrectched limbes they byt, and fed theron.
Then raught they hym, who had his wepon caught

To rescue them; twise winding him about,
With folded knottes and circled tailes, his wast;
Their scaled backes did compasse twise his neck,
Wyth rered heddes aloft and stretched throtes.
He with his handes strave to unloose the knottes,
Whose sacred fillettes all be sprinkled were
With filth of gory blod, and venim rank,
And to the sterres such dredfull shoutes he sent,
Like to the sound the roring bull fourth loowes,
Which from the halter wounded doth astart,
The swarving axe when he shakes from his neck.
The serpentes twain with hasted traile they glide
To Pallas temple, and her towres of heighte;
Under the feete of which the goddesse stern,
Hidden behinde her targettes bosse they crept.

VIRGIL (70–19 BC), *Aeneid*, book II, tr. HENRY HOWARD, Earl of Surrey
(*c*.1517–47)

He was a mongoose, rather like a little cat in his fur and his tail, but quite like a weasel in his head and his habits. His eyes and the end of his restless nose were pink; he could scratch himself anywhere he pleased, with any leg, front or back, that he chose to use; he could fluff up his tail till it looked like a bottle-brush, and his war-cry, as he scuttled through the long grass, was: '*Rikk-tikk-tikki-tikki-tchk!*'

It is the hardest thing in the world to frighten a mongoose, because he is eaten up from nose to tail with curiosity. The motto of all the mongoose family is, 'Run and find out'; and Rikki-tikki was a true mongoose.

He moves in to live in the bungalow of an English family, and soon has his first encounter with a pair of cobras in the garden. They have eaten the fledgling of Darzee, the tailor-bird.

From the thick grass at the foot of the bush there came a low hiss—a horrid cold sound that made Rikki-tikki jump back two clear feet. Then inch by inch out of the grass rose up the head and spread hood of Nag, the big black cobra, and he was five feet long from tongue to tail. When he had lifted one-third of himself clear of the ground, he stayed balancing to and fro exactly as a dandelion-tuft balances in the wind, and he looked at Rikki-tikki with the wicked snake's eyes that never change their expression, whatever the snake may be thinking of.

He spread out his hood more than ever, and Rikki-tikki saw the spectacle-mark on the back of it that looks exactly like the eye part of a hook-and-eye fastening. He was afraid for the minute; but it is impossible for a mongoose to stay frightened for any length of time, and though Rikki-tikki had never met a live cobra before, his mother had fed him on dead ones, and he knew that all a grown mongoose's business in life was to fight and eat snakes. Nag knew that too, and at the bottom of his cold heart he was afraid.

'Well,' said Rikki-tikki, and his tail began to fluff up again, 'marks or no marks, do you think it is right for you to eat fledglings out of a nest?'

Nag was thinking to himself, and watching the least little movement in the grass behind Rikki-tikki. He knew that mongooses in the garden meant death sooner or later for him and his family, but he wanted to get Rikki-tikki off his guard. So he dropped his head a little, and put it on one side.

'Let us talk,' he said. 'You eat eggs. Why should not I eat birds?'

'Behind you! Look behind you!' sang Darzee.

Rikki-tikki knew better than to waste time in staring. He jumped up in the air as high as he could go, and just under him whizzed by the head of Nagaina, Nag's wicked wife. She had crept up behind him as he was talking, to make an end of him; and he heard her savage hiss as the stroke missed. He came down almost across her back, and if he had been an old mongoose he would have known that then was the time to break her back with one bite; but he was afraid of the terrible lashing return-stroke of the cobra. He bit, indeed, but did not bite long enough, and he jumped clear of the whisking tail, leaving Nagaina torn and angry.

Next, Rikki-tikki attacks Nag, who has come into the bungalow at night. Getting his teeth into the cobra's thick neck, he manages to hang on until the man is able to shoot it. He then turns his attention to Nagaina's eggs.

Rikki-tikki heard Nagaina going up the path from the stables, and he raced for the end of the melon-patch near the wall. There, in the warm litter about the melons, very cunningly hidden, he found twenty-five eggs, about the size of a bantam's eggs, but with whitish skin instead of shell.

'I was not a day too soon,' he said; for he could see the baby cobras curled up inside the skin, and he knew that the minute they were hatched they could each kill a man or a mongoose. He bit off the tops of the eggs as fast as he could, taking care to crush the young cobras, and turned over the litter from time to time to see whether he had missed any. At last there were only three eggs left, and Rikki-tikki began to chuckle to himself, when he heard Darzee's wife screaming:

'Rikki-tikki, I led Nagaina toward the house, and she has gone into the verandah, and—oh, come quickly—she means killing!'

Rikki-tikki smashed two eggs, and tumbled backward down the melon-bed with the third egg in his mouth, and scuttled to the verandah as hard as he could put foot to the ground.

Finally, he takes on Nagaina herself, who is threatening Teddy, the son of the house.

The big snake turned half round, and saw the egg on the verandah. 'Ah-h! Give it to me,' she said.

Rikki-tikki put his paws one on each side of the egg, and his eyes were blood-red. 'What price for a snake's egg? For a young cobra? For a young king-cobra? For the last—the very last of the brood? The ants are eating all the others down by the melon-bed.'

Nagaina spun clear round, forgetting everything for the sake of the one egg; and Rikki-tikki saw Teddy's father shoot out a big hand, catch Teddy by the shoulder, and drag him across the little table with the tea-cups, safe and out of reach of Nagaina.

'Tricked! Tricked! Tricked! *Rikk-tck-tck!*' chuckled Rikki-tikki. 'The boy is safe, and it was I—I—I that caught Nag by the hood last night in the bath-room.' Then he began to jump up and down, all four feet together, his head close to the floor. 'He threw me to and fro, but he could not shake me off. He was dead before the big man blew him in two. I did it. *Rikki-tikki-tck-tck!* Come then, Nagaina. Come and fight with me. You shall not be a widow long.'

Nagaina saw that she had lost her chance of killing Teddy, and the egg lay between Rikki-tikki's paws. 'Give me the egg, Rikki-tikki. Give me the last of my eggs, and I will go away and never come back,' she said, lowering her hood.

Rikki-tikki was bounding all round Nagaina, keeping just out of reach of her stroke, his little eyes like hot coals. Nagaina gathered herself together, and flung out at him. Rikki-tikki jumped up and backward. Again and again and again she struck, and each time her head came with a whack on the matting of the verandah, and she gathered herself together like a watch-spring. Then Rikki-tikki danced in a circle to get behind her, and Nagaina spun round to keep her head to his head, so that the rustle of her tail on the matting sounded like dry leaves blown along by the wind.

He had forgotten the egg. It still lay on the verandah, and Nagaina came nearer and nearer to it, till at last, while Rikki-tikki was drawing breath, she caught it in her mouth, turned to the verandah steps, and flew like an arrow down the path, with Rikki-tikki behind her. When the cobra runs for her life, she goes like a whip-lash flicked across a horse's neck.

Rikki-tikki knew that he must catch her, or all the trouble would begin again. . . . and as she plunged into the rat-hole where she and Nag used to live, his little white teeth were clenched on her tail, and he went down with her—and very few mongooses, however wise and old they may be, care to follow a cobra into its hole. It was dark in the hole; and Rikki-tikki never knew when it might open out and give Nagaina room to turn and strike at him. He held on savagely, and struck out his feet to act as brakes on the dark slope of the hot, moist earth.

Then the grass by the mouth of the hole stopped waving, and Darzee said: 'It is all over with Rikki-tikki! We must sing his death-song. Valiant Rikki-tikki is dead! For Nagaina will surely kill him underground.'

So he sang a very mournful song that he made up on the spur of the minute, and just as he got to the most touching part the grass quivered again, and Rikki-tikki, covered with dirt, dragged himself out of the hole leg by leg, licking his whiskers. Darzee stopped with a little shout. Rikki-tikki shook some of the dust out of his fur and sneezed. 'It is all over,' he said. 'The widow will never come out again.' And the red ants that live between the grass stems heard him, and began to troop down one after another to see if he had spoken the truth.

Rikki-tikki curled himself up in the grass and slept where he was—slept and slept till it was late in the afternoon, for he had done a hard day's work.

'Now,' he said, when he awoke, 'I will go back to the house. Tell the Coppersmith, Darzee, and he will tell the garden that Nagaina is dead.'

Rudyard Kipling, 'Rikki-Tikki-Tavi', The Jungle Book, 1894

Ballad of the Totems

My father was Noonuccal man and kept old tribal way,
His totem was the Carpet Snake, whom none must ever slay;
But mother was of Peewee clan, and loudly she expressed
The daring view that carpet snakes were nothing but a pest.

Now one lived right inside with us in full immunity,
For no one dared to interfere with father's stern decree:
A mighty fellow ten feet long, and as we lay in bed
We kids could watch him round a beam not far above our head.

Only the dog was scared of him, we'd hear its whines and growls,
But mother fiercely hated him because he took her fowls.
You should have heard her diatribes that flowed in angry torrents
With words you never see in print, except in D. H. Lawrence.

'I kill that robber,' she would scream, fierce as a spotted cat;
'You see that bulge inside of him? My speckly hen make that!'

But father's loud and strict command made even mother quake;
I think he'd sooner kill a man than kill a carpet snake.

That reptile was a greedy-guts, and as each bulge digested
He'd come down on the hunt at night as appetite suggested.
We heard his stealthy slithering sound across the earthen floor,
While the dog gave a startled yelp and bolted out the door.

Then over in the chicken-yard hysterical fowls gave tongue,
Loud frantic squawks accompanied by the barking of the mung,
Until at last the racket passed, and then to solve the riddle,
Next morning he was back up there with a new bulge in his middle.

When father died we wailed and cried, our grief was deep and sore,
And strange to say from that sad day the snake was seen no more.
The wise old men explained to us: 'It was his tribal brother,
And that is why it done a guy'—but some looked hard at mother.

She seemed to have a secret smile, her eyes were smug and wary,
She looked as innocent as the cat that ate the pet canary.
We never knew, but anyhow (to end this tragic rhyme)
I think we all had snake for tea one day about that time.

KATH WALKER (b. 1920)

Piscator [Angler]. . . . I am to tell you, that there is a great antipathy betwixt the pike and some frogs; and this may appear to the reader of Dubravius (a bishop in Bohemia) who, in his book *Of Fish and Fish-ponds*, relates what, he says, he saw with his own eyes, and could not forbear to tell the reader, which was:

'As he and the Bishop Thurzo were walking by a large pond in Bohemia they saw a frog, when the pike lay very sleepily and quiet by the shore side, leap upon his head; and the frog having expressed malice or anger by his swollen cheeks and staring eyes, did stretch out his legs and embraced the pike's head, and presently reached them to his eyes, tearing with them and his teeth those tender parts: the pike, moved with anguish, moves up and down the water, and rubs himself against weeds and whatever he thought might quit him of his enemy; but all in vain, for the frog did continue to ride triumphantly, and to bite and torment the pike till his strength failed, and then the frog sunk with the pike to the bottom of the water; then presently the frog appeared again at the top and croaked, and seemed to rejoice like a conqueror; after which he presently retired to his secret hole. The bishop that had beheld the battle called his fisherman to fetch his nets, and by all means to get the pike that they might declare what had happened; and the pike was drawn forth, and both his eyes eaten out; at which when they began to wonder, the fisherman wished them to forbear, and assured them he was certain that pikes were often so served.'

IZAAK WALTON, *The Compleat Angler*, 1653

There was room for ten customers around the L-shaped counter. . . . The old man had learned his trade . . . in Tokyo . . . He was a native of Kobe, however, and he made his *sushi* to fit the Kobe taste. Although he did give his customers the vinegared rice and fish any Tokyo *sushi* man would, the Kobe influence was evident in his choice of materials. He always used white Kobe vinegar, never yellow Tokyo vinegar, and always a thick soy sauce not seen in Tokyo. He offered only fish taken before his very eyes, so to speak, here along the shores of the Inland Sea. No fish was unsuitable for *sushi*, he insisted—on that point at least he agreed with the old Yobei. He tried conger eels and blowfish and dace and even oysters and sea urchins, and scraps of halibut or clam, and sometimes red whale meat. Nor did he limit himself to fish: he used mushrooms too, and bamboo sprouts and persimmons. But he was opposed to tuna, that most common of *sushi* ingredients; and scallops and omelettes and the commonplace *sushi* that goes with them were never seen in his restaurant. Though he sometimes cooked his fish, the prawns and abalone were alive and moving when they reached the customer.

The old man cut open a prawn and spread it over a ball of rice, which he then cut into sections an inch or so wide. One prawn was set before Sachiko and her husband, the other before Yukiko and Taeko. They were such large prawns that a whole one per person would have left room for nothing else. . . .

'Eat it up, young lady, eat it up.'

Yukiko had not touched the *sushi* before her.

'But the thing is still moving.' It was always a trial for Yukiko to have to eat as fast as the others. She liked the 'dancing *sushi*' of which the old man was so proud, the prawns that were still moving when they were set out to be eaten; she liked it as well as the sea bream. But she wanted at least to wait until it had stopped moving.

'That is what makes it good.'

'Go ahead and eat it. Are you afraid it will haunt you?'

'Would I be afraid of a prawn's ghost, I wonder,' mused the broker.

'What about a frog's ghost, Yukiko?'

'A frog's ghost?'

'It happened when we were in Tokyo. Tatsuo took us out to have barbecued chicken one evening. The chicken was very good, but for the last course they killed a frog, and it let out a horrible croak. Yukiko and I were as white as two sheets. Yukiko said she could hear that croak the rest of the night.'

'I would rather talk about something else.' Quite sure that it was no longer moving, Yukiko took up a piece of the 'dancing *sushi*'.

> JUNICHIRO TANIZAKI, *The Makioka Sisters*, 1949 (tr. Edward G. Seidenstecker, 1957)

Fish Markets

Nothing will shake my conviction that Genova *la superba* is the noisiest city on earth. . . . The market-place will therefore be quite a rest; here one is oblivious of the uproar, spellbound by the spectacle of the odd fish which come up from these waters. Their names are descriptive enough: the angler or frogfish, the praying-fish, the sea-hen, the scorpion, the sea-cat, the sea-date, the sea-truffle, sea-snails, sea-strawberries, and a mussel with a hair-covered shell called *cozze pelose*. No wonder that anybody with a spark of imagination is prepared to put up with the ear-splitting din of Genoa, the crashing of trams and trains, the screeching of brakes, and even the agonized wailing of itinerant musicians in the taverns, in order to taste some of these sea beasts when they have been converted into *burrida*, the Genoese fish stew, or into the immense edifice of crustaceans, molluscs, fish, vegetables, and green sauce, which is known as *cappon magro*.

Along the coast at Santa Margherita the fish market is famous; here the fish are less forbidding and savage of aspect, but their brilliance of colour is phenomenal. Huge baskets are filled with what from a distance one takes to be strawberries but which turn out to be huge prawns (they are scarlet by nature, before they are cooked); dark green and grey *tonnetto*, gleaming silver with phosphorescence, are thrust head downwards, like so many French loaves, in a high basket; *moscardini*, brown and pale green, are arranged in rows, like newly washed pebbles; the tiny *calamaretti, fragoline di mare*, are black and grey (cooked in a wine sauce they turn a deep pink); the rose-coloured slippery little fish called *signorini* are for the *frittura*; the *scampi* are pallid compared to the brilliant prawns; an orange *langouste* is a tamed beast beside a black lobster, lashing furiously.

Another market with its own very characteristic flavour is that of Cagliari, in the island of Sardinia. Spread out in flat baskets large as cartwheels are all the varieties of fish which go into *ziminù*, the Sardinian version of fish soup: fat, scaly little silver fish streaked with lime green; enormous octopus, blue, sepia, mauve, and turquoise, curled and coiled and petalled like some heavily embroidered marine flower; the *pescatrice* again, that ugly hooked angler fish; cold stony little clams, here called *arselle*; *tartufi di mare*; silvery slippery sardines; rose-red mullets in every possible size, some small as sprats, like doll's-house fish; the fine lobsters for which Sardinia is famous.

ELIZABETH DAVID, *Italian Food*, 1954

Night and Dreams

I

'I come to you in a dream of ages
past,' sings Crab. He swirls his velvet-
seaweed cloak. 'When first we met,
and last, you will recall, I was
imprisoned in your father's house.'

Sea colours on his carapace,
wave-hiss, tide-rustle in his voice.
'Some fiend had tied my fearful claws—'
—Yes, I recall. I must have been
a skinny child of eight or nine

that night my father brought you home—
'No, let *me* tell,' says Crab, 'this is
my aria, *my* party piece.
Grandmother, mother, father, brother
and you, went to the local theatre

leaving me bound in parching darkness.
I prayed: Redeemer Crab, release me
by your own sidelong righteousness
from these straightforward evildoers.
Take me where my transparent children

float in their manifold sea vision.
Silence. Mouse-whisper, cockroach-scuffle.
I felt, not far, the Brisbane River
ebbing to salt creek, mangrove swamp,
and burst my bonds, O yes I did!

and raged through your dark house, and hid.
That night you dared not go to bed

finding me gone when you returned.
Splintered pencils and toys proclaimed
my ocean strength. How soon forgotten

what Stan and Olly did and said!
Time, time. I felt the tide returning
far off. O Salt Redeemer, come
(I prayed) let navies drown to feed me
with rotten stump, decaying belly,

or if I am to die, allow me
one crunchbone tender-balancing foot.'
—My father caught you. 'Ah, he did.
"We'll cook the brute tonight," he said.
"Bring me the hatpin." Someone put

a diamond eye on a steel stalk
into your father's hand to stab
my stalked eyes. O the blaze of pain
eclipsing light's immense mandala!
Seagreen, seablue, I raged to red.

Boiling, crab died. I became Crab.'

II

Crab is dressed for the feast: on lettuce shredded
to seaweed ribbons, cracked claws reassembled,
he lies among parsley curls and radish roses.
Our starchy Sunday-snowy cloth is set
with what remains of Greatgrandmother's china,
translucent white, rimmed with a deepsea blue.
On his great serving dish Crab's at the centre
of a splendid colour wheel: cucumber slices,
tomato, celery, carrot, egg: my work,
duly admired. My grandmother says grace.
'Where would you eat like this,' my father asks,
passing the homemade bread, 'except in Queensland?'
A lovely room. Windows give on the garden,
rose and green panes of bubble-glass enchanting
the dullest day. The sideboard mirror offers
more light. Such light, restoring, recomposing
many who dined here. Most of them are dead.

III

'That's enough of pentameters,'
says Crab, returning to my dream.
—What shall I write, I ask. He writes,
so I won't miss his fearful joke:
THE DIRE BELLY VARIATIONS!

Making himself a cairn of stones
he says, 'This is my own rock group.
O I'm the original punk rocker
with a hatpin through my brain, my brain,
with a diamond hatpin through my brain.'

—Your jokes are awful. 'I know worse.'
—Impossible. 'Shall I rehearse
the names of those who've died from cancer?
O I'm the original merry prankster,
a diamond hatpin's all my eye.

Tell me, where are those who ate
my claws, my tender body meat?
Laurel and Hardy fans, long gone!
You cracked my hardware, ate my software.
Now I'm programmed in your brain.'

IV

More and more of the great questions,
such as: what am I doing here
in gumboots and a summer nightdress
in a moonlit garden chasing sheep?

The sheep are out. It's not a dream.
I'll mend the broken fence tomorrow.
What's left of night? Enough to dream in.
What dreams will come? Who else but Crab.

I ate him sixty years ago.
Ocean of memory, transposing
feaster and feast. He beckons, wearing
seaweed clothes, with sidelong charm.

'Shall we go to a pirate movie?'
—You like the sea? 'I like the bodies,

and "Take the lady below and make
her comfortable", that's what I like.

I can't be bothered with the love scenes.
I've opened hearts. I know what's in them.'
At interval he buys refreshments,
'Two seafood sticks. One without crab.

Come live with me and be my supper
where colours have no boundaries,
where every word is writ in water,
I'll put my arm around your waist.

I'll put my armour round your waist.
Shell after shell my soft self waxes.
Seek help! Sea kelp for drowning sailors.
Great questions all have wavering answers.'

Ghosts crowd to hear. O my lost loves.
Waking to hard-edge sunlit colours,
sharp birdsong, lamb-bleat, I recall
myself among the moonlit sheep

questioning—what? Why should I care
how long ago my death began?
Am I a ghost dreaming I'm human
with herbs to plant, a fence to mend?

GWEN HARWOOD (b. 1920)

Piscator [Angler]. It is agreed by most men, that the eel is a most dainty fish;
the Romans have esteemed her the Helena of their feasts, and some the
queen of palate-pleasure. But most men differ about their breeding: some
say they breed by generation as other fish do, and others, that they breed
(as some worms do) of mud; as rats and mice, and many other living
creatures are bred in Egypt, by the sun's heat, when it shines upon the
overflowing of the river Nilus; or out of the putrefaction of the earth, and
divers other ways. Those that deny them to breed by generation as other
fish do, ask, if any man ever saw an eel to have a spawn or melt? and they
are answered, that they may be as certain of their breeding as if they had
seen spawn: for they say, that they are certain that eels have all parts, fit for
generation, like other fish, but so small as not to be easily discerned, by
reason of their fatness; but that discerned they may be; and that the he and

the she-eel may be distinguished by their fins. And Rondeletius says he has seen eels cling together like dew-worms.

Next note, that the eel seldom stirs in the day, but then hides himself; and therefore he is usually caught by night, with one of these baits of which I have spoken; and may be then caught by laying hooks, which you are to fasten to the bank, or twigs of a tree; or by throwing a string across the stream with many hooks at it, and those baited with the aforesaid baits, and a clod, or plummet, or stone, thrown into the river with this line, that so you may in the morning find it near to some fixed place; and then take it up with a draghook, or otherwise: but these things are, indeed, too common to be spoken of; and an hour's fishing with an angler will teach you better, both for these and many other common things, in the practical part of angling, than a week's discourse. I shall therefore conclude this direction for taking the eel by telling you, that in a warm day in summer I have taken many a good eel by sniggling, and have been much pleased with that sport.

And because you, that are but a young angler, know not what sniggling is, I will now teach it to you. You remember I told you that eels do not usually stir in the daytime; for then they hide themselves under some covert; or under boards or planks about flood-gates, or weirs, or mills; or in holes on the river banks: so that you, observing your time in a warm day, when the water is lowest, may take a strong small hook tied to a strong line, or to a string about a yard long; and then into one of these holes, or between any boards about a mill, or under any great stone or plank or any place where you think an eel may hide or shelter herself, you may, with the help of a short stick, put in your bait, but leisurely, and as far as you may conveniently; and it is scarce to be doubted, but if there be an eel, within the sight of it, the eel will bite instantly, and as certainly gorge it; and you need not doubt to have him if you pull him not out of the hole too quickly, but pull him out by degrees; for he, laying folded double in his hole, will, with the help of his tail, break all, unless you give him time to be wearied with pulling; and so get him out by degrees, not pulling too hard.

IZAAK WALTON, *The Compleat Angler*, 1653

When I was turned fourteen years old, and put into good small-clothes, buckled at the knee, and strong blue worsted hosen, knitted by my mother, it happened to me without choice, I may say, to explore the Bagworthy water. And it came about in this wise.

My mother had long been ailing, and not well able to eat much; and there is nothing that frightens us so much as for people to have no love of their victuals. Now I chanced to remember that once at the time of the holidays I had brought dear mother from Tiverton a jar of pickled loaches, caught by myself in the Lowman river, and baked in the kitchen oven, with vinegar, a few leaves of bay, and about a dozen pepper-corns. And mother had said that in all her life she had never tasted anything fit to be compared with them. Whether she said so good a thing out of compliment to my skill in catching the fish and cooking them, or whether she really meant it, is more than I can tell, though I quite believe the latter, and so would most people who tasted them; at any rate, I now resolved to get some loaches for her, and do them in the self-same manner, just to make her eat a bit.

There are many people, even now, who have not come to the right knowledge what a loach is, and where he lives, and how to catch and pickle him. And I will not tell them all about it, because if I did, very likely there would be no loaches left ten or twenty years after the appearance of this book. A pickled minnow is very good, if you catch him in a stickle, with the scarlet fingers upon him; but I count him no more than the ropes in beer compared with a loach done properly.

R. D. BLACKMORE, *Lorna Doone*, 1869

I . . . speak of *the* Flounder, as though there were only this one omniscient Flounder who advised, taught, and indoctrinated me, who raised me to manhood and told me in no uncertain terms how to keep the women-folk supinely bed-warm and teach them how to suffer in cheerful silence. Actually the word 'flounder' . . . is only a popular designation for the flatfish family, including the brill, the sole, the halibut, the plaice, the turbot, and, of course, the flounder. To tell the truth, my own flatfish was a turbot, closely resembling the brill except for the bony, pebblelike bumps under his skin.

The turbot is found in the Mediterranean, throughout the North Sea, and in the Baltic. As in all flatfish, the axis of the eyes is not quite parallel to the crooked mouth, and that is what gives him his shrewd, malignant, I might say underhanded look: he squints in quick motion. (The Attic god Poseidon is said to have enlisted him in the struggle against Hera, the Pelasgian Athene, and related exponents of matriarchy—as a propagandist.) Turbot or not, tradition demands that I go on calling him a flounder.

The whole flatfish family is tasty. The neolithic Awa roasted his fellows in moist leaves. Toward the end of the Bronze Age, Wigga rubbed them on both sides with white ashes and laid the white underside in ashes strewn over a bed of coals. After turning, she moistened the flatfish either in the neolithic manner, from her always overflowing breasts, or modern-style, with a dash of fermented mare's milk. Mestwina, who already cooked in flameproof pots placed on an iron grating, simmered flounder with sorrel or in mead. Just before serving, she sprinkled the white-eyed fish with wild dill.

He, the one and only, the talking Flounder, who has been stirring me up for centuries, knew all the recipes that had been used for cooking his fellows, first by the heathen and later as a Christian Lenten fish (and not only on Friday). With an air of detachment and a glint of irony in his slanting eyes, he could sing his praises as a delicacy: 'Yes, my son, we happen to be one of the finer fishes. In the distant future, when you imbecilic men, you eternal babes in arms, will at last have minted coins, dated your history, and introduced the patriarchate, in short, shaken off your mothers' breasts, when after six thousand years of ever-loving womanly care you will at last have emancipated yourselves, then my fellows and relatives, the sole, the brill, the plaice, will be simmered in white wine, seasoned with capers, framed in jelly, deliciously offset by sauces, and served on Dresden china. My fellows will be braised, glazed, poached, broiled, filleted, ennobled with truffles, flamed in cognac, and named after marshals, dukes, the prince of Wales, and the Hotel Bristol. Campaigns, conquests, land grabs! The East will trade with the West. The South will enrich the North. To you and to myself I predict olives, refinements of culture and taste, the lemon!'

> GÜNTER GRASS, *The Flounder*, 1977 (tr. Ralph Manheim, 1978)

Silently the daughter-in-law spread cushions on the floor and brought out more saké and snacks—cobs of sweetcorn, pickled Chinese cabbage and fresh soya beans in hairy salted pods. There was also a bowl of large sautéed grasshoppers, complete with legs and antennae. I looked at them uneasily.

Ocaasan picked one up with chopsticks and offered it to me as if it were a special treat. There was a hush. I was going to have to eat the thing. I took a deep breath, shut my eyes and put it in my mouth.

'Lovely!' I exclaimed, picking a little black leg out of my teeth. Everyone roared. I'd passed the test; though I desperately hoped they wouldn't offer me a live one. I had meant it, too, and took another. It was sweet and crunchy, flavoured with soy sauce.

'Karushiyaam,' said Ocaasan approvingly, 'calcium'. Not much in their diet was rich in it, but grasshoppers certainly were.

> LESLIE DOWNER, *On the Narrow Road to the Deep North: Journey into a Lost Japan*, 1989

Triumphs and Trophies in Cookery, to be used at Festival Times, as Twelfth-day, *etc.*

Make the likeness of a Ship in Paste-board, with Flags and Streamers . . . Place your Ship firm in the great Charger; then make a salt round about it, and stick therein egg-shells full of sweet water, you may by a great Pin take all the meat out of the egg by blowing, and then fill it up with the rose-water, then in another Charger have the proportion of a Stag made of course paste, with a broad Arrow in the side of him, and his body filled up with claret-wine; in another Charger at the end of the Stag have the pro-portion of a Castle with Battlements, Portcullices, Gates and Draw-Bridges made of Paste-board, the Guns and Kickses, and covered with course paste as the former; place it at a distance from the ship to fire at each other. The Stag being placed betwixt them with egg shells full of sweet water (as before) placed in salt. At each side of the Charger wherein is the Stag, place a Pye made of course paste, in one of which let there be some live Frogs, in each other some live Birds; make these Pyes of course Paste filled with bran, and yellowed over with saffron or the yolks of eggs, guild them over in spots, as also the Stag, the Ship, and Castle; bake them and place them with guilt bay-leaves on turrets and tunnels of the Castle and Pyes; being baked, make a hole in the bottom of your pyes, take out the bran, put in your Frogs and Birds, and close up the holes with the same course paste, then cut the Lids neatly up; To be taken off the Tunnels; being all placed in order upon the Table, before you fire the trains of powder, order it so that some of the Ladies may be persuaded to pluck the Arrow out of the Stag, then will the Claret-wine follow, as blood that runneth out of a wound. This being done with admiration to the beholders, after some short pause, fire the train of the Castle, that the pieces all of one side may go off, then fire the Trains of one side of the Ship as in a battel, next turn the Chargers; and by degrees fire the trains of each other side as before. This done, to sweeten the stink of powder, let the Ladies take the egg-shells full of sweet waters and throw them at each other. All dangers being seemingly over, by this time you may suppose they will desire to see what is in the pyes; where lifting first the lid off one pye, out skip some Frogs, which make the Ladies to skip and shreek; next after the other pye, whence come out the Birds, who by a natural instinct flying in the light, will put out the Candles; so that what with the flying Birds and skipping Frogs, the one above, the other beneath, will cause much delight and pleasure to the whole company.

Robert May, *The Accomplished Cook, or The Art & Mystery of Cookery*, 1685

The Inheritor

I the sophisticated primate
Have stunted fingers on my feet,
And almost I control my climate,
And Everything is what I eat.

I wrote the story of Creation
when I discovered nudity:
The world is yours for exploitation.
I gave this charter unto me.

I traded in for my survival
My peaceful heart, my flealined coat;
Outpaced my vegetarian rival.
I have Creation by the throat.

GERDA MAYER (b. 1927)

THE HARE—This little animal is found generally distributed over Europe, and indeed, in most parts of the northern world. Its extreme timidity is the endowment which Providence has bestowed upon it as a means of defence; it is therefore attentive to every sound, and is supplied with ears both long and tubular, with which it can hear with great acuteness. Its eyes, also, are so constructed, and placed so prominent in its head, that it can see both before and behind it. It lives entirely upon vegetables, but its flesh is considered dry, notwithstanding that it is deemed, in many respects, superior to that of the rabbit, being more savoury, and of a much higher flavour. Its general time of feeding is the evening; but during the day, if not disturbed, it adheres closely to its *form*.

MRS ISABELLA BEETON, *Beeton's Book of Household Management*, 1861

The Hunting of the Hare

Betwixt two ridges of ploughed land lay Wat,
Pressing his body close to earth lay squat.
His nose upon his two forefeet close lies,
Glaring obliquely with his great grey eyes.
His head he always sets against the wind:
If turn his tail, his hairs blow up behind,
Which he too cold will grow; but he is wise,
And keeps his coat still down, so warm he lies.
Thus resting all the day, till sun doth set,
Then riseth up, his relief for to get,
Walking about until the sun doth rise;
Then back returns, down in his form he lies.
At last poor Wat was found, as he there lay,
By huntsmen with their dogs which came that way.

Seeing, gets up, and fast begins to run,
Hoping some ways the cruel dogs to shun.
But they by nature have so quick a scent
That by their nose they trace what way he went;

.   .   .   .

Into a great thick wood he straightway gets,
Where underneath a broken bough he sits;
At every leaf that with the wind did shake
Did bring such terror, made his heart to ache.
That place he left; to champian plains he went,
Winding about, for to deceive their scent,
And while they snuffling were, to find his track,
Poor Wat, being weary, his swift pace did slack.
On his two hinder legs for ease did sit:
His forefeet rubbed his face from dust and sweat.
Licking his feet, he wiped his ears so clean
That none could tell that Wat had hunted been.
But casting round about his fair great eyes,
The hounds in full career he near him spies;
To Wat it was so terrible a sight,
Fear gave him wings, and made his body light.

.   .   .   .

The great slow hounds, their throats did set a base,
The fleet swift hounds as tenors next in place;
The little beagles they a treble sing,
And through the air their voice a round did ring;
Which made a consort as they ran along:
If they but words could speak, might sing a song:
The horns kept time, the hunters shout for joy,
And valiant seem, poor Wat for to destroy.
Spurring their horses to a full career,
Swim rivers deep, leap ditches without fear;
Endanger life and limbs, so fast will ride,
Only to see how patiently Wat died.
For why, the dogs so near his heels did get
That they their sharp teeth in his breech did set.
Then tumbling down, did fall with weeping eyes,
Gives up his ghost, and thus poor Wat he dies.

MARGARET CAVENDISH, Duchess of Newcastle (1623–73)

Lièvre à la Royale

Ingredients
'You require a male hare, with red fur, killed if possible in mountainous country; of fine French descent (characterized by the light nervous elegance of head and limbs), weighing from 5 to 6 pounds, that is to say older than a leveret but still adolescent.'

This famous recipe for Lièvre à la Royale was invented by Senator Couteaux, who contributed regular articles to the Paris newspaper *Le Temps*. On November 29, 1898, instead of his usual political column, appeared this remarkable recipe. M. Couteaux related at length how he had spent a week in Poitou hunting the right kind of hare; how, the exactly suitable animal at last in his hands, he instantly took the train to Paris, sent out his invitations and hurried off to consult his friend Spüller, who ran a well-known restaurant in the Rue Favart, to arrange the preparation and cooking of his hare for the following day. The dish takes from noon until 7 o'clock to prepare and cook, and Senator Couteaux tells how by 6 o'clock the exquisite aroma had penetrated the doors of Spüller's restaurant, floated down the street and out into the boulevard, where the passers-by sniffed the scented air; an excitable crowd gathered, and the whole *quartier* was '*mis en émoi*'.

> The recipe is translated by Elizabeth David, and introduced in *A Book of Mediterranean Food*, 1950

Giving Rabbit to my Cat Bonnie

Pretty Bonnie, you are quick as a rabbit,
though your tail's longer,
emphasizing suppressed disapproval,
and your ears are shorter—two
radar detectors set on swivels
either side of your skull, and your yawn
is a view of distant white spires—not
the graveyard jaw of this poor dead naked pink

rabbit, who like you, was a
technological success, inheriting a snazzy
fur coat, pepper-and-salt coloured, cosy,
and beautiful fur shoes with spiked toes.
You're both of you
better dressed than I am for most occasions.
Take off your shoes and suits, though,
what have you got?

Look puss, I've brought us a rabbit for supper.
I bought it in a shop.
The butcher was haggis-shaped, ham-coloured,
not a bit like you. His ears
were two fungi on the slab of his head.
He had a fat, flat face.
But he took your brother rabbit off a hook
and spread him on the counter like a rug,

and slice, slice, scarcely looking,
pulled the lovely skin off like a bag.
So, Bonnie, all I've brought us is food
in this silly pink shape—more like me, really.
I'll make a wine sauce with mushrooms, but will
you want this precious broken heart? this perfect liver?
See, protected in these back pockets, jewels?
Bonnie. What are you eating? Dear Bonnie, consider!

ANNE STEVENSON (b. 1933)

MONSTERS

Jabberwocky

'Twas brillig, and the slithy toves
  Did gyre and gimble in the wabe:
All mimsy were the borogoves,
  And the mome raths outgrabe.

'Beware the Jabberwock, my son!
  The jaws that bite, the claws that catch!
Beware the Jubjub bird, and shun
  The frumious Bandersnatch!'

He took his vorpal sword in hand:
  Long time the manxome foe he sought—
So rested he by the Tumtum tree,
  And stood awhile in thought.

And, as in uffish thought he stood,
  The Jabberwock, with eyes of flame,

Came whiffling through the tulgey wood,
  And burbled as it came!

One, two! One, two! And through and through
  The vorpal blade went snicker-snack!
He left it dead, and with its head
  He went galumphing back.

'And hast thou slain the Jabberwock?
  Come to my arms, my beamish boy!
O frabjous day! Callooh! Callay!'
  He chortled in his joy.

'Twas brillig, and the slithy toves
  Did gyre and gimble in the wabe:
All mimsy were the borogoves,
  And the mome raths outgrabe.

LEWIS CARROLL, *Through the Looking-Glass*, 1872

Deep down here by the dark water lived old Gollum, a small slimy creature. I don't know where he came from, nor who or what he was. He was a Gollum—as dark as darkness, except for two big round pale eyes in his thin face. He had a little boat, and he rowed about quite quietly on the lake; for lake it was, wide and deep and deadly cold. He paddled it with large feet dangling over the side, but never a ripple did he make. Not he. He was looking out of his pale lamp-like eyes for blind fish, which he grabbed with his long fingers as quick as thinking. He liked meat too. Goblin he thought good, when he could get it; but he took care they never found him out. He just throttled them from behind, if they ever came down alone anywhere near the edge of the water, while he was prowling about. They very seldom did, for they had a feeling that something unpleasant was lurking down there, down at the very roots of the mountain. They had come on the lake, when they were tunnelling down long ago, and they found they could go no further; so there their road ended in that direction, and there was no reason to go that way—unless the Great Goblin sent them. Sometimes he took a fancy for fish from the lake, and sometimes neither goblin nor fish came back.

Actually Gollum lived on a slimy island of rock in the middle of the lake. He was watching Bilbo now from the distance with his pale eyes like telescopes. Bilbo could not see him, but he was wondering a lot about Bilbo, for he could see that he was no goblin at all.

Gollum got into his boat and shot off from the island, while Bilbo was sitting on the brink altogether flummoxed and at the end of his way and his wits. Suddenly up came Gollum and whispered and hissed:

'Bless us and splash us, my preciousss! I guess it's a choice feast; at least a tasty morsel it'd make us, gollum!' And when he said *gollum* he made a horrible swallowing noise in his throat. That is how he got his name, though he always called himself 'my precious'.

J. R. R. TOLKIEN, *The Hobbit*, 1937

They say that Ethiopia and the Indies possess birds extremely variegated in colour and indescribable, and that Arabia has one that is famous before all others (though perhaps it is fabulous), the phoenix, the only one in the whole world and hardly ever seen. The story is that it is as large as an eagle, and has a gleam of gold round its neck and all the rest of it is purple, but the tail blue picked out with rose-coloured feathers and the throat picked out with tufts, and a feathered crest adorning its head. The first and the most detailed Roman account of it was given by Manilius, the eminent senator famed for his extreme and varied learning acquired without a teacher: he stated that nobody has ever existed that has seen one feeding, that in Arabia it is sacred to the Sun-god, that it lives 540 years, that when it is growing old it constructs a nest with sprigs of wild cinnamon and frankincense, fills it with scents and lies on it till it dies; that subsequently from its bones and marrow is born first a sort of maggot, and this grows into a chicken, and that this begins by paying due funeral rites to the former bird and carrying the whole nest down to the City of the Sun near Panchaia and depositing it upon an altar there.

PLINY THE ELDER (AD 23–79), *Natural History* (tr. H. Rackham, 1937)

We passed very slowly through the woods, partly because Lord John acted as scout before he would let us advance, and partly because at every second step one or other of our professors would fall, with a cry of wonder, before some flower or insect which presented him with a new type. We may have travelled two or three miles in all, keeping to the right of the line of the stream, when we came upon a considerable opening in the trees. A belt of brushwood led up to a tangle of rocks—the whole plateau was strewn with boulders. We were walking slowly towards these rocks, among bushes which reached over our waists, when we became aware of a strange low gabbling and whistling sound, which filled the air with a constant clamour and appeared to come from some spot immediately before us. Lord John held up his hand as a signal for us to stop, and he made his way swiftly, stooping and running, to the line of rocks. We saw him peep over them and give a gesture of amazement. Then he stood staring as if forgetting us, so utterly entranced was he by what he saw. Finally he waved us to come on, holding up his hand as a signal for caution. His whole bearing made me feel that something wonderful but dangerous lay before us.

Creeping to his side, we looked over the rocks. The place into which we gazed was a pit, and may, in the early days, have been one of the smaller volcanic blow-holes of the plateau. It was bowl-shaped, and at the bottom, some hundreds of yards from where we lay, were pools of green-scummed, stagnant water, fringed with bullrushes. It was a weird place in itself, but its occupants made it seem like a scene from the Seven Circles of Dante. The place was a rookery of pterodactyls. There were hundreds of them congregated within view. All the bottom area round the water-edge was alive with their young ones, and with hideous mothers brooding upon their leathery, yellowish eggs. From this crawling flapping mass of obscene reptilian life came the shocking clamour which filled the air and the mephitic, horrible, musty odour which turned us sick. But above, perched each upon its own stone, tall, grey, and withered, more like dead and dried specimens than actual living creatures, sat the horrible males, absolutely motionless save for the rolling of their red eyes or an occasional snap of their rat-trap beaks as a dragon-fly went past them. Their huge, membranous wings were closed by folding their fore-arms, so that they sat like gigantic old women, wrapped in hideous web-coloured shawls, and with their ferocious heads protruding above them. Large and small, not less than a thousand of these filthy creatures lay in the hollow before us.

Our professors would gladly have stayed there all day, so entranced were they by this opportunity of studying the life of a prehistoric age. They pointed out the fish and dead birds lying about among the rocks as proving the nature of the food of these creatures, and I heard them congratulating each other on having cleared up the point why the bones of this flying dragon are found in such great numbers in certain well-defined areas, as in the Cambridge Green-sand, since it was now seen that, like penguins, they lived in gregarious fashion.

Finally, however, Challenger, bent upon proving some point which Summerlee had contested, thrust his head over the rock and nearly brought destruction upon us all. In an instant the nearest male gave a shrill, whistling cry, and flapped its twenty-foot span of leathery wings as it soared up into the air. The females and young ones huddled together beside the water, while the whole circle of sentinels rose one after the other and sailed off into the sky. It was a wonderful sight to see at least a hundred creatures of such enormous size and hideous appearance all swooping like swallows with swift, shearing wing-strokes above us; but soon we realized that it was not one on which we could afford to linger. At first the great brutes flew round in a huge ring, as if to make sure what the exact extent of the danger might be. Then, the flight grew lower and the circle narrower, until they were whizzing round and round us, the dry, rustling flap of their huge slate-coloured wings filling the air with a volume of sound that made me think of Hendon aerodrome upon a race day.

'Make for the wood and keep together,' cried Lord John, clubbing his rifle. 'The brutes mean mischief.'

ARTHUR CONAN DOYLE, The Lost World, 1912

Canst thou draw out leviathan with an hook? or his tongue with a cord which thou lettest down?

Canst thou put an hook into his nose? or bore his jaw through with a thorn?

Who can open the doors of his face? his teeth are terrible round about.

His scales are his pride, shut up together as with a close seal.

One is so near to another, that no air can come between them.

They are joined one to another, they stick together, that they cannot be sundered.

By his neesings a light doth shine, and his eyes are like the eyelids of the morning.

Out of his mouth go burning lamps, and sparks of fire leap out.

Out of his nostrils goeth smoke, as out of a seething pot or caldron.

His breath kindleth coals, and a flame goeth out of his mouth.

In his neck remaineth strength, and sorrow is turned into joy before him.

The flakes of his flesh are joined together: they are firm in themselves; they cannot be moved.

His heart is as firm as a stone; yea, as hard as a piece of the nether millstone.

When he raiseth up himself, the mighty are afraid: by reason of breakings they purify themselves.

The sword of him that layeth at him cannot hold: the spear, the dart, nor the habergeon.

He esteemeth iron as straw, and brass as rotten wood.

The arrow cannot make him flee: slingstones are turned with him into stubble.

Darts are counted as stubble: he laugheth at the shaking of a spear.

Sharp stones are under him: he spreadeth sharp pointed things upon the mire.

He maketh the deep to boil like a pot: he maketh the sea like a pot of ointment.

He maketh a path to shine after him; one would think the deep to be hoary.

Upon earth there is not his like, who is made without fear.
He beholdeth all high things: he is a king over all the children of pride.

Job 41: 1–2, 14–34

The Kraken

Below the thunders of the upper deep;
Far, far beneath in the abysmal sea,
His ancient, dreamless, uninvaded sleep
The Kraken sleepeth: faintest sunlights flee
About his shadowy sides: above him swell
Huge sponges of millennial growth and height;
And far away into the sickly light,
From many a wondrous grot and secret cell
Unnumber'd and enormous polypi
Winnow with giant arms the slumbering green.
There hath he lain for ages and will lie
Battening upon huge seaworms in his sleep,
Until the latter fire shall heat the deep;
Then once by man and angels to be seen,
In roaring he shall rise and on the surface die.

ALFRED, LORD TENNYSON (1809–92)

But here we have something very different. A grown lady is changed straightway into a fox. There is no explaining that away by any natural philosophy. The materialism of our age will not help us here. It is indeed *a miracle*; something from outside our world altogether; an event which we would willingly accept if we were to meet it invested with the authority of Divine Revelation in the scriptures, but which we are not prepared to encounter almost in our time, happening in Oxfordshire amongst our neighbours.

The only things which go any way towards an explanation of it are but guesswork, and I give them more because I would not conceal anything, than because I think they are of any worth.

Mrs Tebrick's maiden name was certainly Fox, and it is possible that such a miracle happening before, the family may have gained their name as a *soubriquet* on that account. They were an ancient family, and have had their seat at Tangley Hall time out of mind. It is also true that there was a half-tame fox once upon a time chained up at Tangley Hall in the inner yard, and I have heard many speculative wiseacres in the public-houses turn that to great account—though they could not but admit that 'there was never one there in Miss Silvia's time.' At first I was inclined to think that Silvia Fox, having once hunted when she was a child of ten and having been blooded, might furnish more of an explanation. It seems she took great fright or disgust at it, and vomited after it was done. But now I do not see that it has much bearing on the miracle itself, even though we know that after that she always spoke of the 'poor foxes' when a hunt was stirring and never rode to hounds till after her marriage when her husband persuaded her to it.

She was married in the year 1879 to Mr Richard Tebrick, after a short courtship, and went to live after their honeymoon at Rylands, near Stokoe, Oxon. . . . The marriage was a very happy one. The bride was in her twenty-third year. She was small, with remarkably small hands and feet. It is perhaps worth noting that there was nothing at all foxy or vixenish in her appearance. On the contrary, she was a more than ordinarily beautiful and agreeable woman. Her eyes were of a clear hazel but exceptionally brilliant, her hair dark, with a shade of red in it, her skin brownish, with a few dark freckles and little moles. In manner she was reserved almost to shyness, but perfectly self-possessed, and perfectly well-bred.

On one of the first days of the year 1880, in the early afternoon, husband and wife went for a walk in the copse on the little hill above Rylands. They were still at this time like lovers in their behaviour and were always together. While they were walking they heard the hounds and later the huntsman's horn in the distance. Mr Tebrick had persuaded her to hunt on Boxing Day, but with great difficulty, and she had not enjoyed it (though of hacking she was fond enough).

Hearing the hunt, Mr Tebrick quickened his pace so as to reach the edge of the copse, where they might get a good view of the hounds if they came that way. His wife hung back, and he, holding her hand, began almost to drag her. Before they gained the edge of the copse she suddenly snatched her hand away from his very violently and cried out, so that he instantly turned his head.

Where his wife had been the moment before was a small fox, of a very bright red. It looked at him very beseechingly, advanced towards him a pace or two, and he saw at once that his wife was looking at him from the animal's eyes. You may well think if he were aghast: and so maybe was his lady at finding herself in that shape, so they did nothing for nearly half-an-hour but stare at each other, he bewildered, she asking him with her eyes as if indeed she spoke to him: 'What am I now become? Have pity on me, husband, have pity on me for I am your wife.'

DAVID GARNETT, *Lady into Fox*, 1923

Ocyrrhoe transform'd into a Mare

Old *Chiron* took the Babe with secret Joy,
Proud of the Charge of the Celestial Boy.
His Daughter too, whom on the sandy Shore
The Nymph *Charicle* to the Centaur bore,
With Hair dishevel'd on her Shoulders, came
To see the Child, *Ocyrrhoë* was her Name;
She knew her Father's Arts, and could rehearse
The Depths of Prophecy in sounding Verse.
Once, as the sacred Infant she survey'd,
The God was kindled in the raving Maid,
And thus she utter'd her Prophetick Tale;
'Hail, great Physician of the World, All-hail;
Hail, mighty Infant, who in Years to come
Shalt heal the Nations, and defraud the Tomb;
Swift be thy Growth! thy Triumphs unconfin'd!
Make Kingdoms thicker, and increase Mankind.
Thy daring Art shall animate the Dead,
And draw the Thunder on thy guilty Head:
Then shalt thou dye, but from the dark Abode
Rise up Victorious, and be Twice a God.'
    Thus entring into Destiny, the Maid
The Secrets of offended *Jove* betray'd:
More had she still to say; but now appears
Oppress'd with Sobs and Sighs, and drown'd in Tears.
'My Voice, says she, is gone, my Language fails;
Through ev'ry Limb my kindred Shape prevails:
Why did the God this fatal Gift impart,
And with prophetick Raptures swell my Heart!
What new Desires are these? I long to pace
Oer flow'ry Meadows, and to feed on Grass;
I hasten to a Brute, a Maid no more;
But why, alas! am I transform'd all o'er?
My Sire does Half a human Shape retain,
And in his upper Parts preserve the Man.'
    Her Tongue no more distinct Complaints affords,
But in shrill Accents and mis-shapen Words
Pours forth such hideous Wailings, as declare
The Human Form confounded in the Mare:
'Till by degrees accomplish'd in the Beast,
She neigh'd outright, and all the Steed exprest.
Her stooping Body on her Hands is born,

Her Hands are turn'd to Hoofs, and shod in Horn,
Her yellow Tresses ruffle in a Mane,
And in a flowing Tail she frisks her Train.
The Mare was finish'd in her Voice and Look,
And a new Name from the new Figure took.

OVID (43 BC–AD 18), *Metamorphoses*, book II, tr. JOSEPH ADDISON (1672–1719)

Welsh Incident

'But that was nothing to what things came out
From the sea-caves of Criccieth yonder.'
'What were they? Mermaids? dragons? ghosts?'
'Nothing at all of any things like that.'
'What were they, then?'
                              'All sorts of queer things,
Things never seen or heard or written about,
Very strange, un-Welsh, utterly peculiar
Things. Oh, solid enough they seemed to touch,
Had anyone dared it. Marvellous creation,
All various shapes and sizes, and no sizes,
All new, each perfectly unlike his neighbour,
Though all came moving slowly out together.'
'Describe just one of them.'
                              'I am unable.'
'What were their colours?'
                              'Mostly nameless colours,
Colours you'd like to see; but one was puce
Or perhaps more like crimson, but not purplish.
Some had no colour.'
                              'Tell me, had they legs?'
'Not a leg nor foot among them that I saw.'
'But did these things come out in any order?
What o'clock was it? What was the day of the week?
Who else was present? How was the weather?'
'I was coming to that. It was half-past three
On Easter Tuesday last. The sun was shining.
The Harlech Silver Band played *Marchog Jesu*
On thirty-seven shimmering instruments,
Collecting for Caernarvon's (Fever) Hospital Fund.
The populations of Pwllheli, Criccieth,
Portmadoc, Borth, Tremadoc, Penrhyndeudraeth,
Were all assembled. Criccieth's mayor addressed them

First in good Welsh and then in fluent English,
Twisting his fingers in his chain of office,
Welcoming the things. They came out on the sand,
Not keeping time to the band, moving seaward
Silently at a snail's pace. But at last
The most odd, indescribable thing of all,
Which hardly one man there could see for wonder,
Did something recognizably a something.'
'Well, what?'
                    'It made a noise.'
                                        'A frightening noise?'
'No, no.'
            'A musical noise? A noise of scuffling?'
'No, but a very loud, respectable noise—
Like groaning to oneself on Sunday morning
In Chapel, close before the second psalm.'
'What did the mayor do?'
                            'I was coming to that'.

ROBERT GRAVES (1895–1985)

[Alice] was looking about for some way of escape, and wondering whether she could get away without being seen, when she noticed a curious appearance in the air: it puzzled her very much at first, but, after watching it a minute or two, she made it out to be a grin, and she said to herself 'It's the Cheshire Cat: now I shall have somebody to talk to.'

'How are you getting on?' said the Cat, as soon as there was mouth enough for it to speak with.

Alice waited till the eyes appeared, and then nodded. 'It's no use speaking to it,' she thought, 'till its ears have come, or at least one of them.' In another minute the whole head appeared, and then Alice put down her flamingo, and began an account of the game, feeling very glad she had some one to listen to her. The Cat seemed to think that there was enough of it now in sight, and no more of it appeared.

'Who *are* you talking to?' said the King, coming up to Alice, and looking at the Cat's head with great curiosity.

'It's a friend of mine—a Cheshire Cat,' said Alice: 'allow me to introduce it.'

'I don't like the look of it at all,' said the King: 'however, it may kiss my hand if it likes.'

'I'd rather not,' the Cat remarked.

'Don't be impertinent,' said the King, 'and don't look at me like that!' He got behind Alice as he spoke.

'A cat may look at a king,' said Alice. 'I've read that in some book, but I don't remember where.'

'Well, it must be removed,' said the King very decidedly, and he called to the Queen, who was passing at the moment, 'My dear! I wish you would have this cat removed!'

The Queen had only one way of settling all difficulties, great or small. 'Off with his head!' she said, without even looking round.

'I'll fetch the executioner myself,' said the King eagerly, and he hurried off.

Alice thought she might as well go back and see how the game was going on, as she heard the Queen's voice in the distance, screaming with passion. She had already heard her sentence three of the players to be executed for having missed their turns, and she did not like the look of things at all, as the game was in such confusion that she never knew whether it was her turn or not.

When she got back to the Cheshire Cat, she was surprised to find quite a large crowd collected round it: there was a dispute going on between the executioner, the King, and the Queen, who were all talking at once, while all the rest were quite silent, and looked very uncomfortable.

The moment Alice appeared, she was appealed to by all three to settle the question, and they repeated their arguments to her, though, as they all spoke at once, she found it very hard indeed to make out exactly what they said.

The executioner's argument was, that you couldn't cut off a head unless there was a body to cut it off from: that he had never had to do such a thing before, and he wasn't going to begin at *his* time of life.

The King's argument was, that anything that had a head could be be-headed, and that you weren't to talk nonsense.

The Queen's argument was, that if something wasn't done about it in less than no time, she'd have everybody executed, all round. (It was this last remark that had made the whole party look so grave and anxious.)

Alice could think of nothing else to say but 'It belongs to the Duchess: you'd better ask *her* about it.'

'She's in prison,' the Queen said to the executioner: 'fetch her here.' And the executioner went off like an arrow.

The Cat's head began fading away the moment he was gone, and, by the time he had come back with the Duchess, it had entirely disappeared; so the King and the executioner ran wildly up and down looking for it, while the rest of the party went back to the game.

LEWIS CARROLL, *Alice's Adventures in Wonderland*, 1865

The Amphisbæna or, The Limits of Human Knowledge

Amphisbæna: a serpent supposed to have two heads, and by consequence
to move with either end foremost.   —Johnson

If you should happen to descry
An Amphisbæna drawing nigh,
You may remain upon the spot,
But probably had better not.
The prudent its approach avoid
And do not stop to be annoyed,
For all who see it are perplexed
And wonder what will happen next.
Both ends, unfortunately, are
So singularly similar.
It has indeed a head in front
(As has the Indian elephant),
But then, to our alarm, we find
It has another head behind;
And hence zoologists affirm
That it is not a pachyderm.
Until it starts, you never know
In which direction it will go,
Nor can you even then maintain
That it will not come back again.
The sportsman, in amaze profound
Collapsing on his faithful hound,
Exclaims, as soon as he can speak,
'The Amphisbæna is unique.'
Unique no doubt it is; but oh,
That is not what distracts me so.
No: when before my musing eye
The Amphisbæna rambles by,
The question which bereaves of bliss
My finite intellect is this:
Who, who, oh, who will make it clear
Which is the front and which the rear?
Whether, at any given date,
The reptile is advancing straight,
Or whether it is hind-before,
Remains obscure for evermore.
Philosophy, with head of snow,
Confesses that it does not know;

Logicians have debated long,
Which is the right end, which the wrong;
But all their efforts are in vain.
They will not ever ascertain.

A. E. HOUSMAN (1859–1936)

Suddenly a dry husky voice in the sand made the children all jump back, and their hearts jumped nearly as fast as they did.

'Let me alone,' it said. And now everyone heard the voice and looked at the others to see if they had too.

'But we want to see you,' said Robert bravely.

'I wish you'd come out,' said Anthea, also taking courage.

'Oh, well—if that's your wish,' the voice said, and the sand stirred and spun and scattered, and something brown and furry and fat came rolling out into the hole and the sand fell off it, and it sat there yawning and rubbing the ends of its eyes with its hands.

'I believe I must have dropped asleep,' it said, stretching itself.

The children stood round the hole in a ring, looking at the creature they had found. It was worth looking at. Its eyes were on long horns like a snail's eyes, and it could move them in and out like telescopes; it had ears like a bat's ears, and its tubby body was shaped like a spider's and covered with thick soft fur; its legs and arms were furry too, and it had hands and feet like a monkey's.

'What on earth is it?' Jane said. 'Shall we take it home?'

The thing turned its long eyes to look at her, and said: 'Does she always talk nonsense, or is it only the rubbish on her head that makes her silly?'

It looked scornfully at Jane's hat as it spoke.

'She doesn't mean to be silly,' Anthea said gently; 'we none of us do, whatever you may think! Don't be frightened; we don't want to hurt you, you know.'

'Hurt *me!*' it said. '*Me* frightened? Upon my word! Why, you talk as if I were nobody in particular.' All its fur stood out like a cat's when it is going to fight.

'Well,' said Anthea, still kindly, 'perhaps if we knew who you are in particular we could think of something to say that wouldn't make you cross. Everything we've said so far seems to have. Who are you? And don't get angry! Because really we don't know.'

'You don't know?' it said. 'Well, I knew the world had changed—but—well, really—do you mean to tell me seriously you don't know a Psammead when you see one?'

'A Sammyadd? That's Greek to me.'

'So it is to everyone,' said the creature sharply. 'Well, in plain English, then, a *Sand-fairy*. Don't you know a Sand-fairy when you see one?'

E. NESBIT, *Five Children and It*, 1902

The Microbe

The Microbe is so very small
You cannot make him out at all,
But many sanguine people hope
To see him through a microscope.
His jointed tongue that lies beneath
A hundred curious rows of teeth;
His seven tufted tails with lots
Of lovely pink and purple spots,
On each of which a pattern stands,
Composed of forty separate bands;
His eyebrows of a tender green;
All these have never yet been seen—
But Scientists, who ought to know,
Assure us that they must be so . . .
Oh! let us never, never doubt
What nobody is sure about!

HILAIRE BELLOC (1870–1953)

Whereas those scattered trees, which naturally pertake,
The fatnesse of the soyle (in many a slimy Lake,
Their roots so deeply sok'd) send from their stocky bough,
A soft and sappy Gum, from which those *Tree-geese* grow,
Call'd *Barnacles* by us, which like a Jelly first
To the beholder seeme, then by the fluxure nurst,
Still great and greater thrive, untill you well may see
Them turn'd to perfect Fowles, when dropping from the tree
Into the Meery Pond, which under them doth lye,
Waxe ripe, and taking wing, away in flockes doe flye;
Which well our Ancients did among our Wonders place.

MICHAEL DRAYTON (1563–1631), *Poly-Olbion*, Song XXVII

Behold now behemoth, which I made with thee; he eateth grass as an ox.
　　Lo now, his strength is in his loins, and his force is in the navel of his belly.
　　He moveth his tail like a cedar: the sinews of his stones are wrapped together.

His bones are as strong pieces of brass; his bones are like bars of iron.

He is the chief of the ways of God: he that made him can make his sword to approach unto him.

Surely the mountains bring him forth food, where all the beasts of the field play.

He lieth under the shady trees, in the covert of the reed, and fens.

The shady trees cover him with their shadow; the willows of the brook compass him about.

Behold, he drinketh up a river, and hasteth not: he trusteth that he can draw up Jordan into his mouth.

He taketh it with his eyes: his nose pierceth through snares.

Job 40: 15–24

Behold Now Behemoth

See the wide-footed, pendant-bellied beast
called Behemoth, burst loose the river weeds
in cloudy mud-mist down the stream; he feeds
grunting, suck-sucking Jordan with his feast
of grass; slow swings his low eyes to the east,
blinks as the sun strikes, turns away; he needs
no such clean light, shafting the trodden reeds;
logs it in water-holes till day has ceased.

Drowse and be comfortable; lie, Behemoth
under the cross-stick shadow, tremulous veil
heat-vibrant, quick in the slant-broken stems.
So has he made you; bone and sinew both
of iron, that his image man may quail
at sight of you, and clutch his garment's hems.

ALLEN CURNOW (b. 1911)

The Woman and the Ngarara

told by Mohi Ruatapu
Ngati Porou, East Coast 1876

There were once two women named Hine-te-pipiri and Hine-te-kakara. One day these women visited a grove of tarata trees, and while they were up in a tree they looked down and saw a ngarara climbing towards them. When they saw him one ran away, but the other was caught by the ngarara and taken to his home.

The woman who had escaped went back to the village and said to the people there, 'My friend has been captured by a ngarara.'

'What sort of ngarara?'

She said, 'He is Te Mata-o-te-rangi; he is ten spans long.'

And so the woman who had been carried off by the ngarara lived with him as his wife. After they had been together for a long time she thought that she would go to see her brothers. She told her husband, 'I should like to visit my brothers.'

The ngarara agreed to this: 'Yes, go and see your brothers.'

So she set off, and reached the village. There she was greeted and wept over by her parents and brothers. When the weeping was finished she said, 'I have come to fetch you to take you to my husband.'

They agreed to this: 'Very well, but bring your husband here.'

Then the woman said to them, 'I will come. You must pile up firewood on both sides of the house, and at the back and the front.'

After this she returned to her husband. When she arrived he asked, 'Did you go to your parents?'

'Yes, I went to them.'

'What did they say?'

She said, 'They agree that we should visit them.'

The monster was delighted at this. And so they set off, and when they were approaching the village the call went out, 'Welcome, fish! Welcome, ngarara!'

The ngarara said, 'Perhaps you are trying to start a fight with me, my brothers-in-law, with this word "fish"?'

Then the ngarara entered the house. He was ten spans long, and so was the house; when he stretched out, he was exactly the same length as the house.

Then they brought him food; there were a thousand basketsful of food, and he ate them all up in a single meal. When his belly was full he went to sleep, and when they saw this someone called out, 'The ngarara is asleep!'

Then they set fire to the house. Now when the ngarara felt the heat he tried to put out the fire. He tried with his mouth, but it was no use—the fire did not go out. Next he tried with his tail, but in vain—still the fire did not go out. And so he was burnt to death.

From *Maori Folktales in Maori and English*, tr. Margaret Orbell, 1968

The Bunyip

You keep quiet now, little fella,
You want big-big Bunyip get you?
You look out, no good this place.
You see that waterhole over there?
He Gooboora, Silent Pool.

Suppose-it you go close up one time
Big fella woor, he wait there,
Big fella Bunyip sit down there,
In Silent Pool many bones down there.
He come up when it is dark,
He belong the big dark, that one.
Don't go away from camp fire, you,
Better you curl up in the gunya.
Go to sleep now, little fella,
Tonight he hungry, hear him roar,
He frighten us, the terrible woor,
He the secret thing, he Fear,
He something we don't know.
Go to sleep now, little fella,
Curl up with the yella dingo.

KATH WALKER (b. 1920)

The Siren

Strange things indeed   Are seen in the sea-world:
Men say that mermaids   Are like to maidens
In breast and body,   But not so below:
From the navel netherward   Nothing looks human,
For there they are fishes   And furnished with fins.
These prodigies dwell   In a perilous passage
Where swirling waters   Swallow men's vessels;
Cheerily they sing   In their changeable voices
That are high and sweet   And hopeful of harm.
This song makes shipmen   Forget their steering
And sink into drowses,   And deeply they dream:
For their vessels are sunken,   Their voyages over.
But wise men and wary   Will turn from these wiles
And often escape   That evil embrace,
Being warned of the mermaids.   Surely this monster,
Half fish and half woman,   Must harbor some meaning.

tr. from *The Middle English Bestiary* by Richard Wilbur, 1952

But centaurs never existed; there could never be
So to speak a double nature in a single body
Or a double body composed of incongruous parts
With a consequent disparity in the faculties.
The stupidest person ought to be convinced of that.

In the first place, it is only a matter of three years
Before a horse is fully grown. Not so with a child!
At that age he may in sleep still grope for the nipple.
Later, when the horse finds his old body grown tired

And his strength is almost gone, the boy on the contrary
Is just at the point where the flower of his age begins
And the down begins to appear upon his cheeks.
So do not imagine that the seed of men and of horses
Together make a centaur, or that such a beast
Could survive in any case; nor that there are Scyllas
With half-aquatic bodies and a chain of mad dogs
About their middles; nor anything of that kind.

LUCRETIUS (*c*.99–55 BC), tr. C. H. SISSON, 1976

Of Griffins

That there are Griffins in Nature, that is a mixt and dubious Animal, in the
fore-part resembling an Eagle, and behind, the shape of a Lion, with erected
ears, four feet and a long tail, many affirm, and most, I perceive, deny not.
The same is averred by *Ælian, Solinus, Mela,* and *Herodotus,* countenanced
by the Name sometimes found in Scripture, and was an Hieroglyphick of
the Egyptians.

Notwithstanding we find most diligent enquirers to be of a contrary
assertion. For beside that *Albertus* and *Pliny* have disallowed it, the learned
Aldrovandus hath in a large discourse rejected it; *Mathias Michovius* who writ
of those Northern parts wherein men place these Griffins, hath positively
concluded against it; and if examined by the Doctrine of Animals, the
invention is monstrous, nor much inferiour unto the figment of Sphynx,
Chimæra, and Harpies, for though there be some flying Animals of mixed
and participating Natures, that is, between Bird and quadruped, yet are
their wings and legs so set together, that they seem to make each other;
there being a commixtion of both, rather then an adaptation or cement of
prominent parts unto each other, as is observable in the Bat, whose wings
and fore-legs are contrived in each other.

As for the testimonies of ancient Writers, they are but derivative, and
terminate all in one *Aristeus* a Poet of *Proconesus*; who affirmed that near the
Arimaspi, or one-eyed Nation, Griffins defended the Mines of Gold. But this,
as *Herodotus* delivereth, he wrote by hear-say; and *Michovius* who hath
expresly written of those parts, plainly affirmeth, there is neither Gold nor
Griffins in that Country, nor any such Animal extant.

Lastly, Concerning the Hieroglyphical authority, although it nearest approach the truth, it doth not infer its existency. The conceit of the *Griffin* properly taken being but a symbolical phansie, in so intollerable a shape including allowable morality. So doth it well make out the properties of a *Guardian*, or any person entrusted; the ears implying attention, the wings celerity of execution, the Lion-like shape, courage and audacity, the hooked bill, reservance and tenacity. It is also an Emblem of valour and magnanimity, as being compounded of the Eagle and Lion, the noblest Animals in their kinds; and so is it appliable unto Princes, Presidents, Generals, and all heroick Commanders; and so is it also born in the Coat-arms of many noble Families of *Europe*.

Sir Thomas Browne, Pseudodoxia Epidemica, 1646

The *Sphinx* or *Sphinga* is of the kinde of Apes, having his body rough like Apes, but his breast up to his necke, pilde and smooth without hayre: the face is very round yet sharp and piked, having the breasts of women, and their favor or visage much like them: In that part of their body which is bare without haire, there is a certaine red thing rising in a round circle like Millet seed, which giveth great grace & comelinesse to their coulour, which in the middle parte is humaine: Their voice is very like a mans but not articulat, sounding as if one did speak hastily with indignation or sorrow. Their haire browne or swarthy coulour. They are bred in *India* and *Ethyopia*.

The name of this *Sphynx* is taken from binding, as appeareth by the Greek notation, or else of delicacie and dainty nice loosnesse, (wherefore there were certain common strumpets called *Sphinctae*, and the *Megarian Sphingas*, was a very popular phrase for notorious harlots) hath given occasion to the Poets, to faigne a certaine monster called *Sphynx*, which they say was thus derived. *Hydra* brought forth the *Chimæra*, *Chimæra* by *Orthus* the *Sphinx*, and the *Nemœan* Lyon: now this *Orthus* was one of *Geryons* Dogges. This *Sphinx* they made a treble-formed monster, a Maydens face, a Lyons legs, and the wings of a fowle, or as *Ausonius* and *Varinus* say, the face and hand of a mayde, the body of a Dogge, the winges of a byrd, the voice of a man, the clawes of a Lyon, and the tayle of a Dragon: and that she kept continually in the *Sphincian* mountaine; propounding to all travailers that came that way an *Ænigma* or Riddle, which was this: *What was the creature that first of all goeth on foure legges; afterwards on two, and lastly on three*: and all of them that could not dissolve that Riddle, she presently slew, by taking them and throwing them downe headlong, from the top of a Rocke.

Edward Topsell, The Historie of Foure-footed Beastes, 1607

The Knight of the Red Cross meets the dragon.

By this, the dreadful Beast drew nigh to hand,
Halfe flying and halfe footing in his haste,
That with his largenesse measured much land,
And made wide shadow under his huge waste,
As mountaine doth the valley overcaste.
Approching nigh, he reared high afore
His body monstrous, horrible, and vaste;
Which, to increase his wondrous greatnes more,
Was swoln with wrath and poyson, and with bloody gore;

And over all with brasen scales was armd,
Like plated cote of steele, so couched neare
That nought mote perce; ne might his corse bee harmd
With dint of swerd, nor push of pointed speare:
Which as an Eagle, seeing pray appeare,
His aery plumes doth rouze, full rudely dight;
So shaked he, that horror was to heare:
For as the clashing of an Armor bright,
Such noyse his rouzed scales did send unto the knight.

His flaggy winges, when forth he did display,
Were like two sayles, in which the hollow wynd
Is gathered full, and worketh speedy way:
And eke the pennes, that did his pineons bynd,
Were like mayne-yardes with flying canvas lynd;
With which whenas him list the ayre to beat,
And there by force unwonted passage fynd,
The cloudes before him fledd for terror great,
And all the hevens stood still amazed with his threat.

His huge long tayle, wownd up in hundred foldes,
Does overspred his long bras-scaly back,
Whose wreathed boughtes when ever he unfoldes,
And thick entangled knots adown does slack,
Bespotted as with shieldes of red and blacke,
It sweepeth all the land behind him farre,
And of three furlongs does but litle lacke;
And at the point two stinges in fixed arre,
Both deadly sharp, that sharpest steele exceeden farre.

pennes: feathers   *boughtes*: folds

But stinges and sharpest steele did far exceed
The sharpnesse of his cruel rending clawes:
Dead was it sure, as sure as death in deed,
What ever thing does touch his ravenous pawes,
Or what within his reach he ever drawes.
But his most hideous head my tongue to tell
Does tremble; for his deepe devouring jawes
Wyde gaped, like the griesly mouth of hell,
Through which into his darke abysse all ravin fell.

And, that more wondrous was, in either jaw
Three ranckes of yron teeth enraunged were,
In which yett trickling blood, and gobbets raw,
Of late devoured bodies did appeare,
That sight thereof bredd cold congealed feare;
Which to increase, and all atonce to kill,
A cloud of smoothering smoke, and sulphure seare,
Out of his stinking gorge forth steemed still,
That all the ayre about with smoke and stench did fill.

EDMUND SPENSER (*c.*1552–99), *The Faerie Queene*, book I, canto IX

'What animal ends in "cora"?'

The Chancellor answered:

'The Manticora, of course.'

'What is he like?' asked the King.

'He is the sworn foe of Dragons,' said the Chancellor. 'He drinks their blood. He is yellow, with the body of a lion and the face of a man. I wish we had a few Manticoras here now. But the last died hundreds of years ago— worse luck!'

Then the King ran and opened the book at the page that had 'cora' on it, and there was the picture-Manticora, all yellow, with a lion's body and a man's face, just as the Chancellor had said. And under the picture was written, 'Manticora.'

And in a few minutes the Manticora came sleepily out of the book, rubbing its eyes with its hands and mewing piteously. It seemed very stupid, and when Lionel gave it a push and said, 'Go along and fight the Dragon, do,' it put its tail between its legs and fairly ran away. It went and hid behind the Town Hall, and at night when the people were asleep it went round and ate all the pussy-cats in the town. And then it mewed more than ever. And on the Saturday morning, when people were a little timid about going out, because the Dragon had no regular hour for calling, the Manticora went up and down the streets and drank all the milk that was left in the cans at the doors for people's teas, and it ate the cans as well.

And just when it had finished the very last little ha'porth, which was short measure, because the milkman's nerves were quite upset, the Red Dragon came down the street looking for the Manticora. It edged off when it saw him coming, for it was not at all the Dragon-fighting kind; and, seeing no other door open, the poor, hunted creature took refuge in the General Post Office, and there the Dragon found it, trying to conceal itself among the ten o'clock mail. The Dragon fell on the Manticora at once, and the mail was no defence. The mewings were heard all over the town. All the pussies and the milk the Manticora had had seemed to have strengthened its mew wonderfully. Then there was a sad silence, and presently the people whose windows looked that way saw the Dragon come walking down the steps of the General Post Office spitting fire and smoke, together with tufts of Manticora fur, and the fragments of the registered letters.

E. NESBIT, *The Book of Beasts*, 1899

To invent from nothing an animal *that can exist* (I mean to say that can physiologically grow, nourish itself, resist the environment and predators, and reproduce itself) is an almost impossible feat. It is a project that by far exceeds our rational abilities and also that of our best computers: we still know too little about existing vital mechanisms to dare create others, even only on paper. In other words, evolution has always proven itself to be enormously more intelligent than the best evolutionists. Every year that passes confirms the fact that the mechanisms of life are not exceptions to the laws of chemistry and physics, but at the same time the furrow which separates us from the ultimate comprehension of vital phenomena grows ever wider. It is not that problems are not solved and questions not answered, but every solved problem generates dozens of new ones and the process gives no sign of ending.

Nevertheless, the experience of three thousand years of storytelling, painting and sculpture shows us that even inventing at whim an animal from nothing, an animal whose ability to exist we do not consider important but whose image somehow stimulates our sensibility, is not an easy task. All the animals invented by mythology in all countries and all epochs are pastiches, rhapsodies of features and limbs taken from known animals. The most famous and most composite was the chimera, a hybrid of goat, snake, and lion, so impossible that today its name is equivalent to 'a vain hope'; but it has also been adopted by biologists to indicate the monsters they create, or would like to create, in their laboratories thanks to transplants among different animals.

The centaurs are fascinating creatures, the repository of multiple and archaic symbols, but Lucretius had already realised their physical impossibility and tried to demonstrate it with a curious argument: at the age of three the horse is at the peak of its strength, while man is still an infant and 'will often seek in his dreams for the nipple' from which he has just been weaned; how could two natures live together which do not *florescunt pariter* (bloom apace) and in any case are not inflamed by the same love?

In more recent times and in a beautiful science fiction novel, P. J. Farmer has indicated the respiratory difficulties of classic centaurs and solved them by endowing the centaurs with a supplementary organ similar to a set of bellows which draw in air through an aperture similar to a throat. Others have dwelt on the problem of nourishment, pointing out that a small human mouth would have been insufficient to feed the animal's equine part.

In short, it would seem that the human imagination, even when not faced by problems of biological verisimilitude and stability, hesitates to venture down new paths and prefers to recombine already known building elements.

In a sixth-grade class not far from Turin they carried out an experiment, having the children describe an invented animal, and the results confirmed this limit to the imagination. Substantially mythological, that is composite, animals were described: conglomerates of diverse limbs like Pegasus and the Minotaur, or flights into the colossal and the supernumerary which bring to mind Job's Leviathan, Rabelais' human and bestial giants, Argus of the hundred eyes, Shiva with his eight arms, Cerberus with his three heads, and the six-legged dog of the ENNI (Italian National Hydrocarbon Authority) logo. But within these limits bold, amusing and alarming intuitions have surfaced.

> PRIMO LEVI, 'Inventing an Animal', *Other People's Trades*, 1985 (tr. Raymond Rosenthal, 1989)

The Death of the Loch Ness Monster

Consider that the thing has died before we proved it ever lived
    and that it died of loneliness, dark lord of the loch,
fathomless Worm, great Orm, this last of our mysteries—
    haifend ane meikill fin on ilk syde
    with ane taill and ane terribill heid—
and that it had no tales to tell us, only that it lived there,
    lake-locked, lost in its own coils,
waiting to be found; in the black light of midnight
    surfacing, its whole elastic length unwound,

and the sound it made as it broke the water
      was the single plucked string of a harp—
this newt or salamander, graceful as a swan,
      this water-snake, this water-horse, this water-dancer.

Consider him tired of pondering the possible existence of man
      whom he thinks he has sighted sometimes on the shore,
and rearing up from the purple churning water,
      weird little worm head swaying from side to side,
he denies the vision before his eyes;
      his long neck, swan of Hell, a silhouette against the moon,
his green heart beating its last,
      his noble, sordid soul in ruins.

Now the mist is a blanket of doom, and we pluck from the depths
      a prize of primordial slime—
the beast who was born from some terrible ancient kiss,
      lovechild of unspeakable histories,
this ugly slug, half blind no doubt, and very cold,
      his head which is horror to behold
no bigger than our own;
      whom we loathe, for his kind ruled the earth before us,
who died of loneliness in a small lake in Scotland,
      and in his mind's dark land,
where he dreamed up his luminous myths, the last of which was man.

                                    GWENDOLYN MACEWEN (1941–87)

Sea Unicorns and Land Unicorns

with their respective lions—
'mighty monoceroses with immeasured tayles'—
these are those very animals
described by the cartographers of 1539,
defiantly revolving
in such a way that
the long keel of white exhibited in tumbling,
disperses giant weeds
and those sea snakes whose forms, looped in the foam, 'disquiet shippers.'
Knowing how a voyager obtained the horn of a sea unicorn
to give to Queen Elizabeth,
who thought it worth a hundred thousand pounds,
they persevere in swimming where they like,
finding the place where sea-lions live in herds,

strewn on the beach like stones with lesser stones—
and bears are white;
discovering Antarctica, its penguin kings and icy spires,
and Sir John Hawkins' Florida
'abounding in land unicorns and lions;
since where the one is,
its arch-enemy cannot be missing.'
Thus personalities by nature much opposed,
can be combined in such a way
that when they do agree, their unanimity is great,
'in politics, in trade, law, sport, religion,
china-collecting, tennis, and church-going.'
You have remarked this fourfold combination of strange animals,
upon embroideries
enwrought with 'polished garlands' of agreeing difference—
thorns, 'myrtle rods, and shafts of bay,'
'cobwebs, and knotts, and mulberries'
of lapis lazuli and pomegranate and malachite—
Britannia's sea unicorn with its rebellious child
now ostentatiously indigenous to the new English coast;
and its land lion oddly tolerant of those pacific counterparts to it,
the water lions of the west.
This is a strange fraternity—these sea lions and land lions,
land unicorns and sea unicorns:
the lion civilly rampant,
tame and concessive like the long-tailed bear of Ecuador—
the lion standing up against this screen of woven air
which is the forest:
the unicorn also, on its hind legs in reciprocity.
A puzzle to the hunters, is this haughtiest of beasts,
to be distinguished from those born without a horn,
in use like Saint Jerome's tame lion, as domestics;
rebelling proudly at the dogs
which are dismayed by the chain lightning
playing at them from its horn—
the dogs persistent in pursuit of it as if it could be caught,
'deriving agreeable terror' from its 'moonbeam throat'
on fire like its white coat and unconsumed as if of salamander's skin.
So wary as to disappear for centuries and reappear,
yet never to be caught,
the unicorn has been preserved
by an unmatched device
wrought like the work of expert blacksmiths,

this animal of that one horn
throwing itself upon which head foremost from a cliff,
it walks away unharmed;
proficient in this feat which, like Herodotus,
I have not seen except in pictures.
Thus this strange animal with its miraculous elusiveness,
has come to be unique,
'impossible to take alive,'
tamed only by a lady inoffensive like itself—
as curiously wild and gentle;
'as straight and slender as the crest,
or antlet of the one-beam'd beast.'
Upon the printed page,
also by word of mouth,
we have a record of it all
and how, unfearful of deceit,
etched like an equine monster of an old celestial map,
beside a cloud or dress of Virgin-Mary blue,
improved 'all over slightly with snakes of Venice gold,
and silver, and some O's,'
the unicorn 'with pavon high,' approaches eagerly;
until engrossed by what appears of this strange enemy,
upon the map, 'upon her lap,'
its 'mild wild head doth lie.'

MARIANNE MOORE (1887–1972)

The Unicorn

(*adapted from Rainer Maria Rilke*)

This is the animal that never existed.
None of them ever knew one; but just the same
They loved the way it moved, the way it stood
Looking at them, in pure tranquillity.

Of course there wasn't any. But because they loved it
One became an animal. They always left a space.
And in the space they had hollowed for it, lightly
It would lift its head, and hardly need

To exist. They nourished it, not with grain
But only, always, with the possibility
It might be. And this gave so much strength to it

That out of its forehead grew a horn. One horn.
Up to a virgin, silverily, it came
And there within her, there within her glass, it was.

RANDALL JARRELL (1914–65)

The first version of the Unicorn is nearly identical with the latest. Four hundred years B.C., the Greek historian and physician Ctesias told that among the kingdoms of India there were very swift wild asses with white coats, purple heads, blue eyes, and in the middle of their foreheads a pointed horn whose base was white, whose tip was red, and whose middle was black. Pliny, more precise, wrote (VIII, 31):

the fiercest animal is the unicorn, which in the rest of the body resembles a horse, but in the head a stag, in the feet an elephant, and in the tail a boar, and has a deep bellow, and a single black horn three feet long projecting from the middle of the forehead. They say that it is impossible to capture this animal alive.

Around 1892, the Orientalist Schrader conjectured that the Unicorn might have been suggested to the Greeks by certain Persian bas-reliefs depicting bulls in profile with a single horn.

In Isidore of Seville's *Etymologies*, composed at the beginning of the seventh century, we read that one thrust of the Unicorn's horn may kill an elephant; this perhaps is echoed in the similar victory, in Sindbad's second voyage, of the Karkadan, or rhinoceros, which can 'carry off a great elephant on its horn.' (We also find here that the rhinoceros's horn 'cleft in twain, is the likeness of a man'; al-Qaswini says it is the likeness of a man on horseback, and others have spoken of birds and fishes.) Another of the Unicorn's enemies was the lion, and a stanza in the tangled allegory *The Faerie Queene* records the manner of their duel in this way:

> Like as a Lyon, whose imperiall powre
> A prowd rebellious Unicorn defyes,
> T' avoide the rash assault and wrathful stowre
> Of his fiers foe, him to a tree applyes,
> And when him ronning in full course he spyes,
> He slips aside; the whiles that furious beast
> His precious horne, sought of his enimyes,
> Strikes in the stocke, ne thence can be releast,
> But to the mighty victor yields a bounteous feast.

These lines (Book II, Canto v, Stanza x) date from the sixteenth century; at the beginning of the eighteenth century, the union of the Kingdom of England with the Kingdom of Scotland brought together on the heraldic arms of Great Britain the English Leopard, or Lion, and the Scottish Unicorn.

In the Middle Ages, bestiaries taught that the Unicorn could be captured by a maiden; in the Greek *Physiologus* we read: 'How it is captured. A virgin is placed before it and it springs into the virgin's lap and she warms it with love and carries it off to the palace of kings.' One of Pisanello's medals and many famous tapestries illustrate this victory whose allegorical applications are obvious. Leonardo da Vinci attributes the Unicorn's capture to its lust, which makes it forget its fierceness, lie in a girl's lap, and so be taken by hunters. The Holy Ghost, Jesus Christ, mercury, and evil have all been represented by the Unicorn. In his *Psychologie und Alchemie* (1944), Jung gives a history and an analysis of these symbols.

A small white horse with the forelegs of an antelope, a goat's beard, and a long twisted horn projecting straight out from its forehead is the picture usually given of this imaginary animal.

JORGE LUIS BORGES, *The Book of Imaginary Beings*, 1970

Lo! in the mute, mid wilderness,
What wondrous Creature?—of no kind!—
His burning lair doth largely press—
Gaze fixt—and feeding on the wind?
His fell is of the desert dye,
And tissue adust, dun-yellow and dry,
Compact of living sands; his eye,
Black luminary, soft and mild,
With its dark lustre cools the wild;
From his stately forehead springs
Piercing to heaven, a radiant horn,—
Lo! the compeer of lion-kings!
The steed self-armed, the Unicorn!
Ever heard of, never seen,
With a main of sands between
Him and approach; his lonely pride
To course his arid arena wide,
Free as the hurricane, or lie here,
Lord of his couch as his career!—
Wherefore should this foot profane
His sanctuary, still domain?
Let me turn, ere eye so bland
Perchance be fire-shot, like heaven's brand,
To wither my boldness! Northward now,
Behind the white star on his brow
Glittering straight against the sun,
Far athwart his lair I run.

GEORGE DARLEY (1795–1846), *Nepenthe*

DEATH AND
EXTINCTION

'Eustace! Eustace!' Hilda's tones were always urgent; it might not be any-thing very serious. Eustace bent over the pool. His feet sank in its soggy edge, so he drew back, for he must not get them wet. But he could still see the anemone. Its base was fastened to a boulder, just above the water-line. From the middle of the other end, which was below, something stuck out, quivering. It was a shrimp, Eustace decided, and the anemone was eating it, sucking it in. A tumult arose in Eustace's breast. His heart bled for the shrimp, he longed to rescue it; but, on the other hand, how could he bear to rob the anemone of its dinner? The anemone was more beautiful than the shrimp, more interesting and much rarer. It was a 'plumose' anemone; he recognised it from the picture in his Natural History, and the lovely feathery epithet stroked the fringes of his mind like a caress. If he took the shrimp away, the anemone might never catch another, and die of hunger. But while he debated the unswallowed part of the shrimp grew perceptibly smaller.

There was only one thing to do.
'Hilda,' he cried, 'come here.'
His low soft voice was whirled away by the wind; it could not compete with the elements, as Hilda's could.

He called again. It was an effort for him to call: he screwed his face up: the cry was unmelodious now that he forced it, more like a squeak than a summons.

But directly she heard him Hilda came, as he knew she would. Eustace put the situation before her, weighing the pros and cons. Which was to be sacrificed, the anemone or the shrimp? Eustace stated the case for each with unflinching impartiality and began to enlarge on the felicity that would attend their after-lives, once this situation was straightened out—forgetting, in his enthusiasm, that the well-being of the one depended on the misfortune of the other. But Hilda cut him short.

'Here, catch hold of my feet,' she said.

She climbed on to the boulder, and flung herself face down on the sea-weedy slope. Eustace followed more slowly, showing respect for the inequalities of the rock. Then he lowered himself, sprawling uncertainly and rather timidly, and grasped his sister's thin ankles with hands that in spite of his nine years still retained some of the chubbiness of infancy. Once assumed, the position was not uncomfortable. Eustace's thoughts wandered, while his body automatically accommodated itself to the movements of Hilda, who was wriggling ever nearer to the edge.

'I've got it,' said Hilda at last in a stifled voice. There was no elation, only satisfaction in her tone, and Eustace knew that something had gone wrong.

'Let me look!' he cried, and they struggled up from the rock.

The shrimp lay in the palm of Hilda's hand, a sad, disappointing sight. Its reprieve had come too late; its head was mangled and there was no vibration in its tail. The horrible appearance fascinated Eustace for a moment, then upset him so much that he turned away with trembling lips. But there was worse to come. As a result of Hilda's forcible interference with its meal the anemone had been partially disembowelled; it could not give up its prey without letting its digestive apparatus go too. Part of its base had come unstuck and was seeking feebly to attach itself to the rock again. Eustace took Hilda's other hand and together they surveyed the unfortunate issue of their kind offices.

'Hadn't we better kill them both?' asked Eustace with a quaver in his voice, 'since they're both wounded?'

He spoke euphemistically, for the shrimp was already dead.

L. P. HARTLEY, *The Shrimp and the Anemone*, 1944

Epitaph on a Hare

Here lies whom hound did ne'er pursue
　　Nor swifter greyhound follow,
Whose foot ne'er tainted morning dew,
　　Nor ear heard huntsman's halloo;

Old Tiney, surliest of his kind,
　Who, nursed with tender care,
And to domestic bounds confined,
　Was still a wild Jack hare.

Though duly from my hand he took
　His pittance every night,
He did it with a jealous look,
　And, when he could, would bite.

His diet was of wheaten bread,
　And milk, and oats, and straw;
Thistles, or lettuces instead,
　With sand to scour his maw.

On twigs of hawthorn he regaled,
　On pippins' russet peel,
And, when his juicy salads failed,
　Sliced carrot pleased him well.

A Turkey carpet was his lawn,
　Whereon he loved to bound,
To skip and gambol like a fawn,
　And swing his rump around.

His frisking was at evening hours,
　For then he lost his fear,
But most before approaching showers,
　Or when a storm drew near.

Eight years and five round-rolling moons
　He thus saw steal away,
Dozing out all his idle noons,
　And every night at play.

I kept him for his humour's sake,
　For he would oft beguile
My heart of thoughts that made it ache,
　And force me to a smile.

But now beneath this walnut shade
　He finds his long last home,
And waits, in snug concealment laid,
　Till gentler Puss shall come.

He, still more agèd, feels the shocks
From which no care can save,
And, partner once of Tiney's box,
Must soon partake his grave.

WILLIAM COWPER (1731–1800)

Myxomatosis

Caught in the centre of a soundless field
While hot inexplicable hours go by
What trap is this? Where were its teeth concealed?
You seem to ask.
              I make a sharp reply,
Then clean my stick. I'm glad I can't explain
Just in what jaws you were to suppurate:
You may have thought things would come right again
If you could only keep quite still and wait.

PHILIP LARKIN (1922–85)

[*Florence, 1892*]

It is early, scarcely more than half-past eight, the voice of the bell clock I always hear from my room has given out two soft little chimes to mark the half-hour. The air feels fresh and cool at starting, but I know that no warm wraps are required, not even a jacket. The city of Florence is wide awake, indeed it must have been awake since sunrise, for the streets are full of people, Italian soldiers in their uniform, tourists of all nations, flower-sellers and beggars. I turn to the left at the end of the Via dei Fossi, and walk along the Arno for a short distance . . . Now I had three objects in view in taking this walk, for the carrying out of each my basket contains the wherewithall; my sketch-book, a small pocket-book with ruled lines for writing, and my butterfly net and pocket box, though I fear it is a little early in the year to make that pursuit very successful. All of a sudden a large butterfly of the *Vanessa* tribe whirled high above my head. 'A Red Admiral,' I think to myself, but that was no Red Admiral, and with a rapture none but a naturalist can ever know I recognize no other than a Camberwell Beauty. It must have come out of its chrysalis this very morning, for it is strong on the wing and after passing rapidly above my head shows no fancy to settle in the road where I stand but at once disappears over the high wall on the other side. I take my net out of my basket and set it up, so as to be quite prepared in the case of another event of equal importance, but no such chance recurs.

After passing through a small village I turn up a little pathway which leads to a country church with flowers growing in wild profusion in the churchyard; roses that look as though they had never known the touch of a pruning knife. Plenty of butterflies here; I caught a splendid specimen of male Brimstone, thinking that though it was common enough in England I should always love to think that it was caught in Italy. It gave me a pang of remorse to take this beautiful creature away from her flowers and her sunshine, which I too knew so well how to enjoy; the death of the butterfly is the one drawback to an entymological career . . .

MARGARET FOUNTAINE, *Love among the Butterflies*, 1892

The Countess of Ossory losing two piping Bull-finches in one day, & having them buried under a rose tree, desired Mᴿ H. W. to write Epitaphs on them: he sent her the following.

> All flesh is grass, and so are feathers too.
> Finches must die as well as I and you.
> Beneath a damask rose in good old Age
> Here lies the Tenant of a noble Cage.
> For forty moons He charm'd his Lady's ear,
> And piped obedient oft as She drew near
> Tho now stretched out upon a clay-cold bier.
> But when the last shrill flageolet shall sound,
> And raise all Dicky birds from holy ground,
> His little Corpse again its wings shall prune,
> And sing eternally the selfsame tune
> From everlasting night to everlasting noon.

> On the other Bullfinch.

> Beneath the same bush rests his Brother:
> What serves for One will serve for tother.

HORACE WALPOLE, 4th Earl of Orford (1717–97), *Miscellany 1786–1795*

Imagine a cricket about the size of an ordinary mosquito, with a pair of antennae much longer than his own body, and so fine that you can distinguish them only against the light. Kusa-Hibari, or 'Grass-Lark,' is the Japanese name of him; and he is worth in the market exactly twelve cents: that is to say, very much more than his weight in gold. Twelve cents for such a gnat-like thing!

By day he sleeps or meditates, except while occupied with the slice of fresh eggplant or cucumber which must be poked into his cage every morning . . . To keep him clean and well fed is somewhat troublesome: could you see him, you would think it absurd to take any pains for the sake of a creature so ridiculously small.

But always at sunset the infinitesimal soul of him awakens; then the room begins to fill with a delicate and ghostly music of indescribable sweetness—a thin, thin silvery rippling and trilling as of tiniest electric bells. As the darkness deepens, the sound becomes sweeter, sometimes swelling till the whole house seems to vibrate with the elfish resonance, sometimes thinning down into the faintest imaginable thread of a voice. But loud or low, it keeps a penetrating quality that is weird . . . All night the atomy thus sings: he ceases only when the temple bell proclaims the hour of dawn.

Last evening—the twenty-ninth of the eleventh month—an odd feeling came to me as I sat at my desk: a sense of emptiness in the room. Then I became aware that my grass-lark was silent, contrary to his wont. I went to the silent cage, and found him lying dead beside a dried-up lump of eggplant as gray and hard as a stone. Evidently he had not been fed for three or four days; but only the night before his death he had been singing wonderfully, so that I foolishly imagined him to be more than usually contented. My student, Aki, who loves insects, used to feed him; but Aki had gone into the country for a week's holiday, and the duty of caring for the grass-lark had devolved upon Hana, the housemaid. She is not sympathetic, Hana the housemaid. She says that she did not forget the mite—but there was no more eggplant. And she had never thought of substituting a slice of onion or of cucumber! . . . I spoke words of reproof to her and she dutifully expressed contrition. But the fairy-music has stopped; and the stillness reproaches; and the room is cold, in spite of the stove.

LAFCADIO HEARN, 'Kusa-Hibari', from Kotto, 1902

Song

I had a dove and the sweet dove died;
    And I have thought it died of grieving.
O, what could it grieve for? Its feet were tied,
    With a silken thread of my own hand's weaving.
Sweet little red feet! why would you die—
Why should you leave me, sweet bird! why?
You lived alone on the forest-tree,
Why, pretty thing, could you not live with me?

I kissed you oft and gave you white peas;
Why not live sweetly, as in the green trees?

JOHN KEATS (1795–1821)

Fly

I have been cruel to a fat pigeon
Because he would not fly
All he wanted was to live like a friendly old man

He had let himself become a wreck filthy and confiding
Wild for his food beating the cat off the garbage
Ignoring his mate perpetually snotty at the beak
Smelling waddling having to be
Carried up the ladder at night content

Fly I said throwing him into the air
But he would drop and run back expecting to be fed
I said it again and again throwing him up
As he got worse
He let himself be picked up every time
Until I found him in the dovecote dead
Of the needless efforts

So that is what I am

Pondering his eye that could not
Conceive that I was a creature to run from

I who have always believed too much in words

W. S. MERWIN (b. 1927)

Pat came swinging along; in his hand he held a little tomahawk that winked in the sun.

'Come with me,' he said to the children, 'and I'll show you how the kings of Ireland chop the head off a duck.'

They drew back—they didn't believe him, and besides, the Trout boys had never seen Pat before.

'Come on now,' he coaxed, smiling and holding out his hand to Kezia.

'Is it a real duck's head? One from the paddock?'

'It is,' said Pat. She put her hand in his hard dry one, and he stuck the tomahawk in his belt and held out the other to Rags. He loved little children.

Tall bushes overhung the stream with red leaves and yellow flowers and clusters of blackberries. At some places the stream was wide and shallow, but at others it tumbled into deep little pools with foam at the edges and quivering bubbles. It was in these pools that the big white ducks had made themselves at home, swimming and guzzling along the weedy banks.

Up and down they swam, preening their dazzling breasts, and other ducks with the same dazzling breasts and yellow bills swam upside down with them.

'There is the little Irish navy,' said Pat, 'and look at the old admiral there with the green neck and the grand little flagstaff on his tail.'

He pulled a handful of grain from his pocket and began to walk towards the fowl-house, lazy, his straw hat with the broken crown pulled over his eyes.

'Lid. Lid—lid—lid—lid—' he called.

'Qua. Qua—qua—qua—qua—' answered the ducks, making for land, and flapping and scrambling up the bank they streamed after him in a long waddling line.

Then Pat scattered the grain and the greedy ducks began to gobble. Quickly he stooped, seized two, one under each arm, and strode across to the children. Their darting heads and round eyes frightened the children—all except Pip.

'Come on, sillies,' he cried, 'they can't bite. They haven't any teeth. They've only got those two little holes in their beaks for breathing through.'

'Will you hold one while I finish with the other?' asked Pat. Pip let go of Snooker. 'Won't I? Won't I? Give us one. I don't mind how much he kicks.'

He nearly sobbed with delight when Pat gave the white lump into his arms.

There was an old stump beside the door of the fowl-house. Pat grabbed the duck by the legs, laid it flat across the stump, and almost at the same moment down came the little tomahawk and the duck's head flew off the stump. Up the blood spurted over the white feathers and over his hand.

When the children saw the blood they were frightened no longer. They crowded round him and began to scream. Even Isabel leaped about crying: 'The blood! The blood!' Pip forgot all about his duck. He simply threw it away from him and shouted, 'I saw it. I saw it,' and jumped round the wood block.

Rags, with cheeks as white as paper, ran up to the little head, put out a finger as if he wanted to touch it, shrank back again and then again put out a finger. He was shivering all over.

Even Lottie, frightened little Lottie, began to laugh and pointed at the duck and shrieked: 'Look, Kezia, look.'

'Watch it!' shouted Pat. He put down the body and it began to waddle—
with only a long spurt of blood where the head had been; it began to pad
away without a sound towards the steep bank that led to the stream. . . .
That was the crowning wonder.

'Do you see that? Do you see that?' yelled Pip. He ran among the little
girls tugging at their pinafores.

'It's like a little engine. It's like a funny little railway engine,' squealed
Isabel.

But Kezia suddenly rushed at Pat and flung her arms round his legs and
butted her head as hard as she could against his knees.

'Put head back! Put head back!' she screamed.

When he stooped to move her she would not let go or take her head
away. She held on as hard as she could and sobbed: 'Head back! Head back!'
until it sounded like a loud strange hiccup.

'It's stopped. It's tumbled over. It's dead,' said Pip.

KATHERINE MANSFIELD (1888–1923), Prelude

Hen Dying

The old grey hen is dying
who once was so cheeky.
For ten years or more
I've not been able to leave the house
without her begging bowl
being thrust in front of me.
You have to be in the mood for hens.
Some days I had my heart set on people.

She's learning now about queues and things
and how the spring sunshine
rests more heavily on some hens
than on others.
She sits by herself over near the byre.
Her head's pulled in like a tortoise's.
Her eyelids are half drawn-down.

The other hens have cast her out.
They batter her with their beaks
whenever they come across her.
Most of them are her daughters.
Hens are inhuman.

She doesn't visit the feed any more.
I lay some grain in front of her
whenever I come across her.
She rummages through her mind,
slowly remembering how to eat.

One of these days she'll fall over.
I'll make a coffin from a shoebox for her
and tie it with a piece of ribbon.
I'll bury her in a corner of the stackyard
between two stooks of corn.

That's holy ground to hens and crofters.
The earth is dry and sandy there
and the worm count is as low
as any place in Ardnamurchan.
For a week or two I'll miss her.

ALASDAIR MacLEAN (b. 1926)

Poor Mailie's Elegy

Lament in rhyme, lament in prose,
Wi' saut tears trickling down your nose;
Our *Bardie's* fate is at a close,
                Past a' remead!
The last, sad cape-stane of his woes;
                Poor Mailie's dead!

It's no the loss o' warl's gear,
That could sae bitter draw the tear,
Or make our *Bardie*, dowie, wear
                The mourning weed:
He's lost a friend and neebor dear,
                In *Mailie* dead.

Thro' a' the town she trotted by him;
A lang half-mile she could descry him;
Wi' kindly bleat, when she did spy him,
                She ran wi' speed:
A friend mair faithfu' ne'er came nigh him,
                Than *Mailie* dead.

                dowie: sad, dejected

I wat she was a *sheep* o' sense,
An' could behave hersel wi' mense:
I'll say 't, she never brak a fence,
      Thro' thievish greed.
Our *Bardie*, lanely, keeps the spence
      Sin' *Mailie*'s dead.

Or, if he wanders up the howe,
Her living image in *her yowe*,
Comes bleating to him, owre the knowe,
      For bits o' bread;
An' down the briny pearls rowe
      For *Mailie* dead.

She was nae get o' moorlan tips,
Wi' tauted ket, an' hairy hips;
For her forbears were brought in ships,
      Frae 'yont the TWEED:
A bonier *fleesh* ne'er cross'd the clips
      Than *Mailie*'s dead.

Wae worth that man wha first did shape,
That vile, wanchancie thing—*a raep*!
It maks guid fellows girn an' gape,
      Wi' chokin dread;
An' *Robin*'s bonnet wave wi' crape
      For *Mailie* dead.

O, a' ye *Bards* on bonie DOON!
An' wha on AIRE your chanters tune!
Come, join the melancholious croon
      O' *Robin*'s reed!
His heart will never get aboon!
      His *Mailie*'s dead!

ROBERT BURNS (1759–96)

---

mense: decorum, sense   *lanely*: lonely   *spence*: parlour   *howe*: valley   *yowe*: ewe   *knowe*: knoll   *tips*: rams   *tauted ket*: matted fleece   *wanchancie*: unlucky   *raep*: rope

One day, whilst our cab and many others were waiting outside one of the parks where a band was playing, a shabby old cab drove up beside ours. The horse was an old worn-out chestnut with an ill-kept coat, and with bones that showed plainly through it. The knees knuckled over, and the forelegs were very unsteady.

I had been eating some hay, and the wind rolling a little lock of it that way, the poor creature put out her long, thin neck and picked it up, and then turned round and looked about for more. There was a hopeless look in the dull eye that I could not help noticing; and then, as I was thinking where I had seen that horse before, she looked full at me and said, 'Black Beauty, is that you?'

It was Ginger! but how changed! The beautifully arched and glossy neck was now straight, lank, and fallen in; the clean, straight legs and delicate fetlocks were swollen; the joints were grown out of shape with hard work; the face that was once so full of spirit and life was now full of suffering; and I could tell by the heaving of her sides and by her frequent cough how bad her breath was.

Our drivers were standing together a little way off, so I sidled up to her a step or two that we might have a little quiet talk. It was a sad tale that she had to tell.

I said, 'You used to stand up for yourself if you were ill-used.'

'Ah!' she said, 'I did once, but it's no use; men are stronger, and if they are cruel and have no feeling, there is nothing that we can do but just bear it—bear it on and on to the end. I wish the end was come; I wish I was dead. I have seen dead horses, and I am sure they do not suffer pain; I hope I may drop down dead at my work, and not be sent off to the knacker's.'

I was very much troubled, and I put my nose up to hers, but I could say nothing to comfort her. I think she was pleased to see me, for she said, 'You are the only friend I ever had.'

Just then her driver came up, and with a tug at her mouth backed her out of the line and drove off, leaving me very sad indeed.

A short time after this a cart with a dead horse in it passed our cab-stand. The head hung out of the cart tail, the lifeless tongue was slowly dropping blood; and the sunken eyes!—but I can't speak of them, the sight was too dreadful. It was a chestnut horse with a long, thin neck. I saw a white streak down the forehead. I believe it was Ginger; I hoped it was, for then her troubles would be over. Oh! if men were more merciful, they would shoot us before we come to such misery.

ANNA SEWELL, *Black Beauty*, 1877

The Bull Moose

Down from the purple mist of trees on the mountain,
lurching through forests of white spruce and cedar,
stumbling through tamarack swamps,
came the bull moose
to be stopped at last by a pole-fenced pasture.

Too tired to turn or, perhaps, aware
there was no place left to go, he stood with the cattle.
They, scenting the musk of death, seeing his great head
like the ritual mask of a blood god, moved to the other end
of the field, and waited.

The neighbours heard of it, and by afternoon
cars lined the road. The children teased him
with alder switches and he gazed at them
like an old, tolerant collie. The women asked
if he could have escaped from a Fair.

The oldest man in the parish remembered seeing
a gelded moose yoked with an ox for plowing.
The young men snickered and tried to pour beer
down his throat, while their girl friends took their pictures.

And the bull moose let them stroke his tick-ravaged flanks,
let them pry open his jaws with bottles, let a giggling girl
plant a little purple cap
of thistles on his head.

When the wardens came, everyone agreed it was a shame
to shoot anything so shaggy and cuddlesome.
He looked like the kind of pet
women put to bed with their sons.

So they held their fire. But just as the sun dropped in the river
the bull moose gathered his strength
like a scaffolded king, straightened and lifted his horns
so that even the wardens backed away as they raised their rifles.
When he roared, people ran to their cars. All the young men
leaned on their automobile horns as he toppled.

ALDEN NOWLAN (1933–83)

In Moulmein, Lower Burma, where he was subdivisional police officer, George Orwell was expected to shoot an elephant that had gone 'must'.

But I did not want to shoot the elephant. I watched him beating his bunch of grass against his knees, with that preoccupied grandmotherly air that elephants have. It seemed to me that it would be murder to shoot him. At that age I was not squeamish about killing animals, but I had never shot an elephant and never wanted to. (Somehow it always seems worse to kill a *large* animal.) Besides, there was the beast's owner to be considered. Alive, the elephant was worth at least a hundred pounds; dead, he would only be worth the value of his tusks, five pounds, possibly. But I had got to act quickly. I turned to some experienced-looking Burmans who had been there when we arrived, and asked them how the elephant had been behaving. They all said the same thing: he took no notice of you if you left him alone, but he might charge if you went too close to him.

It was perfectly clear to me what I ought to do. I ought to walk up to within, say, twenty-five yards of the elephant and test his behaviour. If he charged I could shoot, if he took no notice of me it would be safe to leave him until the mahout came back. But also I knew that I was going to do no such thing. I was a poor shot with a rifle and the ground was soft mud into which one would sink at every step. If the elephant charged and I missed him, I should have about as much chance as a toad under a steam-roller. But even then I was not thinking particularly of my own skin, only of the watchful yellow faces behind. For at that moment, with the crowd watching me, I was not afraid in the ordinary sense, as I would have been if I had been alone. A white man mustn't be frightened in front of 'natives'; and so, in general, he isn't frightened. The sole thought in my mind was that if anything went wrong those two thousand Burmans would see me pursued, caught, trampled on and reduced to a grinning corpse like that Indian up the hill. And if that happened it was quite probable that some of them would laugh. That would never do. There was only one alternative. I shoved the cartridges into the magazine and lay down on the road to get a better aim.

The crowd grew very still, and a deep, low, happy sigh, as of people who see the theatre curtain go up at last, breathed from innumerable throats. They were going to have their bit of fun after all. The rifle was a beautiful German thing with cross-hair sights. I did not then know that in shooting an elephant one would shoot to cut an imaginary bar running from ear-hole to ear-hole. I ought, therefore, as the elephant was sideways on, to have aimed straight at his ear-hole; actually I aimed several inches in front of this, thinking the brain would be further forward.

When I pulled the trigger I did not hear the bang or feel the kick—one never does when a shot goes home—but I heard the devilish roar of glee that went up from the crowd. In that instant, in too short a time one would have thought, even for the bullet to get there, a mysterious, terrible change had come over the elephant. He neither stirred nor fell, but every line of his body had altered. He looked suddenly stricken, shrunken, immensely old, as though the frightful impact of the bullet had paralysed him without knocking him down. At last, after what seemed a long time—it might have been five seconds, I dare say—he sagged flabbily to his knees. His mouth slobbered. An enormous senility seemed to have settled upon him. One could have imagined him thousands of years old. I fired again into the same spot. At the second shot he did not collapse but climbed with desperate slowness to his feet and stood weakly upright, with legs sagging and head drooping. I fired a third time. That was the shot that did for him. You could see the agony of it jolt his whole body and knock the last remnant of strength from his legs. But in falling he seemed for a moment to rise, for as his hind legs collapsed beneath him he seemed to tower upwards like a huge rock toppling, his trunk reaching skywards like a tree. He trumpeted, for the first and only time. And then down he came, his belly towards me, with a crash that seemed to shake the ground even where I lay.

I got up. The Burmans were already racing past me across the mud. It was obvious that the elephant would never rise again, but he was not dead. He was breathing very rhythmically with long rattling gasps, his great mound of a side painfully rising and falling. His mouth was wide open—I could see far down into caverns of pale pink throat. I waited a long time for him to die, but his breathing did not weaken. Finally I fired my two remaining shots into the spot where I thought his heart must be. The thick blood welled out of him like red velvet, but still he did not die. His body did not even jerk when the shots hit him, the tortured breathing continued without a pause. He was dying, very slowly and in great agony, but in some world remote from me where not even a bullet could damage him further. I felt that I had got to put an end to that dreadful noise. It seemed dreadful to see the great beast lying there, powerless to move and yet powerless to die, and not even to be able to finish him. I sent back for my small rifle and poured shot after shot into his heart and down his throat. They seemed to make no impression. The tortured gasps continued as steadily as the ticking of a clock.

In the end I could not stand it any longer and went away. I heard later that it took him half an hour to die. Burmans were bringing dahs and baskets even before I left, and I was told they had stripped his body almost to the bones by the afternoon.

GEORGE ORWELL, 'Shooting an Elephant', 1931–6

Native-born

In a white gully among fungus red
　　Where serpent logs lay hissing at the air,
I found a kangaroo. Tall, dewy, dead,
　　So like a woman, she lay silent there.
Her ivory hands, black-nailed, crossed on her breast,
　　Her skin of sun and moon hues, fallen cold.
Her brown eyes lay like rivers come to rest
　　And death had made her black mouth harsh and old.
Beside her in the ashes I sat deep
　　And mourned for her, but had no native song
To flatter death, while down the ploughlands steep
　　Dark young Camelli whistled loud and long,
'Love, liberty, and Italy are all.'
　　Broad golden was his breast against the sun.
I saw his wattle whip rise high and fall
　　Across the slim mare's flanks, and one by one
She drew the furrows after her as he
　　Flapped like a gull behind her, climbing high,
Chanting his oaths and lashing soundingly,
　　While from the mare came once a blowing sigh.
The dew upon the kangaroo's white side
　　Had melted. Time was whirling high around,
Like the thin wommera, and from heaven wide
　　He, the bull-roarer, made continuous sound.
Incarnate lay my country by my hand:
　　Her long hot days, bushfires, and speaking rains,
Her mornings of opal and the copper band
　　Of smoke around the sunlight on the plains.
Globed in fire-bodies the meat-ants ran
　　To taste her flesh and linked us as we lay,
For ever Australian, listening to a man
　　From careless Italy, swearing at our day.
When, golden-lipped, the eagle-hawks came down
　　Hissing and whistling to eat of lovely her,
And the blowflies with their shields of purple brown
　　Plied hatching to and fro across her fur,
I burnt her with the logs, and stood all day
　　Among the ashes, pressing home the flame
Till woman, logs, and dreams were scorched away,
　　And native with night, that land from whence they came.

EVE LANGLEY (1908–74)

The sun was just peeping over the high forests on the eastern hills, as if coming to look on, and bid us act with becoming fortitude. I placed all the people at the end of the rope, and ordered them to pull till the cayman appeared on the surface of the water; and then, should he plunge, to slacken the rope and let him go again into the deep.

I now took the mast of the canoe in my hand (the sail being tied round the end of the mast) and sunk down upon one knee, about four yards from the water's edge, determining to thrust it down his throat, in case he gave me an opportunity. I certainly felt somewhat uncomfortable in this situation, and I thought of Cerberus on the other side of the Styx ferry. The people pulled the cayman to the surface; he plunged furiously as soon as he arrived in these upper regions, and immediately went below again on their slackening the rope. I saw enough not to fall in love at first sight. I now told them we would run all risks, and have him on land immediately. They pulled again, and out he came,—'monstrum horrendum, informe.' This was an interesting moment. I kept my position firmly, with my eye fixed steadfast on him.

By the time the cayman was within two yards of me, I saw he was in a state of fear and perturbation; I instantly dropped the mast, sprung up, and jumped on his back, turning half round as I vaulted, so that I gained my seat with my face in a right position. I immediately seized his fore-legs, and, by main force, twisted them on his back; thus they served me for a bridle.

He now seemed to have recovered from his surprise, and probably fancying himself in hostile company, he begun to plunge furiously, and lashed the sand with his long and powerful tail. I was out of reach of the strokes of it, by being near his head. He continued to plunge and strike, and made my seat very uncomfortable. It must have been a fine sight for an unoccupied spectator.

The people now dragged us about forty yards on the sand: it was the first and last time I was ever on a cayman's back. Should it be asked, how I managed to keep my seat, I would answer,—I hunted some years with Lord Darlington's fox hounds.

After repeated attempts to regain his liberty, the cayman gave in, and became tranquil through exhaustion. I now managed to tie up his jaws, and firmly secured his fore-feet in the position I had held them. We had now another severe struggle for superiority, but he was soon overcome, and again remained quiet. While some of the people were pressing upon his head and shoulders, I threw myself on his tail, and by keeping it down to the sand, prevented him from kicking up another dust. He was finally conveyed to the canoe, and then to the place where we had suspended our hammocks. There I cut his throat; and after breakfast was over, commenced the dissection.

CHARLES WATERTON, *Wanderings in South America*, 1839

The Quagga

By mid-century there were two quaggas left,
And one of the two was male.
The cares of office weighed heavily on him.
When you are the only male of a species,
It is not easy to lead a normal sort of life.

The goats nibbled and belched in casual content;
They charged and skidded up and down their concrete mountain.
One might cut his throat on broken glass,
Another stray too near the tigers.
But they were zealous husbands; and the enclosure was always full,
Its rank air throbbing with ingenuous voices.

The quagga, however, was a man of destiny.
His wife, whom he had met rather late in her life,
Preferred to sleep, or complain of the food and the weather.
For their little garden was less than paradisiac,
With its artificial sun that either scorched or left you cold,
And savants with cameras eternally hanging around,
To perpetuate the only male quagga in the world.

Perhaps that was why he failed to do it himself.
It is all very well for goats and monkeys—
But the last male of a species is subject to peculiar pressures.
If ancient Satan had come slithering in, perhaps . . .
But instead the savants, with cameras and notebooks,
Writing sad stories of the decadence of quaggas.

And then one sultry afternoon he started raising Cain.
This angry young quagga kicked the bars and broke a camera;
He even tried to bite his astonished keeper.
He protested loud and clear against this and that,
Till the other animals became quite embarrassed
For he seemed to be calling them names.

Then he noticed his wife, awake with the noise,
And a curious feeling quivered round his belly.
He was Adam: there was Eve.
Galloping over to her, his head flung back,
He stumbled, and broke a leg, and had to be shot.

D. J. ENRIGHT (b. 1920)

Can the quagga defy extinction's quagmire?

What looked very like an unfinished zebra, with faint stripes on its hind-quarters, none on its legs, and a brown background? The quagga, hunted to extinction in South Africa a century ago. Yet researchers believe the quagga's genes live on, and they are attempting to bring back this vanished animal by selective breeding.

DNA cloned from preserved quagga skins has shown that the animal was a subspecies of the plains zebra. Scientists suspect that its genes might still be present in southern plains zebra populations. In 1987 they began breeding poorly striped and brownish zebras from Etosha National Park in Namibia and Zululand in South Africa. Some of the ten foals born since December 1988 bear striking quagga-like features, such as reduced striping and a predominantly white tail brush.

JOHN L. ELIOT, National Geographic, July 1992

The Last of the Dinosaurs

Chalky, you've gone—
the only one to see the last
stegosaurus, the blue edged plain
with bald egg-eaters blurring it,
eighty days' rain
before the mating season
and parsley blades neck high—

nice to have known such niceness,
these Cretaceous days!
Tyranno—sore arse—Rex
and other thick necks
thrive. Where's the gentle
ninety ton nonsense
we ate mustard grass beside?

So much time and blue.
That great arc telling
the centuries with its pivotless
movement, tick, tock, tick:
you can watch evolution
in those hairy faces
and poor Protoceratops being sick.

Another gentle day and
nothing to do. When you've lasted
150 million years
you can stand the sound of time.
Some day a mind is going to come
and question all this dance—
I've left footprints in the sand.

Valete and Salvete.
I hear the wintering waters rise
under the hemstitched sky.
Put me in the anthologies,
darling, like Horace almost
killed by a falling tree;
life is a dream or very nearly.

PETER PORTER (b. 1929)

Ichthyosaur

at the exhibition of Dinosaurs from China

Jurassic travellers
trailing a wake of ammonites.
Vertebrae swirl in stone's currents,
the broken flotilla of a pilgrimage.
Bone-pods open their secret marrow.

Behind glass she dies, birth-giving.
Millions of years too late it can still move us,
the dolphin-flip of her spine
and the frozen baby turning its head
to the world at the last moment
as all our babies do, facing the storm
of drowning as it learned to live.

Small obstetric tragedy,
like the death of a lamb at a field-edge
the wrong way up or strangled at birth
by the mothering cord.
Perhaps earth heaved, slapped a burning hand
on both of them as he ducked under her lintel,
leaving only a grace of bones
eloquent as a word in stone.

GILLIAN CLARKE (b. 1937)

The Committee of Missionaries at the Bay of Islands had granted to the Rev. Mr Williams and Mr Colenso a few weeks respite after their arduous labours in connection with the editing and printing of the New Testament into the Maori language. They left the Bay of Islands on 1st January, and returned on 13th February, 1838. While at a village in the Waiapu district, about twenty miles south-west of the East Cape, they heard some stories from the natives of 'a certain monstrous animal; some said it was a bird; others a person; but they were all agreed that it was called a Moa, and that in general appearance it resembled an immense domestic fowl, with the difference, however, that it dwelt in a cavern on the precipitous side of a mountain; that it lived on air; and that it was attended, or guarded, by two immense tuataras who, argus-like, kept incessant watch while the Moa slept.'

The travellers were also told, with fear and trembling, that if one ventured to approach the dwelling of this ferocious creature he would at once be trampled on and killed. A mountain called Whakapunake, at least eighty miles distant, was assigned as the residence of this creature.

Later some Moa bones are discovered. Colenso sets out again.

Quitting Turanga, and travelling still in a southerly direction, Mr Colenso soon came in sight of the fearsome mountain, Whakapunake, the traditional home of the only surviving Moa. He describes it as 'a huge, table-topped, and lofty mountain, covered with primeval forests and gloomy pines, its brow singularly adorned with a horizontal stratum of white sandstone which runs continuously and precipitously for more than two miles.' At the base of the mountain flowed the deep, surging river Whangaroa, so that, viewed from near or far, the spot was well chosen as the scene of an awe-inspiring fiction. Mr Colenso eagerly enquired as to the whereabouts of the bird, with no result except to be told that it was not there, but on a certain high mountain, Tawhiu-au, at Te Whaiti, it would be found. 'If,' says Mr Colenso, 'I was little inclined to believe the story of the bird's existence before, I was much less inclined to do so now. However, as my route lay that way, I determined to make every possible inquiry after it.'

Fifteen days' laborious travel 'on, and up where nature's heart beats strong amid the hills'; over rough Maori tracks and through dense bush, the beauty of which charmed the eye of the botanist, brought Mr Colenso to the village of Te Whaiti, the last stronghold of the ever-retreating Moa. Here, again, the resident natives had never seen a Moa, though they had always heard of it, and believed firmly in its being.

'The following day,' says Mr Colenso, 'I passed close to the mountain where this Moa had resided for so many years, but noticed nothing more than usual (although

I availed myself to the utmost of the use of my pocket telescope) save that this part of the country had a much more barren and desolate appearance than any I had hitherto witnessed.'

So concluded Mr Colenso's second quest for the Moa. Although he had offered substantial rewards for them, he had not been able to obtain any further bones, and in the autumn of the year he returned to the Bay of Islands to study, and muse upon, those he had been fortunate enough to secure.

In the matter of procuring bones, the Rev. Mr Williams was more successful; indeed, he was not infrequently embarrassed by the plethoric supply he sometimes found dumped down at his mission door, and for which he was asked to trade. All this was due to the fact that everywhere he had gone, Mr Colenso had impressed upon the people that should they be so fortunate as to find any relics of the bird they were immediately to carry them to Mr Williams, at Turanga, where they would be suitably recompensed.

T. LINDSAY BUICK, *The Mystery of the Moa: New Zealand's Avian Giant*, 1931

The Skeleton of the Great Moa in the Canterbury Museum, Christchurch

The skeleton of the moa on iron crutches
Broods over no great waste; a private swamp
Was where this tree grew feathers once, that hatches
Its dusty clutch, and guards them from the damp.

Interesting failure to adapt on islands,
Taller but not more fallen than I, who come
Bone to his bone, peculiarly New Zealand's.
The eyes of children flicker round this tomb

Under the skylights, wonder at the huge egg
Found in a thousand pieces, pieced together
But with less patience than the bones that dug
In time deep shelter against ocean weather:

Not I, some child, born in a marvellous year,
Will learn the trick of standing upright here.

ALLEN CURNOW (b. 1911)

The Archaeopteryx's Song

I am only half out of this rock of scales.
What good is armour when you want to fly?
My tail is like a stony pedestal
and not a rudder. If I sit back on it
I sniff winds, clouds, rains, fogs where
I'd be, where I'd be flying, be flying high.
Dinosaurs are spicks and
all I see when I look back
is tardy turdy bonehead swamps
whose scruples are dumb tons.
Damnable plates and plaques
can't even keep out ticks.
They think when they make the ground thunder
as they lumber for a horn-lock or a rut
that someone is afraid, that everyone is afraid,
but no one is afraid. The lords of creation
are in my mate's next egg's next egg's next egg,
stegosaur. It's feathers I need, more feathers
for the life to come. And these iron teeth
I want away, and a smooth beak
to cut the air. And these claws
on my wings, what use are they
except to drag me down, do you imagine
I am ever going to crawl again?
When I first left that crag
and flapped low and heavy over the ravine
I saw past present and future
like a dying tyrannosaur
and skimmed it with a hiss.
I will teach my sons and daughters to live
on mist and fire and fly to the stars.

EDWIN MORGAN (b. 1920)

Speaking of Larks

Suddenly larks are rare. A fertiliser kills
The reasons for their song. Their landscape fills
With whispers that some sharp-eared god enjoys,
Papery music, low botanical noise.

Friends give each other names of fields not drugged, where birds
Still practise their ascensions on transparent words,
　　Still disappear in light and silence where
　　Nobody else can hide: a span of air.

You think of following them. The sound of summer now
Falls only from an aeroplane that echoes somehow
　　In the soft sky. I'll find and interview
A lark with my machine . . .
　　　　　　　　　　　　But will that comfort you?

Nature is leaving earth. The species one by one
Withdraw their voices. Soon the creatures shall have gone,
Leaving the subtle horns of rock for nitrogen
And oxygen and noble gas to play upon.

ALISTAIR ELLIOT (b. 1932)

The Mountain Kiwi

I have very little to say regarding this bird, as I have only seen two of them, and being pushed with hunger, I ate the pair of them, under the circumstances I would have eaten the last of the Dodos.

It is all very well for science, lifting up its hands in horror, at what I once heard called glutony, but let science tramp through the Westland bush or swamps, for two or three days without food, and find out what hunger is. Besides at the time, which was many years ago, I was not aware that it was an almost extinct bird. Had I known so, I would at least have skinned it and kept the head and feet.

> CHARLES EDWARD DOUGLAS (1840–1916), *Mr Explorer Douglas*, ed. John Pascoe

Mankind have generally made swiftness the attribute of birds; but the Dodo has no title to this distinction. Instead of exciting the idea of swiftness by its appearance, it seems to strike the imagination as a thing the most unwieldy and inactive of all nature. Its body is massive, almost round, and coverd with grey feathers; it is just barely supported upon two short thick legs like pillars, while its head and neck rise from it in a manner truly grotesque. The neck, thick and pursy, is joined to the head, which consists of two great chaps, that open far behind the eyes, which are large, black and prominent; so that the animal when it gapes seems to be all mouth. The bill therefore is of an extraordinary length, not flat and broad, but thick, and of a bluish-white, sharp at the end, and each chap crooked in opposite directions. They resemble two pointed spoons that are laid together by the backs. . . . The dodo seems weighed down by its own heaviness, and has scarce strength to urge itself forward. It seems among birds what the sloth is among quadrupedes, an unresisting thing, equally incapable of flight or defence. . . . One would take it for a tortoise that had supplied itself with the feathers of a bird. . . .

This bird is a native of the Isle of France; and the Dutch, who first discoverd it there, called it in their language the *nauseous bird*, as well from its disgusting figure as from the bad taste of its flesh. However, succeeding observers contradict this first report, and assert that its flesh is good and wholesome eating. It is a silly simple bird, as may very well be supposed from its figure, and is very easily taken. Three or four dodos are enough to dine an hundred men.

OLIVER GOLDSMITH, A History of the Earth, and Animated Nature, 1774

The Last Monster

First, the dodo disappeared,
Leaving a legend of a simpleton's head,
Grotesque nut-cracker nose:
But a rum, a rare old one,
With feathers like old clothes.

The great Auk struck out for St Kilda's,
Settled with shaggy Highlanders,
Skin divers and such:
Learned the language of oblivion,
Finally lost touch.

Gone also, as Goldsmith noted,
The bird of Nazareth and the lesser tatou,
Beasts of strange pattern and birds past belief:
Even to number their names, like witchcraft,
Affords sensual relief.

Golden-pawed snowman of Everest,
Wildcat of the Grampians,
Bower-bird of Peru:
Stay hidden wherever you are,
The final inventory is after you!

Somewhere on the ultimate scarp
The last monster will watch
With hooded eyes,
While tiny men trek importantly towards him,
Bristling with strange supplies.

JOHN MONTAGUE (b. 1929)

EPILOGUE

CELEBRATION

The Zebras

To Chips Rafferty

From the dark woods that breathe of fallen showers,
Harnessed with level rays in golden reins,
The zebras draw the dawn across the plains
Wading knee-deep among the scarlet flowers.
The sunlight, zithering their flanks with fire,
Flashes between the shadows as they pass
Barred with electric tremors through the grass
Like wind along the gold strings of a lyre.

Into the flushed air snorting rosy plumes
That smoulder round their feet in drifting fumes,
With dove-like voices call the distant fillies,
While round the herds the stallion wheels his flight,
Engine of beauty volted with delight,
To roll his mare among the trampled lilies.

ROY CAMPBELL (1902–57)

Hast thou given the horse strength? hast thou clothed his neck with thunder?

Canst thou make him afraid as a grasshopper? the glory of his nostrils is terrible.

He paweth in the valley, and rejoiceth in his strength: he goeth on to meet the armed men.

He mocketh at fear, and is not affrighted; neither turneth he back from the sword.

The quiver rattleth against him, the glittering spear and the shield.

He swalloweth the ground with fierceness and rage: neither believeth he that it is the sound of the trumpet.

He saith among the trumpets, Ha, ha; and he smelleth the battle afar off, the thunder of the captains, and the shouting.

JOB 39: 19–25

A rev'rend lady-cow drawes neare,
Bids Amarantha welcome here;
And from her privy purse lets fall
A pearle or two, which seeme[s] to call
This adorn'd adored fayry
To the banquet of her dayry.
   Soft Amarantha weeps to see
'Mongst men such inhumanitie,
That those, who do receive in hay,
And pay in silver twice a day,
Should by their cruell barb'rous theft
Be both of that and life bereft.
   But 'tis decreed, when ere this dies,
That she shall fall a sacrifice
Unto the gods, since those, that trace
Her stemme, show 'tis a god-like race,
Descending in an even line
From heifers and from steeres divine,
Making the honour'd extract full
In Iö and Europa's bull.
She was the largest goodliest beast,
That ever mead or altar blest;
Round [w]as her udder, and more white
Then is the Milkie Way in night;
Her full broad eye did sparkle fire;

silver: silvery or white milk.

Her breath was sweet as kind desire,
And in her beauteous crescent shone,
Bright as the argent-horned moone.

RICHARD LOVELACE (1602–57/8), *Amarantha: A Pastorall*

Goat

The goat, with amber dumb-bells in his eyes,
The blasé lecher, inquisitive as sin,
White sarcasm walking, proof against surprise,

The nothing like him goat, goat-in-itself,
Idea of goatishness made flesh, pure essence
In idle masquerade on a rocky shelf—

Hangs upside down from lushest grass to twitch
A shrivelled blade from the cliff's barren chest,
And holds the grass well lost; the narrowest niche

Is frame for the devil's face; the steepest thatch
Of barn or byre is pavement to his foot;
The last, loved rose a prisoner to his snatch;

And the man in his man-ness, passing, feels suddenly
Hypocrite found out, hearing behind him that
Vulgar vibrato, thin derisive me-eh.

NORMAN MACCAIG (b. 1910)

The boudoir of the Empress was situated in a little meadow, dappled with buttercups and daisies, round two sides of which there flowed in a silver semicircle the stream which fed the lake. Lord Emsworth, as his custom was, had pottered off there directly after breakfast and now, at half-past twelve, he was still standing, in company with his pig-man Pirbright, draped bonelessly over the rail of the sty, his mild eyes beaming with the light of a holy devotion.

From time to time he sniffed sensuously. Elsewhere throughout this fair domain the air was fragrant with the myriad scents of high summer, but not where Lord Emsworth was doing his sniffing. Within a liberal radius of the Empress's head-quarters other scents could not compete. This splendid animal diffused an aroma which was both distinctive and arresting. Attractive, too, if you liked that sort of thing, as Lord Emsworth did.

Between Empress of Blandings and these two human beings who minis-
tered to her comfort there was a sharp contrast in physique. Lord Emsworth was tall and thin and scraggy, Pirbright tall and thin and scraggier.
The Empress, on the other hand, could have passed in a dim light for a
captive balloon, fully inflated and about to make its trial trip. The modern
craze for slimming had found no votary in her. She liked her meals large
and regular, and had never done a reducing exercise in her life. Watching
her now as she tucked into a sort of hash of bran, acorns, potatoes, linseed,
and swill, the ninth Earl of Emsworth felt his heart leap up in much the
same way as that of the poet Wordsworth used to do when he beheld a
rainbow in the sky.

'What a picture, Pirbright!' he said reverently.

P. G. WODEHOUSE, *Heavy Weather*, 1933

Franz, a Goose

It is contagious as a dance,
The morning exultation of the goose
Whose inappropriate name is Franz.
Daily he comes, majestic and snow white,
To put his private pond to use,
To stand alone within the rite
And make ovations to pure self-delight.

As one long waving sleeve, he dips
Soft neck, blue eyes, and orange beak
Deep into waters where the magic sleeps,
Now up, now down, in hieratic bliss,
Gives them the dark caress they seek,
Then lifts that giant arm, weapon and grace,
To shake a rain of diamonds to the grass.

Can one describe superb-as-these ablutions,
This royal pomp as a mere daily wash?
The liquid phrase, the lovely repetitions?
His squawks are murmurs now. He sings.
Then with one huge triumphant splash
Enters the pond and beats his wings:
'I am the goose of geese, the king of kings!'

Who could resist such pride or pull it down?
Yet who resist one tentative caress,

To touch the silken neck that wears a crown?
I dare the irresistible in play,
To meet a cold blue eye and blazing hiss;
His person rises up in terrible dismay,
And talks of the indignity all day.

Followed at just two paces by his queen
(Possessive murmurs lead her gently on),
He makes his progress like a paladin,
Explains, complains of the awesome caress,
And how pomp trembled yet achieved disdain,
Assures her that he gave a fatal hiss,
Assures himself what a great goose he is.

MAY SARTON (b. 1912)

Jenny Wren

Of all the birds that rove and sing,
  Near dwellings made for men,
None is so nimble, neat, and trim
  As Jenny Wren.

With pin-point bill, and tail a-cock,
  So wildly shrill she cries,
The echoes on their roof-tree knock
  And fill the skies.

Never was sweeter seraph hid
  Within so small a house—
A tiny, inch-long, eager, ardent,
  Feathered mouse.

WALTER DE LA MARE (1873–1956)

I was puzzled by the phrase, 'silkworm-moth eyebrow,' in an old Japanese, or rather Chinese proverb:—*The silkworm-moth eyebrow of a woman is the axe that cuts down the wisdom of man.* So I went to my friend Niimi, who keeps silkworms, to ask for an explanation.

'Is it possible,' he exclaimed, 'that you never saw a silkworm-moth? The silkworm-moth has very beautiful eyebrows.'

'Eyebrows?' I queried, in astonishment.

'Well, call them what you like,' returned Niimi;—'the poets call them eyebrows. . . . Wait a moment, and I will show you.'

He left the guest-room, and presently returned with a white paper-fan, on which a silkworm-moth was sleepily reposing.

'We always reserve a few for breeding,' he said;—'this one is just out of the cocoon. It cannot fly, of course: none of them can fly. . . . Now look at the eyebrows.'

I looked, and saw that the antennæ, very short and feathery, were so arched back over the two jewel-specks of eyes in the velvety head, as to give the appearance of a really handsome pair of eyebrows.

LAFCADIO HEARN, 'Silkworms', *In Ghostly Japan*, 1899

The Giraffe

For neck, a tulip-stalk;
Flower-head, far off and elegant;
Tongue, to fill your body's want
Stretched out like hands of a lady
Who takes her own naturally;
Wind netted in your small-paced walk;

Eyes dark and innocent;
Airy beast with flower's grace,
With bird's speed, with human face;
Painted like ground under trees
With light and shade; supple as these;
Horizon's instrument:

Strength flowers, speed, in you.
Speed is your soul's obedience.
Tiger and strolling wolf must dance
To other tunes, obeying God.
Strength is their fruit, who feed on blood;
But the trees kneel for you.

O meshed among high leaves,
Among clouds: I should never start
To see, when clouds or branches part,
Like a wild cherub's, bloom your head,
Serpent wise, dove feathers spread
Brushing the poplar's sleeves.

E. J. SCOVELL (b. 1907)

The Tyger

Tyger! Tyger! burning bright
In the forests of the night,
What immortal hand or eye
Could frame thy fearful symmetry?

In what distant deeps or skies
Burnt the fire of thine eyes?
On what wings dare he aspire?
What the hand dare sieze the fire?

And what shoulder, & what art,
Could twist the sinews of thy heart?
And when thy heart began to beat,
What dread hand? & what dread feet?

What the hammer? what the chain?
In what furnace was thy brain?
What the anvil? what dread grasp
Dare its deadly terrors clasp?

When the stars threw down their spears,
And water'd heaven with their tears,
Did he smile his work to see?
Did he who made the Lamb make thee?

Tyger! Tyger! burning bright
In the forests of the night,
What immortal hand or eye,
Dare frame thy fearful symmetry?

WILLIAM BLAKE (1757–1827)

It is necessary to add that [Tulip] is beautiful. People are always wanting to touch her, a thing she cannot bear. Her ears are tall and pointed, like the ears of Anubis. How she manages to hold them constantly erect, as though starched, I do not know, for with their fine covering of mouse-grey fur they are soft and flimsy; when she stands with her back to the sun it shines through the delicate tissue, so that they glow shell-pink as though incandescent. Her face also is long and pointed, basically stone-grey but the snout and lower jaw are jet-black. Jet, too, are the rims of her amber eyes, as though heavily mascara'd, and the tiny, mobile eye-brow tufts that are set like accents above them. And in the midst of her forehead is a kind of Indian caste-mark, a black diamond suspended there, like the jewel on the brow of Pegasus in Mantegna's 'Parnassus', by a fine dark thread, no more than a pencilled line, which is drawn from it right over her poll midway between the tall ears. A shadow extends across her forehead from either side of this caste-mark, so that, in certain lights, the diamond looks like the body of a bird with its wings spread, a bird in flight.

These dark markings symmetrically divide up her face into zones of pale pastel colours, like a mosaic, or a stained-glass window; her skull, bisected by the thread, is two primrose pools, the centre of her face light grey, the bridge of her nose above the long, black lips fawn, her cheeks white, and upon each a *patte de mouche* has been tastefully set. A delicate white ruff, frilling out from the lobes of her ears, frames this strange, clownish face, with its heavily leaded features, and covers the whole of her throat and chest with a snowy shirt-front.

For the rest, her official description is sable-grey: she is a grey dog wearing a sable tunic. Her grey is the grey of birch-bark; her sable tunic is of the texture of satin and clasps her long body like a saddle-cloth. No tailor could have shaped it more elegantly; it is cut round the joints of her shoulders and thighs and in a straight line along the points of her ribs, lying open at the chest and stomach. Over her rump it fits like a cap, and then extends on in a thin strip over the top of her long tail down to the tip. Viewed from above, therefore, she is a black dog; but when she rolls over on her back she is a grey one. Two dark ribbons of fur, descending from her tunic over her shoulders, fasten it to her at her sternum, which seems to clip the ribbons together as with an ivory brooch.

J. R. ACKERLEY, My Dog Tulip, 1956

The creature that emerged, not greatly disconcerted, from this sack on to the spacious tiled floor of the Consulate bedroom did not at that moment resemble anything so much as a very small medievally-conceived dragon. From the head to the tip of the tail he was coated with symmetrical pointed scales of mud armour, between whose tips was visible a soft velvet fur like that of a chocolate-brown mole. He shook himself, and I half expected this aggressive camouflage to disintegrate into a cloud of dust, but it remained unaffected by his manoeuvre, and in fact it was not for another month that I contrived to remove the last of it and see him, as it were, in his true colours.

Yet even on that first day I recognized that he was an otter of a species that I had never seen in the flesh, resembling only a curious otter skin that I had bought from the Arabs in one of the marsh villages. Mijbil, as I called the new otter, after a sheikh with whom we had recently been staying and whose name had intrigued me with a conjured picture of a platypus-like creature, was, in fact, of a race previously unknown to science, and was at length christened by zoologists, from examination of the skin and of himself, *Lutrogale perspicillata maxwelli*, or Maxwell's otter. This circumstance, perhaps, influenced on my side the intensity of the emotional relationship between us, for I became, during a year of his constant and violently affectionate companionship, fonder of him than of almost any human being, and to write of him in the past tense makes me feel as desolate as one who has lost an only child. For a year and five days he was about my bed and my bath spying out all my ways, and though I now have another otter no whit less friendly and fascinating, there will never be another Mijbil.

Gavin Maxwell, *Ring of Bright Water*, 1960

The Bush-Baby

I would rather hold this creature in my hand
Than be kissed by a great king.
The love for what I do not understand
Goes from me to the slight thing.

The moth-velvet and the round nocturnal eyes
And the unchanging face
Are excellent as an image out of Paradise,
As a flower in a dark place.

There is only mutual inoffensiveness
Between us, and a sense
Here in my heart, of what it is to bless
A simple immanence;

To see a glory in another kind,
To love, and not to know.
O if I could forsake this weary mind
And love my fellows so!

Ruth Pitter (1897–1992)

The Cat and the Moon

The cat went here and there
And the moon spun round like a top,
And the nearest kin of the moon,
The creeping cat, looked up.

Black Minnaloushe stared at the moon,
For, wander and wail as he would,
The pure cold light in the sky
Troubled his animal blood.
Minnaloushe runs in the grass
Lifting his delicate feet.
Do you dance, Minnaloushe, do you dance?
When two close kindred meet,
What better than call a dance?
Maybe the moon may learn,
Tired of that courtly fashion,
A new dance turn.
Minnaloushe creeps through the grass
From moonlit place to place,
The sacred moon overhead
Has taken a new phase.
Does Minnaloushe know that his pupils
Will pass from change to change,
And that from round to crescent,
From crescent to round they range?
Minnaloushe creeps through the grass
Alone, important and wise,
And lifts to the changing moon
His changing eyes.

W. B. YEATS (1865–1939)

For I will consider my Cat Jeoffry.
For he is the servant of the Living God, duly and daily serving him.
For at the first glance of the glory of God in the East he worships in his
    way.
For is this done by wreathing his body seven times round with elegant
    quickness.
For then he leaps up to catch the musk, which is the blessing of God upon
    his prayer.
For he rolls upon prank to work it in.
For having done duty and received blessing he begins to consider himself.
For this he performs in ten degrees.
For first he looks upon his fore-paws to see if they are clean.
For secondly he kicks up behind to clear away there.
For thirdly he works it upon stretch with the fore paws extended.
For fourthly he sharpens his paws by wood.
For fifthly he washes himself.

For sixthly he rolls upon wash.

For Seventhly he fleas himself, that he may not be interrupted upon the beat.

For Eighthly he rubs himself against a post.

For Ninthly he looks up for his instructions.

For Tenthly he goes in quest of food.

For having consider'd God and himself he will consider his neighbour.

For if he meets another cat he will kiss her in kindness.

For when he takes his prey he plays with it to give it chance.

For one mouse in seven escapes by his dallying.

For when his day's work is done his business more properly begins.

For keeps the Lord's watch in the night against the adversary. ·

For he counteracts the powers of darkness by his electrical skin & glaring eyes.

For he counteracts the Devil, who is death, by brisking about the life.

For in his morning orisons he loves the sun and the sun loves him.

For he is of the tribe of Tiger.

For the Cherub Cat is a term of the Angel Tiger.

For he has the subtlety and hissing of a serpent, which in goodness he suppresses.

For he will not do destruction, if he is well-fed, neither will he spit without provocation.

For he purrs in thankfulness, when God tells him he's a good Cat.

For he is an instrument for the children to learn benevolence upon.

For every house is incompleat without him & a blessing is lacking in the spirit.

For the Lord commanded Moses concerning the cats at the departure of the Children of Israel from Egypt.

For every family had one cat at least in the bag.

For the English Cats are the best in Europe.

For he is the cleanest in the use of his fore-paws of any quadrupede.

For the dexterity of his defence is an instance of the love of God to him exceedingly.

For he is the quickest to his mark of any creature.

For he is tenacious of his point.

For he is a mixture of gravity and waggery.

For he knows that God is his Saviour.

For there is nothing sweeter than his peace when at rest.

For there is nothing brisker than his life when in motion.

For he is of the Lord's poor and so indeed is he called by benevolence perpetually—Poor Jeoffry! poor Jeoffry! the rat has bit thy throat.

For I bless the name of the Lord Jesus that Jeoffry is better.

For the divine spirit comes about his body to sustain it in compleat cat.

For his tongue is exceeding pure so that it has in purity what it wants in
    musick.

For he is docile and can learn certain things.

For he can set up with gravity which is patience upon approbation.

For he can fetch and carry, which is patience in employment.

For he can jump over a stick which is patience upon proof positive.

For he can spraggle upon waggle at the word of command.

For he can jump from an eminence into his master's bosom.

For he can catch the cork and toss it again.

For he is hated by the hypocrite and miser.

For the former is affraid of detection.

For the latter refuses the charge.

For he camels his back to bear the first notion of business.

For he is good to think on, if a man would express himself neatly.

For he made a great figure in Egypt for his signal services.

For he killed the Icneumon-rat very pernicious by land.

For his ears are so acute that they sting again.

For from this proceeds the passing quickness of his attention.

For by stroaking of him I have found out electricity.

For I perceived God's light about him both wax and fire.

For the Electrical fire is the spiritual substance, which God sends from
    heaven to sustain the bodies both of man and beast.

For God has blessed him in the variety of his movements.

For, tho he cannot fly, he is an excellent clamberer.

For his motions upon the face of the earth are more than any other
    quadrupede.

For he can tread to all the measures upon the musick.

For he can swim for life.

For he can creep.

CHRISTOPHER SMART (1722–71), *Jubilate Agno*

ACKNOWLEDGEMENTS

The editors and publishers are grateful for permission to reproduce the following copyright material:

J. R. Ackerley, from *My Dog Tulip* (Secker & Warburg, 1956), copyright © 1956 by J. R. Ackerley. Reprinted by permission of Reed Consumer Books Ltd and Beacon Press.

Richard Adams, from *Watership Down* (Puffin Books, 1973).

Joy Adamson, from *Born Free* (Collins & Harvill Press, 1961).

Fleur Adcock, from *Selected Poems* (Oxford University Press, 1983), and from *The Virgin and the Nightingale: Medieval Latin Poems* (Bloodaxe Books Ltd., 1983).

A. R. Ammons, from *Collected Poems 1951–1971*. Reprinted with the permission of W. W. Norton & Company Inc., copyright © 1972 by A. R. Ammons.

Aristotle, *Historia Animalium*. Translation by A. L. Peck (Harvard University Press, 1965–70). Reprinted by permission of the publishers and the Loeb Classical Library.

Neil Astley, from *Darwin Survivor* (Peterloo Poets, 1988).

Margaret Atwood, 'Vultures' and 'Bad Mouth' from *Poems 1976–1986*, Copyright © 1987 by Margaret Atwood. Reprinted by kind permission of the publishers, Virago Press Ltd and Houghton Mifflin Co. All rights reserved.

W. H. Auden, from *Collected Poems* (Faber & Faber Ltd., 1976, 1991). Reprinted by permission of the publisher.

Sybille Bedford, from *A Visit to Don Otavio: A Traveller's Tale from Mexico* (Eland, 1953). Reprinted by permission of the publishers.

Hilaire Belloc, from *Complete Verse* (Gerald Duckworth & Co. Ltd., 1970).

John Betjeman, from *Collected Poems* (John Murray Ltd., 1970). Reprinted by permission of the publishers.

Ruth Bidgood, from *Selected Poems* (Seren Books, 1992). Reprinted by permission of the publishers.

Elizabeth Bishop, from *The Complete Poems 1927–1979* (Chatto & Windus). Copyright © Alice Helen Methfessel, 1983. Reprinted by permission of Farrar Straus & Giroux Inc. and Random House UK Ltd.

Karen Blixen, from *Letters from Africa 1914–1931* (University of Chicago Press, 1981).

Jorge Luis Borges, 'The Unicorn' from *The Book of Imaginary Beings* by Jorge Luis Borges with Margarita Guerrero, trans. Norman Thomas di Giovanni, translation copyright © 1969 by Jorge Luis Borges and Norman Thomas di Giovanni. Used by permission of Dutton Signet, a division of Penguin Books USA Inc. and Random House UK Ltd.

George Mackay Brown, from *The Wreck of the Archangel* (John Murray Ltd., 1989). Reprinted by permission of the publishers.

T. Lindsay Buick, from *The Mystery of the Moa: New Zealand's Avian Giant* (Thomas Avery & Sons Ltd., 1931).

Roy Campbell, from *Selected Poems* (Oxford University Press, 1982).

Elias Canetti, from *The Human Province*. Translation by Joachim Neugroschel. Reprinted by permission of Carl Hanser Verlag & Co.

Angela Carter, from *Nights at the Circus* (Chatto & Windus, 1984). Reprinted by permission of Rogers Coleridge & White Ltd.

Amy Clampitt, from *The Kingfisher* (Faber & Faber Ltd., 1983), copyright © Amy Clampitt. Reprinted by permission of the publisher.

Gillian Clarke, from *Letting in the Rumour* (Carcanet Press Ltd., 1989). Reprinted by permission of the publishers.

Paul Colinvaux, from *Why Big Fierce Animals are Rare* (George Allen & Unwin, 1980).

Jim Corbett, from *Man-Eaters of Kumaon* (Oxford University Press, 1944).

Richmal Crompton, from *William the Detective* (George Newnes Ltd., London).

Allen Curnow, from *Collected Poems 1933–1973* (A. H. & A. W. Reed, 1974). Reprinted by permission of the author.

Elizabeth David, from *Italian Food* (Penguin Books Ltd., 1954), and *A Book of Mediterranean Food* (Penguin Books Ltd., 1955).

Walter de la Mare, from *Collected Rhymes and Verses* (Faber & Faber Ltd., 1989). Reprinted by permission of The Literary Trustees of Walter de la Mare, and The Society of Authors as their representative.

Leslie Downer, from *On the Narrow Road to the Deep North. Journey Into a Lost Japan* (Jonathan Cape, 1989). Reprinted by permission of Random House UK Ltd.

Douglas Dunn, from *Northlight* (Faber & Faber Ltd, 1988). Reprinted by permission of the publishers and Peters Fraser & Dunlop Group Ltd.

Gerald Durrell, from *The Overloaded Ark* (Faber & Faber Ltd, 1953). Reprinted by permission of the publishers. *My Family and Other Animals* (Rupert Hart-Davis, 1956). Reprinted by permission of HarperCollins Publishers Ltd.

Richard Eberhart, from *Collected Poems 1930–1976* (Chatto & Windus, 1976).

John Eliot, from *National Geographic*, July 1992. Reprinted by permission of the National Geographic Society.

Alistair Elliot, from *My Country: Collected Poems* (Carcanet Press Ltd., 1989). Reprinted by permission of the publishers.

Frederick Engels, from *The Origin of the Family, Private Property and the State* (Wishart & Wishart, London). Translation Alick West and Dona Tow, 1940.

D. J. Enright, from *Selected Poems* (Oxford University Press, 1990). Reprinted by permission of the author.

Jean Henri Fabre, from *Insect Life* (Beacon Press, 1991).

Penelope Farmer (ed.), from *Beginnings. Creation Myths of the World* (Chatto & Windus, 1978).

Ian Hamilton Finlay, from *The Dancers Inherit the Party* (Migrant Press, 1960). Reprinted by permission of the author.

Gustave Flaubert, from *Un Coeur Simple*. Translated and reprinted by permission of M. & D. J. Enright.

Paul Fountain, from *The River Amazon from its Sources to the Sea* (Constable & Co. Ltd., 1914).

Margaret Fountaine, from *Love among the Butterflies: The Travels and Adventures of a Victorian Lady* (HarperCollins Publishers, 1980). Reprinted by permission of the publishers.

Roy Fuller, from *Collected Poems 1936–1961* (Andre Deutsch Ltd., 1962). Reprinted by permission of the Estate of Roy Fuller.

David Garnett, from *Lady into Fox* (Chatto & Windus, 1922). Reprinted by permission of the publishers.

Jane Goodall, from *Through a Window: Thirty Years with the Chimpanzees of Gombe* (Weidenfeld & Nicolson Ltd., 1990). Reprinted by permission of The Orion Publishing Group Ltd.

Stephen Jay Gould, from *The Panda's Thumb. More Reflections in Natural History* (W. W. Norton & Co. Inc., 1980). Copyright © 1980 by Stephen Jay Gould. Reprinted by permission of W. W. Norton & Co. Inc.

Günter Grass, from *The Flounder*. Translation by Ralph Manheim (Secker & Warburg, 1978). Reprinted by permission of Reed Consumer Books Ltd.

Robert Graves, from *Collected Poems* (Cassell, 1959). Reprinted by permission of A. P. Watt Ltd. on behalf of the Trustees of the Robert Graves Copyright Trust.

Thom Gunn, from *The Man With Night Sweats* (Faber & Faber Ltd., 1992), copyright © Thom Gunn. Reprinted by permission of the publisher.

Mike Harding, from *Daddy Edgar's Pools* (Peterloo Poets, 1992).

L. P. Hartley, from *The Shrimp and the Anemone* (Putnam, 1944).

Gwen Harwood, from *Collected Poems* (Oxford University Press, 1991).

Seamus Heaney, from *Field Work* (Faber & Faber Ltd., 1979), copyright © Seamus Heaney 1979. Reprinted by permission of Farrar, Straus & Giroux Inc. and Faber & Faber Ltd.

John Heath-Stubbs, from *Collected Poems 1943–1987* (Carcanet Press Ltd., 1988). Reprinted by permission of David Higham Associates Ltd.

Anthony Hecht, from *Collected Earlier Poems* (Oxford University Press, 1990).

Conrad Hilberry, from *Sorting the Smoke: New and Selected Poems* (University of Iowa Press, 1990). Reprinted by permission of the publisher.

E. T. A. Hoffmann, from *Kater Murr: Selected Writings*. Translation Kent & Knight Vol. 2 (University of Chicago Press, 1969). Reprinted by permission of the publishers.

A. E. Housman, from *Collected Poems and Selected Prose* (Allen Lane, 1988).

Sue Hubbell, from *Broadsides from the Other Orders: A Book of Bugs* (Random House Inc., 1993).

W. H. Hudson, from *Birds and Man* (Gerald Duckworth & Co. Ltd., 1915).

Ted Hughes, from *Season Songs* (Faber & Faber Ltd., 1976), copyright © Ted Hughes. Reprinted by permission of the publishers.

Julian Huxley, from *Kingdom of the Beasts* (Thames & Hudson Ltd., 1956). Reprinted by permission of the publishers.

Randall Jarrell, from *The Complete Poems* (Faber & Faber Ltd., 1971), copyright © Randall Jarrell 1971. Reprinted by permission of the publisher.

Joe Joseph, from *The Times*, 25 February 1994.

X. J. Kennedy, from *Cross Ties: Selected Poems* (University of Georgia Press, 1985). Copyright © 1975 by X. J. Kennedy, renewed. Originally published in *One Winter Night in August*. Reprinted by permission of Curtis Brown Ltd.

David Lack, from *The Life of the Robin* (H. F. & G. Witherby Ltd., 1943). Reprinted by permission of Victor Gollancz Ltd.

Eve Langley, from *The Penguin Book of Australian Women Poets* (Penguin Books Ltd., 1986).

Philip Larkin, from *Collected Poems* (Faber & Faber Ltd., 1988). Reprinted by permission of the Marvell Press, England and Australia.

D. H. Lawrence, 'Mountain Lion' and 'Mosquito' from *The Complete Poems of D. H. Lawrence* edited by V. de Sola Pinto & F. W. Roberts. Copyright © 1964, 1971 by Angelo Ravagli and C. M. Weekley, Executors of the Estate of Frieda Lawrence Ravagli. Used by permission of Viking Penguin, a division of Penguin Books USA Inc. and Laurence Pollinger Ltd.

Brad Leithauser, from *Between Leaps: Poems 1972–1985* (Oxford University Press, 1987).

Primo Levi, from *Other People's Trades*. Translation Raymond Rosenthal (Summit Books, Simon & Schuster, 1989).

Hugh Lofting, from *The Story of Doctor Doolittle* (Dell Publishing NY, 1988).

Michael Longley, from *Poems 1963–1983* (Gallery Press, 1985).

Barry Holstun Lopez, from *Of Wolves and Men* (J. M. Dent & Sons Ltd., 1978).

Konrad Lorenz, from *King Solomon's Ring: New Light on Animal Ways* (Methuen & Co. Ltd, 1952). Reprinted by permission of Routledge.

Lucretius, from *The Poem on Nature*. Translation by C. H. Sisson (Carcanet Press Ltd., 1976). Reprinted by permission of the publishers.

George MacBeth, from *Collected Poems 1968–1982* (Hutchinson, 1989), copyright © George MacBeth 1989. Reprinted by permission of Sheil Land Associates Ltd.

Norman MacCaig, from *Collected Poems* (Chatto & Windus, 1990). Reprinted by permission of Random House UK Ltd.

Gwendolyn MacEwen, from *Afterworlds* (McClelland & Stewart Inc., 1987). Reprinted by permission of the Canadian publishers McClelland & Stewart, Toronto and the Estate of Gwendolyn MacEwen.

Alasdair Maclean, from *From the Wilderness* (Victor Gollancz Ltd, 1973). Copyright © Alasdair Maclean 1973. Reprinted by permission of the publishers.

Katherine Mansfield, from *Prelude* (Oxford University Press, 1969).

John Masefield, from *Collected Poems* (Heinemann, 1923). Reprinted by permission of The Society of Authors as the literary representatives of the Estate of John Masefield.

Gavin Maxwell, from *Ring of Bright Water* (Penguin Books, 1974). First published by Longmans Green. Copyright © Gavin Maxwell 1960. Reprinted by permission of Penguin Books Ltd.

Gerda Mayer, from *The Orange Dove of Fiji: Poems for the World Wide Fund for Nature* (Hutchinson, 1989).

W. S. Merwin, from *The Lice* (Atheneum, 1974). Copyright © 1967 by W. S. Merwin. Reprinted by permission of Georges Borchardt Inc.

A. A. Milne, 'Eeyore Loses a Tail & Pooh Finds One', from *Winnie The Pooh*, illustrated by E. H. Shepard. Copyright 1926 by E. P. Dutton, renewed 1954 by A. A. Milne. Used by permission of Dutton Children's Books, a division of Penguin Books USA Inc. and Reed Consumer Books Ltd.

John Montague, from *Selected Poems* (Oxford University Press, 1982).

Marianne Moore, 'Sea Unicorns and Land Unicorns' and 'The Malay Dragon' from *The Collected Poems of Marianne Moore*. Reprinted by permission of Simon & Schuster, Inc. and Faber & Faber Ltd. Copyright 1935 by Marianne Moore, renewed 1963 by Marianne Moore and T. S. Eliot. 'A Jelly-Fish' from *The Complete Poems of Marianne Moore*, copyright © 1959 by Marianne Moore, © renewed 1987 by Lawrence E. Brinn and Louise Crane, Executors of the Estate of Marianne Moore. Used by permission of Viking Penguin, a division of Penguin Books USA Inc. and Faber & Faber Ltd.

Geoffrey Moorhouse, from *The Fearful Void* (Hodder & Stoughton Ltd., 1974).

Edwin Morgan, from *Poems of Thirty Years* (Carcanet Press Ltd., 1982). Reprinted by permission of the publishers.

Edwin Muir, from *Collected Poems* (Faber & Faber Ltd., 1960). Reprinted by permission of the publisher.

Les Murray, 'Bats' Ultrasound' from *The Daylight Moon and Other Poems* by Les A. Murray. Copyright © 1983, 1987, 1988 by Les A. Murray. Reprinted by permission of Persea Books. 'Mollusc' and 'Cell DNA' from *Translations from the Natural World* (Carcanet Press Ltd., 1988 and 1993). Reprinted by permission of the publishers.

Robert Musil, from *Posthumous Papers of a Living Author*. Translation by Peter Wortsman (Eridanos Press, 1987).

Ogden Nash, from *I Wouldn't Have Missed It: Selected Poems of Ogden Nash* (André Deutsch Ltd., 1983). Reprinted by permission of the publishers and Curtis Brown, New York.

Howard Nemerov, from *Trying Conclusions: New and Selected Poems 1961–1991* (University of Chicago Press, 1991). Reprinted by permission of Margaret Nemerov.

Norman Nicholson, 'Cowper's Tame Hare' from *Selected Poems* and 'Plankton' from *Sea to the West* (Faber & Faber Ltd., 1966 and 1981). Reprinted by permission David Higham Associates Ltd.

Dorothy Nimmo, from *Homewards* (Giant Steps, 1987). Reprinted by permission of the author.

Alden Nowlan, from *An Exchange of Gifts: Poems New and Selected* (Irwin Publishing, 1985). Copyright © Alden Nowlan 1985. Reprinted by permission of Stoddart Publishing Co. Ltd., Don Mills, Ontario.

Redmond O'Hanlon, from *Into the Heart of Borneo* (The Salamander Press, 1984).

Margaret Orbell (ed.), from *Maori Folktales in Maori and English* (Blackwood & Janet Paul, 1968).

George Orwell, from *Shooting an Elephant and Other Essays* (Secker & Warburg, 1950). Copyright © 1950 Sonia Brownell Orwell and renewed 1978 by Sonia Pitt-Rivers. Reprinted by permission of A. M. Heath & Co. Ltd and Harcourt Brace & Co.

Jan Owen, from *Fingerprints on Light* (Angus & Robertson, 1990). Reprinted by permission of the author.

Ruth Pitter, from *Collected Poems* (Enitharmon Press, 1990).

Pliny the Elder, from *Natural History*. Translations by H. Rackham, reprinted by permission of Harvard University Press and the Loeb Classical Library; and Philemon Holland (Clarendon Press, 1964).

Peter Porter, from *Collected Poems* (Oxford University Press, 1983).

Beatrix Potter, from *The Tale of Samuel Whiskers* and *The Journal of Beatrix Potter 1881–1897*, translation from her code writings by Leslie Linder (Frederick Warne & Co., 1966).

Arthur Ransome, from *Swallows and Amazons* (Jonathan Cape, 1930). Reprinted by permission of Random House UK Ltd.

Gwen Raverat, from *Period Piece: A Cambridge Childhood* (Faber & Faber Ltd., 1942). Reprinted by permission of the publisher.

Vicki Raymond, from *Selected Poems* (Carcanet Press Ltd., 1993). Reprinted by permission of the publishers.

Peter Redgrove, from *Poems 1954–1987* (Penguin Books Ltd., 1989).

Judith Rodriguez, from *New and Selected Poems* (University of Queensland Press, 1988). Reprinted by permission of the publishers.

Theodore Roethke, 'The Bat', copyright 1938 by Theodore Roethke. 'The Minimal', copyright 1942 by Theodore Roethke. 'The Meadow Mouse', copyright © 1963 by Beatrice Roethke, Administratrix of the Estate of Theodore Roethke. From the *Collected Poems of Theodore Roethke*. Used by permission of Doubleday, a division of Bantam Doubleday Dell Publishing Group, Inc. and Faber & Faber Ltd.

Miriam Rothschild, from *Penguin Science Survey 1967: Biology* (Penguin Books Ltd., 1967).

May Sarton, from *Selected Poems of May Sarton*, ed. Serena Sue Hilsinger and Lois Brynes. Copyright © 1966 by May Sarton. Reprinted by permission of W. W. Norton & Co. Inc.

Siegfried Sassoon, from *Memoirs of a Fox-Hunting Man* (Faber & Faber Ltd., 1928).
Reprinted by permission of George Sassoon.

E. J. Scovell, from *Collected Poems* (Carcanet Press Ltd., 1988). Reprinted by permission of the publishers.

James Scully, from *Avenues of the Americas*. Reprinted by permission of the author.

Penelope Shuttle, 'Zoo Morning' from *The Orange Dove of Fiji: Poems for the World Wide Fund for Nature* (Hutchinson, 1989) and 'Killiow Pigs' from *Adventures with my Horse* (Oxford University Press, 1988).

Stevie Smith, from *Collected Poems* (Penguin Books, 1985). Copyright © 1972 by Stevie Smith. Reprinted by permission of New Directions Publishing Corporation and James MacGibbon.

John Sparks, from *The Sexual Connection* (David & Charles, 1977).

Anne Stevenson, from *Selected Poems* (Oxford University Press, 1989).

Lucien Stryk, from *Collected Poems 1953–1983* (Ohio University Press, 1984). Reprinted by permission of the publishers.

Graham Swift, from *Waterland* (Heinemann, 1983). Reprinted by permission of A. P. Watt Ltd. on behalf of the author.

George Szirtes, from *November and May* (Secker & Warburg, 1981). Reprinted by permission of Reed Consumer Books Ltd.

Junichiro Tanizaki, from *The Makioka Sisters* (Alfred A. Knopf Inc., 1957).

D'Arcy Wentworth Thompson, from *On Growth and Form* (Cambridge University Press, 1917). Reprinted by permission of the publishers and the University of St Andrews.

Johann Heinrich Tischbein, from *Aus Tischbeins Leben und Briefwechsel* by Friedrich von Alten. Translation by D. J. Enright. Reprinted by permission of D. J. Enright.

J. R. R. Tolkien, from *The Hobbit* (George Allen & Unwin, 1937). Reprinted by permission of HarperCollins Publishers Ltd.

Voltaire, from *Dictionnaire Philosophique*. Translation Theodore Besterman (Penguin Books Ltd., 1971).

Kath Walker, from *The Dawn is at Hand: Selected Poems* (Marion Boyars London & New York, 1992). Reprinted by permission of the publishers.

Ted Walker, from *Burning the Ivy: Poems 1973–1977* (Jonathan Cape, 1978). Reprinted by permission of Random House UK Ltd.

Sylvia Townsend Warner, from *T. H. White: A Biography* (Jonathan Cape, 1967) and from *Letters*, ed. William Maxwell (Chatto & Windus, 1982). Reprinted by permission of Random House UK Ltd.

Beatrice Weinreich-Silverman (editor), 'Yiddish Fable' from *Yiddish Folktales*. Translated by Leornard Wolf, reprinted in *The Second Book of Fairy Tales* ed. Angela Carter. Copyright © 1988 by YIVO Institute for Jewish Research. Reprinted by permission of Pantheon Books, a division of Random House, Inc.

E. B. White, from *Charlotte's Web* (Hamish Hamilton, 1952).

Richard Wilbur, 'A Black November Turkey' from *Things Of This World*, copyright 1953 and renewed 1981 by Richard Wilbur; 'Cicadas' from *The Beautiful Changes and Other Poems*, copyright 1947 and renewed 1975 by Richard Wilbur. Reprinted by permission of Harcourt Brace & Co. and Faber & Faber Ltd.

J. H. Williams, from *Elephant Bill* (Rupert Hart-Davis, 1950).

William Carlos Williams, from *Collected Poems 1939–1962* (Carcanet Press Ltd., 1988). Reprinted by permission of the publisher.

P. G. Wodehouse, from *Heavy Weather* (Herbert Jenkins Ltd., 1933). Reprinted by permission of Random House UK Ltd. and A. P. Watt Ltd. on behalf of the Trustees of the Wodehouse Estate.

Leonard Woolf, from *Downhill all the Way: An Autobiography of the Years 1919–1939* (The Hogarth Press, 1967) copyright © 1967 Leonard Woolf. Reprinted by permission of Harcourt Brace & Co. and Random House UK Ltd.

Virginia Woolf, from *Flush* (The Hogarth Press, 1933). Copyright © 1933 by Harcourt Brace & Co. and renewed 1961 by Leonard Woolf, reprinted by permission of Harcourt Brace and Co.

James Wright, from *Above the River: The Complete Poems* (Bloodaxe Books Ltd., 1992).

Judith Wright, from *Collected Poems 1942–1970* (Angus & Robertson, 1975). Reprinted by permission of HarperCollins Publishers, Australia.

W. B. Yeats, from *Collected Poems* (Macmillan Publishers Ltd., 1958).

Andrew Young, from *The Poetical Works* (Secker & Warburg, 1985). Reprinted by permission of Alison Young.

While every effort has been made to secure permission, we may have failed in a few cases to trace the copyright holder. We apologize for any apparent negligence.

INDEX OF CREATURES

adder 134–5, 241–2
alligator 115
    see also cayman
amphisbæna 318–19
anaconda 115
animals: blessing of 145–6
    inventing of 328–9
    language of 195–6
    rebellion of 3–4
ant 72, 257–9
ape 61
archaeopteryx 357
armadillo 286–7
ass 200–1, 201–3

badger 115, 165–6, 277–8
barnacle (tree-geese) 320
bat 30, 165, 192–3, 269–70
beaver 236
bedbug 260
bee 73, 208–10
behemoth 72, 320–1
bird 8, 39–40, 96–7, 243, 302 *and see individual species*
blackbird 154–5
bower-bird 95
bull-dog 142–4
bullfinch 93, 339
bunyip 322–3
bush-baby 369
butter bump 179
butterfly 8–9, 69, 338–9
buzzard 285

camel 53, 248–9
cat 7, 121, 122, 199–200, 252, 252, 305–6, 316–17, 369–70, 370–2
caterpillar 13, 33, 154
cayman (American alligator) 351
cell DNA 2
centaur 323–4, 329
centipede 257
chimera 328
chimpanzee 196–7, 219–20, 235–6
cicada 177–8
clock a clay, *see* ladybird
cobra 288–91
collie 223–4

cormorant 214
cow 101–2, 102, 146–7, 223–4, 224–5, 225–6, 262–3
crab 12, 17, 295–8
cranefly 74
cricket 175, 176–7, 339–40
crocodile 50, 130, 271–2
cuckoo 179–80, 180–1
currawong 186–7

Daddy-long-legs 31–2
death-watch beetle 77
dinosaur 48–9, 353–4
dodo 358–9, 359
dog 13, 13–15, 45–7, 140–1, 141–2, 199, 220, 367–8, *and see specific breeds*
dolphin 129–30, 246
donkey 29–30, 169–70, 170–3, 233
    see also ass
dove 340–1
dragon 326–7
duck (mallard) 66–7, 341–3
dung beetle 205–8

eel 47–8, 298–9
elephant 220–1, 221–2, 248, 348–9
elver 73
emmet *see* ant

fawn 144–5
firefly 107–8
    see also glowworm
fish (various) 103–4, 104, 105, 294–5
flamingo 218–19
flea 69–70, 262–3, 263, 264–5, 265–6
flounder 300–1
fly 150, 152
fowl, *see* hen
fox 56–9, 222–3, 282–3, 283, 312–13
frog 51, 292–3, 302

gecko 250–1
giraffe 366
glowworm 117–18
gnat 9–10, 30–1
goanna 81–2
goat 363
Gollum 308–9

goose 39, 242, 242–3, 364–5
goshawk, *see* hawk
grasshopper 175, 301
griffin 324–5
guanaco 114, 249–50
guinea worm 267
gull 87–90

halcyon, *see* kingfisher
hamster 62
hare 132, 132–3, 303–4, 305, 336–8
hawk 212–13, 213–14
hedgehog 27, 218–19
hen 215–16, 343–4
heron 101–2
horse 166–7, 167–8, 169, 225–6, 226–7, 228–9,
    314–15, 346, 362
hound 222–3

ichthyosaur 354
iguana 114
insect 12, 30–1, 149–50, 176–7, 339–40

jabberwock 307–8
jackdaw 15–16
jaguar 115–17
jellyfish 21

kangaroo 34–6, 60–1, 350
kid 148–9
    see also goat
kingfisher 100–1
kiwi 358
kraken 312

ladybird (clock a clay) 75
lamb 147–8, 148–9
    see also sheep
lark 357–8
leech 211, 267–8
lemming 237
leviathan 106, 311–12
lion 9, 54–5, 170–3, 173–4, 274–5, 275–7, 286
lion-ant 1, *see also* ant
llama 114
loach 299–300
lobster 18 (lapster), 113
Loch Ness Monster 203, 329–30
louse 152–4
lungworm 75–6

magpie 38
Malay dragon 43
manatee 110–12
manticora 327–8

marmoset 164–5
mayfly 32–3
mermaid (siren) 323
microbe 320
moa 355–6, 356
mockingbird 192
mole 86, 87, 91–3
mollusc 20–21
mongoose 288–91
monster 315–16, 359–60
moorhen 65–6
moose 37, 347
mosquito 151–2, 260, 260–2
mouse 4–5, 27–9, 78–9, 79–80, 123–4, 238
mule 230–1

nautilus (pilot-fish) 21, 22–3
ngarara 321–2
nightingale 186

octopus 49
osprey 101
otter 105, 368–9
owl 40, 90–1, 155–6, 179, 180–1, 283–4
ox 146
oyster, pearl 244–6

parasitic worm 266–7
parrot 161–3, 193–5, 195–6
pelican 3, 187–9
penguin 285
phoenix 40–3, 309
pig 6–7, 60, 259–60, 263–4
pigeon 67–8, 216–18, 341
pike 292–3
pit-pony 230
plankton 108–9
pointer 14–15
polar bear 280–1
porpoise 106–8
prawn (sushi) 293–4
primate 302–3
psammead 319–20
pterodactyl 309–10
ptinus fur ('bookworm') 77
puff adder 241
puma 115

quagga 352, 353

rabbit 69–70, 87–90, 133–4, 242, 305–6, 338
ram 53–4
rat 125–9, 238, 278–80
raven 163–4, 189–92
red setter 144

reindeer xii
robin 156–8, 158–60

salamander 119
sandpiper 244
scorpion 253
seahorse 112–13
sea mouse 113–14
seal 47
serpent, *see* snake
shark 270
sheep 85–6, 344–5
shrimp 335–6
silkworm 68, 211, 365–6
siren, *see* mermaid
skunk 255–6
sloth, two-toed 82–3
slug 50–51
snail 23–4, 84
snake 24–6, 241–2, 287–8, 291–2, *and see
    individual species*
spaniel 136–8, 138–40
sparrow 182–6
sphynx 325
spider 151, 210–11, 252, 259–60
starfish 18–19
stonechat 178
stork 62–5, 99–100
swallow 160–1
swan 38–9, 65
swift 97–8

tapeworm 49

tapir 36
termite 68
thrush 181–2
tiger 272–3, 367
toad 26, 26–7
tomineios 98–9
tortoise 83, 239–40
turkey 37–8
turtle 52, 130–2

unicorn 330–2, 332–4, 334

viper, *see* adder
vulture 10–12, 273–4, 286

wasp 33–4
waterbeetle, Dytiscus 270
water-hog 109–10
watersnake 109
wapiti 34
weasel 284–5
whale 105–6, 247
wildcat 55
wolf 56, 197–8, 236–7
wolf-spider 251–2
woodworm 31
worm 72, 238–9
wren 365
wryneck 94

yellowhammer 94–5

zebra 361

INDEX OF AUTHORS

Ackerley, J. R. 45–7, 367–8
Adams, Richard 87–90
Adamson, Joy 170–3
Adcock, Fleur 50–1, (tr.) 186
Addison, Joseph (tr.) 314–15
Aesop 236
Ammons, A. R. 17
Andersen, Hans Christian 62–5
Anon. 186
Aristotle 49, 53, 67–8, 238, 246
Arnim, Elizabeth von 140–1, 199
Astley, Neil 81–2
Atwood, Margaret 241–2, 273–4
Auden, W. H. xii, 80–1

Balzac, Honoré de 264–5
Beddoes, Thomas Lovell 130
Bedford, Sybille 145–6
Beeton, Isabella (Mrs) 303
Belloc, Hilaire 320
Betjeman, John 78–9
Bidgood, Ruth 150
Bird, Isabella 262–3
Bishop, Elizabeth 244
Blackmore, R. D. 299–300
Blake, William 13, 72, 367
Blixen, Karen (Isak Dinesen) 274–5
Borges, Jorge Luis 333–4
Boswell, James 122
Brooke, Rupert 104
Brown, George Mackay 113
Browne, Sir Thomas 324–5
Browning, Elizabeth Barrett 138–40
Buick, T. Lindsay 355–6
Burnett, Frances Hodgson 158–60
Burns, Robert 123–4, 152–4, 344–5

Campbell, Roy 361
Canetti, Elias 3–4
Carew, Thomas 150
Carroll, Lewis 27–9, 218–19, 307–8, 316–17
Carter, Angela, (ed.)8; 219–20
Cavendish, Margaret, Duchess of
    Newcastle 303–4
Cellini, Benvenuto 119, 253
Clampitt, Amy 113–14
Clare, John 8–9, 75, 94, 117, 149–50, 179, 277–8
Clarke, Gillian 47, 354

Cliffe, Edward (Hakluyt) 285
Coleridge, Samuel Taylor 2–3, 109
Colinvaux, Paul 94–5, 251–2, 283
Conan Doyle, Arthur 309–10
Corbett, Jim 272–3
Cowper, William 15–16, 64, 132–3, 336–8
Crompton, Richmal 125–9
Curnow, Allen 321, 356

Darley, George 334
Darwin, Charles 1, 26, 109–10, 118, 169,
    230–1, 238–9, 249–50
Darwin, Erasmus 50, 68
David, Elizabeth 294–5, 305
De la Mare, Walter 169–70, 365
Dickens, Charles 189–92
Dickinson, Emily 24–5, 154, 210–11, 243
Donne, John 70
Douglas, Charles Edward 358
Downer, Leslie 301
Drayton, Michael 103–4, 148–9, 213–14, 320
Drummond, William 263
Dryden, John (tr.) 53, 208–10
Dunn, Douglas 216–18
Durrell, Gerald 106–8, 235–6
Dyer, John 85–6

Eberhart, Richard 54–6
Eliot, John L. 353
Elliot, Alistair 146–7, 357–8
Engels, Frederick 49
Enright, D. J. (tr.) 12–13, (tr.) 161–3; 352

Fabre, Jean Henri 205–8
Field, Barron 34–6
Finch, Anne, Countess of Winchilsea
    9–10
Finlay, Ian Hamilton 18
Flaubert, Gustave 161–3
Fountain, Paul 36
Fountaine, Margaret 338–9
Fuller, Roy 75–6

Garnett, David 56–9, 312–13
Gaskell, Elizabeth (Mrs) 142–4
Goldsmith, Oliver 358–9
Goodall, Jane 196–7
Gould, Stephen Jay 39–40

Grahame, Kenneth 91–3
Grass, Günter 300–1
Graves, Robert 315–16
Gunn, Thom 270

Hakluyt, Richard, *see* Janes, John; Cliffe, Edward
Harding, Mike 267
Hardy, Thomas 101–2, 181–2, 215–16, 224–5
Hartley, L. P. 335–6
Harwood, Gwen 295–8
Heaney, Seamus 165–6
Hearn, Lafcadio 176–7, 211, 339–40, 365–6
Heath-Stubbs, John 77, 87, 250–1
Hecht, Anthony 83
Heyrick, Thomas 98–9
Hilberry, Conrad 62
Hoffmann, E. T. A. 199–200
Housman, A. E. 271–2, 318–19
Howard, Henry (tr.) 287–8
Hubbell, Sue 69
Hudson, W. H. 193–5, 242–3, 255–6, 286–7
Hughes, Ted 74
Huxley, Julian 60–1

Janes, John (Hakluyt) 280–1
Jarrell, Randall 192, 332–3
Jefferies, Richard 13–15, 32–3, 179–80, 228–9, 242, 284–5
Jenyns, Revd Leonard 77, 155–6
Job, Book of 311–12, 320–1, 362
Johnson, Samuel 281–2
Joseph, Joe 230

Keats, John 121, 175, 340–1
Kennedy, X. J. 286
Kipling, Rudyard 56, 288–91

Lack, David 156–8
Langley, Eve 350
Larkin, Philip 338
Lawrence, D. H. 260–2, 275–7
Lear, Edward 99–100, 187–8
Leithauser, Brad 260
Leonardo da Vinci 39, 96–7
Levi, Primo 265–6, 328–9
Lévi-Strauss, Claude (told by) 115–17
Lofting, Hugh 195–6
Longley, Michael 65, 101
Lopez, Barry Holstun 197–8
Lorenz, Konrad 163–4, 236–7, 270
Lovelace, Richard 23–4, 362–3
Lucretius 323–4

Macbeth, George 283–4
MacCaig, Norman 26–7, 178, 223–4, 363
MacEwen, Gwendolyn 329–30
MacLean, Alasdair 285, 343–4
Maeterlinck, Maurice 73
Mansfield, Katherine 341–3
Marvell, Andrew 117–18, 144–5
Masefield, John 237, 282–3
Maxwell, Gavin 55, 105, 368–9
May, Robert 301–2
Mayer, Gerda 302–3
Mayhew, Henry 278–80
Melville, Herman 151–2
Merwin, W. S. 341
Milne, A. A. 29–30
Milton, John 25–6, 71–2, 105–6
Montague, John 233, 359–60
Montaigne, Michel Eyquem de xii, 7, 100–1, 173–4, 220–1, 247–8
Moore, Marianne 21, 43, 330–2
Moorhouse, Geoffrey 248–9
Morgan, Edwin 203, 357
Muir, Edwin 167–8
Murray, Les 2, 20–1, 192–3
Musil, Robert 154–5

Nash, Ogden 33, 34, 52
Nemerov, Howard 68
Neruda, Pablo, *see* Wright, James
Nesbit, E. 319–20, 327–8
Nicholson, Norman 108–9, 132
Nimmo, Dorothy 266–7
Nowlan, Alden 347
Numbers, Book of 200–1

O'Hanlon, Redmond 267–8
Orbell, Margaret (tr.) 321–2
Orwell, George 348–9
Ovid 314–15
Owen, Jan 48–9

Pitter, Ruth 369
Pliny the Elder 21, 30–1, 61, 119, 129–30, 146, 309
Porter, Peter 112–13, 253–4
Potter, Beatrix 40, 133–4, 252, 260

Ransome, Arthur 134–5
Raverat, Gwen 225–6
Raymond, Vicki 238
Redgrove, Peter 152
Rilke, Rainer Maria, *see* Jarrell, Randall
Rodriguez, Judith 110–12, 257
Roethke, Theodore 30, 73, 122–3
Rossetti, Christina 147–8

Rothschild, Miriam 69–70
Roule, Louis 244–6
Ruatapu, Mohi (told by) 321–2
Ruskin, John 93

Sarton, May 364–5
Sassoon, Siegfried 222–3
Scovell, E. J. 38–9, 366
Scully, James 18–19
Sewell, Anna 226–7, 345–6
Shakespeare, William 141–2, 166–7
Shuttle, Penelope, xii 60
Sisson, C. H., (tr.) 323–4
Skelton, John 182–6
Smart, Christopher 370–2
Smith, Stevie 286
Sparks, John 51
Spenser, Edmund 326–7
Sterne, Laurence xii, 201–3
Stevenson, Anne 97–8, 305–6
Stevenson, Robert Louis 231–3
Stryk, Lucien 214
Swift, Graham 47–8
Szirtes, George 31–2

Tanizaki, Junichiro 293–4
Taylor, Edward 53–4
Tennyson, Alfred, Lord 90–1, 312
Thompson, D'Arcy Wentworth 19–20, 22–3
Thoreau, Henry David 257–9
Tischbein, Johann Heinrich Wilhelm 12–13
Tolkien, J. R. R. 308–9

Topsell, Edward 325
Trimmer, Sarah 6–7

Virgil 53, 208–10, 287–8
Voltaire 13

Walker, Kath 291–2, 322–3
Walker, Ted 53–4
Walpole, Horace 339
Walton, Izaak 84–5, 292–3, 298–9
Warner, Sylvia Townsend 65–6, 102, 144,
    179, 212–13, 252
Waterton, Charles 82–3, 269–70, 351
White, E. B. 259–60
White, Gilbert 27, 37, 79–80, 165, 180–1,
    239–40
White, T. H. 38, 144, 212–13
Wilbur, Richard 37–8, 177–8, (tr.) 247, (tr.)
    323
Williams, J. H. 221–2
Williams, William Carlos 130–2
Wodehouse, P. G. 363–4
Woolf, Leonard 164–5
Woolf, Virginia 136–8
Wordsworth, Dorothy 160–1, 211
Wright, James 114–15
Wright, Judith 3, 95, 186–7
Wyatt, Sir Thomas 4–5

Yeats, W. B. 369–70
Young, Andrew 86